KEITH ROWE: THE ROOM EXTENDED

by

Brian Olewnick

powerHouse Books Brooklyn, NY

"If you don't know, why do you ask?"

David Tudor

Prologue

There is the room. It contains an atmosphere, walls, perhaps windows. It is dark, grainy, ill-kept, an elegant theater space, warm and moist, empty and echoing with each footstep, a bit chilly, bustling with the arriving crowd. Traces of past events linger in the form of an abandoned plastic cup, graffiti cut into a table, the wale of crushed velour impressed by thousands of backsides. Each passing occurrence, large and small, has left a subtle tinge that manifests in small material changes, drawing the aura in the room toward comfort, edginess, sadness, vigor, tension, depth. Aspects of the world outside the room have seeped in: the conditions of the local population, their cultures (ancient or transnationalized), their wars, snow on boots, smoke from the processing plant a mile away, traffic, corporate artifacts. The room reflects the small touches of care or neglect meted out over the years; it has an identity as palpable as the several people worrying at their equipment, nestling into their seats. In one corner, against a wall, onstage, just over there, in the middle of the room, rests a table.

The table is strewn with a large number of objects, one of which is an electric guitar. The surface of the table is brown or black, red or silver; it is wooden or metallic or vinyl-covered. Occasionally, it's draped in soft cloth. The guitar, shiny black and trapezoidal, red and whole, sawn into fragmented blocks, only a fingerboard, laid on its back, neck facing left as seen from the seat placed alongside. There is dust in the air, motes glinting in and out of view, settling on odd surfaces, taking off again. Wires fall from the guitar past the table's edge, twining toward, into, and around foot pedals on the floor or amplifiers. A violin bow rests against small, rectangular electronic devices that are obscure in meaning, sprouting sparse orchards of knobs. Several hand-held fans, their lozenge-like bodies in candy shades of purple, winy blue, and pink, stand near the guitar's body, the small engines within waiting to intermingle energy fields. Two of the fans sport smiley faces.

There are various blades and similar items: a butter knife, a nail file, street sweeper blades recently rescued from the gutter, and rasps of different widths, lengths, and grains. Alligator clips, teeth clenched, form irregular borders aligned with screws of many dimensions, some without heads, hemming in two or three rainbow-colored plastic balls that vibrate gently with each nearby foot tread. Washers and springs loll to the side, partially covering half of an American Express card, its missing portion lending an ironic air by its absence. Stones, water-rounded, in soft grays and ochres, lie patiently in wait, mildly suspicious of their too-regularly-shaped neighbors. A computer, perhaps, a couple of mixing boards, radios. The visual aspect of the table presents a picture at once cluttered and purposeful, utilitarian and attractive to the eye, recalling Braque.

The room is not silent. Inside, there are murmured conversations, chair scrapings, ice shavings, exhaled breaths, a cell's cry, the complex hum of amplifiers or the heating system. Infiltrating from without are the ubiquitous automotive sounds, the engines, tires, car alarms, brake squeals, drunken yells, the distant roar of a jet engine or the closer one of a boom box. They osmose through the walls of the room, dispersing into the interior space, forming a dense, pregnant fabric that is, in fact, the beginning of the performance at hand.

Keith Rowe:

> *I can visualise The Room quite well. I know that the walls,*
> *though they are a dark, "Rothkoesque" brown colour, are*
> *in fact transparent and that you can go through them...*
> *so currently the whole conflict in the Middle East would*
> *be a part of The Room. When you are in The Room play-*
> *ing, performing, making a noise, whatever it is you are*
> *doing...what's in that "room" with you is the whole issue of*
> *Iraq, the whole issue of poverty in the world, unfair water*
> *distribution across the world. Part of The Room also is the*
> *activity of someone sitting in front of a canvas making*
> *their work. It's that part of history...the composer sitting at*
> *the table, someone writing a poem.*

There is air between the objects, tensile space fraught with
meaning between the performer and the items on the table. Conscious of all of this, he tries to imagine introducing a sound which
will only tinge the ambience slightly, though perhaps crucially. He
has no idea what he will do, even as his hand descends toward
the table, through the lamina of sights, smells, sounds, thoughts.

Chapter 1

Plymouth, England was a navy town. Crowded housing, narrow, dirty streets leading to industrial shipyards, countless bars serving the working class residents and hordes of visiting sailors. The cutting smell of machine oil hung in the air mixed with other less appealing odors. Jobs, when jobs could be had, were usually connected in one way or another to the navy, from office and food support to repair and cleaning of warships. Sometimes there was work in the renowned Plymouth Gin Distillery, yet another vital area of provision for the naval forces. Though located only 30 or so miles from the English Riviera seaside resorts of Torquay, Paignton, and Brixham, where worldly Londoners idled in the summer, pre-war Plymouth was harsh, gray, culturally isolated, and grimly poor.

The city was slow to drag itself into the 20th century, having undergone an extensive renewal and modernization program begun in the aftermath of the First World War that included the large-scale demolition of slum neighborhoods, only to be replaced with equally dismal "council housing," rudimentary dwellings built on the cheap. Buses began to appear in lieu of the old tramlines, some parks were created, and the population grew swiftly, reaching about 220,000 at the end of the 1930s.

By the summer of 1939, the impending war with Germany had spurred a furious amount of preparatory activity in England. Conscription had been introduced in April, requiring that all males 20 and 21 years of age enter into a six-month military training program. There was a widespread belief that, unlike the "Great War," the battle might well be joined on British soil this time, not solely in distant lands. Plymouth's maritime resources and its proximity to the northern coast of France made it an obvious potential target. Bulldozers and excavators descended upon virtually all open spaces, from schoolyards to public parks to front lawns, constructing a web of trenches and air raid shelters that honeycombed the seaport, imparting to the city a bombed-out appearance before an enemy plane ever crossed the sky.

Military personnel were regularly shuttled through Plymouth. In that spring of 1939, an officer named Valentine Richard (Ricky) Charters-Rowe was bunkered in town. Little has been passed down regarding the specifics of his life, but he was believed to have attained some degree of rank by this time, possibly Lieutenant Colonel. He met a 25-year-old hairdresser named Eileen Tucker, a shallow young lady dazzled by the attention paid her by a dashing officer, and in short course impregnated her. They were married in a civil ceremony late that summer, Charters-Rowe moving into the attached house at 279 North Road which Eileen shared with her mother and sister. On September 3, Great Britain and France issued a joint declaration of war against Germany.

Rationing of ham, bacon, butter, and sugar began in January of the new year and restrictions were placed on the distribution of canned goods and cereals. Staples like milk and eggs were controlled to ensure that expectant mothers and the elderly received a sufficient supply. A general system of meat rationing was instituted on March 11, typically offering a family of four about a quarter pound of meat per week. On March 16, 1940, Eileen gave birth to her first child, Keith Charters-Rowe.

*

When Rowe was about two and a half months old, on June 30, 1940, Plymouth experienced its initial air raid alert, lasting about an hour. On July 6, the first of dozens of bombing raids occurred, destroying three homes, killing two citizens, and wounding six others. For the next several years there would be hundreds of air raids, the sirens a near constant presence mingling with the low, threatening drones of Luftwaffe bombers. These sounds are among Rowe's earliest memories. Families scuttled to the nearest shelter, rarely more than five minutes away, and huddled down in the darkness, singing songs to keep up the spirits ("Roll Out the Barrel" and "Run Rabbit Run" were popular favorites). Some of the shelters were little more than ditches; others were set up with lavatories and food supplies. None would provide protection from a direct hit—several would suffer just such a fate—but the deadly effect of flying shrapnel and debris was greatly mitigated. Peeking out from such a refuge, you might see the underside of a barrage balloon, one of scores, lit up from below by nearby explosions. These devices, enormous blimp-like bags filled with lighter-than-air gas and tethered to steel cables, floated above Plymouth in airborne flocks, creating a bizarrely surreal atmosphere, a panorama out of Magritte. Their function was to frustrate the incoming airplanes' ability to fly low, thereby thwarting to some degree the accuracy of the bombers' arsenal. The success of this strategy doubtless saved the lives of thousands of Plymouth residents.

The Charters-Rowe family tended not to flee to the bomb shelters during air raids, instead opting for home-based protection. Keith and other family members were herded underneath the kitchen table that was wedged against a wall at the rear of the house. The table, wooden with stout legs, was one of the most structurally sound items in the household, likely to retain stability in the event of a ceiling or wall collapse. A makeshift wire cage was wrapped around the table and the whole structure was inserted into a portion of the wall that had been partially hollowed out for exactly this purpose. On the exterior wall of the house opposite the niche in which the table was set, there was painted a large red cross. Should the building suffer a direct hit, rescuers would know precisely where to begin digging for any possible survivors.

Underground shelters were part of the daily existence for most Plymouth citizens for several years as the bombings continued. The sirens sounded unceasingly. Raids generally occurred at night and, once begun, would often recur for several days in succession, subside for a week, then begin anew. During the day, between attacks, people would try to conduct business and affairs in as normal a fashion as could be expected, casting wary glances skyward when German reconnaissance planes circled to inspect the extent of the previous night's damage. Enemy airmen dropped rows of spikes on roadways, hoping to puncture the tires of emergency vehicles. Occasionally, perhaps when the supply of that night's ordinance had been depleted, they tossed out whatever detritus was on hand in the aircraft: bottles, pipe-fittings, tools, etc., lightening the load for the return flight to the continent. The shelters took on the aspect of shadow cities, dark, dank obverse images of the playgrounds and parks directly above them, children playing Boomps-a-Daisy in muddy trenches. Graffiti adorned their walls: Hitler (with breasts or conspicuously lacking a testicle), Churchill, an earring-wearing Goering, drawings of bombs and barrage balloons.

The Plymouth Blitz, some 59 attacks in all with over 600 air raid alerts, continued into 1944. By then virtually the entire center of the city, home to its major markets and churches, had been destroyed. The civilian death count was 1,174 and over 4,500 homes no longer existed. Very few buildings escaped some degree of damage and many were hit more than once. The population had fallen to around 110,000. During 1942, rationing was introduced for soap, white bread, sweets, and milk (three pints a week for "non-priority" consumers, reduced to two in 1944).

The Charters-Rowe family moved out of Plymouth, north into Devon County, itself subject to frequent air raids, sometime in early 1942 where his mother opened a hairdressing shop. Shortly thereafter, the couple split apart and Keith would have almost no contact with his father from that point on. He retained a vague image of being visited while sick in bed as a very young boy, but acknowledged that this might be a false memory. Ricky Charters-Rowe would die in a car crash sometime in the early 1960s, though he was at a great enough remove from his ex-wife at the time that this news was only received by his former family well after the fact. Indeed, it wasn't until many years after his death that Keith would find out that his father had been something of a musician—a guitarist—himself.

Eileen soon engaged in a brief dalliance with an American serviceman, resulting in the birth of her second child, Barry, in 1942. The entire family, including the three subsequent brothers born to Eileen and a third companion, retained the surname "Charters-Rowe," probably for the simple reason that she thought it sounded "classier" than the names of the others. Eileen Tucker fit the "dizzy blonde" caricature almost perfectly, having a scattershot personality, bereft of anything remotely intellectual in nature and, of course, being artificially blonde, something very much the fashion in the late 30s. She had no sense of planning for the future, and what decisions she did make tended to be very self-centered, based on what would gladden her for the next several minutes or hours. Having been abandoned by Charters-Rowe and his successor, she felt unable to continue with child-rearing duties and turned over custodianship of Keith to her younger sister Ascenath (known as Mary, born 11/14/1915), an unmarried woman residing in Plymouth where she was taking care of their blind mother.

Though now living in fairly dire poverty, the Tucker family was only a generation removed from measurable wealth and prominence. Sydney Tucker, father to Eileen, Mary, and Beatrice (another sister who would move in and out of the North Road residence in the years to come), was quite a successful cattle breeder (known as a "stockman") and meat supplier, winning awards for the "Best Butcher's Beef" from the area in the 1920s. He owned one of the very first private cars in Plymouth. Not satisfied with merely being one of a handful of people well off enough to own a car at all, he insisted on an even rarer commodity: an American car, generally preferring a Cadillac or Studebaker. Unfortunately for his daughters, he was a bit of a playboy (hence an early separation from his wife), and managed to squander most of his fortune on the proverbial "wine, women, and song," though keeping enough for himself to continue living in some amount of comfort.

On May 11, 1945, three days after VE Day, Plymouth streetlights were relit for the first time in 5 ½ years. Though the war had ended, rationing continued for several years as part of Britain's Austerity Program, a stringent measure taken to get the country back on its economic feet. Gradually, these strictures were eased: clothing in 1949, gasoline (petrol) in 1950, and basic foodstuffs such as sugar, eggs, tea, and butter throughout the early 1950s until 1954 when the rationing system was finally suspended.

*

"Auntie Mary" was the true parent in Rowe's childhood. She was a very plain woman, never married, sharing most of the conservative prejudices of the rest of her family and neighbors but having just a little more perspicacity, a hint of a discerning eye and ear that would help allow her nephew to carve out a bit more of an intellectual and aesthetic niche in this culturally barren town. She ran a household full of people who might otherwise have had difficulty making day-to-day ends meet. Her mother was blind, a gaunt, elderly woman who rarely left the house and was already suffering from the cancer that would claim her in the mid-1950s. She possessed an acute aural sensitivity however, having the ability, for example, to hear bread being sliced in an adjoining room and being easily able to identify people by the sound of their footsteps. The other sister, Aunt Beatrice, was possibly even more the archetypal empty-headed blonde than Eileen, another platinum-dyed hairdresser married to a stolid, reliable fireman named Charlie Bullock. They owned a parrot and a cockatoo and occupied a bedroom decorated in shades of pink.

The house itself was one of thousands of identical structures built in the early part of the century. Attached on either side to conserve heat, a small front yard sloping down to the sidewalk, row after row of these blank, tired structures lined the streets of Plymouth. One toilet on the ground floor (a washbasin in a separate room) was shared by everyone in the household. On Sundays, a large tin basin was dragged in from its hanging place in the courtyard and filled with hot water so everyone could have his or her weekly bath. Warmth was provided by a coal fire downstairs but wasn't terribly efficient. In the winter, ice would form on the interior of the upstairs windowpanes. Rowe would very neatly fold his clothes and place them under his pillow and blanket, sleeping on them so they'd be a little bit less cold the next morning.

Every so often, one of the rooms was let out and if the renter was a single man, hopes would arise that Auntie Mary might have a suitor. She was thought to have had an affair with a surveyor who the family expected to "do the right thing" and marry her, thus providing more stability, financial and otherwise, to the household but he flew off one day, leaving them to struggle on.

As is always the case, a young child living not only in poverty but also in fairly extreme deprivation has little idea of the misery of his situation. Knowing nothing else, young master Charters-Rowe made use of what was available, scavenging through the bombed-out ruins with his friend Kenny Trevorrow for what small treasures were to be found, playing "army," marveling at motorcars. They developed a game where they'd sit on a front stoop and try to identify the make of an unseen car coming up the road by the sound of its engine.

Due to his grandfather's butcher business, Rowe's family likely benefited a bit more with regard to meat rations than was strictly allowed, but still, nutrition in post-war Britain was spotty at best. Porridge or puffed wheat was the standard breakfast fare. Rowe savored the memory of having a hunk of bread and drippings thrust into his hand as he headed out for school, the "drippings" consisting of congealed pork fat left over from the previous meal swabbed onto the tight, solid loaf. A special dessert was "pine-apple": squares of turnip simmered in pineapple juice. Milk was always a rarity.

> *There's a point at which Beatty and Aunt Mary are in the house and they've got a young man coming over, obviously romantically inclined. So he comes in and they offer him a cup of tea, late in the evening. They go to where you kept the milk—there was no fridge—and there's no milk. The only milk in the house is in the cat's saucer, with cat hair and all sorts of debris in it, so they actually sift the milk into the tea, milk that was lying there all day probably. Horrible.*

Still, the Charters-Rowe family might have had it a little better than many in Plymouth. The house looked out onto an attractive building that served as a nunnery that abutted a pleasant Victorian park. There was a back lane used by tradesmen in which Keith and Kenny could construct imaginary adventures. The family's prior prosperity lingered on in traces, like the fancy silverware set kept in the front parlor that Keith, donning a white apron and gloves, would be required to polish weekly. The parlor, kept under lock and key save for the rare occasion of entertaining a guest, also contained an upright piano on which Auntie Mary would once in a while play popular songs and ditties. No lessons were ever offered to the children, no prodding to learn anything about music.

Of all the activities in Rowe's childhood daily doings, none may have had the lasting influence of the many afternoons spent tinkering with his Meccano set. Similar to the American Erector Set, Meccano was a box full of metal plates, strips, bolts, and wheels from which one could fashion all manner of devices, limited only by one's imagination and the specific materials at hand. Beginning with a goal in mind—a racing car, an airplane, or a rocket ship—you made use of these rather abstract components to fashion the picture in your head. The set was never complete; you always had to improvise with whatever was available to achieve your objective. Fifty years later, Rowe would cite the Meccano set as a crucial source of his creative approach, of working within pared down material limits so as to force oneself to investigate pathways one would have otherwise ignored or never noticed.

An uncle with a job as a chauffeur enabled the family to take the occasional day trip to Torquay or other nearby resort towns, but Rowe rarely otherwise journeyed more than 30 miles from his home until he was a teenager. Already something of a cultural backwater, the post-War austerity program only reinforced the practical character of its citizens and provided virtually no outlet for any creatively gifted youngster. Rowe's graphic impulses were channeled into sketches made in the margins of notebooks, largely revolving around racing cars, though his earliest surviving drawing is derived from a newspaper photograph of the funeral of King George VI in 1952. Exposure to music, aside from his aunt's dabbling on the house piano, playing popular favorites of the day, came through the radio, though again, little if anything of substance was heard. Instead, what this medium did provide was yet another important window into the world outside of Plymouth, albeit one built on fantasy: *Journey Into Space*. This serial, which ran from 1950-56 and might be compared to the American Flash Gordon series, played a central role in expanding Rowe's imaginative powers as he sat by the radio, visually recreating the conquest of the Moon by Captain "Jet" Morgan and company. That sense of wonderment, the delight of exploring outward, never disappeared, and the radio was often a means to do so.

Though not overly involved with athletics, Rowe developed something of your normal teenager's attraction toward sporting events and competition generally. Tall, slender, and fit, he was an enthusiastic bicyclist, eventually taking lengthy rides with Kenny Trevorrow and other friends from Plymouth to Land's End (more than 50 miles). Those childhood drawings of racing cars grew into a fascination with actual car racing, Le Mans in particular. The most important event of his mid-teen years was the radio broadcast of this annual race in France. He'd sit glued to the set, listening to live coverage from a reporter in the pits who would recount the race in what Rowe recalled as an "RAF-type voice," using dogfight terms in his descriptions. The three-year string of victories by Jaguar D-type cars from 1955-57 played a strong symbolic part in Britain's recovering self-image, post-war.

As of 1956, then, we see a fairly normal young boy, somewhat more intelligent and questioning than average, involved in activities that, today, might be described as a bit geeky, living in an extremely poor, culturally reactionary household not very much different from the norm in that time and place. There was little reason to think that he'd go on to further schooling, more likely ending up in either the military or in some grim, naval-related job in Plymouth.

Chapter 2

The Plymouth College of Arts and Crafts (currently known as the Plymouth College of Art and Design) had been in existence since 1855, offering a combined education in the fine arts and, more importantly for the vast majority of its students, courses in the applied arts, areas with practical uses whose mastery might help toward earning a living. It was located in the center of town on Tavistock Road, having survived the bombings of the prior decade largely intact. The arts curriculum was very classically based with an emphasis on the study of Greek and Roman casts and anatomy, while also offering trades courses including book-binding, calligraphy, and printmaking. Though hardly renowned for aesthetic innovation (in fact, one of its "functions" was to serve as a kind of repository for young ladies whose families couldn't afford to send them to fashionable Swiss finishing schools), by the 1940s the college had become a relatively re-laxed institution, affording substantial leeway for student pranks and escapades, and was beginning to acknowledge the virtues of experimentation and the notion that one could always learn something valuable, even from an idea that fails.

In the indifferent, post-war primary education system in Britain, Rowe had shown little out of the ordinary as far as noteworthy skills, performing decently enough in many subjects, poorly in others. The only area in which he evinced any real passion was draw-ing. Granted, this talent was largely expressed in sketches of racing cars and various science fiction-oriented and comic book themes, but his proficiency was pronounced enough to draw the attention of the school guidance counselor. By the mid-50s, having a career in the graphic arts, doing commercial design for advertising agencies and the like, was considered a respectable trade and Rowe's family had no objections to this course of study. The basic attitude was, "It's something he's good at. He may as well pursue it and make the best of it." Always practical, Auntie Mary remarked, "Well, you know, everything has to be designed." Within the provincially conservative outlook of this maritime town, there was absolutely no thought of studying "Art" itself, indeed of seriously engaging in any purely aesthetic, non-practical education. There were no printed sources scattered about that might in any way awaken one's artistic nature. The only reading matter at all to be found in the Rowe household was a three-volume set of *Pear's Encyclopedia,* and even that was very likely in excess of the neighborhood average. Rowe himself could only just read at this point, a common enough situation in English working class families at the time that remedial reading courses were regularly offered at college level.

Getting accepted at the Plymouth College was less a matter of a pre-existing portfolio than a combination of interview and drawing aptitude test. Rowe, adept at shorthand sketching and perceived as being eager to learn, made the grade. In 1956, at sixteen years of age (children then were encouraged to leave school and prepare for a career as early as possible), still living at home and coming from a lower, more proletarian background than the great majority of students enrolled there, he entered the school something of a loner, with none of his childhood friends in tow, walking into a new and strange world where art might be something that mattered.

Following the traditional discipline of learning drawing before all else, and the school having a long-standing life-study course as part of the curriculum, Rowe, during his first week in attendance found himself face to face with a naked female model (his own cheeks doubtless flushing crimson), not only the first unclothed woman he'd ever observed in his young life, but something so far beyond the pale of possibility in working class Plymouth as to arouse cries of disbelief from his friends in the neighborhood when he reported the incident. "I've seen a nude woman," he told Kenny Trevorrow. Kenny just would not believe it, a common-sense response to such a claim there and then. You simply would not have seen a nude woman! In a school classroom, no less!

In addition to getting his initial actual lessons in applied art, Rowe encountered Art History for the first time. Again following a traditional format, the students were schooled in Western art from the Greeks through the Renaissance (Giotto and Fra Lippo Lippi made some impression on Rowe), and on down through Impressionism, just barely edging into the 20th century for a passing mention of Cubism. As would likely be the case with any naive youngster, painters of a more spectacular or "weird" manner tended to pique Rowe's interest the most: El Greco, Bosch, Brueghel. Over time, he found himself exposed to masters from the Expressionist school that had perhaps a more profound psychological influence on him than a purely formal one. Artists like Chagall, Munch, and Nolde became quite important in his development, their clear evocations of intense emotional states limning a very different world than experienced in the drab grayness of Plymouth. Even so, classmates recall him still spending a great deal of time producing drawings of racing cars and bicyclists; that love and appreciation of everyday objects would never be lost.[1]

While the atmosphere in the town as well as the attitudes of many of his friends remained unstintingly conservative, Rowe found himself encountering a very different set of ideas at the college. Even as he retained a love for the sorts of activities and passions typical of young men of his class, Rowe was also beginning to cultivate the image of the rebellious outsider, a stance

---

[1] Biking, indeed, was a major pastime of Rowe's teen years. Lengthy excursions throughout the Devon area were regular and greatly enjoyed affairs. He'd often cycle down to Tavistock and back before attending art classes and avidly followed the Tour de France, regaling friends with stories about Jacques Aquivel.

commonly affected by art school students. His abject poverty made this rather more easy and natural for him, perhaps, than for many of his fellow classmates. Wearing out of necessity a single pair of black jeans for weeks on end and an unchanging black sweater (with an increasingly imperceptible yellow stripe, representing, in fact, the colors of his favorite racing team) went some way toward causing him to stand out from his peers. Tall, slender, and attractive, he carved an alluring, if remote, figure.

He spent the first two years at the college immersed in the study of the arts, honing his drawing ability, doing copies from plaster casts, learning the Latin names for all human muscles and bones, ultimately moving on to painting (courses only available after a year of serious draftsmanship studies as well as learning the technical and chemical aspects of oil painting). He toiled a great deal in the lithography studio, developing a love of printmaking and an appreciation, fitting for one from the working class, for the gritty mechanical aspects of a print's creation. You can hear his fascination with the intensely *physical* nature of the process, something that would echo down through the years:

> You had to spin this disc over the stone, very heavy with sand and water, to clean off the old image. We always inherited the stone from the prior user. You brought it to the "wet" part of the room, sprinkled it with water and sand, and then you had this round disc, probably about 5-6 kilos or more, and it had a handle on one edge. There were holes in it and you dripped sand and water into the holes and basically ground the wax off the stone, grinding it down flat.

From the beginning, Rowe's work was criticized by the school's professors for his insistence on presenting his subjects encased in bold, dark outlines. While some of this stemmed from a new-found knowledge and enjoyment of stained glass artistry, certainly a large portion of his approach derived from an early and ongoing love of comic books, including the classic English strips, "Beano and Dandy" and "Desperate Dan."

*...Almost immediately, in '57 or '58, I made a kind of "Pop
Art," just instinctively. I drew everything with big, heavy
lines around it, everything. It's the only way I could ever see
it. The idea of painting up to the edge, you know, the blue
sky, without this line—I could never conceive of doing that,
I could never do it.*

A crucial discovery for Rowe around this period was Cubism. The
realization, perhaps reinforced by childhood obsessions like the
Meccano sets, that you could look at everyday reality and take
it apart and isolate it into its constituent elements, unearthing a
deeper structure, was enormously compelling to him.

*It was more theoretical than actually practicing it [Cub-
ism]. That would be a huge influence on me, huge. I think
that really, really affected me. That idea that you had two
[opaque] containers that were identical but this one was
full of liquid and this one was empty. But you knew that
was full and that was empty and how do you communicate that knowledge of the fullness? That whole thing of:
it was no longer visual...I really loved the "novelty" of the
new in that sense, I don't think for the sake of it but for the
"finding-out-ness" of it, the investigation, the breaking of
barriers and moving on into new territory.*

At the same time, the school's insistence on a thorough grounding in classic techniques and art history left a lingering tinge
in his work as well. The idea of doing a painting "after" that of
another, of placing oneself within a historical framework, being
aware of a certain "classical" form, however distended, became
something that would never quite leave Rowe's consciousness.

*That's the trick: to remain free but quite conscious of what
you're about, the historical process. You see that in Philip
Guston, endlessly thinking about how the paintings relate
to each other, to him, to history. Cy Twombly, Mark Rothko
will know precisely how all of this fits into Greek culture*

or something. It's certainly true in the compositional field. Composers are certainly aware of what aspects of their work might be Webernesque or Mahleresque.

For Christmas, in 1957, Rowe's next youngest brother Barry received a guitar ("an Egmond guitar or something, a quasi-classical guitar, a dog's-dinner"), a gift in which he quickly lost interest. Keith, intrigued by the small tastes of big band jazz he'd heard over Voice of America radio as well as a BBC program devoted to jazz guitar, snatched it up.

The guitar was in the bedroom and I basically farted about with it, maybe playing the odd little tune, almost like a kid poking fingers at a piano, not knowing what to do. Interested in it but not knowing what to do. I didn't have the motivation. Nothing I'd heard in music really inspired me to the degree that I'd really sit down and learn it.

Actually, there has been no point in my life where I've been interested in learning the songs. Never. I was never interested in playing a tune on the guitar. Obviously there were times when I would...put it this way, a lot of guitar players, they pick it up and they want to play this or that tune and sometimes what they want to do with that is go on the stage or in a bar or with their friends and play that tune. It never interested me to do that. But I somehow learned just a fragment of a tune. I don't think I ever, in the whole of the time I played guitar, I never learned to play a tune...It was highly fragmented. That probably did fit in, in a sense, with the things I was doing in art school, the notion of fragmentation, like in Cubism cutting something up into its parts and assembling it again in a way. The fragments would be like found objects. What the art school training gave me was the ability to believe that I didn't have to do it in the way it said you had to do it.

Though it would be far more of an interest later on, Rowe was already intrigued by the visual aspect of the instrument, that he could see it while playing and that it was at a remove from his head, an object to be observed as opposed to an attachment on one's mouth or neck. There was an early sense of respectful separation, of acknowledgment that the guitar was an entity of its own. In a sense, it was already beginning to be conceived as a sound-producing device as opposed to "his music maker."

Early rock and roll had begun to make its way over the airwaves and into the record shops. Rowe was aware of it (the movie *Blackboard Jungle* was a big hit, among other sources) but pretty much dismissed it with an attitude possibly born of a burgeoning snobbishness toward popular culture engendered by the art school atmosphere.

> *I think there probably is something quite deep in me, the fact that I come from a very poor kind of background, maybe as an adolescent you reject it. If you're very rich, you reject richness, you slum around, adopt a working class accent, that sort of stuff. If you're very poor, one of the possibilities is that you actually reject the values of the poor and their culture. Could well have happened in my case. For example, Elvis Presley I would identify as music that was associated with the people who rejected the things I really liked. So I really liked Picasso and Braque and they would be the laughing stock of people who liked Elvis Presley so therefore I would reject Elvis Presley. This may be dumb, but that's probably what I did.*

This inclination also contributed to a growing disenfranchisement with his childhood friends, all of whom were wending their way down standard working class career paths, such as were available. Among the neighborhood clan, Rowe was beginning to alienate himself.

> *I think that happened with Kenny [Trevorrow] and myself. When I went to art school and he didn't, he worked on a*

*building site. Kenny really liked Duane Eddy, for example, I
remember he was one of his great heroes and I thought he
was all very nice but, basically, compared to Barney Kessel,
was not on the same plane. That's how it evolved but the
seeds were already there.*

Still, had it been a situation of Rowe alone and adrift, with little
real formal education, this headlong lunge into art, art history,
and the acquisition of even the sketchiest of musical awareness,
having been catapulted from such a dearth of area culture, may
have resulted in more confusion and misdirection than a true
learning and growing experience. Luckily, his tenure at the Plymouth College of Art coincided with that of a remarkable number
of intriguing, intelligent, and intensely experimental young men
and women. Chief among them was Mike Westbrook.

Westbrook (along with future filmmaker Malcolm Le Grice)
arrived in Plymouth for the fall 1958 semester. Four years older
than Rowe, he came from an entirely different, far more upper
class background, having received a prior arts education at Kelly
College. By the late 40s he had heard jazz and developed a pas-
sionate interest, collecting 78s, teaching himself piano and taking
trumpet lessons, developing a special love for Ellington, Basie,
and the nascent West Coast school.

> But in those days in my school...jazz was actually forbid-
> den. The immediate post-War atmosphere in England
> hadn't really changed and jazz was pretty much frowned
> on in polite society.[2]

Westbrook left school, struggled to learn accountancy, performed
miserably at that, did his National Service in the Army,[3] and
eventually managed to gain acceptance at Cambridge University

---

2   Westbrook, 2004.

3   Rowe: He'd gotten called up to invade Egypt but luckily for the British,

to study geography. But he wasn't able to sustain interest in any of these areas, ultimately failing in the courses and acknowledging the growing realization that his only real passion had to do with the arts. At the Plymouth school, he plunged into the visual arts program with relish but couldn't avoid the musical itch and, after meeting fellow student and fledgling trombonist Ron Hills, decided to form a band. Group members fluctuated of course, but in addition to Hills, often included Stan Willis on tenor, Malcolm Le Grice or Rob Lord on guitar, Graham Russell on piano, Dave Webb on bass, and Terry Lidiard on drums, with Westbrook playing both trumpet and some piano. Many of these young men had no notion of being "musicians" and had little if any previous schooling on their instruments. Instead, they were transfixed by the new jazz they were hearing and, seizing on a particular instrument, went out and bought one. Thus, Hills viewed *The Glenn Miller Story*, became enamored with the trombone, and found a beat up old Selmer for 25 pounds. Terry Lidiard, on the other hand, was a young electrician who had played drums off and on in local skiffle bands and would stop in the pub to catch some of the regional talent, eventually being asked to sit in with Westbrook's group.

The raging debate in much of the jazz world, especially outside of the United States, was still between traditional forms like Dixieland and "modern" idioms like swing and early bebop. As difficult as it may be for 21st century listeners to imagine, in the mid-50s, you would often find writers bemoaning bebop as the sound of chaos, of pots and pans being flung against the wall, casting it in "end of the world" terms. In a relative backwater city like Plymouth, Dixieland and early forms of swing embodied the idea of "jazz." Little by little, however, the "new music" began to seep in through the cracks. By far the most important site of these local fissures was Peter Russell's Hot Record Store, an establishment located in Plymouth's red-light district on Union Street, nestled

---

the Americans persuaded England that it was a bad idea! I think Westbrook was put on the boat for a few days. I remember him saying, "Ruined my weekend!"

among the pubs where the local and visiting navy personnel would congregate. Russell was himself a jazz drummer, a follower of the New Orleans tradition, and an admirer of Sammy Penn, the rhythmic foundation of the New Orleans All Stars, as well as swing drummers like Chick Webb, Zutty Singleton, and Cozy Cole. Additionally, he was a critic for England's leading jazz magazine, Jazz Journal, and had his ears open to the newer strains of music, selling such imported labels as Blue Note, Contemporary, and Atlantic. The Hot Record Store, conveniently attached to the local musical instrument shop, Clarke & Chinn's, became the gathering spot for the town's younger musicians and jazz fans, including Rowe. They'd hang out in lieu of attending classes at art school, listening to everything they could though rarely having the wherewithal to actually purchase a recording. Russell was quite the jazz proselytizer, eagerly playing the latest releases for the kids, selling them at a cheap price on the rare occasions when one had some extra money, and taking Keith on drives up to Bristol, allowing him to see bands like Count Basie and Stan Kenton in concert. It was at this store that many of these young men received their first tastes of such revolutionary music as Ornette Coleman's "Something Else!," John Coltrane's "Giant Steps," the classic, late 50s Charles Mingus sides, and the under-appreciated but extremely adventurous Jamaican-born alto saxophonist and composer, Joe Harriott, all of which (and more) proved enormously influential.

Le Grice had come from a background similar to Rowe's, "working class—maybe even more lumpen than that—families on the verge of 'just about legal,'" and the two hit it off quickly and well, collaborating on a welded wire sculpture that caused a bit of a scandal when they decided to "exhibit" it on the roof of the school. His father had operated a small scrap metal business which likely led to his having one of the very few automobiles owned by any student, an enormous luxury. Le Grice had also played guitar and banjo with Rod Mason's band, a group playing New Orleans-style jazz, before joining Westbrook's school ensemble as one of two guitarists often employed.

In late 1958 or early 1959, one of those guitarists, probably Rob Lord, left Westbrook's band and Rowe was asked to join. By this time he'd learned a few jazz chords, enough to fake his way through most pieces, and settled into the role of rhythm guitarist. He'd recently gone to see the tenor Peter Pears performing Elizabethan songs with Julian Bream, most likely on lute, and found the idea of "the accompanist" very intriguing and attractive, a concept that would reverberate down through the years into his work of the next century. Despite the increased prominence of soloists like Charlie Christian (several solos by whom Rowe had learned by heart), the role of the jazz guitarist was still more often as a rhythm player, something that was a natural fit for Rowe's personality. Still, his relative lack of "chops" and natural inclination to go off on irregular tangents caused some amount of tension within the band. Westbrook's music was highly influenced by Ellington (in addition to some originals, the band would regularly perform standards by Ellington and Basie) and the rich, smooth arrangements didn't accommodate any sort of off-key or irregular playing, even if it was just the comping of a rhythm guitarist. Malcolm Le Grice remembers:

> I came to jazz from Armstrong and the Hot 5, Hot 7 so I needed some education into [the] more progressive stuff. I was in the Westbrook band before Keith started playing, but he came in with a more advanced idea of jazz guitar— Charlie Christian. Keith did not seem to bother to learn the guitar before he started playing in public—he learned on the stage and so his style was very wild and quite disruptive, but a challenge. I knew more about chords and sequences than Keith, but he was doing something more committed and dangerous.

Opinions vary on Rowe's degree of technical proficiency, or lack thereof, probably depending somewhat on which phase of his tenure with Westbrook is being cited. Rowe himself tended to denigrate his ability, at least as far as "jazz" playing goes, thinking that in addition to not really mastering the necessary rudiments, he never quite acquired the appropriate feel.

> *What I did do, because I was in Westbrook's band, is that I learned chords, I learned the changes (I've completely forgotten most of them now). I was kind of interested in doing the improvisations on the tunes but I would muck about with them so much that I was never really...I mean, if they were playing a 12-bar blues, mine would often be, like, 13 or 11.*

Some of his co-musicians would, in retrospect, grudgingly agree. Westbrook, asked if Rowe's playing at the time was crude, replied:

> Well, yes. I'd have to agree, viewed in any conventional terms. But people were interested in what he was doing or where he was aiming. He didn't really have the technique or the ear for conventional playing. He sort of bypassed it. He got the chords, but in terms of improvisation over set harmonies it was a very uneasy relationship. He was trying to reconcile the irreconcilable. But there were elements beginning to happen, an exciting electronic sound that I dimly recall now. He was into something, that was clear to everybody...He got a Barney Kessel chord book and proceeded. I think the actual graphic design of the chord symbols and of the guitar itself was as much of an attraction to him as the musical side!

Stan Willis recalled, regarding Rowe's playing:

> He was very strange. There were members in the Westbrook band who were sort of hostile to Keith's way of playing. I wondered about it at times. Certainly, he would at times produce quite a good, conventional jazz solo, but most of the time he would deliberately avoid that, just as he did in his art. He would avoid anything clichéd.

The band practiced fairly often, at least weekly, at the Plymouth Arts Centre, a building adjacent to the college, and played the odd dance or pub gig, the group swelling to between twelve and fourteen members at times. True to the nature of snarky art students everywhere, they gave their ensemble absurdist names to create an aura of oddness. So they might appear one day as Hieronymus Bosch and the Burghers, on another as Emily Stomp: Music in a Modern Manner. Terry Lidiard remembers seeing a listing at the Plymouth Jazz Club for a group called the Palace Court Jug Blowers and wandering in to discover it was the Westbrook band who, sure enough, in addition to their standard repertoire, did a piece that featured the ensemble blowing into bottles of Scrumpy's hard cider, the rotgut of choice in that neck of the woods.

One day, likely in 1959, Rowe and friends were hanging out, as usual, at the Hot Record Store/Clarke & Chinn's Music Shop.

> *This young guy comes in. Whether he was in shorts or not, I don't know, but it's possible. He comes in and he's looking for an instrument to play. He already played clarinet, classical clarinet, in school and he had this thick Devonshire accent and he says, "I need a bloody instrument to play, I like saxophones, you got any bloody saxophones?" And the guy says, "Well, we've got this one here" and it's a huge green [verdigris] baritone saxophone. [Surman: "Contrary to Keith's memory, it was big, gold and shiny!"] So Surman picks it up and immediately just goes off. So I said we've got this band that plays down at the art school and he came down.*

John Surman, several years younger than the rest of the musicians, was an instant hit with them, both for his ferocious attack on the baritone and his huge enthusiasm. His youthful image and boys' school togs lent themselves to many a humorous vignette:

> *One of the first gigs we had [with Surman in the band]*

was opposite a guy called Humphrey Littleton, a trad jazz trombonist. We did the warm-up and John and the baritone player from Littleton's group basically end up doing some kind of duel on the stage and Surman just wipes this guy away. This other guy's slick and cool with sunglasses and Surman's this youngster in short pants!

The thing is, he wasn't trying to put it over on anyone, he would just stick the thing in his gob. He had amazing lungs, John. I remember him having to go to a hospital with a lung infection. He's in bed and the nurse comes up and says, "We have to test your lung capacity with this instrument" that's basically a rubber hose attached to a glass tube filled with mercury. "Blow as hard as you can." He says, "No, I shouldn't do that." She says, "No, it's not a problem, just blow." So he blows the top off the thing, mercury all over the place.

Westbrook, in conjunction with Russell's record store, prepared a small flyer for a performance that describes the band's approach around this time. It provides an interesting view of the context in which "progressive" jazz viewed itself (in England) in the late 50s.

BEHIND THE TIMES

The Mike Westbrook band has been in existence for nearly four years. Abandoning New Orleans early in its career, the band arrived quickly at Jazz's middle period, where it has since remained. Ignoring the so-called Trad. Boom, the band persisted in this unpopular style, retreating further and further from the public eye and eventually arriving at the situation when a gig was almost an annual occasion. Tired of holding sessions in front rooms and on deserted beaches, of playing second fiddle to juke boxes, of trying to foist their music on indifferent and sometimes hostile ears (there is scarcely a hall or coffee bar in town where the band hasn't appeared once) the musicians abandoned their search for an audience.

The Arts Centre offered a refuge, a cellar known as Potter's Bar. Re-named the Plymouth Jazz Workshop, it quickly became a haven for the forgotten men of jazz. From local dance bands, military bands and rock groups came thwarted jazzmen in search of musical asylum. Saxophonists of every denomination queued up for solos in some astonishing jam-sessions at which many jazzmen met musically for the first time.

Soon the MWJB acquired the eight-piece line-up which was to prove the most successful. This new sound, while rooted in the rhythm-guitar era, and owing much to Duke Ellington and Count Basie, was never a carbon copy of any style. The repertoire consisted largely of original compositions and arrangements, tailored for that particular set of musicians. Soloists were allowed full reign, yet equally important was the kind of group feeling and intuition that can only come from keen mutual understanding.

New arrangements came thick and fast during the band's brief Golden Age (which included a memorable performance at Torquay Town Hall), but before the end of the summer began that partial disbandment that was to rob the group of four members.

Undaunted, the Quintet has kept the door of the Jazz Workshop firmly open, and the exiles have had to content themselves with an occasional reunion.

The young enthusiasts of the original Palace Court Jug Blowers have become the Grand Old Men of Plymouth Jazz, yet, despite increased musical assurance and changes in personnel, the line-up before you tonight remains faithful in every way to the spirit of the group that began to see the light in the Autumn of 1958.

At the beginning of the fall 1959 term, a young woman arrived at the college, someone who was entirely uninterested in its "finishing school" attributes. Krystyna Nelson née Dziegielewska (pronounced: Jag–uh–LEV–ska) was the daughter of an English woman and a Polish fighter pilot who had been shot down and killed over Nantes, France on May 19, 1943, when she was eleven months old. She was born and raised in England, her mother remarrying Olaf Nelson when she was twelve. By her early teens, Krystyna was determined to attend the Royal Academy of Drama and Arts with the intention of becoming an actress. When her drama teacher approached her parents to advise them on her application to the school, her stepfather, a hardheaded pragmatic conservative, declared, "Certainly not! Young ladies do not go to drama college!" The unspoken addendum being, "They marry officers and gentlemen." The distraught (and quite headstrong) Krystyna left home and signed herself up at the Plymouth School of Arts and Crafts after an art tutor suggested that by studying stage design, she might work her way into the theatre. She knew the academy already, having taken some drawing classes there and, in fact, having noticed a certain tall, attractive student in the class.

She entered the Fine Arts program, concentrating in exactly the same principal areas as Rowe, painting and lithography, becoming quite proficient in the latter. She was drawn to him from the start.

> Keith had a presence; he was magnetic, with a very laid back approach to life. Whereas everyone else seemed to undergo forms of angst to achieve results, Keith just did it. There was an intensity about him; it was a strange contradiction, almost two forces working within one being. It was like being with a constantly taut violin string. I think this is what enabled him to break things apart, look beyond the accepted, the obvious, and the conventional. He was an explorer, a challenger, a questioner, and an unraveller.[4]

---

4   Krystyna Roberts, 2004.

The combination of extreme poverty and willful bohemianism was readily apparent.

> He was almost plastered into or sewn into these dreadful trousers and this dreadful black sweater and a black leather jacket like a bomber's jacket. He did not give a rat's ass about people's opinion of him.[5]

The "grotty" black sweater with a yellow horizontal stripe is recalled by virtually everyone who knew him at the time; he was rarely seen without it. Still,

> He was tall, he had beautiful hands. I remember being very struck by his hands. I was absolutely in awe of him. He taught me everything I know about jazz. I mean, I was a rock and roller. I've always loved, absolutely loved, dancing and I had a sense of rhythm, but I knew nothing about jazz. I was very awestruck by his work. I thought his paintings were absolutely fantastic. I suppose I followed him around rather like a schoolgirl. It's a wonder he didn't kick me off. Quite a few female students at the time fancied Keith. I think it was a combination of the sense of humour, the laconic attitude, his work, and the music.[6]

While Rowe's visual art was somewhat under the influence of painters like Munch and Nolde, Chagall gradually became a predominant force. He created a series of floating nudes in a Chagall-like style for an exhibition in the Plymouth Art Gallery which was adjacent to the local museum but the local administrators, led by the head of the Art School, Fred Forrest, and assisted by area Freemasonry groups and the Plymouth Brethren, a Christian organization of great influence, found them unacceptably offensive and had the show canceled.

---

5   Ibid.

6   Ibid.

Forrest was a popular brunt of antics and practical jokes on the part of the art students. One day, Rowe and Le Grice constructed an enormous, shocking pink "Cadillac" out of scrap wood and other detritus, depositing it on the roof of the Art College, the next they'd parade through a posh department store carrying a huge painting of a particularly lascivious nude.

But the professor with the longest lasting influence on Rowe was Ben Hartley, who began teaching in Plymouth in 1960. A quiet, religious man, he stressed understatement and the lack of self-importance, choosing to paint the majority of his own work on brown wrapping paper. His subjects were local ephemera done in a primitivist style but always with a care for placement of shapes and muted colors.

> *...in my mind's eye, I'm always surrounded by a virtual world of experiences, people/things, objects/stories, etc. and Ben has always stood behind me high to the right hand side, a long shape, always, always there. If I ever thought about him, my mind's eye would immediately locate him there. Or if I thought about the issues, "promotion-projection-presentation-your reason for doing something," etc. my internal world would locate Ben's long, dark shape and Ben's ethics would have to be addressed. I think how I've realized Ben's "reticence" is obliqueness— delayed interpretation—no rush to express—no need to express—to do your work honestly—there is no hurry, etc., resistance, preferring obscurity.*

In addition to a profound ethical influence, Hartley's formal approach would also resonate down the years. Rowe's cover painting for the *Duos for Doris* album bears a striking resemblance to a work by Hartley from the Plymouth period, titled "Dragonfly and Legs," including a pair of black shoe-clad lower limbs descending from the upper edge of the painting.

Still, Rowe's adolescent obsessions with bicycling and car

racing were difficult to shake and he'd often sneak a representation of one or another into a painting no matter how inappropriate. Ron Hills recalls:

> When we were practicing pictorial composition, he'd always manage to stick one in somewhere in the piece. And I'd go across and say—this was a routine we had—"Excuse me, Keith, that looks very much like a BMW" and he'd say, "No, no, it's a star."

The students also staged the odd "happening" in public areas to the bafflement of local citizenry. An undated photo (likely from around 1959) from the local newspaper shows three students in an outdoor square, Rowe clad in bowler and omnipresent yellow-striped dark sweater, kneeling on top of a pile of large, abstract drawings participating in an obscure put-on ritual, the others sporting lab-coats and long straw wigs. A crowd of amused-looking onlookers is in the background. The charming caption reads:

> This startling form of "art" is evidently fascinating the bystanders, or perhaps they are just as intrigued by the antics and ultra-Bohemian garb of the "artists." This almost-Parisian scene, in Plymouth City Centre today, was just one of the facets of Plymouth and Davenport Technical College students' Rag Week activities.

Krystyna and Keith quickly became a pair. Bitten by the jazz bug and particularly overwhelmed by her discovery, through Keith, of Billie Holiday, she sang once in a while with the Westbrook band.

> Just a little bit. When the Westbrook band started up, they didn't have a singer. Westbrook's first wife, Caroline, sang for a bit and then they decided to let me have a go. I remember singing at a concert they did, I think at the Athenaeum Theatre in Plymouth, and I sang three

songs that John Surman scored for me. I was wearing my mother's red evening gown![7]

A program for a concert by the Westbrook Band at the Athenaeum Theatre on June 30th (presumably 1960) listed the following personnel and program:

Mike Westbrook	Trumpet
Ron Hills	Trombone
Mike Lloyd	Tenor Saxophone
John Surman	Baritone Saxophone
Graham Russell	Piano
Keith Rowe	Guitar
Terry Liddiard [sic]	Drums
Miles Scott	Bass
Krystyna Nelson	Vocals

[Songs]

Juno
Tomato
Potter's Bar
Master Copy
The Big Four
Farewell Blues
The Good Noise
Giant Grim
Doodlin'
Behind the Times
How About You?
Little Darlin'
Trombone in the Basement
Mood Indigo
Duke's Dinner

---

7   Roberts, 2004.

Browsing in Clarke & Chinn's music shop, Rowe found a dusty and dirty Gibson guitar. It cost about 25 pounds, a tidy sum in those days, but he scraped together the cash, cleaned it up, and became quite attached to it. "That was his first baby, his first beautiful guitar," as Krystyna recalls. The two would sit in her studio on the Barbican, she painting, Rowe playing, doggedly learning to play "proper" jazz guitar from records and the occasional how-to book. The Westbrook band continued to practice with some regularity, still very much a local band and rough enough around the edges that more established musicians on the scene, members of dance bands who worked routinely, wouldn't likely find it of enough interest or competence to sit in with. Westbrook made a point of introducing modern fare like "Lullaby of the Leaves," "Poinciana" or "Chelsea Bridge," pieces that tested the limits of the young musicians.

Still, painting was Rowe's primary focus, though occasionally music would find its way into a given work. For a while, he fell under the spell of the early 20th century English Impressionist Walter Sickert, a student of Degas and an odd character whose name sometimes surfaces when people ponder the identity of Jack the Ripper. For an examination, Rowe created a painting of an imaginary musical performance, viewed from a skewed angle over the stage, of Ella Fitzgerald, Oscar Peterson, Herb Ellis, and Ray Brown that owed much to Sickert. He also began to refine his working materials down to only a handful of colors, enamel house paints, and Masonite board, using large, flat areas of tone with little painterly expression.

> I know this will be weird, but probably toward the end
> of this time, people like Chagall would be a big influence.
> Quite romantic, in a way. I remember doing a few paint-
> ings which would be called The Lovers. Kind of European,
> in that respect. And that, invariably, they would be rather
> long paintings and it would be almost like a wave, almost
> like a Henry Moore, like Reclining Nude, like that [drawing
> a curving figure in the air] and then maybe another one

would be like that and this would, say, be blue and that would be red and this would be white. [It was] a kind of figurative abstraction, but with no eyes or teeth or hair. Almost like a painted version of Brancusi, like that kind of European curve. I also, oddly enough, was very interested in square paintings. I would take fruit pie covers or take, for instance, you know the "K" in Kellogg's? I'd take that "K" and take half of it and base a piece on that. There's a painting we studied we knew as "The Watering Can Solution." The painting would "dribble out" of the corner if it wasn't for the fact of the watering can there which actually brings your eye back up, the spout makes you eye go up. The whole "watering can solution" became quite important and cropping—absolutely decisive. Those angles in the corner that are keeping things from leaking out of the space.

A requirement for one's final presentation, in addition to a finished "thesis" painting, was to incorporate all the various fields one had learned during the course of study into one project, generally taking the form of a "book" of some sort. Not only did the student have to actually create the physical book itself (bookbinding being one of the areas of study), but he or she would have to include examples of calligraphy and illustration in addition to the paintings, drawings, and lithographs produced over the years. Rowe, true to form, cobbled together this document the weekend prior to its due-date, almost daring the professors to decipher his chicken-scratch handwriting (no typewriters around). His dissertation involved perhaps the earliest definitive glimmer of his idea of the non-differentiation between music and visual art. It was called, *The Guitar*.

It was the guitars of Braque and Picasso as seen in their various paintings. Particularly Braque, but all artists, including Juan Gris. The guitar was a very important visual element in those paintings along with glasses and bottles, the man with the guitar, pipes. But something about those strings combined with the curves...And what I wrote about, because by then I was actually playing the guitar, I tried to imagine how they [the guitars in the paintings] would actually sound. What would this guitar actually sound like, what would this music be like?

It passed.

Chapter 3

In the summer of 1960, Rowe found himself with a degree in Fine Arts and every bit as penniless as before. Westbrook had also graduated and was still in town (he would move to London in the spring of 1962) and band members practiced and performed sporadically but the notion of any ongoing group had begun to evaporate. With the intention of eventually getting to London himself, Rowe set about acquiring a job in order to save up the necessary money to make the trip. A choice soon presented itself: window dresser at The Coop, a local department store, or laborer in the dockyard in Devonport. He chose the latter.

The grimness of the job cannot be overstated.

> *I worked in a gang. It was a shipyard for warships and there was an aircraft carrier called the HMS* Eagle; *I worked almost exclusively in that period on the* Eagle. *As you know, aircraft carriers have a kind of central island which is set to one side. This island was being reconstructed and made lighter and to counterbalance that island there's pig iron between the armor plating and the superstructure and, obviously, there was too much pig iron once the island was lightened. So myself and a couple of other people had to make a hole in the side of the ship, like a couple of feet square, and then you slid down inside this gap, which is about a foot, two feet wide. You have a pair of rub-*

ber gloves and a light bulb at the end of a lead, a very long lead, and a crowbar and you crowbarred the pig iron out of there. And you passed it up one by one and threw them outside the hole. That pretty well took up one summer.

Things didn't improve as Rowe moved on to the next job at the docks.

Then they emptied the diesel fuel tanks. The diesel tank was a huge square, like a football stadium-sized square, full of baffles at different angles to prevent the fuel from sloshing too much during transit. They open up a hatch on top of the fuel tank a couple of feet across. Diesel fuel is really slippery stuff, really greasy. My job was that when they pumped the tanks dry, in fact there's still a couple of inches of diesel fuel on the bottom that can't be pumped out. And that had to be got out and the only way of getting it out is that you go into the tank—and the smell is horrendous—with a light bulb at the end of a piece of flexible rod. You go down these slippery ladders, and they're really slippery, you get to the bottom and then, with a rag, you mop it up and wring it into a bucket. You pull the string and the person at the top pulls the bucket up and puts its contents into a container and then the bucket comes back down. It was so horrible that you could only do it for 18-20 minutes and you had to come up for fresh air. Now, aside from that—you obviously had the smell—but what's really horrendous is the noise because you're in a huge metal chamber and on the outside there are these things called corkers. They're taking a pneumatic drill with a huge chisel at the end of it and they're taking the tops of rivets off and inside the noise was absolutely horrendous.

[Author: Worse than an early AMM performance?]

Right! I mean, this explains a lot, yes? So there I was, this student with a fine arts degree, very ambitious, wanting to do all this music but because the kind of poverty of my situation had to do that work to save up for train fare [to get to London]. It took me a year and a half because the pay was so bad.

There were awakenings in the middle of the night, admiralty police banging on the door of the Rowe household, rounding up 1,000 men to manually tow a carrier from one berth to another. But there were also the odd jobs that could encourage a calmer, more meditative outlook as when he was assigned, on his own, to sweep the enormous flight deck of the ship, an endless, peaceful kind of work amidst chaotic surroundings. On occasion, while entombed in the bowels of the carrier, Rowe could hear songs being played on transistor radios on the deck outside, filtered in and metallically distorted, creating an alien sound world at once evocative and disorienting.

Working among the dock laborers, the cultural split between his origins and the kind of atmosphere he was aiming to enter grew ever deeper. The worldly cynicism of men who might never get very far beyond the dockyards, the total ignorance of any notion of "Art" or of the idea that life could be different, made working there, physical issues aside, a wrenching experience for Rowe's psyche.

> *In the dockyard, the men who worked there said, once you get in the dockyard you never escape. Basically, you go in there, you never come out. And they could not believe that anyone could go in there out of choice and then go out and I said, "Well, I am. I don't know what the date is, but I'm going to leave and go to London." "Yeah, yeah." And that whole kind of humor there was a kind of homophobic humor, was all to do with fake homosexuality where all the men would pretend to be gay, make gay jokes, touching men on their bums and all of that. I mean, really an extraordinary culture, with foul language, unbelievable foul language, swearing, "fucking" and "blimey," they couldn't speak without swearing. Except, on Sunday mornings you'd actually see them in the center of Plym-*

outh with their wives, pushing a push chair, being utter gentlemen, saying, "Hello, Keith, how are you this morning?" whereas back in the dockyard they were absolutely awful. I think if they were ever actually faced with a gay guy who had come out they would run a mile, they'd be really scared! I never quite worked all that out when I was there but I remember the culture.

United States naval vessels docked regularly in Plymouth. There would often be a few musicians on board who would make their way to the local music bars to sit in with whoever happened to be around. In early 1962, the USS *Wasp* pulled into harbor. One of the sailors was the baritone saxophonist (and future tuba player extraordinaire) Howard Johnson:

> Leslie Watts, [who worked] in a good record store...put me on to John Surman, a very shaggy schoolboy who played a pretty beat-up baritone very, very well. When I let him play my new Selmer, it was the first time (and only time outside of the movies!) I ever heard an Englishman say, "Blimey!" So we did hang out and play a bit. A little too much is made of whatever my influence was at the time because even then John was his own man. But it was kinda trippy for him. I think [so] because he said at the time that I was the first American he had ever met, the first black person, and the first baritone player. His way and his independence had a positive impact on me too. So on the most important level we were no more than peers striving together.

Johnson apparently sat in with Westbrook's band on at least one occasion (as did, according to Stan Willis, Joe Harriott a couple of times) and his presence had an impact beyond the purely musical. The mere fact that an American jazz musician played with these "locals" as an equal was quite important for their self-regard. Virtually every musician from that scene at the time recalled Johnson's visit with fondness.

Rowe's romance with Krystyna Nelson, still a student at the Art School, continued unabated, though not without stiff resistance from her parents. It was bad enough that she was going out with this weedy would-be artist/musician, worse yet that he was earning a paltry living cleaning fuel out of the hulls of ships. Olaf Nelson was a state agent (a real estate agent, in American parlance), though apparently not a very good one as his income was erratic. They kept up appearances however, living in a fancy house in a very nice neighborhood. Rowe was required to submit to a kind of dinner/interview, arriving in borrowed formal wear and having his silverware skills closely scrutinized while eating. Both he and Krystyna would later acknowledge that at least part of the fuel that stoked their relationship was her intense desire to revolt against her family's mores.

Both his painting and music suffered from lack of attention during these years. Not having access to a studio space drastically curtailed the former, though he'd already switched from canvas to hardboard and had begun using enamel house paints in a minimal range of primary colors. But even that low level of documentation was pretty much left by the wayside in favor of music and the reasons had something to do with a burgeoning philosophical attitude toward the idea of "commodity":

> With music, I didn't have the commodity. I didn't have the luggage of the canvas. I hit the guitar and made a note, and the note disappeared into air, I didn't have anything. It was completely fluid. I could constantly change it. I really enjoyed that.[8]

He still occasionally played with the remnants of the Westbrook band, including John Surman, and Westbrook himself came back from London several times, generally organizing a few rehearsals and a show if possible, but the majority of music making was

---

8   Interview with Rowe by Dan Warburton in *Paris Transatlantic*, January 2001.

confined to practicing the guitar by himself in the small bedroom at Auntie Mary's house. He continued frequenting Peter Russell's shop, still listening to Woody Herman and Stan Kenton but becoming increasingly drawn to the new music of Ornette Coleman, Cecil Taylor, and Charles Mingus. His art school background came in handy when dealing with Coleman's concept, recognizing it for its boundary-breaking aspects and, partially because of this, finding it not nearly as difficult to "hear" as many did at the time. Voice of America radio also provided an ongoing stream of American jazz, and Rowe kept his ear pressed to the box as much as possible. But a professor's admonition, "Rowe, you cannot paint a Caravaggio. Only Caravaggio can paint a Caravaggio" gnawed at him, causing him to continue to question the whole idea of, for instance, trying to play like Jim Hall. He did, however, manage to acquire a mono record player in 1962. His first piece of vinyl: a Django Reinhardt/Stephane Grappelli 7" 45 rpm.

By late 1962, enough money had been saved to quit the dockyards and make the move to London. Rowe and Surman hopped on the train and arrived to sleep on the floor in Westbrook's two-room apartment that he held with his first wife, Caroline. Krystyna, still a student, remained back in Plymouth but the two corresponded via letters every day. Surman enrolled as a clarinet student in the London School of Music and Rowe went on the dole.

Soon, on a tip from Westbrook, they found an apartment on Tavistock Crescent in Notting Hill, two tiny rooms, a kitchenette, and bath in the basement of a building that otherwise housed the neighborhood prostitution trade.

> *...on the first floor above us was a white prostitute with a white partner, above them a white prostitute with a black partner. In the front of the house was a Canadian couple who never came out of their room! Above them was a white, gay hustler and in the front room [on the third floor] lived Phil Minton [presumably a bit later, beginning around 1963], who was working in a psychiatric hospital at the time.*

The building's garbage was stored immediately outside their flat, in cans so rusted the bottoms often disintegrated, leaving mounds of refuse for the great benefit of the local rodent population. Hustlers and strong-arm men were always about, forcibly or by guile relieving innocents of their worldly goods. The rear of the house abutted a rail yard, reachable by a nearby footbridge. A public toilet was positioned on the near side, a convenience that also served as a contact place for the area's gay population. At night, the prostitutes would pick up a mark on the opposite bank and take some money, telling them, "I'm going to walk over the bridge and I'm going to turn left. Three doors along is my apartment; we'll meet there." Of course, they'd get over the bridge and quickly turn toward the toilet and then surreptitiously leave the area. Rowe and Surman would hear the clop-clop-clop of the eager paramour followed by the slam of a door and shouts of, "You fucking slag! I'll fucking kill you!"

But the ladies took a shine to these unusual boys practicing jazz in their basement, coming down for chats, flashing the occasional bum as they deposited their trash and generally taking them under their wing to protect them from the sleazier characters that frequented their house. With virtually no money, they subsisted on scraps the local butcher would throw their way—meat pies and some mashed potatoes—while they practiced and talked music all day. Well, that and the odd Rube Goldberg construction:

> There was one day when I went there and Keith and a couple guys living there, maybe John Surman and Phil Minton, had rigged up the flat with strings. So, you opened the door to the room, a teaspoon would come out of a cup and a bell would ring. They'd spent the whole day rigging this room up because they had nothing else better to do.[9]

Malcolm Le Grice moved in during 1963, joining Rowe, Surman,

---

9   Roberts, 2004.

and Minton in the basement performances as well as dealing with the day-to-day outside their room.

> I had an old Ford van—the kids put sand in the fuel tank—no malice, just boredom. Keith and I took the fuel tank off and drained it—then dried it out by setting light to it—we could have both been killed as it exploded a jet of flame—however we were not—as is obvious—I put the tank back but the carburetor was never really clear of that sand.

> Drinking Advocaat—that yellow egg spirit—attacking a mouse with a wire coat hanger—huge paintings—the smell of turpentine, a canvas camp bed—no routine.

Rowe would occasionally make surprise visits to Krystyna back in Plymouth but in lieu of that they kept up the constant stream of letters. She graduated in June 1963 and applied for teacher training at several colleges including Goldsmiths College of the University of London to which she was accepted, beginning her studies there in September, allowing the couple to be reunited. Eventually she obtained a job as a teacher and, with Rowe having gotten off the dole and making a little bit of money working in an advertising agency, decided to get married, doing so in a civil ceremony on December 19, 1964. This was his exit out of the miserable flat as the two settled into a small but adequate place in Vauxhall still with just enough income to live on. In the meantime, it was life in the hovel livened with the odd performance that Westbrook could rustle up.

Minton, who by 1963 was also performing in the Westbrook band, had likewise been pointed to the apartment. He had first encountered the group about a year earlier at one of the gigs organized by Westbrook with his Plymouth band members.

> The first time I heard Keith was at the Taunton Jazz Festival in 1962. I was playing in a group called the Brian Wilson Quartet and part of the festival had a ridiculous

thing: a jazz contest. A stupid, fucking idea. Well, we did it. We didn't think we stood a chance because we knew this famous band from Plymouth would be there, a band led by this guy called Allen Rowe [no relation]. He was a very hip, fantastic saxophone player, brilliant. We get up there in the morning in front of a prestigious group of judges, all London musicians. I was just playing trumpet then and it went better than we thought. Then the [Allen] Rowe band went up and it didn't really happen. I was amazed. They just set up a phenomenal tempo, like playing "I'll Remember April" at 100 mph and they did it too fast. Then I heard this other band, the Mike Westbrook Workshop band from Plymouth, and I'd never heard anything about them at all. I was blown away! I was listening to Coltrane, Dolphy, and Ornette and you could hear some of that in there.

What blew me away were Keith and John Surman. I just couldn't believe it. These guys were from Plymouth?! Keith may not have sounded like he wanted to sound then, but it was strong. It was strong, it was something. There was a freedom to it that wasn't being held back by, like, people wanting to play jazz riffs. He's a kindred spirit, really, that's what you knew. And John Surman was out of this world! At 17 years old! Incredible! I didn't talk to Keith then. Nobody talked to anybody, they just sort of scowled at each other. About a week later, out of pure coincidence, I went to a jam session at Newton Abbot Art College with a few friends and who were playing there but John Surman and Stan Willis. Keith wasn't there, I don't think. I was doing my Jimmy Rushing pantomime, the bel canto blues singing I could sort of do. And John said, "Why don't you come up to London? We have a band up there, the Mike Westbrook band, and we have a gig at the Marquee." So, I packed my job—I was a laborer working for the Southwestern

Electricity Board—and I was up in London in a week.[10]

Gradually, the Plymouth-based musicians were superseded by those from London, the group coming to include trumpeter Henry Lowther, trombonist Malcolm Griffiths, French horn player Tom Bennellick, the ferocious young altoist Mike Osborne, tenor saxophonist Lou Gare, pianist Ken McCarthy, bassist Lawrence Sheaff, and drummer Alan Jackson.

Rehearsals with the Westbrook band were far more numerous than actual gigs and when the latter did come along, they could be a little odd. Westbrook had been working as a "visualizer" for an interior design company. That is to say, clients would describe the sort of look they were interested in and he would sketch out several variations in sundry colors from which they could choose. One of them heard that he led a jazz group and invited them to play for a party, one of their very first paying gigs. The group, numbering about twelve musicians plus assorted girlfriends and pals, rented a van and drove to the address in an extremely posh area well outside the city. They arrived mid-afternoon and set up for the first part of the job, performing in front of the swimming pool, playing things like "C Jam Blues" and some originals. Several guys appeared and began fooling around in the pool, splashing the musicians a bit. This irritated the already grumpy Osborne and Surman who were peeved at both the absence of food and apparent lack of women in attendance. Rowe was afraid to look closely at what was going on in the pool. "Anyway, I'm the rhythm player so my head was down!" That portion of the event eventually finished and the host asked the band to set up once more inside, in the marquee area, a kind of ballroom with chandeliers and a bandstand. More importantly, there was food and drink. Come evening, guests were arriving by the dozen, 100-200 men of all ages, dancing and jiving to

---

10   That festival, held August 25, 1962, also featured the Joe Harriott Quintet. It's interesting to note that on Rowe's copy of the program, Harriott's is the sole autograph, one of only two or three that Rowe ever sought.

the band. Things loosened up enough to the degree that every time one of the musicians took a solo, guys would come up onto the stage to embrace and kiss him.

> "So it gets to the point where no one is soloing, like Music Minus One and the Minus One is the guy doing the solo. And Westbrook is frantically pointing to people to stand up and solo but no one would do it!"

At one point the pianist decided to use the toilet, disappeared for about fifteen minutes and returned ashen and in shock. Making his way to the house in search of the facilities, he'd encountered all manner of indiscreet activities taking place behind bushes, in foyers, almost wherever he looked. In the house, he spied a group of men gathered at the base of a large staircase looking up, wandered over, and witnessed a man having intercourse with a French poodle by the name of Chocolate. He dared not venture into the toilet. They finished the gig and prepared to leave but the van was stuck in the grass. Several of the guests assisted the crew pushing it free, helping themselves to more than a handful of grabs in the process. One of the friends of the band, Eric Morby, the hardest drinking member of the bunch, was missing. The musicians went back to search for him and soon the front door opened and Morby, unconscious, was thrown bodily from the house. When he came to, they discovered he'd vomited and passed out on a bed and had been beaten and raped. As a wry postscript, about a week later, the band was practicing in the basement apartment, there came a knock on the door and it's the guy with the poodle, come to say hello to Westbrook. For a backwater boy from Plymouth, this was quite the London eye-opener.

Though that may have been the most bizarre gig, it wasn't the most dangerous. Shortly afterwards, the were offered the opportunity to play two Saturday night shows in a dance hall at the Mercury Theatre in Nottinghill Gate as a replacement for the regular group there. This was around the time The Beatles were beginning their early rise to fame and the crowd that arrived to the dance was hardly one geared to appreciate modern jazz.

> *So we're part of the way into the gig and there's two guys come up and ask us to play "Twist and Shout" and Westbrook kind of goes over, with his educated voice, and says, "Sorry, we don't play 'Twist And Shout,' this is a jazz band." So these guys start yelling, "'Twist and Shout"! C'mon, "Twist and Shout!"' So we play some more of Mike's stuff and they come up again, "C'mon, we want 'Twist and Shout' not this fucking rubbish you're fucking playing!" And Surman says, "Well, fuck off! We're not playing fuck all for you wankers!" So they leave, we carry on playing the gig. It finishes and we're getting set to leave, packing up, chatting, when the doors burst open and in come maybe ten guys, all drunk, led by the two guys who wanted to have "Twist and Shout" played. They get fire buckets off the wall, full of water, and throw them at us and a huge fight takes place on the dance floor. Westbrook and Surman are held by some other guys while one hits them over the head with a music stand. Westbrook looks like he's been in WWII, he's got water and blood all over him and Surman, he had to be taken to the hospital for stitches. Now this club had a kind of theatrical bar at the side and in the bar that night was working a man who was an actor, the guy who played Larry the Lamb on this children's program.[11] He comes in, sees this huge fight going on, and in his top theatrical projection and voice, shouts, "STOP IT!" like Charlton Heston or something and they all stopped and ran away. That was a good gig. And these guys said, "If you fucking come back next week, we'll kill you!" So, not being cowards, we came back and I have a great image of Osborne, who was as much of a coward as the rest of us, sitting there on stage with his coat and hat on, his music case all the way open to drop his saxophone into and get the hell out of there! Eyes*

---

11   Possibly Derek McCulloch.

on the door. It was somewhat ironic that later, Westbrook
actually did do a Beatles album.[12]

The band caught the odd gig at local community centers but it
was tough to break into the jazz club scene in London; they were
actually more popular outside of the city where audiences, even
if they had less exposure to "progressive" jazz, were more relaxed
and accommodating. Surman complained that London audiences were too blasé and indifferent: "I remember one session in a
suburban club where we couldn't get any kind of a reaction at
all. I started making the most awful noises possible, but no one
even put their hands over their ears!" They also performed some
pieces that went beyond simply standing on-stage, including a
45-minute calypso where band members wandered amongst the
dancing audience, improvising freely. The program for a March 9,
1965 concert at the 11th St. Pancras Arts Festival in London lists
an extended work by Surman titled, "Jazz Legend," based on a
poem by Doreen Moore and featuring thirteen additional musicians as well as four actors.

The Westbrook band still returned on occasion to Plymouth,
mostly for small affairs. One flyer proclaimed: "Jive! Wyndham
Hall Rock! Two Bands!! Rock & Jazz!! Mike Satan and the Demons
– The Mike Westbrook Band." Peter Russell, who was writing for
Jazz Monthly at the time, did manage to organize a larger event
that was recorded for telecast in Plymouth in August of 1965 and
wrote it up in the September issue of the magazine. Despite his
involvement, Russell offers a very even-handed evaluation of the
performance, admiring the general conception and direction
(including the complexities of Westbrook's charts), while taking
note of the less-than-mature caliber of several of the musicians.
He notes the modernist tendencies of Surman and trombonist
Malcolm Griffiths, apparently enjoying the contrast they provided
on otherwise mainstream pieces like "Chelsea Bridge" and "Come

---

12   Also perhaps a subsidiary source of Rowe's lifelong antipathy towards
the Fab Four.

Rain or Come Shine." Surman brought in a piece of his titled "Galata Bridge," inspired by a recent tour of Turkey, [13] which featured a solo section for Rowe. Russell wrote:

> After several years of bizarre playing in a sort of anti-jazz style that always ill-suited his supposed role of rhythm guitarist, Rowe now seems on the point of demonstrating that his individual approach to jazz guitar is fully vindicated. As an original and completely uncompromising artist his musical future will be worth watching. The strong Turkish flavor he injected into his solo here was perhaps a bit of conscious programming, but it also managed to be a masterful snatch of jazz playing.

Little by little, Westbrook's band began to attract notice in the jazz press, most of it quite favorable. Derek Jewell, in the *Sunday Times*, reviewed a performance at the Kensington Music Society noting a "fiercely modern, consciously muscular" style. "You hear echoes of Ellington, Mulligan, Monk, Mingus and, most nostalgically, the 1949-50 Miles Davis Capitol band." He also noted that the band "did not swing enough and turned its back on the blues," and quoted an unnamed bandleader derisively remarking after their sixth number, "That was the first major chord tonight." Michael Shera wrote a detailed, two page article for *Jazz Journal* (complete with photographs of all the band members) in early 1965, comparing the group to Mingus' ensembles. He was one of many who sensed that connection, a comparison Westbrook certainly appreciated. When asked to cite his favorite musicians, Westbrook responded:

> Duke mainly, and more recently Mingus. I feel an affinity with Mingus, and I see in him an artist whose every per-

---

13   In 1964, Surman had the opportunity to go to Turkey with the London Students Madrigal Choir. As they were in dire need of a bass singer, Phil Minton, by then the regular trumpeter in Westbrook's band, also went along but enjoyed himself enough there to not return to London until 1966.

formance is a defiant affirmation of the true jazz values. At a time when jazz is being widely betrayed, compromised and abused in the public's mind, I think that the jazz musician must constantly clarify his artistic position in positive terms. This is not the time for mincing matters if the music we love is to retain its identity and dignity. I also admire Duke and Mingus for their ability to use a group of musicians to explore themes that extend beyond the music itself.

Of Rowe's playing, Shera simply wrote:

Guitarist Keith Rowe is the first avant-garde guitarist I have heard, and he is an entirely convincing and exciting exponent of the genre.

Happily, Rowe retained possession of a tape of a live performance of the band, probably from 1964. The date makes sense insofar as Rowe was still being given substantial solo opportunities; his playing hadn't moved *quite* outside enough to be relegated to the back bench. Indeed, the opening track is a rendition of "Chelsea Bridge" on which Rowe's comping has much the globular, bubbling style of Jim Hall, not offensive in the slightest, and very much accommodating to the changes, though clearly conscious of his obbligato role, commenting subtly on Surman's baritone solo. Westbrook announces the ensuing piece as a multi-part composition that incorporates free playing. It begins in a kind of Mingus-y mode, settling into a quick, modal vamp with a tenor solo (Lou Gare?) before the free section kicks in. It's pretty much a free-for-all and only lasts for a minute, but Rowe can be heard knifing through, though again without distortion and in a relatively traditional manner. When the next theme enters, a soft, Gil Evans-like song, he plays some lovely chords that belie any notion of an inability to play things straight.

The Surman piece "Galata Bridge" very much anticipates the sort of fare the Willem Breuker Kollektief would develop some ten years hence. Rowe takes the first solo and here, one briefly gets a strong sense of what all the bother was about as he sends icy needles into the loping composition, heedless of its own "style." There follows a medium tempo blues, again featuring Rowe, who plays quite ably, if traditionally, in his first chorus but begins splintering things in his second. Another slow, modal piece, somewhat in the manner of Coltrane, affords an opportunity for Rowe to take things further out—single notes that begin on key, but gradually splay out into foreign realms, including intimations of feedback. It's "simple" in terms of the clarity of the notes, but verging on the entirely atonal; one can imagine the sort of looks he might have been receiving from the more conservative members of the band.

A later number, another slow blues, finds Rowe in an extremely harsh mode, ripping out a solo, managing to retain the bluesy feel while at the same time incorporating a kind of pointillism that seems reminiscent, as will be seen, of Webern. The set also contains some notably ferocious bass work by Lawrence Sheaff, giving clear notice that Rowe wasn't the only forward-looking member.

On the home front there was a development with Krystyna's elderly grandmother. She was a rather wealthy widower, having been married to a successful builder/developer. Krystyna's parents had, for some years in fact, been living well above their means in anticipation of soon receiving a hefty inheritance. Apparently the grandmother had been in touch with a savvy solicitor who informed her that she could avoid the inheritance tax by "jumping" a generation in her will, i.e., leaving her estate to her granddaughter. She followed his advice and shortly after she died, early in 1965, the young couple woke up and found themselves sitting on quite a little stack of money. Her parents, needless to say, were distraught to the point of physical illness.

> *Obviously, we had no option in a sense; we did the decent thing and gave them [her parents] the money. It would have been part of me; I wasn't that interested. It wouldn't*

bother me. We were reasonably OK at this point, both hav-
ing jobs. I think the morality of it was more important than
money. I suppose it's possible that Krystyna said that she'd
inherit it one day anyway, so...

The couple went in a matter of days from possessing a fair
amount of wealth back to a state of hand-to-mouth living. To help
make ends meet, Rowe did some off-hours babysitting for Alan
Cohen, a teacher at the Royal Academy of Music and a musician
who straddled both the contemporary classical and jazz scenes,
as well as turning in the occasional pop arrangement for band-
leaders like Joe Loss, whose "March of the Mods" was something
of a hit in 1964. He also led a big band, somewhat more experimental in nature than Westbrook's, which Rowe and Surman
would play with now and then. Cohen's record collection became
an enormous source of inspiration for Rowe, providing his first
exposure to 20th century classical composition, particularly that
of Anton Webern.

Combined with his ongoing interest in the further reaches of the
jazz avant-garde, this growing appreciation for non-jazz experimen-
talism only made the already burgeoning musical tensions in the
Westbrook band that much more severe. Webern-esque began to
creep into his playing, resulting in spatters of pointillistic notes high
up on the fretboard, clinky sounds that bore little relation even to
Ornette-inspired jazz, much less to the sort of progressive mainstream model that Westbrook had in mind. In terms of transferring
this newly acquired knowledge to the guitar, Rowe still found his
output to be a little too polite, with less energy than he wanted
to bring to the fore. "I quite liked the idea of ripping it along." It's
reasonable to speculate that some of this desire to play loudly
and aggressively, something that would continue on and even be
an issue of sorts in upcoming years, stemmed in part from the
electrification of the nascent rock scene and the increased decibel
levels thereby achievable. Rowe was very familiar with the British
jazz/blues bands that were beginning to appear around this time
and would go see groups led by Graham Bond, Alexis Korner, and

Manfred Mann. In retrospect, it's not difficult to imagine these three strands—the freedom of avant-garde jazz, the structural and philosophical connotations of serial and post-serial classical music, and the protean power offered by rock amplification—conspiring to produce an attack that might confound, and conceivably transcend, aspects of all three approaches. Around this time,

> ...I made a New Year's resolution not to tune the guitar anymore. As the months rolled on, the guitar became more and more out of tune. Westbrook would give me scores and I would cut out images from magazines and fruit pie packets and glue those onto the score and solo from the fruit pie covers.[14]

> I'd take a Paul Klee drawing and make a tracing of it, put that tracing paper underneath the strings, and where the Klee drawing intersected with the strings on this kind of grid, I would use those points as the ones I'd use during a particular solo. The bridge would be D7, G7, C7, F7 type of stuff. And I would have these notes to play, for me, in that bridge, that would be completely crazy, based on some alien information that was from the Klee drawing. They obviously didn't quite meet and match.[15]

> ...for me, there had been a contradiction for some time between what I had learned in the history of plastic arts and what I was actually doing in a jazz group. In the plastic arts the idea is to find out who you actually are and what you have to say, and the idea is not to be like somebody

14   Warburton, 2001. It's worth noting that Rowe's use of pie packets and other detritus from the commercial world (as well as reproductions of Paul Klee paintings) as scores predated any knowledge on his part of the graphic scores pioneered a decade or so before by composers like Earle Brown. Instead, they were an early manifestation of his desire to merge the visual and the abstract; a primitive attempt perhaps, but an intriguing one nonetheless.

15   Gino Robair, 1991.

else. Whereas in the jazz world it seemed that you had to be like somebody else. I had to play like Jim Hall or, say, Wes Montgomery and this seemed like a contradiction. In the plastic arts you have a list of criteria; one of the criteria is about originality and not so much an emphasis on craft and technique vís a vís the whole history of the found object (Marcel Duchamp). In the plastic arts it got away from the idea that you had to display your technique and that there was a difference between technique and virtuosity. Whereas in the jazz world there was no difference. In fact, there was often little virtuosity but lots of technique.[16]

It was logical for Rowe to view the guitar as something "very open," like a canvas rather than something that had somehow been completed. He also began concentrating on extenuating the percussive aspects of the guitar, the plectrum hitting the strings at more of a vertical angle than stroked across, digging into the idea of "something striking the guitar."

As experiments in this direction continued, members of the Westbrook band found themselves in one of two camps: on the one hand were those comfortable with the progressive ideas as represented in the bulk of the leader's compositions but on the other, Rowe, along with Lou Gare and Lawrence Sheaff, were becoming more and more dissatisfied with what they felt were restrictions on their freedom as improvisers. For Rowe, there was a growing disconnect between the unfettered freedom found in the work of abstract expressionist painters he had come to admire and the constraints always in effect with not only Westbrook's music but modern jazz as such; as much as it might be compared in the popular press to abstract art, it was clearly a far more repressed form than, say, a Jackson Pollock painting. In Rowe's case, attempting to break through these barriers resulted in an obviously decreased frequency of solo opportunities.

---

16   Interview in *Avant* magazine, 1997.

...his solo playing was unlike anything I had ever heard. He would turn up the volume and spray notes around in a very lively manner, with seeming disregard for the tempo, time or changes, though they were probably hidden in there somewhere. He would often bring the rhythm section to a bewildered halt. They would complain to Mike that it was impossible to play with him.[17]

Keith Rowe was a different kettle of fish! I think in those days I didn't really know what it was he was trying to do. I could appreciate free ideas in music and frequently played free music myself but Mike Westbrook's band was a quite straightforward conventional band in many ways and it seemed to me that if you play in somebody's band perhaps you should try to play the music they have in mind. Hearing Keith play in that band was like hearing three minutes of Stockhausen in the middle of a Mozart symphony. His anarchy used to make me smile however and he was very determined.[18]

And we began to react against the notion of the 32 bars and the 16 bars and the 8 bars, feeling I think that life didn't actually neatly break itself up into 16 bars, that life was a much more open-ended system. And we reacted against the restrictions by playing in different keys, injecting what would then have been regarded as arbitrary kinds of notes, and experimenting, taking ideas...Lou and I had been to art school, and for example in painting you can paint something any colour, as long as you get the tone right, then overall the landscape will work. Tonally you can do a colour-shift on it, shifting yellow to green, and green to purple, and purple to blue, so you shift all the colours around but tonally it's right so the painting still works.

---

17   Gare, 2004.

18   Lowther, 2005.

Then we took those sorts of ideas and said, let's forget the pitch, but get the timing of the note right. Of course this was chaotic in the context of jazz music! And of course, then dropping the bar-lengths too just created havoc. Well, in the end we had to leave.

Lawrence Sheaff describes multiple events when the rhythm section would become so befuddled by Rowe's solos that they'd stop playing entirely. In Sheaff's case, this was combined with awe and appreciation; not necessarily so with drummer Alan Jackson. Sheaff laughingly recounts an occasion when Surman happened on him, Jackson, and Ken McCarthy simultaneously making use of a pub urinal and quipped, "That's the first time I've seen the rhythm section together."

Westbrook recalled:

I think there was a time when somehow it was possible to keep all the elements together: the more mainstream players and the more experimental ones could somehow coexist in the same group. Then things got a bit more specialized and people drifted off into their particular area. I do remember at some stage organizing some sessions, very informally, which Keith and Lou were involved in, which developed very rapidly into totally improvised situations, which was a contrast to the more arranged work we did in the band. And so there was a kind of split and I was in the middle of it. There was a good overlap but then it split. We played once in a while like this at the canteen of the Royal College of Art, once a week or something—hardly anybody ever listened or was interested, but it got going. After a while, I got into the position where I had to choose. It sounds very grand! I think, on the whole, I liked the composing situation, of having all these elements together. I wasn't content with the purely straight-ahead thing but finally I wasn't satisfied with the wholly improvised thing either. In the end, I did stop going to the improvised sessions.

It likely wasn't as cut-and-dried as some of those involved might think in retrospect. Surman points out that Westbrook always stressed personal originality and self-expression to his band mates and, given that several members came from art school backgrounds and already possessed an open mind toward art in general, the eventual fracturing of the group was inevitable. There was also the musico-philosophical rift between those following a more virtuosic instrumental path à la Coltrane (Osborne and Surman, for example) and those whose concern was for a more environmental, less individualistic kind of sound. Rowe and Gare found themselves organizing side events, sessions where they could freely improvise, roughly in the manner of the American jazz musicians they so admired. Informal invitations went out into the jazz community, seeking other musicians of like mind.

Chapter 4

Edwin Prévost was born in 1942 and had studied drums since his youth, beginning in the Boy Scouts. He'd been interested in bebop from his early teens but, the technique being a bit more than he could handle at such a young age, worked with various trad (that is to say, New Orleans style) and skiffle bands until he was around 18, at which point he began to organize and lead his own hard bop ensembles. They were tough, driving groups, generally with a sax/trumpet frontline, performing pieces gleaned from the Blue Note catalog, especially those from the Bobby Timmons songbook. In the early 60s, the groups began to make something of a name for themselves on the London scene, a milieu still dominated by swing and trad bands but starting to open up to more modern trends. A newspaper reviewer referred to Prévost as "the Blakey of Brixton" and the sobriquet stuck.

As was the case with many forward-thinking younger players, Prévost began listening to the American avant-garde jazz that was just beginning to filter into the local record shops, discovering a particular affinity with the music of Ornette Coleman, Albert Ayler, and especially, the drumming of Ed Blackwell. He had seen Mike Westbrook's band in performance (even subbing for the drummer once) and found himself very much taken with the muscular, Rollins-esque approach of the tenor player Lou Gare, soon corralling him into joining the group he currently co-led with trumpeter David Ware. Still, the band tended toward playing hard bop in concert, restricting their freer tendencies to rehearsals. In the spring of 1965, Gare invited Prévost to attend some loose sessions, up until that point drummer-less, that he and other members of the Westbrook band had begun holding.[19]

It's reasonable to surmise that the same independence of spirit and action that Westbrook had demonstrated in trying to maintain a band while performing relatively adventurous material had rubbed off on his younger colleagues who in turn quite naturally took it upon themselves to organize situations that offered a wider range of playing options. Indeed, far from being put off at the notion of "his" musicians working out their own issues, Westbrook, in addition to often providing or securing a venue for the weekly get-togethers (the sessions were generally open to the public wherever they were held, usually at the Royal College of Art as it had a piano), would sometimes sit in, evincing a genuinely high regard for the goals of free playing even if he'd prefer not to hear such sounds erupting during performances by his own band and would, ultimately, return to composition himself. Other musicians from the group also participated, including Surman and Lowther as well as various instrumentalists from the London scene like bassist Mal Hawley, but the prime instigators of this experiment were Rowe and Gare, having become increasingly frustrated at their reduced and constricted playing time with Westbrook, and the routine, repetitive nature of their repertoire-based concerts. For Prévost, it was an open door inviting him to plunge into the musical world he'd been aiming toward, one which took the discoveries of the black American avant-garde of Coltrane, Coleman, and Sun Ra as a given, a starting point from which these musicians were determined to continue outward.[20]

---

19   The drummer in Westbrook's band, Alan Jackson, was one of its more musically conservative members and had no interest in these experimental get-togethers. Rowe recounts running into him in the late 60s and Jackson inquiring, in a friendly manner, "Are you still putting those fucking knives in the guitar?"

20   At almost the same time, Muhal Richard Abrams and others were founding the Association for the Advancement of Creative Musicians (AACM)

Right from the beginning of these sessions, several crucial decisions were made. First and foremost, the music was explicitly, totally improvised, albeit initially jazz-based. They not only never entertained the thought of performing their own compositions, much less standards (including contemporary pieces that had become virtual standards such as Coleman's "Lonely Woman" or Coltrane's "Naima"), as a platform for freeform experimentation, still the common practice among many "free" musicians both in the US and Europe, but also tended to push things further, specifically de-emphasizing to the point of abandoning any overt, consistent rhythmic pulse as well as eliminating "solos" as such early on, concentrating on a group sound from which an individual voice might or might not emerge. A rougher-edged Jimmy Giuffre ensemble could be imagined as a point of reference, Giuffre's drumless trio work having become known to them by that time, mixed in with a hint of Gabor

---

in Chicago, an organization for black musicians generally operating out of jazz. While it shared some of the same concerns (an initial premise was, "Original music only!"), it necessarily evolved from the black experience in the United States, one that generated a culture in which strong individualist statements emerged from a collective unity, each being an important survival mechanism. In England, deriving from a European culture where individualism was a given for at least the majority of the educated classes, it was something that could be more easily dispensed with, operating as they were from a more stable cultural position. The AMM musicians didn't fully understand, perhaps, this basic need underlying the black American avant-garde (at least, at that time), hence their subsequent bafflement at why others didn't follow the path they discovered— an attitude that could, with some justification, be interpreted as arrogance.

There are other parallels between both the philosophies and the resultant music of each group, including a stress on the collective (at the expense of nominal leaders), a de-emphasis on stridency and pro forma loud playing, the inclusion of "non-musical" (theatrical, dance, etc.) events during a performance and the influence, musical and otherwise, of the ideas and practices of both John Cage and Sun Ra. George E. Lewis' excellent history of the AACM, *A Power Stronger than Itself*, documents in detail the history of the AACM and, while not mentioning AMM, nonetheless presents a picture wherein it is not difficult to perceive some striking similarities between the American organization and this small band of British thinkers/musicians. Joseph Jarman, in particular, had overlapping interests and interacted with Cage and post-Cagean musicians and artists in "non-jazz" contexts as early as 1966 and within three years several AACM-based ensembles such as the Anthony Braxton/Leroy Jenkins/Leo Smith trio dealt with many similar musical concerns.

Szabo and Chico Hamilton. The startlingly new nature of these decisions must be understood in the context of a London which was a great deal more conservative with regard to avant-garde jazz than an American city like New York, where there had been a gradual move toward similarly focused ideas for at least several years prior. For musicians in England, most of their knowledge of the burgeoning free jazz movement was still via records as there were only a handful of local musicians, such as Joe Harriott, who had ventured in that direction while maintaining any sort of public presence. It's probable, in fact, that Harriott was more of a direct influence than Ornette Coleman because, as captivated as they were by his music, Coleman at that time wasn't perceived as he would be later on, as having actually solved the problems he was attacking. He was still, even for adventurous musicians, a problematic figure who was posing provocative questions, whereas Harriott was known and admired in England for solidifying the ideas of free jazz into coherent, imaginative structures. Contemporaneous musicians in London such as Derek Bailey (whose work had certainly been heard by Rowe at this point) were also finding themselves at something of a crossroads and tending to choose a different path, embarking on the development of a nervous, agitated approach and style that, while quite abstract, had concerns that at least in retrospect allowed their music to be placed more firmly in a jazz tradition, as decidedly difficult as that would have been to grasp at the time. Generally, the music produced by Rowe, Prévost, Gare, and the rest, even this early on, was less fragmented and darker, more amorphous and elastic, as might be expected from Westbrook alumni who had absorbed their bandleader's admiration for the rich, broad brush textures of Ellington and Mingus. To the extent that certain musicians with a stronger dedication to jazz forms were participating on a given occasion, grooves might develop and a quasi-modal form would persist for a while, but it would usually be broken up in short order or the rhythm would shift, never resting in one place for long.[21] The conscious desire *not* to merely imitate free jazz

21   This "finding a groove and quickly abandoning it" strategy would persist for a long time in Rowe's use of radio, particularly when happening on

formulations, as enormously as they were admired, was always in the forefront of their thinking, though, naturally enough, some musicians would every now and then fall back upon that with which they were most familiar.

> *Having said the most significant thing we dropped was the rhythm, I mean that there wasn't a constant rhythm. Like in the Westbrook band, you'd start off with 1-2, 1-2-3-4, clomp, clomp, clomp and that would exist all the way through. And every, every set would have nothing else but that. But here, you'd get periods where there might be some rhythm but it would actually dissolve into some thrashing around or whatever. I think it genuinely was experimenting to see where you could go if you didn't put limits on it.*

They intuitively arrived at a similar point of view to that of John Cage (of whom they were entirely ignorant), that jazz-based improvisation, however ostensibly free, would necessarily always revert to remembered patterns and styles, hemming in the potential creation of truly free music, unfettered by memory. In even the freest of free jazz of the time, in the most "Ascension"-like situation, *everything* wasn't in play. There were avenues that, at least implicitly, were not open to exploration.

The decision made by the group not to have a repertoire of any kind, looked back on decades later, might not seem to be anything of great moment but was, in the context of the era, nothing short of revolutionary.[22] Rowe would later refer to this as "a seismic shift

---

a catchy pop theme and chopping it off just as the listener was getting dangerously close to using it as a foothold of sorts. This is also one indication of what might be described as a puritanical streak in AMM, which we will discuss later.

22   Nothing occurs in a vacuum and there are at least two possible exceptions with regard to the uniqueness of AMM's approach. One is Larry Austin's New Music Ensemble that had formed in the summer of 1963 in California. Austin visited Italy in 1964, importing certain ideas into the nascent

in mentality in music." It is difficult indeed to think of any working ensemble around this time that utilized the idea as an underlying principle of its essential structure. John Stevens' Spontaneous Music Ensemble, often mentioned in the same breath as AMM in this regard, didn't form until early 1966, for example. This was certainly a step into the void and one taken resolutely, as an understood premise not to be reneged upon. Repertoire was a crutch that simply would not be used. From the onset, Rowe, Gare, and Prévost were exceptionally conscious of exactly what they were doing and the reasoning and aesthetical underpinnings behind it. No compositions, no riffs, no regular rhythms, no preset patterns or agreements. No nothing. But not a Dadaist "nothing," instead one imbued with the romantic notion that, having eliminated the accumulated detritus of the ages, a new form of beauty might arise, one that would flower in directions that weren't heretofore available. Additionally, aside from Rowe's limited (though perhaps crucial) exposure to the work of Webern and a handful of other early 20th century composer/theoreticians, the three had virtually no working knowledge of contemporary trends in Western art music when they set out, although the awareness of modern painting helped mark out conceptual territories that might be mapped onto

---

Gruppo di Improvisazione da Nueva Consonanza. Cornelius Cardew interacted with both Austin and GINC while studying in Italy in 1964-65 and presumably brought ideas learned there into AMM when he joined. The New Music Ensemble's self-titled release from 1964 on NME Records (Billie Alexander, soprano (voice); Larry Austin, trumpet and flugelhorn; Jon Gibson, flute, clarinet, soprano saxophone; Wayne Johnson, clarinet and bass clarinet; Stanley Lunetta, percussion; Richard Swift, piano; Arthur Woodbury, flute, alto saxophone, bassoon) is entirely improvised and, while clearly showing awareness of the contemporary classical sonic palette and dispensing with regular rhythms, nonetheless retains a strong amount of modern jazz phrasing (that is to say, the kind of phrasing which had itself been influenced by trends in modern European music, like that heard in Cecil Taylor's roughly contemporaneous work) and is structured in an episodic or "conversational" rather than laminal manner; in many ways, it impressively anticipates upcoming work by musicians such as Leo Smith and Roscoe Mitchell.

The other clear antecedent is Group Ongaku, founded by Takehisa Kosugi and Yasunao Tone in Japan in 1960.

musical ideas. To a remarkable extent, the group managed to carve out a music that owed little to any particular idiom, where all improvised sounds were given equal weight and importance, where almost anything could occur.

It was no easy task. Prévost would later write:

> ...I had been terrified for weeks when AMM first began to play. You see in this new playing situation which I suddenly found myself, I was being asked to produce more than I thought I had. But...I had to go back, although there were many times when I felt that it would be easier and simpler not to.[23]

The three musicians (Sheaff would join somewhat later) had a rather extensive amount of self-awareness and purpose, something that seems to stem, in large part, from Rowe's and Gare's study of the visual arts, particularly the "revolutions" of Cubism and Abstract Expressionism. Not so much the particular formal elements of each (though these were undoubtedly fundamental to the music now being produced) but to the underlying idea of beginning anew, of projecting one's own individual personality into one's art without regard, insofar as it's possible, for previous traditions and structures. Moreover, not being content to treat the music as something isolated from their lives and general thought processes, they'd sit down afterwards and talk about what had been played at the previous session. Less, perhaps, about how this or that element did or didn't work, more about the overall trend of the improvisation, the ways discovered around restrictions, the increased openness to the appearance of any sound.

> I think it [the discussions] did become very formal. Once we decided that we had this group, we actually set off to be serious or scientific about it. Not trying to do it in the way all our other jazz experiences had been, you know, going to

---

23   Edwin Prévost, "AMM Music – The Unknown Factor Is You," January 1973.

the pub, getting drunk, playing, going home and that was it. I think we all felt there was something more to be done than that... [We were] trying to understand it from different viewpoints so it wasn't just music. Not just the sound but something more than that.

It was logical to begin by a process of dismantling, of observing, and dissecting the form with which they were most familiar, jazz, and paring elements that might act as constrictions. As mentioned, a steady rhythm and the idea of soloing were two of the first items to begin to evaporate. Though the solo/accompaniment idea and the notion of the subservient rhythm section had been crumbling in jazz since at least Ornette Coleman, Rowe and Gare (and, later, Sheaff), with their art school backgrounds, came at the problem from another perspective, that of the Cubist model—breaking something down into its constituent parts then reassembling it in a manner that provided different glimpses into its core reality.[24] What if you "inverted" the solo, burying it underneath an element that, before, was subsidiary, allowing one to investigate the properties of that hitherto unnoticed piece of sound? Could you "hear through" a solo, rendering it transparent?

We tried to break away from things that didn't have an openness to them. What there was, was perhaps a growing appreciation that you could make a sound and the sound that you were making could either accommodate, live alongside other sounds or that they were so exclusive that you couldn't do other things beside them. I think we were searching out the kind of sounds that would allow material to fit with them. So if you were going [hums "C Jam Blues"], it didn't allow anything else to go along with it. We were trying to get away from the restrictions of that kind of language.

---

24   This relates specifically to Analytical Cubism. Soon enough, principles of Synthetic Cubism, especially the translation of collage forms to the importation of exterior objects to use with the guitar, would become even more important.

This would lead to misconceptions among public and press alike that AMM had a long tradition of being somehow "anti-jazz," an idea that couldn't be more wrong. The notion that you could hugely admire a form and, at the same time, understand that you were in no position to step into that particular cultural stream but instead could use it as a more general, almost subconscious element of great inspiration seems to have had trouble finding purchase in the minds of many listeners (and musicians).

> When we asked ourselves, being critical, say, of the stuff being too jazzy, I think it's true that it wasn't actually that we were being critical of jazz. I think we just wanted to move away from that, finding the positive things there and gluing more onto it. I don't think we ever criticized jazz as such. I think the jazz players, and they'll say this to this day, thought that we were. Like Peter Brötzmann's stuff about how we hated Americans. It was our admiration of what was great about black jazz musicians that led us.

> We realized that jazz sprang from and reflected a culture, predominantly black American community ethos, with which we as young, white English men could know nothing about, except through the vicarious experience of the vinyl. The search thereafter was for a method of making music that arose out of our own culture and reflected our own aspirations. Part of that was, of course, informed by our admiration for the strength we perceived in the (mostly) black American responses to cultural and political exclusion.[25]

George E. Lewis gets at the nub of the basic difference in approach with regard to improvisation between the black American avant-garde and musicians such as these in his *A Power Stronger Than Itself*, first citing Cage's remarks:

---

25   Prévost, "Visual Sounds Live."

It is at the point of spontaneity that the performer is most apt to have recourse to his memory. He is not apt to make a discovery spontaneously. I want to find ways of discovering something you don't know at the time that you improvise—that is to say, the same time you're doing something that's not written down, or decided upon ahead of time. The first way is to play an instrument over which you have no control, or less control than usual. [Kostelanetz, *Conversing with Cage*]

Lewis then observes:

In contrast, AACM improvisors viewed even an instrument as "little" as a triangle, or as large and seemingly unlikely as the set of tuned "garbage cans" that Anthony Braxton shipped to Europe in the 1970s, as embodying potential for sonic invention that could be fully realized through the familiarization process known as "practicing." On this view, which sees pure spontaneity as a chimerical ideal of autonomy that has little to do with the historical, social, and cultural situatedness of actual improvisation, sustained and rigorous study is generally seen as the most likely way to "discover something you don't know." To use the everyday phrase, "chance favors the prepared mind."[26]

While black American musicians may have, quite rightly, been suspicious of any kind of standards being imposed on them by a white composer drawing from both Eurocentric traditions and a position of power and confidence derived from being a member of the dominant culture in that place and time, Rowe and his companions found it odd in the same sense that British or other European improvisers would seek to conform with standards from a culture just as essentially alien to them, as much as they

---

26   George E. Lewis, *A Power Stronger Than Itself: The AACM and American Experimental Music*, University of Chicago Press, 2008.

admired its creations, instead of building on the legacy left for them by someone like Cage who had opened new perceptual doors for artists working in that lineage. Wouldn't it be presumptuous to attempt to replicate Coltrane if you shared nothing with his culture, with what nurtured his art?[27]

> *So you've sat on the chair in front of a blank canvas and you make your first mark...then you make a second mark... but it's too much like Chagall. Chagall paints Chagalls... you can't paint a Chagall. So you start again and you make some marks and the professor comes along and says, "That's too much like a Caravaggio...only Caravaggio can paint like that." So you are left on your own with a blank canvas for hours and hours and hours, wondering what you can contribute to the history of painting. In the evenings, while I was at Plymouth School of Art, I went to jazz clubs where there was a very strong American contingent and they would invite you to "sit in." So I spent about four years playing basically Black American dance music. But what I learnt there was how to imitate these players and whereas over at the Art School I was really struggling to find a voice, here if you could play a really good copy you were really well respected. The difference was in the element of craft. Because Duchamp had got rid of the idea that you needed to make art with craft and skill, I knew then (as a guitar player) that it was really important to me to make music where no one could tell where the sound came from.[28]*

---

27   Even so, much of the influence on AMM's thought derived from Chinese sources, particularly after Cardew joined the group. He and Prévost would go so far as to study Chinese itself, partially as a way to apply a language with few phonetic indicators to renditions of "Treatise." Ideas from Taoism and Confucianism infiltrated the group as well. Rowe would later wonder if one of the underlying reasons for the lack of attention paid them was this Eastern rather than African basis for much of their music.

28   Phil Mouldycliff, 2002.

Several other concerns that would later be central to AMM were naturally manifested in the early weeks and months of this assemblage. One was a deep, abiding interest in the formal properties and almost sculptural use of silence. At this point, mid-1965, none of the musicians was aware of the innovations of the New York School of composers, particularly John Cage. Indeed, Prévost would be asked by a journalist a short while later if Cage was an influence and innocently responded, "He's a drummer, then?" However, both Rowe's background in painting, specifically in Cubism within which the notion of negative space was deeply embedded, and Prévost's own probing into Buddhism, Kabbalah, and other Eastern and Middle Eastern belief systems led almost automatically to an appreciation of silence as an element entirely as musically important as audible notes or sounds. Often the music would dwindle to a point where the musicians were just barely playing, each eliciting the most tenuous of sounds, and those moments might stretch out to several minutes. The use of silence or near-silence was akin to some developments in what would become known as Conceptual Art, where an event's non-occurrence, given the anticipation and imaginative thoughts that it would engender in an observer, was as important as its actually taking place. A later installation like Walter de Maria's *Lightning Field* might, in a given stretch of time, attract no bolts, but the experience of sitting there, thinking about what might happen would lead one into areas of imagination that would not otherwise have been reached. Similarly, listeners—as well as the musicians!—attending an event by this pre-AMM band would enjoy a giddy tension wondering what, if anything, would happen next and would construct possibilities themselves, those notions becoming part of the experience. There was likely still a bit of uneasiness about this, an uncertainty whether or not this area was a valid one in which to explore, but the idea of silence as a potentially rich resource was definitely planted quite early in the group's gestation. Just as importantly, that silence would not be a foreordained goal but rather something that would arise naturally, or not. There was no "Hey, that silent bit worked very well there, let's try it again" sensibility.

A side issue developing from the use of silence or near-silence had to do with the size of the ensemble. In 1965, the idea of a musician involved in free improvisation "not playing" for any length of time was a new one. There was an interesting question of balance with regard to, on the one hand, the amount of individuality one could effect in a smaller band versus the freedom *not* to contribute (for a time) afforded by a larger grouping.

> *If you're in a group of five people and you don't play for 20 minutes, you're actually hardly noticeable. Whereas in a duo or trio, it is quite noticeable. In a way, your individual power is reduced on one level, in the sense of the effect you have on the totality but it also gives you another kind of freedom in terms of stopping or starting, finding radically new ways of coming in, etc. You have more thinking space.*[29]

> AMM could create a value of silence that I've never found in any other group. I remember sometimes we'd have quite a full audience and somehow everything, the sound would just have to stop. And that silence, and you could maintain that silence for say, twenty minutes. Nobody could move, nobody could do anything. It wasn't an emptiness. It was as full as the sound that had preceded it. That was unbelievable.[30]

On the other hand, when the music did grow loud it was less a matter of spiritual or psychological catharsis as was, arguably, often the case with American free jazz post-Coltrane, and more simply a matter of reaching points in the performance where loudness happened to occur, where it became necessary. The ebb and flow of volume that would come to characterize a "typical"

---

29   Rowe would always maintain that five was the ideal number to comprise AMM, even after the "mature" AMM trio of post-1980.

30   Sheaff, 2005.

AMM performance later on was a natural response not only to the lack of any sort of repertoire but also derived from the refusal to use jazz modes or vamps as platforms from which to improvise. At this point, the concept of stasis, of not having to "get from point A to point B" was too removed to really grasp; there was still the idea of conveying a narrative arc, however abstract, in one form or another. But more so than any other improvising ensemble of the time, they retained a sense of emotional distance, of being witnesses to phenomena rather than instigators of same; it was already a fundamental element of the as-yet-unborn AMM. Things became "loud" the way a day becomes windy—not for a "reason" but only because situations change. As Rowe would later say, "The music is not in time, it's of time."

This idea of reticence, of the non-gestural (the gesture of non-gesture?), was basic and always present. Certainly the traditional British sense of reserve may have played into this attitude, as well as something of a puritanical attitude, but it was also a reaction against the flamboyant, bravura displays of jazz musicians, the individual showcased at the expense of the group and becoming, at least for the moment, the "leader" to which the other musicians deferred. The concept of a musical collective was given a great amount of lip service over the years by many musicians but was something that often deteriorated in practice, egos having their way of making their presence felt. The "pushing forward" nature of much jazz, the desire to impel, was anathema here, the musicians preferring, if necessary, to merely nudge and watch. Additionally, there was the developing idea of the group's sound emerging from the time and space surrounding it at the moment, peaking and then subsiding, leaving only ripples. Deep awareness of the physical and psychological space in which the music was being created and consideration of the "outside" world making itself known in that space was a key concept; the slightly later introduction of the radio would be a clear way of funneling the larger world into the performance space. To this extent, to absorb and internalize as much of the surrounding environment as possible, they preferred performing in darkness or as close as they could manage, trying to eliminate the "show" aspect (although, of course, in the end simply creating a different kind of performance), ridding the stage of individual musicians, leaving only music. Music, moreover, whose direct source might be difficult to determine by an audience member. With a little effort on the part of the listener, the music might be able to be heard as a "natural" extension of the existing space.

> *I think the darkness thing makes sense. What you do is that you shut out the principal way that humans' perceptions are guided. We're primarily visual animals. If that information is closed off, it would feel like you'd become more sensitive about the other things, like hearing. We'd gotten rid of all this décor that went with rock and roll, all the presentation. Whether you're black or white, however you are, when it's dark you're all the same; that kind of feeling, of getting away from the image.*

This stage manner, however, easily engendered charges of arrogance from some less sympathetic or perceptive segments of their (eventual) audience, small though it was. And there was, to be sure, a kind of aloofness at play, a desire to be separate from the herd. This distancing, which may well have been necessary to cut as many psychic ties to the contemporary jazz scene as possible, made the appreciation of their music, already quite extreme, that much more difficult for even a willing audience, something that continued to surface in the reactions of both the general public and other musicians for decades to come.

At least two other musical concerns formed in this period of incubation, concerns that were relatively foreign to the avant-jazz world but which were, unbeknownst to these musicians, coming more to the fore in the experimental classical scene: small sounds and sounds of long duration. In both of these areas, Rowe was at something of an advantage over his partners due simply to the electrification of his instrument. Electronic amplification allowed sounds that were extremely tiny and difficult to hear to be brought into the foreground and magnified multiple times, making for an almost perverse inversion of normality. Iannis Xenakis, in his "Concret ph" from 1959, had hyper-magnified the all but inaudible popping of air pockets within chunks of burning coal, discovering hitherto unobserved sound-worlds as rich and detailed as those found in "normal" volume ranges. Though presumably unknown to any of the nascent AMM members, that fascination with making prominent sound-events that were formerly, necessarily, obscure was a major component of their work. For Rowe, this concentration on the incidental, on the previously-considered-unimportant, had strong parallels with modernist movements in painting, particularly in purely formal, anti-subject frames of reference, wherein *what* an object was became less important than *that* it was. He was fascinated by Robert Rauschenberg's combines of the previous decade where a painted panel might be set directly alongside a ladder, a wooden chair, or a piece of piping, making clear the aesthetic equivalency of the two when looked at with a discerning enough eye, much as Cage (among others, at least since Russolo) had championed the equivalency of traditionally musical tones and "noise." Accidental and uncontrollable sounds, from the chance scraping of a rasp across guitar strings to feedback caused from the proximity of two power sources became elements every bit as vital, perhaps more so, as intentional activity as did the "hidden" sounds capable of amplification via contact microphones.

> *...I can justify it in terms of Duchamp. I know the history of the Armory Show and I understand the whole notion of difference between Synthetic Cubism and Analytical Cubism. The notion of a Synthetic Cubism for me is a very powerful notion which then relates to, say, Rauschenberg's screen prints. I would understand all that more than I would understand the equivalents in the musical world. So that when I'm actually working on the guitar, am I actually a painter working with materials which are not the traditional plastic materials? Are all my judgments painterly decisions and am I still painting? Is my playing actually a*

painting activity using the medium of sound rather than any plastic materials?[31]

In order for the non-amplified musicians to also be able to consider these quieter, smaller sources, it became necessary to sustain prolonged periods of extreme pianissimo, where it might be possible to hear the barest flick of a bass string (or tap on its body), the merest whimper from a tenor saxophone, or the gentle scrape of stick against drumhead. Prévost developed an entire arsenal of soft attacks, including especially his protean mastery of the bowed cymbal.

In addition, the group became very interested in the investigation of long, sustained tones. The idea of *drone*, perhaps inspired by an exposure to Indian classical music but also being "something in the air" with regard to the work being done by the post-Cage American avant-garde, particularly La Monte Young, Tony Conrad, and the Fluxus group, descended on AMM. Once again, Rowe, by virtue of the instrument he happened to play, was uniquely situated to take advantage of this direction. Once sought, sustained tones and feedback were readily achieved on the electric guitar. In some crucial ways, this idea harked back to the pedal point, providing the necessary glue to cement elements that may otherwise have been disparate enough to render a performance incoherent and formless. Prévost, by means of bowing and lengthy drum rolls, could also contribute along this line, and Gare, to the limits of his breath, was able to generate long, steady tones. But the possibilities revealed by electronics and amplification, once appreciated, became a central element of the ensemble, integrated into the fiber of its music. Here, as in other areas that we will come to see, one can perhaps begin to pick up on the influence of Sun Ra's bands of the early 60s when his use of primitive electronic keyboards became prominent.[32]

---

31   Mouldycliff, 1995.

32   Although entirely unknown to the musicians at the time, possibly the

In the fall of 1965, Victor Schonfield wrote what is likely the first appreciation of AMM (*avant les lettres*), though it didn't appear in print until April of the following year. He refers to them as a trio (Rowe, Prévost, and Gare) and describes their music in the context of a post-Ornette Coleman world, in fact a David Izenzon-oriented one, Izenzon just having been named *Melody Maker*'s New Musician of the Year. He's quick, however, to recognize the gulf that's already been widening between AMM's music and most anything else around:

> In melody, the number of notes has been increased from twelve to infinity, by annexing the spaces in-between, and by using notes of multiple or indeterminate pitch... For example, Keith Rowe...combines the manipulation of amplifier feedback with that of violin-bow, steel ruler or drumsticks on the guitar strings, which have often previously been loosened to sagging point. By such means he acquires the melodic resources of sounds like those made by flocks of birds, dogs, sirens, rain on a tin roof, buzz-saws, bubbling lava, giant insects ripping and slashing at steel doors, or electrified cats and babies... AMM does not build up to a final climax, or work up and then down again; levels change imperceptibly or abruptly

---

most direct antecedent to the general sort of music being created here had taken place several years earlier in Japan by Group Ongaku. The music developed in 1960-61 by Takehisa Kosugi, Syuko Mizuno, Yasunao Tone, Mieko Shiomi and others, replete with radio captures, abstract electronics and saxophone and an improvised, non-thematic structure is remarkably similar to areas AMM would explore in its first several years. Their music can be heard on a recording, *Music of Group Ongaku*, issued on CD in 1996 by Hear Sound Library (HEAR-002) and LP in 2011 by Seer Sound Archive (seer 001)—one set from May 8, 1960 and another from September 15, 1961. They gave the first performances in Japan of the works of Cage, Feldman, Wolff and Brown. It is therefore tempting to think that Cardew may have been aware of their work and brought some of their ideas into AMM when he joined, but there exists no documentation of this supposition, although he would, with the Scratch Orchestra, take part in a performance of Kosugi's 1964 work, "Anima 7," the score consisting of the instruction, "perform any action as slowly as possible." In any case, the four original members of AMM had no such awareness.

throughout, all the way from utter silence to passages of overwhelming and terrifying cacophony. Rowe, drummer Eddie Prévost, and the tenor player and violinist Lou Gare, who comprise AMM, like to play continuously for two hours at a time, and reject even the Coleman school's loose discipline of relating by mood or cadence to some theme. Their discipline is the logic of the human flesh, and their scope and complexity reach beyond nineteenth-century forms and notation to include every instrumental possibility; only those criteria which can be applied to all patterns in any media remain valid. AMM does not build up to a final climax, or work up and then down again; levels change imperceptibly or abruptly throughout, all the way from utter silence to passages of overwhelming and terrifying cacophony. The group creates music as gripping, as demanding, as amazing and as exhilarating as any that improvisation can offer; to follow one of its relentless voyages is to undergo a permanent change in one's perceptions.

Although they wouldn't have explicitly portrayed it as such, there was something of the idea of a "tryout" in these weekly sessions, an effort to determine who could really play this freer-than-free music and who couldn't. By the early fall of 1965, after several months of intense consolidation, the core group had been whittled down to Rowe, Gare, and Prévost ("One wonders whether it was a process of consolidation of ideas or whether we were the only ones left!" –Prévost). As a trio, they played at least a gig or two before Lawrence Sheaff finally bolted the Westbrook band to join in. One, Prévost remembers, was before an audience of three people: Alexis Korner and two friends, Korner being impressed enough to ask them to play at a birthday party he threw, not the likeliest of performance opportunities. Rowe recalls looking up from his guitar while playing there only to see all four Beatles sitting on a couch in front of him. A second performance, perhaps their first gig proper as a quartet, came courtesy of Westbrook himself. Despite any lingering animosities between him and his disgruntled musicians, Westbrook actually invited the as-yet-un-named AMM to a concert in Warrington near Liverpool that his orchestra was sharing with a John Surman-led group. They were asked to appear as the opening act. Trundling their gear into a van and making their way up, the four encountered various logistical difficulties en route including a flat tire. By the time they arrived, a couple hours late, the Surman and Westbrook bands had already performed, leaving the proto-AMM to appear lastly. Some suspicion was voiced as to whether or not their delay had been intentional in order to secure the "star" slot, hackles were raised, and the concert fared rather poorly.

For Sheaff, also an art school graduate, the music was a revelatory mirror of the visual work he'd been studying and producing:

> I think what you can say is that, like abstract painting, there were still some references to "figurative" things. Also, occasionally, you'd break into a 4/4 rhythm and have a bass line going but still in that mode of very free improvisation. Gradually, all those kind of presences of some kind of traditional structure dissolved away completely. They weren't things that any of us in the group at that time were interested in. We didn't want the mind to get caught up in any kind of repetitive value that has the tendency to hold the mind on the surface or surface levels of experience. Any kind of rhythmic values that came up were...I think it was more like this destructive value maybe. When you look at it in terms of conventional structures in music, the process or entities that would come up in terms of sound would always have the tendency to break any kind of rhythm. The mind never knew what was going to come up next so, in the end, you just had to let go. The music just *had* to flow like that. And that takes you to deeper levels.

Soon, a bulky Grundig tape recorder was purchased and the group got into a routine of recording the week's session then regrouping a few days later, listening to the performance, and commenting on various aspects, often on a purely musical level but sometimes venturing into deeper, more philosophical areas. Prévost:

> I don't know how critical we were but I think the occasions for meeting up afterward to discuss the session in particular and music in general were fairly invaluable events. They seemed to me to, in some respects, be as valuable as the playing itself. They went on for quite a long time. You have to remember that tape machines weren't as ubiquitous as they are now and so just to hear what you did was a fairly rare and unique event. Just to be able to do it was quite a breakthrough and a different kind of experience, adding a dimension to it that couldn't have happened five or ten years before…There was a definite social element to it as well. We were young people who formed a friendship. It was good to be in each other's company anyway. But it was certainly something that is endemic in British culture, the idea of "discussing it" in music was right out the window. It's very difficult even now to get people to discuss it! …The discussion evolved to some extent. It became an appraisal of what was going on, what the mechanics were, what the relationships were in the making of this music as opposed to playing bebop or any other kind of music…Going hand in hand with the actual playing was also a good deal of individual and collective discovery of ideas inside and out of the art world. I'd been introduced to the Gurdjieffian school and then, as a consequence, Lou, Keith, and Krystyna too got involved for a while. There was this ferment of ideas that weren't just musical but they informed the music. They helped us to evolve because sometimes the language of ideas that came out of the music was inadequate to discuss what it was we thought we were doing. I think it [Gurdjieff] gave us a grasp of an explanation of what we felt when the music was really working well. This whole

sense of being and of being in the moment, which you can't talk about. You're not even allowed in musical theory of thinking of it as an important thing. What we felt in those moments of stillness, those early AMM silences, was so much…tension's the wrong word but so much… difficult to explain.

Asked if there was a conscious attempt to dissolve structures and whether this was discussed in any post-performance talks, Sheaff answered:

Well, I think in those discussions it was more like…the thing about AMM was that you could do anything. You could go stand on Westminster Bridge while the other guys are somewhere else in London and you'd be part of the performance, you know what I mean? It was so completely wide open. Talking about any restriction of anything on that level isn't what we would talk about. We'd talk about what kind of feeling that gave, a particular thing, and do we connect to those things. It was more like observing what was going on and commenting on it.

*

In November of 1965, an unusual opportunity afforded itself. Several decades later, it's difficult to understand how confusing and readily open to misinterpretation this end of experimental improvisation, and what would become the hard and/or psychedelic rock scene, were to an innocent observer of the time. While the pop phenomenon was in full swing and audiences, by and large, could fit bands like The Beatles and Rolling Stones into a framework that made rough sense and continued a certain musical/cultural history, there was an enormous amount of ferment and cross-fertilization going on in London (as elsewhere), a time and place where standard labels made little sense, pop mixing with jazz combining with blues and electronic contemporary music. Bands lead by John Mayall,

Graham Bond, Alexis Korner, and others were incubating a wide variety of as-yet-unknown musicians who would splinter off into various genres themselves, including the future founders of bands like Cream, players who would come to incorporate into hard rock ideas gleaned in blues and jazz groups. Henry Lowther would play with Manfred Mann's pop band; Lol Coxhill might be considered for membership in the Kinks. Roles were ill-defined. "Rock" had yet to be deemed a high-profit business and where its definitional boundaries were actually to be drawn was very much up in the air. Average citizens ignorant of all but the shiniest pop music really might see as little difference between a harsh, loud blues-rock band and a Stockhausen concert as they would between a painting by Franz Kline and one by De Kooning. It was all noise.

Bob Guccione had recently founded the British edition of *Penthouse* magazine, at the time less the skin publication that it would later become and somewhat more in line with the long tradition of "men's magazines" like *Argosy* and *True*, designed to keep the dashing young gent abreast of all things manly and modern, including what was happening on "the scene." Tony Common, an ex-classmate of Rowe's from art school, was a young photographer beginning to make a name in the movie and fashion world. *Penthouse* assigned him the task of searching out hip, young musical acts to shoot and record for possible inclusion in the first issue of the magazine as a flexidisc insert. Common had attended several performances by the ex-Westbrook musicians and thought they might fit the bill. Odd as it may seem today, the mere fact that an electric guitar was present might have been enough for Common to reasonably put them forward as part of the "new thing" scene. In all likelihood, his editors wouldn't have had any standards by which to accept or reject his recommendations anyway; who could understand what these kids were up to? Common arranged for one of the group's weekly sessions to be recorded onto acetate, only about ten copies ultimately being pressed. In addition to the four regulars, a pianist friend of Prévost's was in attendance for the session though no one, 40 years on, is certain of his name![33] The recording never made it into *Penthouse*, leaving unanswered for the ages a "What if?" question as to how the music might have been judged by a substantially wider audience at the time. The handful of copies languished in a few collections, in various states of listenability, for decades.[34]

As the earliest surviving recorded material of this proto-AMM ensemble, it provides an invaluable example of how much progress had been made, how far from their roots in Westbrook and free-ish bop groups they'd traveled. That said, the first sounds one hears are Gare and Rowe engaging in a very jazzy conversation, the latter making oblique references to "Softly As In a Morning Sunrise," Sheaff soon entering with dark arco patterns, Prévost then on brushes. Within two minutes, however, Gare has switched to violin and a far more abstract area has been entered. This string interplay (it's possible that Rowe is playing cello here and elsewhere) foreshadows a good deal of what would be a typical element of AMM performances in the coming few years. That string drone works to produce a constant thread—a center line?—that gives the musicians a gossamer sort of structure with which to work. For the great majority of the time, one hears absolutely no regular rhythms and, of course, no thematic material whatsoever. Already, there's a latent idea of space-expansion, of the merging of instrumental sound into a single entity that would billow out into the room, attenuating here, thickening there, possessing a nature more ambiguously gaseous than atomistic. This produces something at least tangentially akin to the sort of music Ornette Coleman, when on violin, was creating around the same time in his trio with David Izenzon and Charles Moffett.

---

33   Prévost thinks "Ellis" rings a bell. Whatever his name, he's recorded quite low in the mix and is difficult to discern aside from some muffled clusters.

34   In early 2006, Prévost had a digital copy made from this acetate and graciously sent an extract to me. This consisted of two "tracks," comprising about 15 minutes of material. I later received the entire session from Rowe. It is difficult to say how representative of pre-AMM music this is with any certainty but I'm acting on the assumption that it is more or less typical.

Gare, in addition to constructing dizzying, dervish-like spirals, also gets a little bit into the sort of drones that Tony Conrad was noted for: high, keening lines with subtle tonal fluctuations. Sheaff is all over the place on bass, seesawing between arco and pizzicato, high-pitched and low, providing an enormous amount of depth and texture. His weaving counterpoint to the violin lines is stunning though he's quite capable of instantly dropping into brutally contradictory thuds and thunks. Prévost, still on a traditional kit at this stage, is clearly doing whatever he can to avoid overt rhythms, jazz or otherwise, but has yet to develop the more coloristic approach that would soon manifest. If any of the musicians sound a bit tentative at this point, at least when the group is in more astringent, sparser territory, it might be Prévost; it's clear that a more expanded percussive palette would become necessary. When engaged in relatively spare improvisation, as near the beginning of the set, Rowe seems more at ease insofar as pushing the boundaries furthest away from any jazz origins, abstracting his sound to a striking degree. He's already taking the bow to the guitar, creating plaintive, keening cries but even when picking the strings in a normal manner, the pacing and choice of notes is at an enormous remove from the modern jazz tradition. Sometimes one gets the impression he might be playing the guitar with a stiff-haired scrub brush; harsh clouds of noise emerge, though even at this point there's a willingness to remain "back" in the mix, not to dominate the proceedings. It can be read as a perverse response to the sort of comping he was consigned to in the Westbrook bands, scrabbling furiously at the strings, vainly searching for the right rhythmic accents in an environment in which regular tempi have become extinct.

Gare switches to tenor late in Side One for some spirited work possibly more out of John Gilmore than Coltrane, but when he's on that instrument for most of Side Two, this pre-AMM group produces a stellar improvisation that nonetheless lies more clearly within the free jazz tradition, except that were it played for the unwary present-day listener, it's a decent bet that he wouldn't bat an earlash if told that it was created in

1995 instead of 1965. Prévost seems to be very much more in his comfort zone here, producing free drumming on a par with the best being created elsewhere, sliding in and out of pulses and urging the group along without a trace of overbearingness. Rowe is much more up front, utilizing a far more "traditional" attack (that is, picking out notes linearly). He sounds like a portent of some area midway between what Sonny Sharrock and Terje Rypdal would be doing four to five years hence. The notes are plucked out in harsh chirps, ripped off in rapid staccato fashion. At one point, he and Gare (whose sound can be heard clearly coming into its own here, influences being sloughed like old skin) engage in a whipsaw battle of contrapuntal notes, Prévost quickly picking up the beat but, just as quickly, tossing it aside as they move into a freer section. Interestingly, there's little sense of any arc here, no building up or easing down, no real tension and release. Instead, like a mature Morton Feldman piece, it's simply *there* as though one had thrown open a door to the sounds of an ongoing event which would continue to go on after one had left, a separate presence living and functioning on its own terms. It's fascinating to hear the contrast in the two sides. As "advanced" as the free jazz performance heard on Side Two is in the context of music being created in late 1965, it's actually very retrograde in terms of where this pre-AMM ensemble was aiming. It almost reads as a concession of sorts, a fallback position that could always be assumed when trepidation set in. It's intriguing to think what might have occurred had the session been included in the magazine and had this jazzier portion been greeted enthusiastically by a fairly large number of listeners. Happily, for the future history of creative music, this potential success was narrowly avoided and the whole idea of the flexidisc insert was abandoned.

*

As much consideration as was given to discussion about musical content and philosophy, a similar amount of thought went into choosing a name for the ensemble. It's worthwhile understanding that, in 1965, arcane and/or obscure names were not the rule in most music genres. Rock bands still generally used cute plural forms (groups with monikers like The Cream or Pink Floyd—originally "The" Pink Floyd—were yet to appear) while jazz bands strongly tended toward names emphasizing the group's leader and the number of musicians under his command.

In choosing a name consisting of three capitalized, undefined letters, it was understood that the average observer at the time might well be put off. Outside of the contemporary classical world and the more avant-jazz circles, music was still by and large an entertainment form, with groups doing their utmost to get their name "in lights," to have a catchy tag that would both relate to pre-existing names (giving the audience a sense of comfort) and differentiate themselves just enough so that fans knew which band's records to buy. The name "AMM" throws up a blockade, denying ready interpretations or associations. While euphonious enough to be (mis) read as a word connoting the Cockney pronunciation of a pork product (and, more deeply, resonating with both "am" and "om"), the capitals imply an unknown, unspoken acronym that was, in fact, the case.[35]

Deliberations were long and detailed among the four original members[36], engrossed as they were with the philosophy of Gurdjieff. They made sure that the acronymized words expressed an affinity toward the goals of that belief system which included a desire for an almost Zen-like mastery of one's life

---

35   In a short amount of time, acronymic ensemble names, especially among improvisatory groups, would become somewhat popular: SME (Spontaneous Music Ensemble), MIC (Music Improvisation Company), MEV (Musica Elettronica Viva) and ICP (Instant Composers Pool) to name just a few, though in most cases, they were as often referred to by the full name as the abbreviated one.

36   The name was probably chosen right around the time Cardew joined the ensemble, but even if he was more or less a member at this juncture, just as he didn't participate in the post-session musical discussions, so he wasn't involved in the group's selection of a name.

and art. Additionally, the words had to possess a numerological significance related to Prévost's study of Kabbalah.

Gurdjieff's teachings placed great value on secrecy or, more properly, on the non-necessity of telling what you knew. The musicians made the clear and considered decision to keep the three words a secret, known only to permanent AMM members.[37]

AMM: a sheer, blank wall for those needing some extra-musical handhold. Even for some listeners who understood that the name of a musical group is of minimal importance when all is said and done, it presented something of a dilemma. If unimportant, why take such pains in both its formation and subsequent withholding of meaning from the public? The gesture of non-gesture, one of many contradictions the ensemble came to embody. This obscuring of information of some interest to observers has roots at least as far back as Duchamp's "À Bruit Secret" in which a noise-making device was hidden in a block of wood, ineluctably arousing people's curiosity while at the same time saying, "No, you cannot know." Proffering and withholding, causing a delicious little itch in the audience—this was a regular element of AMM's worldview.

*

It was through Alan Cohen that Rowe was introduced to Cornelius Cardew.

Cardew (1936-1981) had already established a reputation for himself as the *enfant terrible* of the British avant-classical scene, having served as Stockhausen's assistant from 1958-60 and worked with the four chief proponents of what had come to be known as the New York School: John Cage, Morton

---

37   John Tilbury, informed of the name's meaning when he joined in 1980, claimed to have subsequently forgotten it. Rowe and Prévost, presumably with sly humor, chose not to tell him again.

Feldman, Earle Brown, and Christian Wolff. He was entirely conversant with a bewildering array of post-serialist structures and philosophical issues as is amply demonstrated in the writings from 1959 through the early 60s collected in *Cornelius Cardew: A Reader* (Cupola, 2006) as well as John Tilbury's monumental biography published in 2008. Many of the problems and projects with which he'd preoccupied himself were at a distant conceptual remove from the controversial matters that avant-garde jazz was grappling with around the same time. But just as jazz was navigating past the once liberating but now stultifying series of rules set in motion by bebop, some in the avant-classical world were seeking their way out of the excessive dryness and academicism of post-serialist strictures. Cardew was very aware of and involved in the issue as seen from the point of view of post-Cage composers in the United States such as La Monte Young, Henry Flynt, and Tony Conrad. All were consumed with navigating their way toward a new and vital approach in the wake of "4'33"" (indeed, how to deal with and "get past" Cage in general) and other stratagems that called into question how one went about creating music when the notion of authorship was apparently resting on severely shaky ground. Despite generating hundreds of "instruction pieces" (such as, famously, Young's "Composition 1960 #10," "Draw a straight line and follow it"), almost all of these works retained at least a vestige of compositional authority; someone was dictating an order for someone else to follow. Cardew had recently finished a year of study with the Italian composer Goffredo Petrassi and had embarked on his own path, one which was heavily involved with the creation and investigation of graphic scores and the possibilities they opened to musicians, following the examples laid out by Brown, Wolff, and others. One could simply present musicians with a set of "illustrations" having no instructions, much less commands, about what to do with it. Still, the score—since it certainly would be perceived as such—carried an aura of authority. "Treatise," his graphic masterwork, was begun around 1963 and performances of its first pages were being staged by

1964[38]. His notes for the piece as collected in his *Treatise Handbook* deal with all manner of problems with regard to interpretation of symbols (or whether "interpretation" was a proper mode of attack at all), orientation within the score, signal sequencing, and gaming rules, but never quite touch on improvisation. There's a deep, abiding respect for structure, even if that structure is amorphous and subject to a prismatic translational approach. On March 11, 1965, Cardew asks and answers: "Treatise: What is it? Well, it's a vertebrate."

Possibly the first public performance took place in June of 1964 in Florence, where pages 57-60 and 75-79 were played in brief episodes lasting only a couple of minutes each by Frederic Rzewski (piano and other noises), Mauricio Kagel ("reading aloud"), Italo Gomez (cello), and Sylvano Bussotti (percussion), with Cardew on whistles. Cardew's notes from that time already indicate the extensive attacks and approaches that were being considered and acted upon. For example, "Rzewski played the central line (one of the few times [it] has been interpreted) as a continuous sound. At each break in the line he would start a new sound." On the other hand, there seems to have been a certain amount of reaction on the part of the musicians against even these vague constraints as the composer mentions, with a hint of annoyance, that Kagel appeared unconcerned with the score, and "insisted on his freedom." The concept of serious, complete improvisation was, perhaps, beginning to scratch at Cardew's door despite Cage's well-known aversion, possibly gleaning a way around those admittedly common and "dangerous" traps.

---

38   "Treatise" is a 193-page graphic score. It contains absolutely no instructions for any potential interpretation. The fact that two sets of staves runs along the bottom of each page might indicate that whatever the interpretation is, it perhaps should be musical in nature. A "center line" (backbone?) tends to be present running horizontally through the middle of every page, though not always. Otherwise, pages range from extremely spare and clean to extravagantly baroque, containing shapes and symbols, including numbers, which repeat in various guises. The shapes include multitudes of circular forms, recognizable musical typography, line patterns and even representational figures, all very elegantly drawn.

Cardew and Robin Page, in the November 1964 issue of the *ICA Bulletin*, published a lightly tongue-in-cheek "manifesto" of sorts in the context of a program notes for a concert that included works by Feldman, Cage, Young, and Giuseppe Chiari as well as Cardew and Page which, playful though it may be, provides a look at the kind of subversive activity they were engaged in, subversive both to the established academy as well as the recent avant-garde:

MAKE YOURSELF A MASTER OF EXPERIMENTAL MUSIC

...THE ART of RELINQUISHING THE CONDITION OF CONTINUOUS CONCENTRATION. The method of composition kept SECRET because of its deadly power to disable and kill—WITH NO BODILY CONTACT! Now these devastatingly brilliant secrets that require NO STRENGTH OR EXERTION are revealed to you through Experimental Music Masters who dare to perform AT THEIR RISK!

Experimental Music is the most DEADLY form of TOTAL ABSTRACTION ever devised. Even a BEETHOVEN, SCHONBERG or STOCKHAUSEN SHUDDER at the thought of meeting an Experimental Music Master because they KNOW who the winner will be. INSTANTLY you will see how to DESTROY ILLUSION AND DRAW ATTENTION TO FACTS.

NEVER BE AFRAID AGAIN!

You no longer have to be helpless, ashamed or humiliated and look pitiful in the eyes of your friends. ACTIVATE THE MEDIUM OF SOUND-PRODUCTION and protect yourself, family, girl friend from DETERMINED SONOROUS EFFECTS.

BECOME A NEW MAN!

In these items your personal Experimental Music Master takes you by the hand and leads you THROUGH THE CONCERT HALL AND OUT.

You learn how to PROVIDE OPPORTUNITIES FOR RANDOM EXPERIENCE in a small mob of audience who are fully armed and even pinning you to the ground so you can't move. You pay nothing if you can't disarm one critic...send another flying through the air to CONCENTRATE ON THE WAY STATES ARE ENTERED and slam a third into the ground. Experimental Music can be DEADLY, CRIPPLING and DISASTROUS to any unfortunate critic foolish enough to suggest ATTACHING MEANING TO COMBINATIONS OF ELEMENTS, etc., etc.

In May of 1965, pages 89-106 of "Treatise" were played at the Walthamstow Forest Technical College in London along with La Monte Young's "Poem" and Michael von Biel's "World II," by an ensemble that included John White (tuba), Roger Smalley (piano), John Tilbury (piano), David Bedford (accordion), and Cardew on guitar. Again, it's interesting that so early on in its performance history, some of the musicians involved were compelled to stretch even the ultra-liberal guidelines of a graphic score that seemingly left itself open to infinite translations. Cardew writes:

On this occasion John White set the precedent for "perverse" interpretation by reading the ascending lines as descending intervals.

The notion of interpreting a symbol or direction in a manner intentionally opposite to one's initial reading, reinvigorating even the sort of instructions that one would otherwise expect to prove impossible for generating ruts or habits in the first place, was one that greatly appealed to Cardew.

Around September, 1965, Cardew was looking for players to realize a performance of "Treatise" at the Theatre Royal in Stratford, an event organized by Mark Boyle.[39] Via Cohen's record collection, Rowe had already been delving into 20th century serial and

39   Boyle would, later in that decade, achieve renown for his hyper-real

post-serial composition with great relish, gradually working his way toward the relatively recent work of the New York School composers. Additionally, his utilization of commercial illustrations, as well as fine art prints, as graphic launching pads for his rare solo opportunities in the Westbrook band indicated that he was primed for some real-time work in graphic score interpretation. Cohen, who had in fact studied and performed with Cardew as a fellow student at the Royal Academy of Music in the mid 50s, suggested that Rowe go down and see if participating as part of Cardew's ensemble would be a good fit. He did so, and the two hit it off immediately.[40] They were very much kindred spirits, arriving in a similar musical territory from two very different directions, each sensing that the other held knowledge he desired. Cardew needed musicians who could improvise without the baggage that almost necessarily came with those who had studied in academia, however ostensibly "avant" their leanings were. Cardew was absolutely fascinated by modern jazz (he was a big fan of Thelonious Monk and Horace Silver, eventually naming a son after the latter), and was eager to utilize jazz musicians with avant tendencies in his work. Having a background in art and graphics, as Rowe did, was all the better, as it might lead him to read the calligraphic forms found in "Treatise" with greater, or at least different, perspicacity.

For this event, the musicians were Tilbury (piano), Cardew (cello), Kurt Schwertsik (horn), John Surman (saxophones),[41] Rowe (guitar), and Peter Greenham (conductor). At the three rehearsals that preceded this performance, the group went over the score, discussing how the various symbols and drawings were to be read on that occasion. Cardew wrote:

---

castings of London curbsides and other detritus.

40   It was here that Rowe also likely met John Tilbury and John White for the first time.

41   Another indication of Surman's continued openness to new ideas.

This was the first performance in which the pauses (numbers) are read as repeated chords. Briefly, the system is this: at each number, each performer selects a note at random and plays it as softly as possible, repeating it as often as the number indicates and holding each repetition for a number of seconds corresponding to the number of repetitions. For example: 5 equals five repetitions of the same chord each lasting five seconds (the repetitions are coordinated by the conductor). The number 1 is regarded simply as a silence.[42]

Once he'd chosen his musicians, Rowe observed that Cardew tended not to be openly critical of their playing or the choices they made, preferring a passive-aggressive mode of operation.

If things were going in a direction he thought appropriate, he'd give some sort of positive encouragement or sign. But if someone suggested a reading that didn't sit well with him, he might say, "Well, that's good, but the only problem with that is…" or, "That's fine, great. But you might want to think about…"[43]

> *He wanted you to articulate the score, not interpret it, not taking into account his intentions. If he had intentions, he would have written it out. "I want you to do this thing this way." So to articulate it, in a sense, you paint it. The numbers are different from the shapes, for instance, they relate directly to things in reality, how you're paid, how you identify things, etc. No matter what Cornelius was about, that's a fact of reality and, I think, one should treat them like that. I might know what he means, but does it*

---

42   Cornelius Cardew, *Treatise Handbook*, London, Edition Peters, 1971.

43   One invariably recalls the classic Morton Feldman story wherein a student orchestra was performing a graphic score of his and the violist came to a box in which was written, "Play three notes." Upon seeing Feldman's grimace in his direction after that section, he defensively said, "But it just says, 'Play three notes!'" Feldman, sourly replied, "Not those notes."

have a reality in fact?

He would also take advantage of John White's innovation and talk about approaching the score "perversely." For instance gongs, round objects, might be associated with squares in the graphic score. This line of attack opened up entire new avenues and modes of thought for musicians like Rowe. The already enormous sense of freedom of interpretation (or, rather, articulation) one had when translating shapes into sound suddenly became multiplied manifold when one realized that there didn't have to be a "one-to-one" correspondence between shapes and sound. You could read the graphic in an opposite or tangential manner. Naturally enough, this could lead to similarly decoding entire sections, allowing the drawn score to increasingly flower out into the "real world." White, for example, would make a practice of injecting "rude" or "banal" sounds into performances, producing the sort of noises that "one simply wouldn't hear" in art contexts.

> Cardew was one of the first Europeans to grasp not just the musical but also the social implications of the new American aesthetic. And this was because his response to the music was not merely a cerebral rejection of the predominant western European compositional method— total serialism—but a deep-seated reaction to content and meaning, to the new ways of thinking and feeling, to the idealism, both moral and philosophical, that seemed to inform the new American music. "There is no room for the policeman in art," Cage said in one of his polemics against Europeans.[44]

The sheer elegance of Cardew's "Treatise" score was a marked contrast to the pie illustrations Rowe had previously attempted to use as improvisatory launching pads (though that was arguably not the case with the Klees). The enormous creativity of the

---

44   John Tilbury, *Contact*, Spring 1983.

drawings, the mystery of the numbers and symbols, and the overt beauty of the images, ranging from hyper-spare to lushly extravagant arabesques, exposed a depth of intellect that could, and would, nurture Rowe for decades. But there was also a kind of systematic approach, one could almost say a type of classicism in the score that appealed greatly to Rowe, an artist who had been schooled in a classic fashion and who would always retain an ongoing appreciation of the probative forms that antedated his own work. This balance between an orderly, Apollonian investigation of aesthetic psychology and the immediate, non-aesthetic appreciation of the ready-made was a gestalt of Rowe's art that loomed quite consistently over the course of his career, providing a sense of structure and purpose that was as viscerally apparent as it was difficult to quantify. In the few months prior to Cardew joining the group, Rowe had already begun importing these kinds of ideas and concerns into the simmering brew of the proto-AMM ensemble. At the same time, Cardew began to see pure improvisation, despite its derision by Cage, as a possible solution to the compositional authority problem. As exemplified by the ongoing conflict that would erupt between La Monte Young and Tony Conrad, issues of authorship and propriety were very difficult for even the most forward-looking of musicians to abandon at the time; few would simply give it all up as a logical next step, sublimating their egos within an ensemble, negating separable claims of individual creation. Even among the most extreme artists of the era, a sense of careerism was never entirely absent.

*

Around January of 1966, Rowe invited Cardew to join their as yet nameless group. It's impossible to overstate the fortuitousness of this conjunction. You have four musicians searching for ways to improvise outside the boundaries of jazz looking to other forms, including contemporary classical ones, for inspiration and, coming in the opposite direction, there's a composer sick and tired of the strictures imposed by the avant-classical world, looking to free jazz for salvation. Cardew may well have had the idea that he was, essentially, joining a jazz band. In contrast to his classical roots and training, he was extremely fascinated by the notion that there were these musicians who could "just play" and that it could be interesting to juxtapose this approach alongside music derived from more formal models.

In an unpublished interview (questioner unknown), probably conducted in early 1966, Cardew recollects hearing this nascent AMM:

> I remember that Keith's playing then was very different from what it is now. He used to play a lot of notes and it was very gestural. Figures would have a very particular shape, a very characteristic dynamic shape, and now they don't have so much. And every now and then at the end of the session, Lou and Eddie used to be like playing jazz, and I used to like that very much, it used to be nostalgic.

Cardew was several years older than the AMM members and came from an entirely different social stratum, having descended from a well-known family (his father was a master ceramicist), and having attended nothing but first class schools throughout his life. He had a forceful personality that could easily prove excessively, if unintentionally, domineering but, venturing into what was for him unknown territory, a certain balance was reached, at least for a while. Indeed, there was some suspicion voiced, Lou Gare opining that he wasn't at all sure Cardew was up to what they were doing.[45] The fact that the four initial members were all from working class roots and had risen by dint of hard labor through the jazz milieu as well as barely scrimping by materially in their personal lives gave them several reasons for looking askance at this well-off "composer." Rowe admitted of this possible aspect of Cardew's persona, that

> ...there's definitely a part of Cornelius that would be like when a rich guy goes out with a cheap woman, slumming.

45   Prévost, 2005.

I think there's a touch of that with the highly regarded
avant-gardist who's hanging around with the riff-raff.

But Cardew, bringing along his cello and sitting at whatever piano happened to be available at that week's gig location, proved to not only fit in with the direction they were pursuing but to bring to the venture an incalculably valuable *other* point of view. If he thought he was essentially joining a jazz ensemble, he also felt that he managed the transition fairly well: "...when I joined in I had no jazz experience whatever, yet there was no language problem." He was observant enough (and aware of some amount of truth in Cage's view of improvisation) to recognize that although they espoused an openness "to admit all sounds," they retained a goodly amount of historical preferences, many of which came part and parcel with the instruments they employed. There were doubtless vestiges of jazz affectations still clinging to everyone's playing, something that Cardew, as an outsider, was in a better position to perceive and point out. Still, it was invigorating for him.

> I compose systems. Sounds and potential sounds are around us all the time—they're all over. What you can do is to insert your logical construct into this seething mass—a system that enables some of it to become audible. That's why it's such an orgiastic experience to improvise—instead of composing a system to project into all this chaotic potential, you simply put yourself in there (you too are a system of sorts after all) and see what action that suicidal deed precipitates.

Though he certainly would have been invited, Cardew never participated in the weekly discussions held by the other members. It's possible he felt that, with his far vaster theoretical background, he would have dominated any conversation-oriented proceedings and that matters would proceed more smoothly if he stayed away. This didn't hinder the frequent talks he'd have with Rowe, however, introducing him to the works and theories of Feldman and David Tudor, among others, which ideas Rowe would necessarily import into the group's sessions. This was an action that may have produced a minute fracture between Rowe and Prévost that never quite healed, a crack that would expand to a chasm decades on. But as these sorts of discussions were soon to cease, once and forever, any resentment could only bubble beneath the surface.

> I think one of the observations that Eddie would probably make about this is that you have people who are from "the art school set" and the people who are not. And in the AMM you had Lou, Lawrence, and myself who were from the art school and Cardew who wasn't but was from that kind of "art set," Cage and Rauschenberg, and in fact was very art school-ish, very conceptual, and Eddie wasn't. I think Eddie often made, not explicitly, but that he always felt underneath, "Oh, these bloody art school...vague...bunch of toffs." But very subtle, something that I picked up that Eddie often felt. In the very later years, he really does take umbrage at all the art school ideas, of being interested in novelty, in the new and constantly breaking down and moving forward, not allowing things to settle...That was also one of the issues, the increasing degrees of abstraction that were happening and the move away from—it was rather hard-edged abstraction as opposed to the lyrical abstraction you get from sax players. I think that's one of the things you get from Eddie and Lou—Lawrence even—not so much Cornelius—they were very much glued to their instruments and the instruments were to be played. In fact, Eddie and Lou maintain that to his very day. They really are, their instruments are highly identifiable. We [Cornelius and I] didn't really care about those sort of things, about the instrument's sound; the technique went to the wall.

However far in any quasi-similar direction AMM may have proceeded without the introduction of Cardew, his presence served to launch them down pathways that they had been "feeling out," and others besides. His own graphic scores, as well as those by

Cage and Brown, offered a deep balance between control and freedom. By showing that the subset of interpretations of a score could be both infinite and *different* than the set of the infinite possible sounds likely to be produced in historically weighted improvisation, Cardew got across something of the Cantorian idea of nested infinities. For Rowe, as strong as was his desire to hurtle out into the unknown, his upbringing and schooling, as well as his nature, flowered in an environment where there were *some* kinds of restrictions, even if those borders were utterly hazy, amorphous, and open to interpretation and restructuring. The possibility of bringing in extra-musical notions into the readings of "Treatise," of understanding that numeric symbols might deal with everyday externalities like money, for instance, was liberating in a way beyond merely abandoning rhythms or chord structures. It allowed the music being created to connect far more closely to the living environment in which it was incubated, to approach an ideal state where it, the music, would in a deep way be undifferentiated from its surroundings. Cardew helped Rowe free himself from the idea that music had to be *music*. He also introduced the group to work by Alvin Lucier, La Monte Young, and Yoko Ono. Pieces like "Make a Long Sound" or "Make a Sound and Follow It" sparked all manner of ideas and illuminated new areas to explore.

One of those "infinite containers," those circumscribed sources of unlimited information, was the radio.

John Cage, at least since his "Imaginary Landscape #4" (1951), had used radios as a prominent element in his works, and Cardew likely alerted his compatriots to this area of sound investigation. In that piece, however, the twelve performers were obliged to follow extremely strict instructions as to where the radios were tuned and at what volume level they were played. This in itself created an intriguing balance between order of a particular sort, and chaos, as a certain overall shape would manifest due to the directions being obeyed but, of course, what would actually emanate from the radio speakers could be, within the parameters of what the station typically broadcast, virtually anything at all.

Before we were AMM, we'd been using them in "Treatise" performances. For me, it was like when someone does something that makes absolute sense, on every criterion I could think of. Yeah, this just makes total sense to me. And from that second on, that's it.

As much lip service as the idea of ceding control and "accepting anything" was being given by the ensemble, actually taking concrete steps in this direction was more psychologically difficult at the time than might be perceived in retrospect. Rowe was about to introduce taped pop songs into the mix as one vehicle for getting to the point of accepting any sonic elements from outside the performing space. It was another step, a small but critical one, to have a radio in hand and to integrate whatever happened to be incoming on the airwaves into one's music. Even when using the most extreme of techniques, a musician generally has at least some notion of what sound is likely to emerge. Short of happening to know what program is on at a particular time on a certain station (which could easily be avoided), one has no real idea what will come forth from the speaker when twirling the dial and flicking on the radio, less still when a short-wave is employed. What's required is the confidence that whatever occurs, you'll be able to "place" it in a sound-field where it makes sense, is beautiful, or doesn't make sense but works somehow, etc.[46] The exposure, via Cardew, to the activities being pursued by the Fluxus group wherein the entire notion of what performance was was being stood on its head, had a deep impact. The expansiveness of what a "musical" group could include as part of a performance, demolishing notions of what was and wasn't art or music, proved as liberating as it was daunting. Faced with the idea that any sound (or other activity) was potentially fair game, the seed was planted for the developing strategy of "sound placement," of seriously considering the multitude of choices available and honing one's aesthetic sense to choose the most appropriate (beautiful, ugly, or otherwise) one(s). Or, of course, the most inappropriate.

---

46   Years later, Rowe would prepare a list titled, Why I use the radio: Found Object.

An article appeared in the *Dover Daily Mail* on March 9, 1966 (author unknown) previewing an AMM concert to be held at the Institute of Contemporary Arts on March 13 (the ICA bulletin for March also noted the event and included in its 24-page publication a full page photo spread consisting of dark, blurred individual shots of the members—Rowe notably still holding his guitar in the vertical position):

> On Sunday evening the Institute of Contemporary Arts in Dover will reverberate to the music of a quintet, three of whom—including modern composer Cornelius Cardew—will perform on transistor radios.

————

Unpredictable content
Fixed to a time and place
Part of a global culture and at the same time a local culture
Part of the process of shifting the object from utilitarian to the aesthetic
Allows vulgar materials to be incorporated into the performance
Difficult to determine whether it elevates, degenerates or celebrates the sources of materials
Creativity at the point of juxtaposition
Integration of other media
Helps to produce a layered sensation
Independent
Perpetual variation
Modular
Reproduces certain aspects of daily life
Synthetic
Challenges the notion of authority that came from technique
Adds to the polyphony of timbre
Has its own unique texture
A question of reality and a question of art: the artistic fact
Engages in imitation
Replaces the exterior contribution of the composer in some aspects
Environment and noise
Provides melody for the guitar
Lack of uniqueness in contribution
Helps with the act of music making, or organising in front of you
Changes the perceptions of the performance

It is called "AMM Music," but the group's guitarist and chief organiser Keith Rowe refuses to reveal what AMM stands for.

"Everything we do is part of the performance," he says.

Their performance takes in the noise of bells, sirens, horns (of the motor variety) and the sound of brightly painted pieces of wood being banged together.
"I think the colour makes the sound different, though I don't suppose it does really—not if you were blindfolded."

His philosophy is based on the reasoning that if modern paintings can include ready-made objects, then music should use all types of sound. Tunes and compositions are out.

Every now and then everyone stops playing. "Silences are part of the performance. It's great when you hear things that have been drowned out by whatever we've been playing—like the sound of a 73 bus outside."

There are moments when the audiences participate. "I'd like them say, to smash up matchboxes or switch the lights on and off. Someone once used an electric drill. It was great."

"But we have to be careful," says Mr. Rowe. "We don't want to pander to the audience. Not like Sir Malcolm Sargent." [47]

AMM played the ICA on March 13 and printed a small flyer for the event, reading *in toto*:

AMM - 13. 3. 66

SOUND IS ESSENTIALLY YOU

---

47   At the time, the conductor of the BBC Symphony Orchestra.

ESSENCE BEING YOU, NOT YOUR YOU

SOUND IS A REFLECTION OF YOU

A reckoning of what appears to have been the March 13 concert at the ICA forms part of an article by Francis Newton (the pseudonym used by Marxist historian Eric Hobsbawm) in the March 25 issue of *New Statesman*. He begins with a brief and doubtful summary of the New Thing in jazz, giving bebop its due and grudgingly admitting that Ornette Coleman, Cecil Taylor and, possibly, Archie Shepp may end up having something to offer but that the movement was in serious danger of following the Albert Aylers of the scene down a pathway toward chaos and a monotonous chaos at that. His paragraph on AMM is worth reprinting for several reasons. Not only do we get a decent first-hand, objective appraisal of what was being manifested but also an honest, if short-sighted attempt to come to grips with the music that was occurring by someone with at least a partial working knowledge of the avant-garde of the time, if not a particularly sympathetic ear:

> Such boredom could be observed spreading though the guaranteed avant-garde audience—long-haired girls dressed for demureness, young men in the gloomy colours of serious hipsters—at the Recital of AMM music at the ICA, a combination of the British New Thing and non-jazz avant-gardists. It was conducted by Messrs Cornelius Cardew, Lou Gare, Eddie Prévost, Keith Row [sic] and Laurence Sheaff with an instrumentation—according to the programme—of cello, piano, tenor-sax, violin, drums, xylophone, bass, electric guitar, sitar, and three transistor radios turned on from time to time to allow us casual snatches of mainly religious discussion. An inventory on the spot also revealed an accordion, a metronome, a tape-recorder, two alarm clocks indicating different times, and something which looked like a burglar alarm but which wasn't used in the first 70 minutes of the first number. The piano was played in the main with the fore-arm [sic] and by striking

the strings by hand, the xylophone mainly on one note, the guitar with the aid of a red plastic spoon, a picnic tin and a steel ruler, the sax along he lines of a ram's horn. It was possible to guess that Mr. Gare is not only a devoted but perhaps also a capable saxophonist. From time to time the sounds were attractive, but the occasion had its longueurs. The yawns began in the female sector of the audience, but by the time this critic admitted defeat had spread visibly among the young men. The main object of the avant-garde had been attained. They were alone and not understood.

Utilizing the tape recorder the group had purchased to document their weekly sessions for subsequent analysis, Rowe had embarked on a new strategy. The notion of incorporating aspects of the outer, non-immediate-performance world into a concert led him to the idea of recording a couple of pop hits of the day, the Beach Boys' "Barbara Ann" and Lou Christie's "Lighting Strikes," for use as a sound element. In a manner that would seem charmingly primitive decades on, he recorded short stretches of the song, sometimes slowed down, sometimes speeded up, here loud, there soft, portion after portion onto a single length of tape until he had ten or so minutes of fractured pop music. Forty years later, the effect is still both powerful and a little hilarious and this is well after any contemporary ironic effect has worn off, the songs having acquired the patina of nostalgia. One can only imagine how an audience in early 1966 reacted, attending this "serious" event only to hear vestiges of, in all likelihood, exactly the kind of music from which many were there to escape. Of course, as with much of Rowe's music, the direct influence of currently produced visual art is easy to perceive. Pop Art had blossomed in the several years prior to these shows and Andy Warhol's soup cans, Lichtenstein's comic strips, and Wasserman's pin-ups and lipstick tubes were common currency in that adjacent aesthetic world. Why shouldn't an evocation of Lou Christie occur in a performance of improvised, abstract music?

The concert of March 28, 1966 at the Royal College of Art provides a rare recorded example of this tape usage as well as giving an intriguing snapshot of where exactly AMM was, conceptually, two or three months after Cardew's joining and some three months before their first "official" recording. [48]

The performance can be considered as being roughly divided into three sections. At the beginning, high, droning strings are heard (presumably Gare on violin, Sheaff or Rowe perhaps on cello, Prévost possibly bowing cymbals) accompanied by Cardew on piano. Unlike the November 1965 date, this state is sustained for a good ten minutes, the strings wavering gently between adjacent pitches, some deeper, darker rumblings emerging in the form of heavy-handed bangings on the guitar from Rowe along with some amount of feedback. The piano, also staying in the high register, is played quite delicately, lending a kind of "raindrop" ambience to the affair. It's already somewhat remarkable how long this stasis is allowed to hold, how intent is the investigation into "minor" variations in sound and, in retrospect, how predominantly the strings are in the forefront. There's a taffy-like attenuation and recompression of the violin, several times stretched out to a vanishing thinness before regrouping.

Suddenly, about 12 minutes in, Rowe produces a raucous yawp and Cardew pounds out a couple of brutal chords, leading to the next section. Prévost emerges full-blown from his drum kit as the performance takes on more of the quality of some of the most extreme avant-jazz being produced at the time. If one is searching for a comparison in that area, perhaps the closest one comes is in Sun Ra's more cacophonous music from around the same period, works like "The Magic City" where electronics and free jazz were combined in riotous and sublime fashion. Very soon in the AMM show, however, you hear the disembodied and blurred voice of a

---

48   A small portion of this concert was published as part of the *Leonardo Music Journal*'s CD insert accompanying the issue (Volume 11, 2001) devoted to "Not Necessarily 'English Music'" (curated by David Toop). My thanks to Eddie Prévost for making the recording of the entire event available.

radio commentator at high volume. Moments after this unexpected entrance, here comes "Lightning Strikes." It wells up into the mix, the falsetto vocal first sounding like a misplaced squeak of feedback before it becomes apparent that the performance space has been invaded. There's something of a battle between Christie and Prévost's drums (as well as the still-present radio voice), the pop song appearing and disappearing in fractured iteration. Gare begins screaming on tenor, Prévost furiously attacking the snares but Christie will not be denied. "I can't stop, no I can't stop." Rowe seems to be operating the tape recorder and thrashing at his guitar simultaneously, attempting to generate as thick a wall of sound as possible. Eventually, "Lightning Strikes" becomes the backbone of this section, as steady-state as the string drones earlier on, supported by snare rolls, roiling tenor, pounding piano and thrummed bass. It's an overwhelming, draining assault.

> It was our version of the "sheets of sound." We would play it as loud as we possibly could and try to climb over it like a wall. It was a barrier to get through.[49]

> I think for me it was the equivalent of Andy Warhol's Marilyn portraits or the electric chair or two views of Liz Taylor getting married. It was much more to do with a statement about reproduction. We were just starting in that period of the best seller, of things being reproduced in multiples.

Events do subside, however, the tape and radio voice fading out, and the initial string drones replaced by similar ones from tenor and, apparently, bass clarinet (Sheaff?), punctuated by clear, single notes from the piano. We hear the stretches of silence previously alluded to with sounds more overtly being placed into position rather than continuously played. It ultimately settles, via some lovely chords from Cardew, into an almost tonal, rather melancholy atmosphere, a surprising but, after the central maelstrom, quite satisfying conclusion.

---

49   Warburton, 2001.

A question almost routinely arises: Was there anything comparable to a performance like this being done anywhere, by anyone, around this time? As previously mentioned, Sun Ra's work from this period was similar in some ways and was certainly known to the musicians by then. The lengthy improvisations, the integration of electronics and acoustic instruments, and the presence, however rarified, of free jazz elements make the comparison a salient one. But there are elements in AMM that were rarely if ever present in Sun Ra's music. The stasis heard in the early string drones, the willingness to remain in "one place" for extended periods, is rare in Sun Ra whose music tended to bustle and boil throughout. And although Rowe's use of feedback and noise from his guitar might be said to be roughly analogous to Sun Ra's use of distortion on his claviolines and other electronic keyboards, there was never anything like the introduction of "Lightning Strikes," no direct reference to the grubby (though enticing—it is, after all, a good song) commercialism rampant outside the walls of the performance space. Sun Ra sent out his messages, tongue in cheek or otherwise, to astral beings and spirits; that notion would never, ever even come to mind amongst AMM members, nor the kitschy evocations of "space age" ephemera.

One might suspect that earlier concurrent and contemporary electro-acoustic explorations by composers like Karlheinz Stockhausen could have been influential and, to be sure, something of his approach was likely carried in by Cardew. But Rowe doesn't remember specifically listening to Stockhausen until a year or two later and, in any case, it's difficult to draw purely auditory parallels between AMM in 1966 and works like "Gruppen" or "Telemusik." Their subsequent frequent use of contact mics, however, quite conceivably owes more than a small debt to the two "Microphonies."

*

As he transitioned from the Westbrook band into the nascent AMM, Rowe was playing his guitar in the traditional manner (whatever odd sounds were emanating from it), that is, sitting down and holding the instrument vertically. When he performed in Cardew's ensembles, he became exposed to the new-to-him idea of pianists extending what their instrument could do, including utilizing the piano's interior by means of Cagean preparations and direct interaction with the strings and body. These notions were likely percolating in the back of Rowe's head for a little while and it only took some happenstance occurrence to actuate the idea:

> *I think the very, very first time would have been just laying it on my lap, instead of the vertical position, then working with coins and stuff on my lap. And then graduating to having another chair in front of me, facing me, and having stuff on that chair. And then there's a point of actually putting it on the chair, then it goes on the table, then down to the floor, then back onto the table...I think without Cornelius, or the kind of information Cornelius brought, I'm not sure how or when I would have done that. I just don't know. It was certainly my wanting to find another way of using the guitar which was there, but it probably came from looking at somebody like Cornelius or Tilbury using the piano, extending it, something like that. I didn't take notes at the time so I don't know exactly what was going on in my head, but I think it's that kind of process: seeing pictures of Cage or seeing Cornelius inside the piano really got me to think of different ways to use the guitar.*

There were at least two main ramifications to this move. One was, simply, the physical reality that things could be placed on the guitar without dropping off!

> *When you lay the guitar down flat, it allows you to work with gravity a lot more. Therefore when you put an object over the guitar, string over the pickup, they stay there, they don't fall off, so I could integrate one of the most important things from my art school experience, the found object. This idea of the found object, of discovering something and rather than trying to re-represent it in a still life, [to] actu-*

ally use the object itself, using knives, spoons, pan cleaners, brushes, rather than representing them, was an important thing for me.[50]

Secondly, perhaps more profoundly, was the removal of the guitar from direct bodily contact, of its ceasing to be an appendage and being allowed a more individualized, even autonomous, position. Following the example of Jackson Pollock, Rowe was able to liberate his instrument (canvas) from the absolute reins of his wrist and hand, automatically reducing the degree to which he could control its output. By physically removing a substantial portion of muscular memory from the equation, Rowe couldn't fail but to free himself from at least a certain amount of the tendency to fall back into known routines. The electric guitar was uniquely accommodating to such an idea in that its electronic nature allowed for sounds to emanate from it for a given period without the direct application of breath, hand/finger manipulation, etc. He could at one blow virtually eliminate the sort of instrumental control issues that dominated—and would continue to dominate—most improvising musicians while at the same time opening up an entirely new and vast area of choices which would have less to do with the specific instrument involved and more with the group sound as such, a recession into the kind of "egolessness" that would become a vitally important element of the finest electro-acoustic improvisation of the coming decades, very different from the virtuosic practices of many others in ostensibly the same field. Too, by laying objects atop the guitar, the listener is hearing more their interaction with the instrument than Rowe as such. As he put it in a recorded letter to Gino Robair in 1991, "What are you hearing? Nuts and bolts! Not Rowe."

Rowe's decision was directly in line with one of the guiding principles of AMM: allowing any sound equal footing, accepting what occurred and working it into the whole. So if he laid down a tin can on top of his amplified strings, he might have a general idea

---

50   Oren Ambarchi, 2000.

of what sort of sound would likely result, but never quite an exact one, much less how it might sound if he gave the can a kick.

> *I would put the guitar on the other end of the stage, roll wooden balls or marbles toward it, and they would hit and, obviously being highly amplified, it was uncontrollable as to how the scream would die down.*

You could also lay the instrument in such a position to generate varying amounts and timbres of feedback, supplying an ongoing drone while Rowe would be able to move on to another sound generator.

More broadly, and more deeply important for his subsequent work, placing the guitar on a flat surface, at a distance from his body, allowed him to reconnect to the ideas investigated in his art school thesis: how the guitars represented in paintings by Braque might actually sound. By being able to *see* his instrument as a formal, visual element, framed by the generally rectangular tables upon which it would lie, Rowe could attempt to incorporate structural elements (via the guitar's interaction with the various accoutrements that would amass over the years) from a visual aspect and educe musical aesthesia from them, blurring the boundaries between forms. It's a tough proposition for the listener, if not so much for the creator who is already so attuned. How to get across the idea of negative space, the shape formed, say, by the space between the curve of the guitar's body and a transistor radio, in purely aural terms? How can a listener possibly be expected to intuit that idea through auditory input? Did Rowe expect the notions to somehow percolate through to the attentive audience member in some poetic fashion that might be difficult, if not impossible, to quantify but which would be somehow felt, like an ultra-subtle tingeing of the atmosphere?

Some of this derived from a growing appreciation of Eastern philosophies:

You could say we were involved in a much more mystical set of ideas, more of a Taoist notion that you can place any sound in whatever context and it will work if you are fully in tune with what's going on within that context. This is close to the Taoist idea of being so much in touch with what's around you that whatever action you take is... correct or appropriate. I think that was there, consciously and not. I think you developed your consciousness to such a degree that you were incapable of it not working; you couldn't produce a sound that didn't work because you'd reached such a high level of integration. The idea was that your sensibility wouldn't allow you—it would edit out stuff that wouldn't work. So the idea that any sound, strictly speaking, wasn't possible because your internal system would edit out sounds you oughtn't to have made. Therefore you'd be completely free to do whatever you wanted and it wouldn't be bound by genre except that many of the genres wouldn't be possible because they themselves were inappropriate actions. There was actually no limit to the kind of sounds that AMM could have made. It could be anything. A lot of that would come from the radio. The radio could emit the James Last Orchestra and it might actually be one of the most repulsive pieces of music that you could hear but it would work in that circumstance somehow. That made it different from composition. If you were composing a piece of music and you said, after 3 minutes and 52 seconds, play James Last, it probably wouldn't work. That was one of the main things about improvisation for us, that moment.

Rowe had been witness to a demonstration of *kyudo*, usually known in English as Zen Archery. In this exercise, several blind-folded monks would send arrows toward targets, apparently hitting around or exactly in the center of the bull's eye with some regularity by virtue, they maintained, of an extreme awareness of the room in which they found themselves—the objects therein, the way the sounds and the air itself interacted with those objects, etc. This made an enormous impression on Rowe, leading him to adopt, insofar as he was capable, a similar hyper-awareness of *the room*, feeding into the sort of self-filtering he refers to above. He later studied Buddhism for a while under a monk named Sangharakshita. As he explained:

> *What I wanted to be able to do was look at something and understand it, or to be able to understand the tension between those two things [searches around for objects on the café table] between the corner of this [ashtray] and that round thing [back of the chair]. I wanted to be able to walk into a space and immediately comprehend what the space was about. To be able to talk to you now and have part of my brain listening to what the coffee machine is doing or what the person is saying over there. Part of Taoism was being able to do the right thing at the right time. You develop a sense of what to do.*[51]

Sheaff, who had become seriously involved with transcendental meditation at this point, found that the music resonated with experiences he'd had in that area:

> The mind never knew what was going to come up next so, in the end, you just had to let go. The music just *had* to flow like that. And that takes you to deeper levels. I realized one day—because by this time I'd already started meditating, so I was having that experience anyway—I realized how deep we were going, all of us, in those sessions. I remember there was a time when we had a rehearsal in the Royal College of Art, in the basement, and it had been going for probably an hour and a half, and suddenly there was a moment where everything stopped just for a second and Cornelius played one note on the piano and it was just the funniest thing I've ever experienced in my life. It was so incredibly humorous. I realized we were

---

51   Warburton, 2001.

on a deep level here, just floating on a note. That was a beautiful thing about playing with AMM because we were exploring those deeper levels of consciousness.

Playing in darkness or as close to that condition as possible was one approach that both helped foster this extreme sensory-conscious environment and also played into the secrecy aspects of the Gurdjieffian worldview. Just as the idea of solos had been subjugated to group expression in the hope of forging a *whole* sound, removing their visual presence necessarily furthered this goal as far as the audience was concerned. Whereas it may already often have been difficult to ascertain whence the source of a given sound, it now became next to impossible to do so. More than that, it drove home the idea that it was pointless to even try or worry about such a thing. It didn't matter to the musicians; it shouldn't matter to the audience. The ensemble becomes part of the room, the room emits the sound.

Not that AMM didn't employ contradictory tactics. At some point, one of the members, possibly Sheaff, brought in some butcher's coveralls and caps made from rugged white material replete with old blood stains, which the group would don for performances, sometimes with bright red sashes for emphasis.

> *I know the image could look like you're in a laboratory, experimenting or something like that, but I don't think that was it. It was a much hotter kind of feeling, the slaughterhouse.*

Clearly, this worked against the idea of subsuming themselves (and their egos) to the room and, indeed, served only to further isolate themselves from both room and audience, erecting another barrier against any possible comprehension. The dress also served to differentiate the group from other rock bands of the time who would be just as likely to appear in brocade jackets with ruffled shirts and skintight knickers. No teen idols here. At the time, such garb served to play down the "musical performance" aspect of the group (although it heightened a desired perception of class consciousness), to further isolate the musicians from any notion the audience might have that they were witnessing an "act" though, of course, a few years on such dress would become an entirely different signifier. Cardew never adopted this garb. It says something about the nature of this ensemble that, having decided to utilize this "costume," to some extent certainly as a shield masking their individualities for the sake of a nebulous group presence, they would have no problem with one member deciding not to go along. This may have played into the notion taken up by less well-informed reviewers that AMM was a quartet of musicians "backing" Cardew.

It should also be noted that, at this early stage, AMM was almost entirely non-political, at least in any overt manifestation short of inferences derived from things like the coveralls. This went for Cardew as well. Indeed, if anything, more so for him than the others.

> In a way, Cornelius was the most non-political. He was the one who wouldn't want politics to raise its ugly head. In fact, that went up into the early Scratch Orchestra before he changes but then, of course, it becomes the main part of his approach. In the early period, he was very resistant to that. Goodness knows what AMM would have been like without him. Maybe Lawrence's humor and jokiness would have sent us along a line like Misha Mengelberg or the ICP Orchestra. I think Lawrence's personality was really, really important. I think Eddie's kind of strictness, in a way—I don't mean meanness in a bad sense—I mean in terms of discipline was really important. And then the art school factor. The chemistry of all that was able to produce this extraordinary music at the time. I think Cardew unlocked. His knowledge and experience kind of gave you permission to exercise the ideas and thoughts you might have had. And then, in turn, AMM gives permission for Syd Barrett or Pink Floyd to do what they want to do; there's a whole lineage

between the avant-garde and popular forms. It always goes back to that political question. There are the political type bands, like the People's Liberation Band, that play for a rally and have some immediate effect: "When do we want it? Now!" There's another kind of politics by playing Beethoven or Brahms or AMM, like a slow burning thing that ultimately has more effect. Cardew's influence was an immediate effect but was much more percolating in the long term. Sometimes you don't realize it until way afterwards.

*

A press release[52] lists a number of aphorisms in effect for the ensemble:

> Does group direction or authority depend on the strength of a leading personality, whose rise and fall is reflected in the projected image; or does the collation of a set of minds mean the development of another authority independent of all the members but consisting of them all?

> An AMM performance has no beginning or ending. Sounds outside the performance are distinguished from it only by individual sensibility.

> The reason for playing is to find out why I want to play.

> Given a certain amount of experience, it is not difficult to assimilate any object.

> Every noise has a note.

> The past always seems intentional, but at the time it appears to be accidental.

---

52   Dated April 11, 1970.

Playing in AMM sometimes produces a state where you feel sounds in a completely different way from usual. Seeing as if for the first time this reddy brown object with all the strings going away to the left, a bow going across the strings on the right hand side and interwoven amongst the strings various little things, on the top of that a plastic lid, and you just watch the sounds happening.

There is no guarantee that the ultimate realisation can exist.

To play and arrive at the state where you no longer need to play.

AMM started itself. It was there a few minutes before we though of it.

Within the time span of a performance the nearness of sound-beauty becomes laughingly obvious, the players merely indicators of what is here already.

Mistakes in and towards AMM could be due to constant reference to sets of standards.

There is no certain knowledge in relation to your development, that the effort you are making at the time, is the right effort.

Chapter 5

[*From a previously unpublished interview of Rowe and Cardew conducted in 1966. Rowe thinks the interviewer was David Sladen but Sladen doesn't recall having conducted it.*]

How did AMM get started?

Rowe: Most of us were in the Westbrook band, and I suppose traditions of big bands are that you always split off into little groups. We played at the Royal College of Art for six months, and we just started off with normal standards like "Baubles, Bangles and Beads," just jazz standards…My big thing in the Westbrook band was that I always used to muck everything up, because if he (Westbrook) wrote a composition, I used to finish it long after they finished it; if they gave me a two-chorus solo it would usually be three and a quarter choruses, because I didn't take any notice and it was an extension of this. The centrepieces became longer and longer in the smaller group, until we would play continuously for two hours.

Cardew: So you would play a chorus at the beginning, and then it would just take off?

Rowe: Yeah. We just gradually got out of it; it wasn't conceived in any way.

Were you playing in the Westbrook band as you're playing now?

Rowe: No. There's a big visual difference. I had the guitar that way up (vertical), I used to tune the strings as they should be tuned, I used a pick and I worried about the edge of the pick. I used to buy new strings every month.

Cardew: [*referenced in previous chapter*] I remember that Keith's playing then was very different from what it is now. He used to play a lot of notes and it was very gestural. Figures would have a very particular shape, a very characteristic dynamic shape, and now they don't have so much. And every now and then at the end of the session, Lou and Eddie used to be like playing jazz, and I used to like that very much, it used to be nostalgic.

Did you think of yourself as a jazz musician when you were with Westbrook? Is jazz your background?

Rowe: Oh yeah. I can't read music whatsoever, I can't read a note. In fact I don't honestly know what a crotchet is. I've tried, but I gave it up after a week; I just hate the idea. I'm a jazz musician now really…But I don't know, I'm just a person. I don't see things like that really.

You're not interested in what what you're doing is called?

Rowe: No, not really.

People can call it jazz if they want?

Rowe: Yeah. But I think they'd be wrong.

Cardew: It's a very familiar situation in straight music that people argue, "is it music?" The answer to that is that it's music because I'm a musician and I've always played music and this is what I play now.

Rowe: Jazz musicians worry like hell about jazz.

Cardew: Has it ever before this period achieved stability?

Rowe: No, it's never been as stable as it is now. I suppose I don't like it being stable now.

Cardew: You don't want it to crystallise?

Rowe: No, I mean last week: in one sense I hated it because I knew I could do it. I'd rather destroy it, I'd rather not do it than know...This is the feeling I had with Westbrook—I knew that we could go to a concert, we could play "Plymouth Sound" and then go straight into "Chelsea Bridge," and it used to be a fantastic feeling and it was always sure to hit it off, you could always make it work. There was no problem whatsoever, you just did it. And I suppose I don't like that.

It's playing in a set style?

Rowe: It is really, yeah...suppose I was depressed about Conway Hall in a way because I suddenly woke up about half way through and felt I was playing in a group, which I didn't like.

Cardew: What is it that disturbs you, because in the group there's a terrific solidarity? It's terrifically reassuring to feel that Lou is backing me.

Rowe: I know what you mean and I get that as well. I suppose that was my one role in the Westbrook band—whatever they did I always used to muck it up. It's always been my one thing. I never used to tune up to the same notes as they did, and if they ever went anywhere where it was a bit risky, like an audition, they wouldn't let me solo, so I'd mess everything up in the background and play half a tone lower than the pianist. And this is what I tend to do here lots of times.

Are you an anarchist who likes breaking things up for the sake of breaking them up?

Rowe: No, I'm not really an anarchist or an iconoclast.

In fact you're looking for new forms. As soon as something becomes set into a style you're dissatisfied with it because it seems too predictable?

Rowe: I am in a way, but I get fantastically pleased at someone like Charlie Christian who's perfect in this respect, and I like it sometimes when everything's really closely knit and works well, but a lot of the time I feel I want to do the exact opposite.

Cardew: It's great to be doing the same as everybody else for a while, then there comes the period when you do the opposite to everybody else. You can't be in the same relationship to the people around you all the time.

Rowe: I see the group in two groups really. I see Lou, Eddie and Lawrence as one set of people because they're all interested in Zen.

Does this affect their music?

Rowe: I couldn't tell you because I never ask them. They all meditate.

Cardew: If there's any personal tension between any members of the group, it's been me and Eddie and Lou and Laurie [Sheaff] because they expect to be drowned in it, to be involved in it to such an extent, whereas Lou in my opinion is a much more Zen character because he can stop things, he can say something which just finishes you.

Rowe: I never like talking about AMM as a person because AMM is five people; it's got to be those five people. If you take one or two out then it isn't AMM in a sense. But then I also think that the whole world is AMM and every one little thing is as well.

Cardew: I have a guilty conscience about talking about these people because everything you formalise about them threatens their existence...For a cameo picture of what I have found in AMM that I haven't found before is just the fact that I can go there and play, and play exactly what you want, and that's something I've always wanted to do, and here's the opportunity, and I think that Keith's sound-world is related to mine. I don't associate myself with a particular sound-world, but his sound experience is similar...I think I often arouse opposition in the group because I play more traditionally. Keith's often very shocked because for a whole session I play nothing but notes.

You don't like notes, Keith?

Cardew: He doesn't <u>know</u> notes.

Rowe: Really, I'm not interested in music at all. I get really dragged off by music.

Cardew: What it is, is that there's real music and there's not music, and that's what Keith doesn't accept, and I don't accept either. I think everything's music and Keith thinks music's nowhere...I think there are things in the world besides AMM. I think La Monte Young is different from AMM, but, of course, AMM is the whole of life. La Monte Young has had a big influence on AMM through me.

Who is La Monte Young?

Cardew: He wrote a piece called "Poem" which is simply a list of instructions on how to use a random number book to establish durations inside a total duration, and each of these durations is occupied with an action, a continuous action—it might be a sound or combing your hair. It started off by being the sound of chairs and tables being pushed around; each duration was one, and they overlapped. And he said that in this piece, in versions lasting several months, it would be useful to have a reserve stock of people to carry out the actions. That was the beginning of the music that goes on forever. I think it's more recent than Cage. Cage is still very selective.

How selective is AMM?

Cardew: It's only selective insofar as the people in it object...I think it's selective in the fact that you can't do it forever, that after two hours you're exhausted.

Rowe: I suppose there's a difference between your limitations and your selectivity.

Cardew: I think it's crowded, and that's excellent.

Rowe: I'm pretty sure if lots and lots of people came to play I'd get fed up. They'd just change it because it'd become so loud you couldn't hear them. That's what usually happens.

What was your reaction to the extra contributions at the Conway Hall concert?

Rowe: None really.

Cardew: I think there was a general reaction. When the audience starts to react in a way which you think is stupid, you reduce the scope of the activity, and I think that happened at Conway Hall. You consolidate on a narrow strip and you hold that.

How do you feel about people sitting in?

Rowe: I suppose there's a lot of snobbishness about AMM because if someone came along and sat in you'd feel very irate. It's a kind of self-preservation. It's the only thing I've got, outside painting. I work 42 hours a week at a lousy job so I can have a few hours a week free to do exactly what I want. So when some-body comes along and starts mucking around, I get annoyed and turn on the feedback or something.

You wouldn't mind a non-human contribution occurring at all? Say someone knocked over a pile of chairs. That wouldn't annoy you?

Cardew: There's something completely perfidious about a musical interruption. A musical intervention is very disturbing because it's musical, whereas a pile of chairs being knocked over is part of <u>our</u> music.

Rowe: I get a feeling that if you added something else to it, it would be duplicating some of it. There's only one person I can think of, Robin Page, who could come along and actually do something extra; lots of other people would just come along and sort of play with us. I think people just come along and do what you expect of them. A pile of chairs would do something different.

A pile of chairs falling over doesn't have any intention behind it?

Rowe: I suppose not.

When you play, it's obviously something different from becoming an automaton. Can you tell me what happens?

Cardew: I don't know.

Rowe: It's not absence of intention really.

Do you mean absence of expression? You obviously intend to do things and do them.

Rowe: There's no absence of one thing. You see, there's no 100% of everything.

Do you evaluate playbacks?

Cardew: I don't think there is any value in playbacks.

Is there such a thing as a mistake in AMM?

Cardew: I make them…I know one thing that I enjoy very much about playing. In composed music, there is always something beyond you, some authority which you are trying to fulfill, and I would never have imagined this was possible in improvised music, but sometimes that happens. I don't want to be all alone, that's why I think composed music is great, why I think, in many cases, composed music goes further. In AMM I find you get close to it because Keith's playing is something I can't break. I can decide that's enough, but he doesn't, he goes on. That's just like composed music.

Rowe: There is no such thing as non-composed music. You can never get away from some form of composition.

Cardew: When you play a composition by La Monte Young, there is this definite thing you have to do.

Rowe: Yes, but then again, everybody in the group has a definite thing they have to do; it's just a different sort of thing.

Cardew: Just being what they are. It's (AMM's) being what it is. When I first started to play with you, you were talking about using tapes as a sort of acoustic score. Now I see that I'm reading Lou like a score. That is the composition.

Rowe: I mean, you get legs dangling down there and arms floating around, and there are so many fingers and one head. I find that is enough limitation for me. It's very strict composition.

Do you like listening to sounds—say traffic noises or railway noises?

Cardew: If I'm going along the street and hear an extraordinary sound I will listen to it, and if an ordinary sound happens I don't take much notice. This is the course that is followed by AMM quite often—through the most extraordinary sounds you come to a place where you can make ordinary sounds and they are of the same quality as extraordinary sounds, the become extraordinary. I enjoy being able to play sometimes with it, slowing down off it. This was costing me real effort on the cello using very heavy bowing, when I suddenly realised this rocking sound was being caused by the touch of a finger.

Rowe: This is like Lou you see. During that fantastic loud piece Lou couldn't be heard whatsoever, yet he really enjoys it. There's something about going flat out and not being able to be heard; I've never experienced it actually.

Cardew: That fantastic feeling that nobody's listening, and that's great….

Could you say more about intended or unintended sounds? Could you say categorically that you're more interested in unintended sounds than human, intended sounds?

Cardew: I'm more interested in animal intended sounds (hilarity)

Rowe: If I close my eyes and someone pushes a lot of chairs over, I can't tell if it's intentional or not just from the sound.

Is it just the sound you're concerned with?

Rowe: Yes…

Cardew: I reserve the right to respond to certain facets of experience, certain things that happen; certain things I'll respond to, others I don't, and I'm answerable to absolutely no one.

Are you divorcing the sound from any intention it might have?

Cardew: Yes, could be. But look, it could be someone unloading a heap of bricks. A lorry might do that periodically, and you might come to rely on it.

Rowe: You can get into a lot of trouble by dwelling on that too much.

*

Well, that's certainly a fascinating little document! The year "1966" is written on the front page of the transcript. Mention is made of the concert at Conway Hall[53] which, according to the AMM "factsheet" time-line published in the liner notes to *The Crypt*, occurred on May 21 of that year. Given that no mention is made of the Elektra recording sessions that took place on June 8 and 27, one is fairly safe in placing this conversation in late May or early June. It's illuminating on several levels, including the acknowledgment of tension-generating issues between band members this early on in AMM's tenure, issues that surfaced repeatedly over the next several decades.

Rowe clearly brooks no debate as to whether AMM music is jazz or not. It's not. Further, in saying that "Jazz musicians worry like hell about jazz," he hints at an early awareness of both the futility of labeling and the over-protectiveness of musicians (and, presumably, others) who worry about the sanctity of some arbitrarily defined form. It can also be read as an understanding on Rowe's part that "jazz musicians" were possibly developing an inkling that there might be less new ground to explore, within their own definitions of the genre, than they'd thought.

---

53   The cover of the CD issue of *The Crypt* was originally painted by Rowe for this concert. The empty yellow word balloon issuing from the transistor radio is a wonderfully evocative statement of, at the least, the element of silence

There's a surprisingly early understanding of the possibility of "ruts," even within as ostensibly free an environment as was afforded by AMM. Not so much in the sense of the repetition of set formulas as was the case with the Westbrook band, but with the more general danger of growing comfortable at producing a "good" improvisational performance, the balancing act that tends to occur between the undemanding creator/consumer in a situation where "anything goes" and the insistence on quality, in other words, that "not anything goes." He says that he's not really an anarchist and that's very true; there's certainly a strong element of the classicist in his nature, albeit an uncomfortable one. It's clear that he saw one of his roles within AMM as an agitator, to foment disruption when things became too smooth (even if "smoothness" is certainly in the ear of the behearer), as evidenced by his worrying whether or not things have already become too stable.

Rowe says he was, "depressed about Conway Hall, in a way, because I suddenly woke up about half way through and felt I was playing in a group, which I didn't like," drawing the subtle distinction between the notion of a *musical* grouping and the baggage that implies, and existing in a space with several other people, some of who are creating sound but also understanding the multitudes of other elements at play—things well outside the staid notion of a musical performance. He later explains the conflict he feels between AMM as five people and AMM as *everything*. You can pick up on the frustration of, psychically, not being able to quite reach the conceptual point that he thinks he *should* have attained. Cardew, perhaps, has been there and is circling back by once again playing "notes" on occasion, to the bafflement of Rowe. In certain respects, he may have "lapped" Rowe. There's a slight sense of, if not condescension, gentle tolerance from the elder artist watching his younger friend grapple with issues that he has already dealt with, or at least thinks he has. It's possi-

in AMM's music, not to mention the vacuousness of what usually emanated from popular media.

ble that some of the resentment, under the table though it was, felt by several of AMM's members (Sheaff, in particular and by inference, probably Gare and Prévost as well) stemmed, at least in part, from an implicit air of superiority in matters aesthetic emanating from Cardew.

The influence of La Monte Young is mentioned, probably for the first time in print by an AMM member. It's not unreasonable to speculate that many of the less overtly musical elements in early AMM performances derived from Cardew's importation and explication of Young's more conceptually oriented works, ones that involved instructions for activities that had no obvious musical nature.

The falling chairs sequence is a marvelous encapsulation of AMMMusic in the world, of the exquisite difference between intentionality's unerring ability to hit a sour note and happenstance's perfect tone and timing. "A musical intervention is very disturbing because it's musical, whereas a pile of chairs being knocked over is part of our music." Even there, however, he pauses to take a look at the notion from another angle, realizing that, eyes closed, he couldn't discern the difference between certain intentional or unintentional acts; things are rarely simple. Similarly delightful is Rowe's idea about the compositional aspects of having four limbs and a head; who else was taking into account such a breadth of understanding in improvised music at the time, even to the extent of recognizing the biological limitations of improvisation?

Rowe apparently thought some ideas that emerged from this conversation worth saving, even improving, as he kept several pages of excerpts (under the heading, "AMM on AMM") which he edited in pen. They're nitpicky in a way. For example, in the original sentence, "Jazz musicians worry like hell about jazz," "musicians" has been replaced by "people," "like hell" has been crossed out and the second "jazz" has been replaced by "what is and what isn't jazz." Even "isn't" was first penned in, "is not." We see here an early instance of the primacy of the aphorism, making sure that the sense imparted is *precisely* the desired one when it comes to the written or spoken language, as opposed to the panoply of sensations they would expect to affect with their music.

*

The weekly sessions had always been open to the public and, little by little, listeners began to trickle in, a few of them liking what they heard enough to return. One of those who returned was Victor Schonfield, a young fan of avant-garde jazz who had also begun exposing himself, a bit dubiously, to contemporary "classical" music. He'd caught the Westbrook band during the previous year and had especially enjoyed the oil and water effect of Rowe's presence, as well as admiring Westbrook's tolerance for this disruptive element. Alan Cohen, the same man who had urged Rowe to play in Cardew's ensembles, coaxed Schonfield to give a listen to this offshoot group. He attended a performance or two and expressed some enthusiasm for what he'd heard. The next thing he knew, Prévost was knocking at the door of his flat, urging him to purchase one of the ten or so copies of the acetate recording done for the *Penthouse* session. Schonfield was poor, a recent college graduate with no job and little discretionary monies to spend frivolously, but Prévost nonetheless prevailed on him to buy the disc—he didn't recall whether he was allowed to give it a listen first or not.

It served to further whet his appreciation of the band and he became a regular attendee at the concerts. Late in 1965 he was on hand when Cardew was invited in, having also just begun getting a handle on music from that end of the spectrum.

> I probably came to terms with it and started liking it just about the time Cornelius came to AMM and I was really excited to hear that they were really doing the same thing! Without any signs that either of them had moved one iota to accommodate the other, like they'd come up

opposite sides of the mountain and met at the top.[54]

He was quick to recognize the tensions that had already developed in the band:

> Keith would rampage; he would trample over everybody like an utter Fascist! He would often choose to do it when everyone else was at their most delicate and responsive. He wouldn't budge, he did what he wanted to do and they did what they wanted to do and when he stopped, they would still be doing what they had been doing underneath. The thing I always valued about AMM is that there was room for all sorts of differences. People could co-exist. Part of it was that the society was wide enough to incorporate thugs and mavericks, which was Keith's musical personality to some extent.[55]

Schonfield would drag whomever he could to the performances, including Steve Lacy. It had been Lacy who had broken down his resistance to some of the elements culled from the avant-classical world that AMM was incorporating, particularly the use of radio, which Schonfield was having a difficult time accepting as a valid musical instrument. Lacy even sat in on a session (*see photo, p. 242*), though, as many musicians would come to realize, sitting in with AMM was a daunting task; there was just too much in terms of group philosophy to assimilate as if it was merely a jam session. After several minutes, Lou Gare asked him to stop playing.[56] Schonfield collared Ornette Coleman into attending another performance, but the saxophonist ignored the music on stage, spend-

---

54   Schonfield, 2005.

55   Ibid.

56   Possibly more rudely than that. Some sources have Gare telling Lacy to "piss off." Gare was especially dubious about "guests" contributing to AMM performances, telling Melody Maker in 1971, "What really brought [the difference] home to me was people sitting in with AMM, and I'd suddenly think how

ing several minutes talking to Schonfield before Gare stopped the music and asked them to leave the room, conversation apparently not falling into the ambit of acceptable room noise at that point.

The whole idea of audience participation in an AMM performance was often misunderstood from the beginning, many listeners assuming that what was occurring in the room was a "happening" in which they were free to participate. As indicated in the preceding dialogue, the musicians distinguished between intentional and happenstance occurrences. Phil Minton recalled:

> I saw one of the first AMM gigs, in early '66. It wasn't quite exciting enough. There was something there, it was on its way, but not there yet. It was tentative as though they didn't know what they'd started. But something happened on that gig. I was there with my wife at the time and maybe we had our little son with us. There weren't many people there, but Henry Lowther was there with [saxophonist] Lyn Dobson and I remember while AMM was playing, Lyn and Henry started to join in from the audience. And Lou Gare told them to shut up. Very strong about it. They weren't trying to destroy it or anything. One of the guys asked, "Why?" and Lou said, "Cause you're fucking about."

---

incredibly crude they sounded. It's difficult to pinpoint why. I think they were somehow unable to hear their own playing."

Somewhat more notoriously, Schonfield thinks it was he who, in September '66, coaxed Paul McCartney to a show, the surprisingly adventurous Beatle gently tapping a coin on a radiator as his contribution to the evening. Later, McCartney would say, referring to that evening, that one didn't have to like something to be influenced by it. He also attended the launch party of the underground newspaper, International Times, on October 15, 1966 where music was provided by AMM, Pink Floyd, Yoko Ono, and others. In November they played at Ono's *Unfinished Objects* exhibition at the Indica Gallery, the occasion when Lennon met his future wife for the first time. As Rowe recalled, "We had a very good relationship with Yoko. She used to stay at Cornelius Cardew's flat...we knew her quite well."

Schonfield soon became a virtual apostle of AMM music, telling all and sundry who would listen that something new and amazing was occurring, quickly assuming the role of (for lack of a better term) their manager, getting them occasional gigs for larger audiences as opening "act" for adventurous nascent rock bands like Pink Floyd and Cream. In January of 1966, they'd appeared at the Marquee Club as part of a "Spontaneous Underground" happening along with Pink Floyd, Donovan, the Pete Lemer Trio, and others. The former's Syd Barrett took some special notice of Rowe's extended guitar techniques, several of which he would later incorporate into his own arsenal such as rolling ball bearings down the amplified guitar strings or sliding a plastic ruler along the instrument's neck.

> A great thing about AMM is that they didn't *perform*, with occasional exceptions, they just did it. And they did it for themselves. That was why you couldn't tell if it had begun until after it had begun and you couldn't tell if it ended until after it had ended. Because there was nothing marked. It was the attention level and focus of the listener. There wasn't the business of playing the first phrase and the last phrase and people listening to you on the edge of their seat ready to applaud. Even though the audience might only be me.[57]

Things were brewing in the spring of 1966, interest being generated in quarters desperately seeking the new, the "happening." Cardew and Rowe were interviewed by a television station from Granada.

> *I remember being at work and the phone rang and this kind of snotty girl said to see my boss and he was already kind of angry and told me that Granada TV wanted to do an interview. And they were really impressed because a chauffeur-driven limo came to the front door of the office and I went out and was driven up to Euston and sat in a*

---

57   Schonfield, 2005.

*completely blank room, just me with a camera that was
being controlled from Manchester and this pair of speakers
was asking me questions. Kind of insulting! Then I went
back to work. I think Cornelius was interviewed too but I
don't know where he was.*

British Vogue did a small feature on AMM in their May 1966 issue.
On their "Spotlight" page was a photo of four of the five members
(Gare refused to show up for the picture taking) looking casual-
ly dapper, Sheaff in a turtleneck, the other three in shirt and tie,
along with a text in which some of their ideas were allowed to see
the light of day in the popular press. Rowe is quoted: "The music
exists. All the time we manifest it. It's part of the fact that music
is happening all the time and everything has music in it." Articles
like this along with Schonfield's proselytizing began to get the
word out about the band and interested observers of the London
experimental scene started to show up at gigs, many wondering if
this was all yet another manifestation of the burgeoning "psychedelic" arts epidemic. One was John "Hoppy" Hopkins.

Hopkins (1937–2015), a photographer, concert organizer, and general gadabout (he had a day job as a nuclear physicist), had known
Cardew in the late-50s when they were both living in Oxford. His
main passion at the time was jazz, though he'd also developed a
working knowledge and appreciation of contemporary Cagean and
post-Cagean music. He was also in the midst of the London rock
scene, being an early and principal photographer of the Beatles
and the Rolling Stones. In 1965, he participated in the founding of
the "London Free School," a community group that hoped to organize various public activities on the order of concerts, dances, car-
nivals, street theaters, etc. Other members included Peter Jenner,
Ronald Atkins (the jazz critic for the *Guardian*), and Elektra engineer Joe Boyd. Eventually, Hopkins, Atkins, Boyd, and another old
friend of Hopkins with extremely adventurous tastes in jazz and
avant-garde music, Alan Beckett, formed the loose-knit production
company DNA, its intention to promote the latest in forward-looking music. Hopkins recalls his first exposure to AMM music:

In the late 50s or early 60s there was a movie made called *Shadows* by John Cassavetes. What struck me about that was that when I walked out of the cinema, it was as if it was still going on. Like walking out of the movie into the movie of your life. It was quite an unusual movie for its time. AMM did the same thing to me as far as audio goes. They were playing at the boundary between music and noise or music and sound. Sitting through a performance or a rehearsal—same thing—with them was like meditating for an hour. If you really let yourself go it would take you to all sorts of places. That would be the best comparison I could make...I perceived them as a sort of open-ended set, sort of unfinished. Heisenberg and Gödel come to mind.

Having the "in" at Elektra via the presence of Boyd, they arranged with him and Schonfield to record AMM. It seems likely that, on some level, there was the idea that AMM might be "sold" to the powers that be at Elektra as representative of the outer fringe of the psychedelic rock scene, a step or two left of bands like Pink Floyd. While it might seem a quixotic gesture in retrospect, it's necessary to remember that there was no surety whatsoever at the time that bands like Pink Floyd or Cream would go on to the renown and fortune that eventually transpired; AMM was one of many "strange" groups then active in London. Whatever the intentions, they booked studio time at Sound Techniques for June 8, 1966.

Unsurprisingly, the engineers had little notion of how to accommodate an ensemble such as AMM in recording studio environs, what with the numerous instruments and noisemakers and the musicians' habit of wandering around the performing area in pursuit of different sounds. The whole idea of discreetly separating the players into isolated booths just wouldn't work. The results of the first session were deemed a disaster and a second was scheduled for June 27.[58] They brought in Jac Holzman, Elek-

58 The first performance of Prévost's composition, "Spirals," took place

tra's founder, who had experience recording much unusual (to Western ears) ethnic music, perhaps figuring that, if anyone, he could get a handle on what was occurring here. As always, AMM simply played as they had for every week since the previous fall, only now in a studio instead of someone's loft, a music practice room, or a small concert hall. A smattering of attendees was present, including Rowe's wife Krystyna and Syd Barrett. They played for some 75 minutes.

Befitting an ensemble who would later use the epigram, "An AMM performance has no beginning and no end," *AMMMusic*, the recording, seems to have been in existence before the engineer flicked the switch. It's much more like opening a window; the action has been there all along, it's only now that you, the listener, have become aware of it. The string drones are there, Gare is honking away, a radio is playing snatches of syrupy symphonic music, a piano is being hammered. Even the title appended to the track itself, "Later During a Flaming Riviera Sunset" infers prior activity.

At the beginning, the piano is up front enough that one could perhaps see why the reviewer who later referred to AMM as the "Cornelius Cardew Quintet" might have been confused.[59] Cardew, amidst a swarm of high strings and whistles, quickly introduces the prepared piano. His playing is clearly indebted to Cage's "Sonatas and Interludes" and also strikingly prefigures John Tilbury's contributions decades later; his touch and that of Tilbury, both profound, have much in common. Rowe joins the strings in

---

between these two dates, on June 15 at the Commonwealth Institute, with Rowe, Gare, Cardew, John Tilbury, and Christopher Hobbs performing, the latter interesting for seemingly having played with, essentially, AMM, two or so years before becoming a member of the ensemble. See Appendix A for further notes on the piece. Hobbs, however, says that he first met Cardew when he became his student in September 1967, so there is some confusion of dates/personnel in play.

59   Although the description here is derived from the CD version which contained the entire set. The music on the original LP begins about seven minutes into the session.

their drone, churning things up significantly with some low, fuzz-based hums. The bright piano chords contrast beautifully with this dark underpinning, like a ship's lantern in a night storm. It's powerful, eerie, and utterly immersive. The listener *believes* in what is happening as a living thing. It's all the more shocking, then, when the schmaltzy orchestra intrudes some 20 minutes in, gauchely elbowing its way into these "serious" proceedings.

But that's the genius of AMM, expressed even in its infancy: that there's a real world out there and it's every bit as meaningful as what's occurring on stage, even when it's "awful."

Gare's saxophone doesn't emerge for another five minutes (near the end of the original Side One) and when it appears, it's almost as disquieting as the muzak, bearing as it does the only overt allusions to jazz as yet encountered. It's soon subsumed beneath a growing barrage of percussion, radio, and harsh guitar. (From this point, there were some 20 minutes left off of the LP release.) The exchange between guitar and tenor continues with radio interjections, including an Arabic song. In retrospect, the section entitled "Ailantus Glandulosa" on the CD issue is one of the most amazing kernels from the session, a dense knot of disparate sounds forming a marvelous, vibrant whole. That track actually fades out, the next (also unissued on LP) looming from the darkness in a smoky haze, Lawrence Sheaff on what seems to be bass clarinet (though only clarinet is credited on the disc sleeve) engaging Gare in a forlorn duet, Rowe and Prévost summoning growling clouds via feedback and stroked cymbals. The radio, probably being controlled by Rowe (and apparently playing Roy Orbison's contemporary hit, "Lana") as one can simultaneously hear heavy piano bangings by Cardew, is on absolutely equal footing with any of the instruments, a striking testament to how far the ensemble had come from their Westbrook days. There's also an early example of the serendipitous radio capture a bit later when a male voice is picked up saying, "...being some very interesting mischief" and other snatches of...interesting mischief. It's worth noting that Rowe had already abandoned the usage of his tape recorder and the wall-of-sound, spliced pop songs that had figured so prominently in AMM concerts only several months before. Shortly thereafter, we encounter the first real example of extreme sparseness in AMM with percussion, accordion, and guitar scratching out bare livelihoods in a barren setting. One can understand, perhaps, why sections like this were left off the initial release. It's one thing to confront a maelstrom; there are always multiple ways in which one can assimilate the complexity. But when the matter is laid in front of one so nakedly, it's either take it or leave it—a decision that may have been well beyond the capacities of even the most adventurous of listeners in the summer of 1966.

At the beginning of Side Two, "After Rapidly Circling the Plaza," one can hear Rowe employing an approach that would become fairly constant throughout his career: the subtle, underlying drone. Here, beneath the welter of chaotic activity occurring above, it threads its way, undulating and bristling if listened to closely but, more likely, being picked up subconsciously, serving as a gelling agent, a sonic undercoating providing a constant reference point. It assists greatly in generating the sheer massiveness of this portion, combining with the more upfront saxophone and string drones, all buttressed by an extraordinary percussive display from Prévost. By the end of the track (and the conclusion of the LP), there is something of the return to that Sun Ra-ish comfort zone that they'd previously settled in but even here, there's a clarity of purpose that had been lacking on earlier dates. The CD appends a three-minute cut consisting of a steady-state drone anchored by Sheaff's deep arco bass momentarily interrupted by radio, as though someone had opened a door to an adjacent room and quickly closed it once again. It ends with gentle taps on a celesta.[60]

*

---

60   Rowe painted the cover image for the album, as he would do frequent-

From the "lofty heights" of a recording session for a major label, it was back to the workaday world immediately thereafter. Rowe was employed as a production artist for a fairly large conglomerate that produced "point of sales" graphic and design work for advertising agencies and the like. It was his first real job after having been on the dole and, though it could be physically taxing, it had its interesting aspects as well. They were contracted to build a mock-up of the first Concorde SST for the Paris Air Show, for example, a model designed to give people an idea of what it would be like to actually sit inside. They'd do everything, from designing and painting enormous signs over 100-feet long for Wembley Park, to developing logos for new companies. It was Rowe's first salaried job since working the docks in Plymouth and even included overtime pay, something he took advantage of by working absurd hours. There were stints when he went in on a Monday and didn't return home until Friday evening.

> In the 60s, advertising had a very pushy atmosphere, kind of a romantic profession to be in at the time. But I used the skills I had, painting, color. As I was someone who was obviously interested in Pop Art, I would do it as art, painting the sides of buildings, on massive scales.[61] I did a lot of cut-out men, spacemen for example. I did them at work and would go home and do them as well. I made strange furniture also, like from bits of plastic signs. Like, you'd print these signs and they'd go wrong, so you'd have a sheet of

---

ly from then on. Of it, he wrote in 2005, "The yellow lorry is delivering AMMMusic to the world. That's how the image was first arrived at, yellow being the colour of AMM, here cadmium yellow. The image contained references to the work of Gurdjieff and Ouspensky, AMM's study topic at the time, referencing the "Law of Three" (triads): Carbon/Nitrogen/Oxygen. On the truck we have three sets of wheels: at the front wheels that set the direction (harmonic/piano?), in the centre the propulsion (percussion?) and at the rear the load bearing wheels (guitar continuo?), though at any moment these roles might be shuffled."

61   Unfortunately, no photos of these works were taken.

plastic that would otherwise have gone into the bin and I'd go home and fashion it into a table. I'd make very large, plastic letters, much like what contemporary artists were making at the time, someone like [George] Segal.

Still, the couple was as well off as they'd been thus far into their lives—they were even able to afford a car—and the relative comfort allowed Rowe to devote a good deal of time to AMM. He also had access to a printing factory into which he and Cardew would sneak late in the evening to run off silkscreen posters announcing the next AMM gig. In a way, the working methodology of AMM, never "practicing" or otherwise playing one's instruments outside of an actual performance, at least as far as Rowe was concerned, fit rather well into the lifestyle of someone who actually had to work a day job to support himself. AMM had begun to be invited to play the same one-off gigs—at universities, in squats, at protest rallies—at which other up-and-coming rock bands would appear. Many of the musicians, being young and relatively adventurous, would pick up ideas from hearing them play, especially Rowe, as a guitarist. Much has been made of his influence on Syd Barrett and, indeed, Barrett was one of the most keenly interested in AMM out of all the young rockers, but it was a much more casual thing than legend has it, nothing to do with "tutoring" in any sense.

That gives the impression of this one person telling the other what to do. It was just talking. He could see it, and I think he did; he immediately saw what the possibilities for him were. Like I would look at a Duchamp and say, "Yeah!" or I can look at a Braque guitar and think what I could derive from that. And I think Syd...we'd chat about something. Even "chat" is the wrong word. We'd pass comments about something and he could see it with his eyes and then go off and do his thing.

I think you could be influenced by people without ever having seen or heard them, though. Someone could say to you, "Hey, shit, I heard this guy and he's got knives and ball bearings that he's rolling down the neck of his guitar!" "Yeah, fucking amazing!" Well, you don't have to see that, you just go and do it! The influences were really free-flowing. No one was worried about copyrighting what you were doing.

I think Barrett was genuinely interested in what AMM was doing but I don't think the others [members of Pink Floyd] were. I think quite a few pop musicians were interested. Didn't particularly like it, but were interested. There was quite a large psychedelic scene. A lot of the psychedelia was very drone-based and AMM had become something of a drone-based band. So we were the kind of group you'd have along. Plus we hardly got paid for that stuff, there was no money, so the organizer would pay the famous groups loads of money and pay AMM nothing.

There was actually less positive reception from the jazz community, even that part of it with avant leanings, than from the progressive rock crowd. While Prévost and Gare maintained good relations with that scene, AMM was essentially shunned. If you run down the gig list (as printed in the booklet released with the CD version of *The Crypt*), you see arts centers, colleges, and the odd concert venue but nary a jazz club. One might have expected them to be sharing bills with SME or Derek Bailey but it didn't happen. Certainly at least part of the reason was the aloofness (perceived and actual) with which AMM members operated and the extreme seriousness of their aesthetic views.

No, AMM was completely ostracized—not ostracized, just ignored by European free jazz, although Evan [Parker] and AMM always had a good relationship. I think Derek was OK, don't think he had a particular problem with AMM. He didn't want to have anything to do with it, he didn't want to listen to it or play in it or play alongside it, but I don't think he had a problem with it. As I've admitted before, we were quite arrogant at times. We had an audacious agenda. We didn't see ourselves as trying to do what they were doing.

AMM always had a special aura about them, but it was not because of extra-musical things or the packaging but that they were using, they were deliberately associating themselves with the ideas of chance and indeterminacy and the aleatoric, and that was different because the rest of us were playing with intentionality. Those distinctions are a little less clear nowadays partly because the music of AMM has become a legitimate field for the application of intentionality. And anyway, what does it mean to use a chance procedure? That also has intentionality involved.[62]

It was likely a combination of things: the arrogance certainly, perceived or real, fed into this feeling. More, it may have been difficult for jazz musicians to appreciate a music in which there was no clear extension from precedent the way there was in even the freest English and European improvisers. Making the leap from mid-60s Coltrane, Coleman, or Pharoah Sanders to Parker or Brötzmann wasn't, for attuned listeners or musicians, an insurmountable difficulty; the lineage, if not crystal clear, could be discerned at least dimly. Bailey's approach to the guitar had less direct precedent in jazz (more in Webern perhaps, but he definitely knew his jazz standards and that knowledge doubtless seeped through to an extent), but he had the advantage of playing an instrument that was undergoing an enormous revolution within rock. Rock fans gave far more latitude to odd sounds emerging from a guitar than they did from the more directly human-sounding reeds. It's not difficult to imagine an avant-jazz fan attending an AMM gig, enjoying the portions dominated by Gare and Prévost—being able to fit a good deal of what they were playing into a pre-existing context—but being "offended" at the seeming contradictory contributions from the other members,

---

62   Evan Parker, 2003.

particularly Rowe and Cardew. The ability to take in AMM in its entirety, to reconcile all of the elements, might simply have been beyond the capability of a great many listeners as well as musicians, and AMM wasn't about offering helping hands.

That sense of arrogance put people off as well. There was the notion, at least implicit if not precisely explicated, that the musicians in AMM, when they had come to the same conceptual fork in the road as most people conscious of contemporary art and music, had not only made a different decision than just about anyone else, in their minds there was no question but that they had made the *right* one. Their refusal to merely extend existing jazz-based improvisational strategies but to use the essences *behind* the innovations of the Minguses and the Dolphys, as well as the Cages and the Feldmans, as springboards into a vastly freer music was as clear to them as it was baffling that others didn't view things the same way. While they didn't overtly scoff at the musicians making their way down the—to them—far less vital and rewarding pathway, their music was, if considered at length, a difficult-to-avoid refutation. Better not to consider it at all.

As early as 1966, Prévost had begun writing about AMM and doing so in a manner that was far more serious (and self-serious) than anything one was likely to find in other "mere" musical groups on the jazz scene. One 32-page set is titled "Theses," subtitled "A series of short expositions, prompted by certain aspects of AMM." In its text can be glimpsed the nascent formulations that aficionados of the ensemble would come to know and enjoy in ensuing years, but it's the postulation of AMM as an *entity*, as a thing moving and breathing of its own accord, that's striking. "AMM have the quality of producing sounds which people respond to…"; "But the effect of sounds produced by AMM seems, at least, to evoke new images, new thoughts and a new way of hearing and seeing things"; "If a listener can be transported to the realms of childhood memories or be sent on flights of fancy by AMM he must have remembered the other times he has been to these places and how easy it was. AMM may be able to provide this, but it is not concerned with doing this and it should be remembered that any listener should not expect, (and has not the right to expect), AMM to do anything." While these are all interesting and reasonable perspectives, it's pretty heady stuff for a group of five musicians whose band is not yet a year old. One can see where accusations of arrogance might begin to gain solid footing. More, within AMM, we begin to see perhaps another seed of the tension that would continue to brew between Rowe and Prévost. Prévost was a reasonably good writer and would get better as time went on, becoming very interested in verbally explicating what AMM was about, as well as probing his own deep ideas on music, especially its communitarian nature. Rowe was never very good at explaining himself through writing; it was something at which he'd have to work hard, as it didn't come naturally. But he was brilliant at getting ideas across via example and comparison in conversation, as often with music and image as with words, and, as time went on, was far more gregarious and more open to speak about things, thus, much later (especially with the advent of the internet and discussion groups therein) becoming the *de facto* spokesman for both AMM and, more widely (and not necessarily fairly) for post-AMM improvised music in general.[63]

AMM's explorations continued apace. Cardew, interviewed on the BBC Radio program *Music in Our Time*, said:

> In the summer of 1966 Lawrence Sheaff and I invested the proceeds of a recording session in a second amplifier and loudspeaker system. The new equipment was intended to balance the range of sounds produced by Keith Rowe's electric guitar...With the new amplifier we began to explore the range of small sounds made available by using contact microphones on all kinds of mate-

---

63   Gare was also expressing some thoughts about music in writing around this time, including a small treatise on ways of listening. As Cardew consistently kept notes and wrote essays as well, it seems that Rowe was the only regular AMM member who didn't write down very much of anything.

rials—glass, metal, wood—and a variety of gadgets from drumsticks to battery-operated cocktail mixers. Instrumentation was further expanded by Eddie Prévost using xylophone and Lou Gare playing violin and occasionally flute, as well as a stringed instrument of his own design. Both Lawrence and I were using cellos in addition to and in conjunction with the electronic devices, and Keith Rowe was developing a preoccupation with coffee tins.

In late July, AMM was invited by the Canadian documentary filmmaker Alan King to record a soundtrack for *Warrendale*, a work depicting new treatment techniques for disturbed children, involving their placement in family-like settings instead of institutions. More accurately, Cardew, who had had a prior working association with King, was asked to provide the music and decided to do it as an AMM project. The film was unflinchingly honest (though not exploitative) in its depiction of the children, causing something of a furor upon its release even as it was acclaimed as an outstanding achievement. Indeed, it was banned from Canadian television until 1997. They played along to a very lengthy rough cut of the film, Rowe remembering it going as long as four hours, not likely restraining themselves in a manner that may have befitted accompanying a motion picture. Unfortunately, King chose not to use a soundtrack at all (Rowe: "It probably came across as the most raucous and horrible noise to the producers.") and the AMM session has disappeared. On the surface, the subject matter of the documentary, particularly its psychological force and its steady, lucid depiction of a certain reality, would have seemed tailor-made for the music of AMM, though perhaps the combination would have been "too much," overwhelming the viewer. In practical terms, the non-use of the soundtrack was doubly unfortunate given the high esteem the film eventually came to enjoy.

The Destruction in Art Symposium took place at the Africa Centre in Covent Garden, London in September of 1966. It was organized in large part by the artist Gustav Metzger, who specialized

in varieties of "auto-destructive" art, and included the participation of a number of major figures, including Hermann Nitsch,
John Sharkey, Yoko Ono, and other Fluxus members as well as
representatives of the French Situationists and similar art provo-
cateurs from around Europe. It was quite an extreme affair and
attracted an enormous amount of media attention due to the extravagant and gruesome nature of potential performances, such
as Juan Hidalgo's penchant for slicing the heads off of live chick-
ens and tossing the results to the crowd. Though Hidalgo bowed
to public pressure and resisted decapitating any fowl, others
didn't fail in their aim to appall. As reported by *Time* magazine:

> ...top honors of the show undeniably went to the four
> Viennese men from something called the Institute for
> Direct Art. Black-shirted Hermann Nitsch gave a demon-
> stration of his popular Blutorgie (blood orgy), in which he
> tore apart the cadaver of a freshly slain lamb, also gave a
> learned lecture on the "liberation of violent urges through
> catharsis." His colleagues, Otto Muehl and Günter Brus,
> held an audience of 100 spellbound in St. Bride Foundation
> Institute when they smeared Susan Kahn, a visiting New
> York schoolteacher clad only in a black strapless bra and
> black panties, from head to toe with flour, crushed ripe
> tomatoes, beer, raw egg, brightly colored powdered paints,
> cornflakes, half-chewed raw carrot, bit of melon and melon
> seed, milk, and tufts of moss and grass.[64]

Somewhat less spectacularly but perhaps more subtly effective,
Yoko Ono performed her "Cut Piece" in which, clad in a paper
costume and sitting onstage alongside a pair of scissors, audience
members had the "opportunity" to approach and shear away as
they pleased, an excuse seized upon to a dismaying extent—the
point of the work. She also spread out large cloths next to people, drawing the outlines of their shadows, then folding it up
and leaving, taking their shadows "prisoner." Metzger's artwork

---

64   September 23, 1966.

consisted of nylon sheets upon which he poured various acids, so that the sheets gradually disintegrated in visually fascinating ways, eventually leaving no material at all.

Both of the above performances had a strong effect on Rowe, who was in attendance because AMM had also been invited to play. They prepared a "press release" of sorts for the event:

> AN EXCERPT FROM A CONTINUOUS PERFORMANCE will take place at the Commonwealth Institute at 8 pm on Thursday 15th September 1966.
>
> A M M [sic] will perform and improvise upon a constant theme set by the limits of time, materials and environment. Every musical instrument, every piece of equipment and furniture, every person actively or passively playing will determine this particular concert. .

Victor Schonfield penned an additional pre-concert flyer that pushed things a bit further:

> This concert is a conscious attempt by AMM to publicly concern themselves and involved their audience with the universe of sound; to try and secure the understanding and accompanying sense of realness which eludes most of us most of the time.
>
> Within the time span of a performance the nearness of sound-beauty becomes laughingly obvious, the players merely indicators of what is there already.
>
> AMM is a group concerned with exploring the full range of possible sounds. Every performance is a continuous sound improvisation; it has no beginning or ending, and sounds outside it in space or time are distinguished from it only by the individual sensibility. A member of AMM does not know what any of his colleagues will play next, and is free

to alter an emerging pattern in any way he wishes. Often he is not sure what sounds he himself will produce, or even if a sound which has just been produced was his. The results are juxtapositions of similar and contrasting shapes and colours which is the substance of all art, and all life.

The back of this flyer was an advert for the upcoming Elektra LP, a rather psychedelic series of comic book panels by Bradley Martin. In the scheme of things, it's likely they didn't create much of a stir given the abundance of strewn lamb parts and such, not to mention the subsequent police action and arrests. AMM probably came across, to most, as just so much noise, just another element in a scene open enough to accept almost anything.[65]

Reviews of the performance emphasized its episodic nature, the prolonged periods of wild, cacophonous frenzy alongside equally extended sections of near inactivity and silence. "Wipeout," the popular surf instrumental, was apparently plucked from the airwaves at one point, the group obligingly joining in for a couple of swinging minutes. But a theatrical aspect was also noted, the group members "bouncing balloons back and forth and rolling tin cans off the edge of the stage." That writer continued:

> There is something to be said for seeing how deeply and sustainedly one can bore people before some reaction is evinced; it is, after all, the complex and largely uninvestigated emotion of boredom that is at the root of destructive art.
>
> AMM is not so much atonal as amusicological. To describe is as music is less a description of AMM than a comment—a valid one—on Music itself.

---

65   Pete Townshend reported attending the symposium, crediting it with affirming in him the idea of destruction being a valid aesthetic element, which he proceeded to freely utilize in performances by The Who. It's not known whether he also heard and saw AMM, but certain guitar techniques that soon became part of his arsenal cause one to wonder if indeed he may have.

Ultimately, however, AMM fails. At the end—half an hour before the advertised time—the musicians fell prey to the inertia they had been generating all evening, and gradually drifted off the stage; the houselights went up; the saxophonist, who had for the previous 15 minutes been

mutilating tin cans with a length of wood, idly rolled one up and down the xylophone. For the audience it required considerable effort of will to concede that the thing was over, and leave. If one accepted what had been happening, one could do nothing but listen to whatever sounds were available, regardless of how unintentional they might be. The disadvantage of this kind of experimentation is that it very quickly exhausts its potentialities. Go out on a limb and you all too frequently find yourself up a blind alley.[66]

In the December 1966 issue of the *ICA Bulletin*, a "dialogue" concerning AMM appeared in the form of a conversation between A and B. David Sladen is "B"; "A" is likely Cardew. As with the conversation that opened this chapter, it sheds valuable light on the thinking processes and ideas in play at the time:

A. What you see first, when you can see, because they often play without much light, is a seated figure poring over a guitar held across his knees, and, in a way which takes you some time to work out, producing by, for example, slow bowing across the strings, a harsh screaming loudness screeching out at you through the amplifier.

B. And then?

A. Then you make out the other players, you can see one or two other amplifiers, maybe you notice Lou walking about at the back, playing his saxophone, you see

---

66   Peter Willis, *Peace News*, September 30, 1966.

the man at the piano treating it in a new way...

B.   From the instruments it sounds rather like a jazz
group.

A.   Yes, the group does derive from a jazz background,
but musically there is very little in common. Think
of AMM more as a total music, total in sound variety,
and also in emotional reach.

B.   I wanted to ask you what AMM stands for?

A.   I don't know. You can make something up to suit
yourself.

B.   What music do they play?

A.   Their own. They play continuously till the music
stops.

B.   Is it written down?

A.   No, it is not. In fact, you might say it couldn't be, because each time they play, they extend their range of
sounds.

B.   What sort of present day music is it like?

A.   If anything, it belongs with the type of music which is
written down in the form of instructions, where you
leave enough up to the player to make sure no two
performances sound the same. I mean, it sounds like
that, but of course there aren't any instructions.

B.   How would another group play it?

A.   Their own way. You need only go along and hear

them. People can go home and develop the concept of music created by AMM, and take it in their own particular direction.

B. Where has this music come from?

A. The insight that the radio is a kind of musical instrument too. Just as painting was changed by photography, so sound transmission and recording has done something to music. I think AMM could only exist in the time of these inventions.

B. So technical change has done more than change in the realm of ideas?

A. Yes, I think so. Or rather, that's a fact that has to be interpreted.

B. What non-musical event does AMM compare to?

A. A concert by AMM has something in common with a sporting event, an athletics match where the players are competing against each other and against past excellences: perhaps a pentathlon where the events and not the people vary: five players and any number of events to go in for.

B. How is a transistor radio used as an instrument?

A. Sparingly. The effect of hearing a snatch of tune from a transistor, in the midst of the other sounds or by itself, is to make you realise what a long way AMM has travelled. I think that the presence of the transistor also works as an irritant upon all the players to prevent the music settling down—like wearing a chain of spikes under your shirt.

B. What if you bring along your own transistor and join in?

A. An irritation of a different sort. Think of the use of the transistor as a sort of mirror within the music of the overall who-knows-what's-next idea.

B. What's the most striking thing about a performance of AMM?

A. In the loud parts, that it is so <u>loud</u>. Louder than anything you've heard before—and much worse—that is to say the noise is all screeching and screaming and squealing loudness, deriving mainly in the early days from Keith's playing of the amplified guitar. But the other players now do their share.

B. And people get up and walk out?

A. In the loud bits, sometimes, yes. But since it's just as loud for the players themselves, they won't keep it up forever either. Essentially, they change it into something not so loud and harsh.

B. What are the merits of loudness?

A. It's something to explore, to see how far you can go, and what you find along the way.

B. Why isn't it all loud?

A. Maybe it will be one day. At the moment they are introducing loudness into the traditional softness or comfortableness of listening. The "unbearable" loudness is easier to bear the second time you hear it; and occurs not only a modest length of time in any performance.

B.   What's the answer to the question, why not loudness all the time?

A.   Because, as you can imagine, it wouldn't work. On the other hand, they might still do it. It might work. I don't know. It's up to them.

B.   But the loudness is so unbearable, so excruciating, it defeats itself. When something is really unpleasant how can you go on defending it?

A.   I agree, it's terrible, like trains going round curves, and so on, like working in a factory, metal on metal grinding and boring you out of your mind—well, you just have to change the metaphor.

B.   What's it like otherwise?

A.   In the quiet bits you're concerned to catch the sounds and yet to be always prepared against a sudden outbreak of loudness—so, in the words of Rene Char, your listening attitude must be one of "tensed serenity."

B.   In other words, even when the loudness has stopped, it puts you in an anxious state in case it starts again.

A.   Something like that. But I exaggerate. In the quiet bits you become aware of another problem, or manifestation. You're following one particular sound which you like, and you are hearing another sound which you only wish would stop, so that you could enjoy yours and everything would be perfect for ever and ever.

B.   But of course it does not stop. You make it sound like the whole listening experience is an exercise in frustration and pain.

A.   Curiously enough, it isn't. At least not for me. For me, what it has given me is, for the first time in my life, the experience of hearing something being played and meant, and that I'm part of it, I'm helping them by being in their audience.

B.   That's very nice, no doubt. But suppose you didn't feel that? Could you sit in the audience, turning off when you didn't like it, and turning on when you heard an interesting effect?

A.   In a way that's what you do, i.e. you choose the sound you hear. But listening for effects is only first steps in AMM listening. After a while you stop skimming, start tracking, and go where it takes you.

B.   Trusting that it's all worthwhile.

A.   Funnily enough I don't worry about that aspect.

B.   That might mean you <u>do</u> trust it.

A.   Yes I suppose I do.

*

In February 1967, *London Look* published a lengthy, largely condemnatory article on its city's current hippie/freak scene titled "Raving London" ("raving as in "mad"). It's a silly, condescending piece filled with photos of pot protesters and a naked man (Mike Lesser) sliding in jelly. Listing some of those held in esteem by these odd people, we find

> ...Williams Burroughs, author of *The Naked Lunch* [sic], now living in London, Paul McCartney who attends their raves, groups like the Move, the Cream, the Pink Floyd and AMM, Negro comedian Dick Gregory, writer Norman

Mailer, and poet Allen Ginsberg. Composers John Cage and Cornelius Cardew are lit brightly in the *avant garde*. This is a collection of tremendous talent which is squandered in the interests of experimentation and exploration.

The article ends with a description of an AMM event and some quotes from their manager.

> The AMM group were performing behind a canvas screen onto which is [sic] projected colour slides. The slides are packed with ink and chemicals which become fluid under the heat of the projector. The result is beautiful colour and movement which resembles a biological slide.

> The AMM's manager, Victor Schonfield, watched as his group spread-eagled themselves around the floor with musical instruments—I saw drums, a clarinet and a piano—and a weird collection of objects which they banged together with ear-piercing clarity. It was rubbish. For two hours people listened as though it were a concert at the Festival Hall. Sometimes through the banging, grinding, screeching came the noise of a radio which one of the group switched on. Said Schonfield: We are exploring the indeterminacy of sounds and forms.

> It is like watching the sea, waves breaking on the shore, sounds rising and dying in all directions, yet somehow part of an organic whole. You couldn't call it anything else but music. The group used to perform conventional music, but now improvisation is important. Artists who want to create something ought to be giving us something we don't know about.

An AMM performance at the Commonwealth Institute on April 10 was actually recorded by the BBC and a fourteen-minute excerpt was released by David Stapleton on United Diaries (UD012) in 1982 as part of the compilation, *An Afflicted Man's Musica Box*.

When the music is first heard—no telling how far into the actual concert—the listener is confronted with the strains of Herb Alpert and the Tijuana Brass playing the theme from *Casino Royale*. This rapidly subsides into drones, a very beautiful section with grainy arco cello and bell tones, occasionally interrupted by Prévost's drumming thunder. The "sweet and sour" approach is fascinating, playing off silvery whistles and chimes against harsh bowing and other noises of an indeterminate nature. The snare is a bit up front later on, tapping small rhythms in a restless manner, but the drone persists and ends up carrying the day, at least in the portion heard here, a very tantalizing one, full of detail. It concludes with a brief assault by Rowe, all screech and feedback, one of the clearest recorded examples of his playing from the period.

Critical reaction to the Elektra album, which was issued in the late fall of 1966, was beginning to appear. Barry McRae, in *Jazz Journal*, would be among the first to perpetuate a common error, referring to the ensemble as the Cornelius Cardew Quintet. As one of the basic precepts of the group was to get away from the ego-driven mentality as evinced by common jazz group names such as The [Musician X] Quartet, this was particularly grating. McRae does, however, deal very honestly with the difficulties that a purely jazz-based critic might necessarily have with AMM music and focuses in on exactly that relevant issue:

> The jazz critic is perhaps the worst person to review such an album. The tremendous projection of "self" that is his yardstick for the jazz musician is not to be found in the work of these five men. Their aim is music that does not project their ego and involves the audience at a participatory level. In the final reckoning I do not like what I hear because my mind applies the wrong standards.

Similarly, G.W. Hopkins, writing in the August 1967 issue of Musical Times, referred to AMM as "Cardew's...group" but was dubious about the results, doubting "the advisability of perpetuating such a performance as anything but a document."

A perhaps surprisingly appreciative appraisal of *AMMMusic* appeared in the *London Times* of August 4, 1967 written by Stanley Sadie, who would go on to become one of Britain's most eminent musicologists and editor of the Sixth Edition of the *Grove Dictionary of Music*. Sadie traces a brief history of contemporary music as the preeminence of the composer gradually gives way to the interpretations of the performer, logically arriving at a point where the composer vanishes altogether. He doesn't so much describe the music as give a relatively accurate overview as to its creation, and seems to cautiously admit to its validity. "Listening to a performance, or to the record, one does in fact sense the players' interactions, and a sort of corporate ebb and flow of mood and idea." After enumerating some details of Cardew's "Tigers Mind," a piece written for AMM, he concludes,

> Possibly the idea seems far-fetched, but it is a perfectly logical extension of the recognized and accepted processes of aleatory music. We may dislike the result, which is likely (indeed is intended) to be both disturbing and physically very uncomfortable. But its aesthetic justification, as a form of contemporary expression, is difficult to deny; though we may prefer to call it something other than "music."

A smidgen of international acclaim appeared that summer as well. Buried deep within the August 24, 1967 issue of *downbeat*, Critics Poll participant Max Harrison (then a *Jazz Monthly* contributor) listed Gare, Sheaff, and Cardew numbers 1, 2 and 3 in his ballot for "Miscellaneous Instrument" (for violin and cello work, one assumes), and Rowe second behind Jimmy Raney on guitar.

Chapter 6

It may be objected that from this point of view anything goes. Actually, anything does go but only when nothing is taken as the basis.

John Cage

In November of 1967, the first independent project from an AMM member not named Cardew appeared: Eddie Prévost's *Silver Pyramid*. It's interesting in several regards, not the least of which is as an example of one end of the range of approaches that Prévost would investigate in coming decades. For all his future distrust of "art school" concepts, he would test these waters on several occasions himself, right up through *Entelechy* in 2005 and beyond. *Silver Pyramid*, in which much of the sound was generated via performers' interactions with a large construction covered with potential noisemaking objects and symbols to be interpreted, was in some ways the diametric opposite of the more intuitive and jazz-oriented music he'd soon create in duo with Gare or in other bands he'd organize in later years. His notes on the work clearly indicate someone pursuing larger game:

Addenda and Afterthoughts on Silver Pyramid—A Mystery

Because it may be expected or perhaps because I might forget, there are some explanations due. These can only be partial, not because I want to be mysterious or because I am vague, but because it is doubtful whether we are capable of ever fully understanding anything. Also because the score is only partial; both the mystery and its solution required for a complete entity.

At this moment there is a great deal that I do not understand about this piece. What it conveys, as far as I can understand, is a description of some universal symbols. These symbols are as lucid as the observer. The deeper he looks the more he will find. All things are as men see them.

I would like SILVER PYRAMID to be considered firstly as a musical score. However, I would not like it to be trapped by this image. I can see no reason why the philosopher cannot find in it the source of many speculations, why the priest cannot see it as a ritual, the scientist as an experiment. Perhaps it will be all these things at all times. To exclude the possibility of any of them and more, would I feel, render any performance completely ineffective.

How is it to be played? That is up to those who may want to play it, but if the score is reconstructed absolutely literally there will arise a situation. Movement will then follow. The result will give as much to the player as he is ready for. The way of things fortunately allows the real player to proceed and even learn, from those who always try to see with their eyes only or who foolishly stumble around.

Whatever quasi-mystical attributes it may have countenanced, a more lasting impact of the work was to open up AMM-style music to a somewhat wider audience as well as an increased amount of participation by other musicians. Performances of *Silver Pyramid* drew dozens of players at times (although the 1969 recording issued on Matchless in 2001 apparently consists of eight or nine) and were far less hermetic, far more public than the average AMM session. While the music, at least judging from the available recording, falls easily into what may be considered general AMM-like territory, the mere fact of its greater physical accessibility makes it, perhaps, an initial cognitive step in the process that would lead to AMM musicians joining and co-founding the Scratch Orchestra. *Silver Pyramid* shows were widely reviewed as well, perhaps feeding into the notion that there were ways to deliver this sort of music using platforms with far greater public accessibility as well as serving a more communitarian ethos.

In the spring of 1968, Lawrence Sheaff left AMM. The reasons behind his departure were complex and included both musical and personal issues, though Sheaff himself might not have been entirely comfortable with the ensemble since Cardew joined, believing that it had been "perfect" before that point. On a purely musical level there was the nagging suspicion on the part of some members that Sheaff's contributions were becoming increasingly redundant. While he was the only member playing the string bass, cellos were frequently utilized by both Rowe and Cardew and the areas being covered by his violin and clarinet work were essentially being duplicated by Gare.[67] More troubling, aspects of his conduct and demeanor were a growing concern for his companions. Stories differ and the accuracy of memories is disputed, but there was certainly an increased dissatisfaction regarding his dealings with female friends. Sheaff was a tall, very attractive, and charismatic individual but, in the opinion of some, displayed an overly cavalier attitude toward women enamored of him, "using" them as it were. There was a decidedly "high-minded," even puritanical, mindset among AMM members, one that may have perceived any even moderately callous treatment of certain individuals as more horrible than it in fact was, but in any case Sheaff was taken aside and spoken with, probably by Prévost as he was always the "action taker" of the group, and essentially asked to leave.

---

67   Sheaff felt that Rowe "was…the embodiment of the thing in AMM

Prévost, in later years, would dispute this sequence of events, claiming that Rowe "maneuvered" Sheaff out of the ensemble. Given the subsequent guests who would be asked to play with AMM, almost all from non-improvising, "classical" backgrounds (with the notable exception of Evan Parker), he characterized the removal of Sheaff as the initial step in this series. It's not difficult to imagine that this perception has at least a partial basis in fact, given Rowe's growing fascination with the musical and conceptual world embodied in Cardew and his more forceful separation from all things jazz-derived, a break that Prévost never wholeheartedly embraced. Add to this that Sheaff's replacement was Christopher Hobbs, a student of Cardew's and yet another member with no jazz or improvising experience, one can see how troubling such a development may have been to Prévost.[68] Though in Rowe's view, a replacement was needed:

> There was probably always the feeling that the perfect number for AMM was five and not four or three. But there were a lot of practical difficulties in finding the proper musicians to get five. We had the general feeling that we should always be on the lookout for people who could join AMM. But people who were able to join AMM were so rare that you always had to keep looking, so you shouldn't miss any possible opportunity. In those early days, I haven't fully worked it out, but I've realized that it was better to have

which I found most exciting...because of my sympathy and understanding about what Keith was doing and how I completely identified with that in my own personality, I think I became almost redundant in the group. At some point, Keith felt I was just doing the same things he was doing, his area. And it was repetitive. My reaction to that, as a member of AMM, would be, fight your way out of it. Don't tell the person to leave. That's there for you to do something with it. See, that's the way I thought about AMM." Rowe, on the other hand, opined, "Maybe Lawrence's humor and jokiness would have sent us along a line like Misha Mengelberg or the ICP Orchestra. I think Lawrence's personality was really, really important."

68   As mentioned in a footnote in the previous chapter, Hobbs had in fact played in the premiere performance of Prévost's composition, "Spirals," in 1966.

*someone who had no experience of improvisation because
the improvisers in those days were all out of free jazz. Hugh
Davies might have been the only person, but Hugh and I
overlapped a lot in the kind of bricolage type of electronics.*

This might be a case, however, where memories of the individuals involved have been tinged by other disagreements over the
intervening years, more so with AMM than with most groups
given their habit of non-discussion and their relative lack of
extra-musical association. Rowe, for instance, recalls that Cardew
simply ushered Hobbs into AMM "without filling out the formal
applications, if you like!" and thinks that the original musicians
may have exhibited a bit of "snottiness," privately thinking that
he wasn't so much *in* AMM as simply Cardew's assistant. In his
mind, this action also helped justify the slight wariness felt by
Prévost and Gare toward the increased presence of non-impro-
visers in the ensemble. Hobbs, however, specifically remembers
being approached by Gare after performing at an "anti-Univer-
sity" concert on the 4th of April, 1968 and asked to join. Perhaps
keeping the number of members at five had a numerological
component that drove matters for certain members. One does
suspect some kind of urging on Cardew's part as, during his
brief tenure with AMM, Hobbs tended to concentrate on musical
aspects that had previously occupied Cardew, especially with
regard to hung percussive objects (stones, bells, brake drums,
and other items, natural and manmade, that could be struck or
otherwise excited), freeing him to devote himself more to the
piano, cello, and electronics. By liberating him from a certain
amount of purely musical responsibilities, the addition of Hobbs
may also have allowed Cardew to further investigate extra-musical aspects of performance, for instance sitting back, pulling out
a tin of tobacco, rolling himself a cigarette, and smoking. Hobbs
remained with the group through 1971.

*

In early March of 1968, Ben Patterson (1934–2016) of Fluxus

invited AMM to perform in New York City.[69]

> *It was pretty momentous for us. For me personally, it was*
> *the first time I'd ever been abroad, at 28 years of age. I re-*
> *member Cornelius, when I was getting my passport, kind of*
> *saying, "Shocking!," kind of apologizing that I was leaving*
> *the shores of Great Britain for the first time.*

The group was slated to play at Steinway Hall on 57th St, the third event in a series titled "January through June 1968," which included concerts by the Terry Jennings Band, La Monte Young/ Marian Zazeela, Jon Higgins, and Terry Riley. Visa problems arose, prompting the following plea to be published in the *Village Voice*:

> AMM will make their New York debut…IF, the US Immi-
> gration and Naturalization officials can be convinced that
> the contributions of AMM to contemporary music are
> serious (we do admit that every major rock group in Lon-
> don studiously attends AMM recitals), and distinguished
> (the Arts Council of Great Britain and the Foundation for
> the Contemporary Performing Arts, New York also admit
> to providing financial support for AMM recitals), At this
> moment distinguished American musicians, compos-
> ers, scholars and critics are forwarding affidavits to the
> US Immigration officials in an attempt to reverse their
> current denial of an "H-1" visa granted to artists of dis-
> tinguished merit. If these recognized musical authorities
> are successful in their attempt to curb this gross artistic
> censorship, we will publish a picture of AMM next week
> in celebration. So bear with us and we thank you for your
> support,
>
> Signed, Benjamin Patterson

---

69   The invitation was likely more specifically directed at Cardew who decided to go as part of AMM.

Somehow, Patterson succeeded in convincing the authorities to allow this odd bunch of musicians entry into the US and the *Voice*, true to its word, printed a celebratory photograph of the group's arrival in New York as they wended their way through customs, treating them in mock pop star fashion.

Almost immediately after touchdown, Cardew vanished without a word to his companions. The performance had been confirmed for 8 p.m. Saturday, a few days hence, so no one was unduly concerned though his disappearance was a bit disconcerting, especially as he was the only person who had had any experience in the country. At about 4 p.m. on the day of the concert, Cardew reappeared, "cool as a cucumber," claiming that he'd been visiting Native American mound builders and, in fact, began incorporating aspects of Native American rituals into performances on occasion, drifting into lengthy vocal incantations.[70]

AMM performed an extract from "Treatise" (which had only just been published in its complete form), as well as an improvisation. During the soundcheck, Mark Boyle, who had been doing psychedelic light shows for Soft Machine, came down and said that he'd heard that Jimi Hendrix was to be playing at some nearby bar later in the evening. The whole group trudged through a messy snowfall and waited at the bar until 3 or 4 in the morning when Hendrix finally showed. Rowe was impressed, a rarity with regard to rock performers, calling the show "extraordinary." For decades, Hendrix and the Beach Boys remained among the few rock or pop musicians he actually enjoyed.[71]

Upon arriving home, they were greeted by an in-depth article written by Victor Schonfield for *Jazz Monthly*, May 1968, in advance of a performance at Queen Elizabeth Hall, titled "Cornelius Cardew, AMM and the path to perfect hearing." As possibly the

---

70   John Tilbury, *Cornelius Cardew: A Life Unfinished*, Copula 2008.

71   The band also took in a Cecil Taylor performance during this trip.

most comprehensive analysis of AMM and the music around it up to that date, it's worth reprinting in full:

> "Contemporary" and "new" are treacherous words: they imply that a qualitative change is taken place, but all they assert is the existence of something at a particular time. "Experimental" also poses problems; many actions whose outcomes cannot be foreseen are performed to extend the boundaries of the known; many others are performed to escape those boundaries.
>
> If "contemporary" means something like "different in kind from anything twenty years older or more," and "experimental" means something like "designed always to produce unpredictable results," then the only contemporary European music today is wholeheartedly experimental (or "indeterminate" or "aleatory") music, deriving from the work since 1950 of John Cage and his associates. This generalization, of course, excludes not only all the most established or most fashionable living composers, but virtually everywhere except the US—and so much the better; the proportion of the human race engaged in creating its own time is always a small one, and the task of locating its members is too important to be left to future historians.
>
> Perhaps the most significant exponent of experimental music outside America has been Cornelius Cardew, who is based in London. Over the last ten years his work as a performer, concert-producer and commentator has introduce British audiences to the whole field, his periods of personal association with leaders of its widely-divergent schools giving his interpretations authenticity as well as immediate shock-value. Cardew's status nowadays is described by one of indeterminacy's founding fathers, the composer Morton Feldman, as follows: "Any direction modern music will take in England will come about only through Cardew, because of him, by way of him. If

the new ideas in music are felt today as a movement in England, it's because he acts as a moral centre." His most ambitious undertaking to date takes place this month in a series of four concerts, entitled, "SOUNDS OF DISCOVERY: experiments in indeterminacy, live electronics, improvisation" at the behest of the Institute of Contemporary Art, where the first three are given. The type of experimental music which uses static patterns to evoke a feeling of timelessness is represented on Sunday May 18th by La Monte Young's "Death Chant" and Terry Riley's "In C"; Young was the first composer to explore this area nearly a decade ago, and Riley (the welcome if unexpected subject of an article by Keith Know in last July's *JM*) was one of his first associates. Musica Elettronica Viva's collective improvisation "Spacecraft" the following day should be not only a definitive but an entertaining introduction to the resources of live electronics, since this group of American and Hungarian composer-performers from Rome works as happily in pop contexts as concert-halls. The third concert on Wednesday 22nd is devoted to the music of Christian Wolff, directed by the composer; Wolff wrote the first piece ever to use chance methods, and is known to be still breaking new ground, but his professorship of Greek at Harvard has made him more of a legend than a presence, and the concert is the first of its kind anywhere in the world.

Cardew's missionary activities in this country, however, are only an adjunct to his work as a composer, which accounts for his international reputation. Although they leave many of the most vital musical decisions to the interpreters, each of his most familiar pieces has a rich emotional colour and its own clear-cut identity, which might be relatively traditional as in "Three Winter Potatoes," an adventure in musical space as in "Solo with Accompaniment," or even an adventure in visual space as in "Memories of You."

Through them all runs the thread of Cardew's distinctive vision of indeterminacy, which he seems to see above all as a means of stimulating performers. For years, Cardew scores would combine precise rigour with permissive open-endedness, and use both verbal and graphic means to express his instructions and suggestions. In a recent article one of his interpreters wrote that the implications of these scores were so complex that "far from being free, as one might suppose at a casual glance...the performer finds himself enmeshed in an ever-narrowing field of possibilities wherein it eventually becomes difficult to do <u>anything at all.</u>

Since 1963 Cardew has also been producing major scores which give absolutely no indications as to performance. "Treatise" is simply a continuous drawing 193 pages long, concerned with graphic elements alone. Any number of any instruments could play any section for any length of time, relating sounds to shapes in any way they chose; the sole (yet sufficient) rule, that whatever sound-shape relationships are chosen for a particular performance should be maintained throughout it, is supplied by the moral sense of the reader. With "Treatise" (a score in the form of a design treating of a group of graphic shapes) or "The Tiger's Mind" (a score consisting of verbal discussions of half a dozen characters in a drama), Cardew clearly takes experimental composition as far as it can go, though the music's eventual form and content will still reflect the intentions of a composer. Even at this level, however, the predicament to which all indeterminate music is ultimately a response remains unsolved- the difficulty of leading players and listeners to realize that music consists primarily of "sounds," not intentions, and that it is to sounds that the response must be made. So long as there is an idea of any kind behind the performance, the ideal state-perfect hearing of whatever takes place- must be frustrated by metaphysical speculations on the nature of the idea which the sounds reflect, leading to inadequate hearing.

A solution to this predicament does seem to me, however, to have been found by three musicians taking part in the last of the May concerts, at the Queen Elizabeth Hall on Thursday 23rd. These men are Keith Rowe, Eddie Prévost and Lou Gare, who formed AMM in London during 1965, and then invited Cardew to join the group. Since jazz was the sole musical background of these three, and since the formulated AMM's approach as one of continuous improvisation without restrictions of any kind, it might seem that jazz (at least free jazz) holds the answer. It doesn't. But then neither does improvisation from the alternative—separate but equal—segregated musical culture of the European tradition. Nor could improvisation based on any other set of assumptions. Even if improvisers were able to break free from the ulterior distractions of agreed plans and standards, and then top break free from the ulterior distractions of purposes or reflexes arising spontaneously in performance, they would still be tied to the cultural associations of the sounds which their musical conditioning would lead them to produce. What makes AMM so far unique is that its improvisations are directed away from members' past experiences towards finding "new" sounds, ways of making them, and ways of combining them—new in the sense that they appear without history, and are prevented from acquiring one.

The listener to AMM music finds himself functioning more perfectly. Once you sense that the four musicians have for some time been fully involved with their sound-sources, you close your eyes and gradually reach an uncanny state of aural awareness and attention. From then until you sense that this trance (in AMM and/or yourself) ended some time before, your hearing seems to unite with the sounds themselves in a musical experience which in some ways transcends any other—the feeling that you are simultaneously inhabiting and discovering the whole multi-dimensional field of aural possibility; an analogy might be with the way one's overall consciousness would be transcended if barriers of space, time and separate identity were suddenly to vanish. Such at least has been my own experience of over half the forty or so AMM performances I have attended, and that of many friends and acquaintances—most of them involved, like myself, with more stylized music as well. I see no reason why AMM's Queen Elizabeth Hall concert should be any different.

They played three shows in April and May before the concert on June 12 at The Crypt on Lancaster Road in London. Fortunately, the concert was recorded by Bob Woolford. Unreleased until 1981, it's the strongest capture of early AMM, a furious behemoth of an event, giving the fullest picture of the capabilities of the ensemble. Looking back, Rowe cites this recording as the purest expression of AMM music caught on tape.

Since its formation, AMM had made much of the idea of "emerging from the room," of integrating its music into the sounds that were pre-existent in the space they occupied, of attempting to attain a similar level of being. Typically, both for AMM and for the many ensembles that would eventually follow in its wake, this meant beginning quietly, at a volume level indistinguishable from the general environs, gradually becoming more of a discrete entity, and ultimately melting back into the ambience. Less often, things might start with a bang, though ideally that would allude to the sort of clamor that might have occurred in that space anyway. Rarer still, but perhaps the most rewarding, was when AMM's music appeared as though someone had just opened a sound-proofed door into an adjacent space, one containing these musicians who had been going about their business for some indeterminate time, the listener only just happening to become aware of it. It's the sort of magical effect you get with some Feldman, for example, "For Samuel Beckett," a certain sense of eternal activity, of which you're encountering a slice. This is the case with *The Crypt*. It wells into existence, surging out of the nothingness fully formed and writhing, long past its infancy, feedback squalling like sheets of rent metal. Things ramp up from there. There's a point some twenty minutes into the music where one encounters as visceral an aural image of a roaring, devastating windstorm as can be imagined, complete with detritus being hurled against the sides of buildings at 200 mph. "Maelstrom" is perhaps an overused term in describing music with a chaotic edge but, if appropriate anywhere, it's here. They've now journeyed well beyond even the nethermost Sun Ra, beyond the grating cacophony of Stockhausen's "Mikrophonie," out past Cage's "Atlas Eclipticalis," entirely and thoroughly into AMMMusic. It's enormously assaultive, oppressively so, the screeching feedback unrelenting, the percussive clatter ear-shattering, every cubic inch of sonic space occupied. Yet the sheer magnitude of the sounds generates a richness, a depth of immersion in which one can—admittedly with some fortitude—absolutely lose oneself in the glorious panoply of noise. There's not a trace of tentativeness. Instead what comes through very clearly is a conviction, a true sense of confidence that whatever transpires, they'll be able to grasp it and work it convincingly into the whole.

Not until a half hour or so has elapsed, following some raging guitar work from Rowe, does the group "settle" into a softer drone territory, though a no less disturbing one. The strings create a shivering set of high, held tones while various percussive elements rattle nervously around them. One notable difference between this set in 1968 and previous recordings from the 1966-67 period is that, despite the obvious difficulty in determining who's doing what, Prévost has clearly dispensed with even the slightest vestige of "jazz drummer" baggage. The drum rolls and other jazz-based drum set explosions have been jettisoned entirely. Additionally, Gare's tenor work, when it can be discerned through the morass, retains virtually nothing of any Ayler-related tinge, no emotive moaning, more of a heady drone, at least in the first half of the set. But he seems unable to maintain this stance for an extended period as later on in the recording those tendencies do still creep into the picture now and again.

The agitated drone continues into the second half of the concert though its nature grows raspier and more diffuse. Matters remain on a fairly low simmer for quite a while, eventually evolving into a section isolating cello and saxophone, each bellowing. This one portion does still hearken back to Sun Ra and the like more than a little bit. It might be justifiably said that, perhaps due to the inherent nature of his instrument, Gare faced the most difficult obstacles in freeing himself entirely from the musical code of his past, a problem that beset innumerable saxophonists attempting to ply this area for decades to come. The "human cry" of the instrument that lent itself so well to blues and jazz is too insistent in this world, too demanding of center stage; the listener has great difficulty not thrusting it to the fore as a "lead" voice. That brief flurry subsides once again to an even sparer, quieter level, space flowing into the music, punctuated by a spasm of clatter here, an electronic quaver there. It might be the first instance on record of the "almost nothing" kind of music Rowe reinvestigated much later, a true even ground between what was occurring on the stage and what was already in the room. The hum (presumably from Rowe) could almost be that of fluorescent lights, the quiet banging the sound of a game of billiards next door, the soft clangs of a cord buffeted by the breeze, hitting the side of a flagpole. It ends like that, having virtually disappeared, entirely subverting any standard arc.[72]

---

72   The thought occurs while listening to David Tudor's recording of Cage's "Variations II" that it might have been an inspiration for the intensity of attack heard in the performance at The Crypt. There's a similar sense of "controlled violence," of a torrent of sound deployed with an incredible balance of rigor and abandon. Tudor's version, recorded in 1961, was released on Columbia's *Music of Our Time* series in 1967 but, according to Rowe, he didn't hear the recording (which he later often cited as, in his opinion, one of the greatest recorded moments of the 20th century) until about 1974. He grants that it's posible that he could have heard a friend's copy but cannot recall anyone he knew owning it at the time, including Cardew.

The additional track appended to the CD release of *The Crypt* largely stays in that very quiet, scraped strings area, very beautiful in and of itself, though, in the context of a documentation of an otherwise organic performance, an isolated gem.

> *I think that period, up until 1968-69, is really the most creative period of AMM. I think just the raw material for going on from what's there. I'd be the first to recognize that at the age of 25 or 26, you've probably made all the material inside you that you're going to use. I think there's a lot of stuff there which kind of germinates in that period.*

Michael Parsons, writing in *Musical Times* (May, 1968) observed:

> [AMM] go out of their way to produce sounds obliquely, and try to get away as far as possible from the conventional associations of their instruments. By putting the sounds at one remove from the actions and gestures which give rise to them they avoid anything directly expressive, which gives the result a quality of sound discovered rather than planned and intended.

Increasingly, AMM participated in concert events that featured music by contemporary "classical" artists. In May of 1968, they were part of a multi-day event presented by Music Now that included works by La Monte Young ("Death Chant"), Terry Riley ("In C"), and Christian Wolff. The following year, the same event drew Gordon Mumma, Alvin Lucier, David Behrman, and Robert Ashley and featured performances of work by Young, Terry Jennings, Cage ("Atlas Eclipticalis"), Prévost's "Silver Pyramid," Wolff, Howard Skempton, Hobbs, and George Brecht ("Candle Piece for Radios").

Wolff, in fact, had come to London in the fall of 1967 on a year-long academic sabbatical. He'd known Cardew since meeting him in Cologne in 1960 and had remained closely in touch. Shortly after his arrival, he participated in a performance of Cardew's "The Tiger's Mind" along with members of AMM, and became a regular attendee of their weekly sessions. During 1968, he played with AMM on two occasions (playing bass guitar), both when Hobbs was absent, composed a piece, "Edges," with AMM in mind,[73] and had his work "Burdocks" performed by them as well. This composition consisted of

> ...a wide variety of material, much of it available to "non-musician," or non-readers of standard notation. [It] could be a problem with the classically trained, unaccustomed to taking initiatives. Of course with AMM they worked just fine.[74]

A recording of a very intriguing project only surfaced in 2009. Laurie Scott Baker, who would co-found People's Liberation Music a few years hence, organized a performance of his own piece, "Gracility" (issued in a 2-disc set under the same name by Music Now, MNCD012) during 1969, the four musicians consisting of Rowe and Derek Bailey on guitars, Gavin Bryars on bass guitar, and Baker on double bass. It's a lengthy work, some 71 minutes in 10 sections. Though improvised, there is one restraint: "The amps are set on the edge of feedback, but the playing is very gentle. The text calls for feedback to be avoided, a bit like trying to contain a genie in a bottle!" (from the liner notes by Baker). Aside from being the sole documentation of Rowe playing with Bailey, possibly the only such occasion, it's fascinating to hear him outside the AMM context at this stage. As indicated in the instructions to the piece, his playing is quite delicate for the most part, very abstract but not so harsh until well into the work. Indeed, he and Bailey are fairly indistinguishable, each sublimating their sound to an extent. But when they let loose, and they

---

73   "Edges" would fascinate Rowe for decades and he'd return to it again and again. He had particular admiration for the instruction: "The signs on the score are not primarily what a player plays." You can see the score and instructions here: http://www.blockmuseum.northwestern.edu/picturesofmusic/pages/wolff/edgesinst.html

74   Wolff, 2008.

do several times (as during the aptly titled, "747 at Keithrowe Airport"), the resulting sound storm is as violent as anything on *The Crypt*. Rowe appears to be quite at home here, comfortable in a non-AMM situation, not dominating the proceedings by any means. To the extent it's possible to say, given the lack of recordings in the period, one is tempted to note that his playing sounds rather different than it did with AMM, more transparent and lucent. Much more so than other available examples, his playing here seems to clearly anticipate that of Fred Frith some five years in the future.

Recorded evidence of AMM's progression during the next few years is slim. A concert in Aarhus from December 19, 1969 with the same personnel as *The Crypt* was issued as Disc One of the three-disc set, *Laminal*, released by Matchless in 1996 to mark the group's thirtieth anniversary. While one wouldn't want to draw overarching conclusions from a single set, based on what's heard here, AMM had not moved very far along from that recording a year and a half earlier in one sense, though one might say, whether considered as a positive or otherwise, that there's a greater degree of smoothness in the moment to moment transitions. From the beginning, the balance between percussive elements, strings, flute, and Rowe's scrabbling guitar is quite even. It's not a drone, really, but is very much steady state for the first ten or twelve minutes. The music remains harsh and bleak, however, the squalling bowed strings, probably including the guitar, reaching particularly angst-ridden heights. Gare's flute and recorder still seem out of place, the sprightly tootling too light for the general ambience, and when he comes out with a few notes from Monk's "Well You Needn't" over some unusual and strident koto-like plucks from Rowe, the effect is deflating. Prévost is marvelous throughout. Still largely on the drum set, he's nonetheless moved even further away from any tinge of jazz form and the interplay between he and Rowe's groaning feedback during the first third of the concert is a major highlight. There's a lovely subsidence about midway through, when Gare's low tenor (far more effective than his flute) winds itself around some deep cello pizzicato, each settling into a quiet eddy of stroked cymbals and electronic hum. It's a rare glimpse into the sort of music that AMM as a trio would create more than a decade hence. Rowe often remarked later on that the cello epitomized AMM music and it's featured prominently in the concert's second half, presumably wielded by both Cardew and Rowe, rip-sawing above the percussive clatter. Several times during the performance, one hears overtly guitar-like sounds emerging, plucked and strummed tones that are surprisingly "normal" sounding. At the least, it indicates that Rowe hadn't totally abandoned that aspect of his instrument. Interestingly, on what was released as the first track on the disc, comprising some fifty-one minutes of music, there's no sign of either piano or radio. Piano does seem to be among the jumble of sound making up track two, a fifteen-minute excerpt from, one guesses, another point in the concert. This portion resides in an area similar to the beginning of *The Crypt*, all massed percussion, ferocious, growling guitar, and whistles. As was often the case when AMM ventured into louder, more raucous territory, the listener can't help but pick up vestiges of Sun Ra, especially when Gare sets his tenor a-wailing. The final track is a lovely denouement, a restrained, hushed drone of bowed objects, created with great sensitivity. On its own, it's as unique and beautiful a piece of music as was being created in the improvised world in 1969.

Two recordings survive (and have been available for download) from January 20 and February 3, 1970, each taped in London. Both are extraordinary sets on their own merits and for the fact that, as far as available evidence goes, they more clearly presage the AMM music of the 80s and 90s than any other recordings from this period. Indeed, one wonders if it's Tilbury at the keyboard here, on one of his occasional substitutions for Cardew. No personnel are provided and attempting to decipher exactly who's present can be a bit baffling. Rowe's contributions aren't obvious when there's no guitar to be heard; perhaps he's playing cello, perhaps percussion, maybe nothing at all. The earlier event immediately establishes a contemplative mood that one hadn't previously heard on works like *AMMMusic* or *The Crypt*, a gentle cascade of sonorous, hollow objects, softly struck, with an underlying hum which is not agitative. There's almost a sense of reverie, of floating, the piano remaining in a more or less tonal area, small right-hand bouquets offset by bass rumblings. A clean, arco note on cello (Rowe?) advances and retreats as the music thickens, the percussion continuing to percolate, both drum and objects (suggesting Hobbs' continued participation). But the entire effect is one of slightly troubled serenity, the sense AMM often achieved on much later recordings such as *Newfoundland*. Prévost is far more coloristic during this concert, rumbling and tumbling rather than utilizing snare rolls, lending a delightfully bumpy undercurrent. Chimes are sounded, gongs worried with padded sticks, the whole far less confrontational than heard before. The separation between instrumental sounds is somewhat more apparent than in earlier examples, the violin, percussion, and piano during a segment midway almost giving the impression of a free jazz kind of environment, each musician "soloing." The piano and quietly droning violin come to predominate, fairly singing over the others, wafting out into the atmosphere. It's not until 22 minutes into this half hour set that one hears a radio, a muffled male voice, but even that can't quell the lapping sonority. Electronics, probably Rowe's guitar in one form or another, enter even later, providing an edgier ground that serves to make the upper level sweetness all the more piquant, ending the date in marvelous fashion, between unease and bliss.[75]

The recording of the February 3, 1970 concert appears to kick in during mid-performance, Rowe exciting his guitar strings with some iterating device, Prévost thundering distantly underneath. While somewhat more assertive than that music from a couple of

---

75   The downloaded version appends about seven minutes of what seems to be a field recording, out of doors in an urban area, with nothing in particular occurring (though, of course, filled with all sorts of things occurring). Whether this was on the original tape or not, it serves as a fine bookend, an "opening of the door" to a quiet exterior world from this relatively quiet interior, created one.

weeks earlier, there remains a smoothness of surface, a certain flowing quality. Even after that initial drone breaks, it's replaced by cello/violin and percussion that move contiguously, without the kind of harsh juxtaposition that characterized the more violent sections of *The Crypt,* and with a richer, more melodious sound palette than that found in its more subdued second half. There's a delicate segment with prepared piano, soft drumming, and radio (spoken male commentary) which isn't all that distant from the sort of free improvisation being championed at the time by Bailey, Parker, et al. indicating that AMM wasn't entirely isolated from the musical currents circulating elsewhere in London. Frankie Valli's "Silence is Golden" rears its falsetto head for a bit, as does a voice intoning, "Save us from sin" and a snatch of older jazz trumpet. The performance on the whole is quite low key. The elements are similar to earlier concerts—the scrabbling guitar, rustling percussion, sawing strings—but everything is lowered a few notches in volume. Perhaps as a result of this more circumscribed approach, the music unfurls in a very organic manner. Evan Parker's description of AMM's music as "laminal" can be clearly appreciated here, each stratum emerging to the surface, abiding, and returning to the soft depths in an almost regular fashion. A portion near the close, with high tones, bowed metal, and guitar, possesses the kind of beauty AMM so often attained, ethereal and earthbound at once, and is strikingly similar to the general area of music Rowe would immerse himself in some thirty years later.

Sadly, this is the latest extant recording of the ensemble prior to the split of early 1972.

Reviews of performances indicate that AMM continued steadfastly along and around the pathways suggested by The Crypt session, at least until political issues began to infiltrate. Reviewers were still baffled and/or horrified (several curiously complaining about the lack of a coffee break intermission), though sometimes one, like the jazz critic for the *London Sunday Telegraph*, Peter Clayton, achieved a kind of understanding almost by osmosis as in this colorful review of a concert performed on June 10, 1971:

> Assuming they remained walking wounded, and had
> not grown so rigid with boredom that they had become
> stretcher cases, at the end of AMM's recital at the Queen
> Elizabeth Hall on Thursday night the entire audience
> could probably have been driven home in one dou-
> ble-decker bus.
>
> I didn't see their departure because after an hour and
> a quarter of chance noise made by two cellists (one
> doubling on a small drum), a man who divided his time
> between producing those yawning metallic groans that
> sawmills make and prowling about blowing a tenor sax-
> ophone, and a drummer, I was driven home by a com-
> pound tedium, an affliction I rarely suffer from.
>
> The rain slashing down on the terrace outside the hall ap-
> plauded my action, the wheels of the train squealed their
> approval on the curve outside London Bridge. And the
> point of all that high-flown nonsense is that the clapping
> rain and the grinding flanges made by accident sounds
> that were infinitely more pleasurable than the ones AMM
> were making on purpose.
>
> This is not idle facetiousness, either. The object of the
> AMM quartet is, I gather, to make rich sounds. "They im-
> provise." Say their apologists, a form of recommendation
> based on the arrogant premise that the first thing that
> comes into a man's head is automatically better than the
> second or third, and on the even more arrogant assump-
> tion that the things he thinks of are inevitably worth
> hearing anyway.
>
> All I can do is try to describe what happened during the
> decade or so I sat there. It began with a note—impro-
> vised of course—played quietly on the cello and held for

maybe three minutes. This was joined by some scraping noises and a burst or two of feedback. The drummer stirred uneasily, and the other cellist made a few almost inaudible passes. He later transferred to a small drum, and at the end of about three-quarters of an hour went and switched the organ on. Didn't play it, simply set it so that it played a chord. Having no need to stop for breath, it continued to do this for the next half-hour. By this time the saxophonist was up and about.

I needn't go on, though AMM did. "It got better," somebody told me the next morning. Well, it could hardly have got worse.

I arrived home just as "Man of Aran" was starting on the television. The sea made its random music from the little screen. The gulls made theirs. Genuine human beings were seen fighting nature every inch of the way. Flaherty had made the picture nearly 40 years earlier and it was still compelling, possibly because he'd shot miles of film and done us the courtesy of selecting, of editing, so that we should not be bored. After what felt like a lifetime in AMM's wastebasket, I could almost smell the fresh air coming out of the set.

Max Harrison, writing in *The Times* of the same event, makes the following observation, interesting in light of future developments:

> ...Yet there are frustrating discontinuities also, lines of exploration that are broken off too near the beginning.

> Usually this seems to be due to one of the players, through inattention, bringing in a sound, a thought, which does not fit, and the music is deflected from its path. Most often it is the drummer, especially last night. Whereas the tenor saxophone has been completely divested of its

jazz overtones, the percussionist, through his too limited range of effects, roots this music again and again to its past, and to the ground.

Prévost, in an interview with *Melody Maker* (June 1971), gives a cogent summery of where AMM's musical consciousness was at the time:

> The problem with AMM is that we're not interested in music. Everyone else has this professional attitude, which we simply can't understand. It seems totally irrelevant when people ask you what equipment you use or how you get a particular sound—though they usually ask Cornelius or Keith rather than us, because their stuff looks more technical. And when we tell people there's no leader, and no scores or plans, they just think we're naïve. So even if they're trying to praise us it comes out condescendingly. After one of our Berlin concerts I overheard a German composer telling a friend we could only play that way because we were high. I felt I really couldn't let that pass, so I explained we were always dead sober, and he was absolutely amazed. But somehow I felt this made us seem even more naïve to him. We just don't fit in the same category as other musicians, though we've begun to see a few connections, with Cage, and the Gagaku music, and some records of Buddhist ceremonies.

In July 1971, AMM gave a workshop in Ghent, Belgium at the Royal Academy of Fine Arts. It was a sparsely attended event, more so when the professor under whose aegis the concert had been booked got up and left in mid-performance, followed en masse by a number of his students. Eventually, the two dozen or so audience members remaining ventured on stage (invited by the group) and began experimenting with the objects they found there. A free bar was opened and the small crowd wandered back and forth between the drinks and the music. However, when the time came to leave, a difficulty was encountered: the exit doors had been chained shut. The fire brigade had to be called in to free the attendees and musicians. Some placards were discovered outside the venue sporting slogans like, "We want to lock up the elite," the work of the "Logos workgroup," an organization founded by the Belgian composer Gottfried-Willem Raes that apparently sympathized with those listeners who had earlier left the premises. Though admirers of the musicians (and, indeed, they'd performed pieces of Cardew in the past), the Logos group was more concerned with a larger issue, that of a reactionary musical establishment promoting shows whose ticket prices were far out of the range of the young students in the city. AMM was sympathetic to their position, but found themselves in the awkward position of being unable, or not quite willing, to do anything about it, something that couldn't have sat well with Rowe's and Cardew's burgeoning politicization (see below).

AMM's second trip to the US included a concert on November 20, 1971 in Brooklyn at the Spencer Memorial Church. Tom Johnson, then writing for the *Village Voice*, covered the event. While appreciating it overall, he was somewhat bothered by what he felt was its hermetic, non-inclusive properties, oddly yearning for a bit of virtuosity or some snatches of rhythmic regularity. As a fascinating composer in his own right, it's interesting to quote his review in full, illustrating the divergences that had taken place between AMM and the contemporary classical world, especially the post-Young and post-Fluxus areas, to which they'd been marginally adjacent earlier on:

> Many performances these days seem more concerned with creating a kind of group performing experience than with creating a presentation for an audience. When I can make myself stop wanting to be entertained, and just be satisfied with a vicarious experience, I can see a fresh and very special kind of beauty. It is sort of like listening to birdcalls. You can't tell what they mean because, after all, they are not singing for your benefit, but sometimes you can latch on to something, and then, for a while anyway,

you can drift right along and it all seems very natural and exciting.

AMM Music, a free form quartet from London, is a lot like this. The most gratifying thing about the group's concert at Spencer Memorial Church in Brooklyn on November 20, was simply the degree of cooperation and sensitivity among the four players. They have worked together for some time now, and their music could drift easily and naturally wherever it wanted to go without having to be pushed there by anybody. The performers' egos were always subordinate to the sound itself, which flowed on and on, more or less non-stop, for almost two hours. It was almost as if no one really had any control over what would happen next.

In one way or another, the music went through a wide variety of colors, from the most delicate single-note passages, to the loud feedback noises created by Keith Rowe on his electric guitar amplifier, and some raucous textures with everybody playing his loudest and fastest. Most of the time the sounds were atonal, but occasionally very simple chords and melodies would creep in. One such sequence finally grew into an Ivesian version of "Loch Lomond," the melody sung very straight by Cornelius Cardew while Lou Gare interspersed fragments of the tune on his tenor sax[76]. Particularly memorable was a soft squealy texture with Eddie Prévost bowing a cymbal, while Cardew and Gare mixed in some very high cello and violin lines. The sound meandered around for some time until it found a particular chord, and then just sat there for a long time.

---

76   An article by Rena Fruchter, documenting a workshop and performance at Rutgers University from the same tour makes no mention of the appearance of any song forms, her write-up describing what seems to be a very "typical" AMM concert.

The players never get in each other's way, and have evolved a rather amazing group sensitivity as to what should happen next. It is a remarkable process by which their music unfolds, but it does take a long time. And the main problem is that it really is just a process rather than a product in the sense of a statement. So, as a member of the audience, not allowed to participate, I felt very remote most of the time. I was not, after all, a part of this process. What was going on didn't really have a thing to do with me. And after an hour or so, I found myself wishing for some of the things that musical products usually have: like maybe a genuine bit of virtuosity, or a repetition of something that happened earlier, or a rhythmic thing that I could get into my feet, or something intricate and calculated which might challenge the intellect for a while.

Morton Feldman once said that the highest goal of the composer should be to let the music compose itself (or at least to get out of its way that it seems to be happening that way). By that criterion, AMM Music has to be considered very highly, because their music is so free, unfettered, and untampered with that it really does seem to be composing itself. But while they come very close to achieving this particular ideal, they have done so at the cost of other things and cut out some of the audience's enjoyment at the same time.

Roger Sutherland wrote a perceptive account of AMM for the April/May 1972 issue of *London* magazine, entitled "AMM Music—Beyond Electronics," wherein he noted:

> ...During all these passages is was often difficult to discern which instruments were producing which sounds, an ambiguity which was enhanced by the darkened stage. This ambiguity of sound is one of the most fascinating aspects of AMM music. The players employ a wide range of techniques to dissolve or blur the identity of their instruments,

creating a continuum of timbre in which the sounds of the piano, 'cello and saxophone shade off into one another. The bass strings of the piano, when bowed, resemble the 'cello with added resonance, while the 'cello, when amplified, sounds grating and metallic, similar to a scraped gong. The AMM thus seem to be trying to merge all the differentials of instrumental timbre into a single vast sea of ambiguous and shifting colours. Such monochromaticism is, of course, familiar from electronic music, where the atomization of sound permits continuous gradation between the sounds of, say, wood, skin and metal, thus obliterating any distinctions between them. However, it is a tendency which can be traced back as far as Debussy's hazy, impressionistic treatment of orchestral colour. Paradoxically, it is an effect which only works when the composer fully understands the instruments he is writing for and can feel their different qualities; only then can he submerge these differentials into a single, undifferentiated sea of sound. The chromatic ambiguity of AMM sound thus not only places it within a European tradition, but also attests to a very high level of musicianship.

Adrian Jack, in an article for *Music & Musicians* (March 1972) that covered the general experimental group scene in London, noticed a certain evolution in AMM's recent music:

> For a time the problem of dwindling audiences evoked extremes "which overrode all possible conditions"—playing very loudly or very softly, for instance—extremes which Cardew now considers only cut them off from the audience. Now they seem to be cultivating an out-going attitude. Their mood is optimistic and constructive, and this suggest a modesty and lack of irony that may be surprising and hard to accept, for where artists live dangerously or unusually, people invariably expect to find arrogance.

To understand how this change in attitude and approach had

manifest, one has to go back a couple of years to concerns formed outside of AMM.

*

During the late 60s, Rowe had been devoting increased time to the study of Chinese history, art, and philosophy, along the way imbuing himself with an appreciation of the sense of the collectivist ethic that had been emerging in China since Mao's rise, a convergence of Russian communist thought and historic ideas of Chinese identity that appealed strongly to him. Among the Left in Britain and elsewhere, there was a growing conviction that the next phase of humanity's progress lay in China and that the Cultural Revolution was the doorway to that stage. Mao's idea of ostensibly vesting power and culture in the peasant class exerted increasing influence on Rowe's thought and necessarily began to chafe at the kind of art he was creating, much as it would for several composers with a strong leftist bent during that decade and afterwards. While AMM was a tightly contained unit of relatively like-minded individuals, there was no denying its essentially arcane nature and the fact that the music was reaching a tiny handful of listeners and members, of the aesthetic elite at that, providing not a whit of improvement in the life of the working class, essentially not touching them whatsoever. The opportunity to engage with a much larger set of people as part of a group whose creations would exist in the public arena was exactly the kind of soil that allowed these nascent ideas a chance to flower. On June 12, 1969, Cardew sent out a short form letter to "about 85 people" including Rowe and Krystyna, inviting them to join his newly formed Scratch Orchestra, enclosing a copy of the Draft Constitution for their consideration, a document that had also been printed in the June issue of the Musical Times.

The history of the Scratch Orchestra is well-documented elsewhere (most recently and with a great amount of detail in John Tilbury's biography of Cardew). To a large degree it was formed by Cardew with several of his students from Morley College, including Howard Skempton and Michael Parsons, for the purpose of widening their musico-philosophical horizons, much of it heavily influenced by the ideas and activities of the Fluxus group in preceding years, and it soon incorporated all of the AMM members as well as numerous other persons, musicians, and non-musicians alike. There were several salient differences between the activities engaged in by Scratch and those of AMM, each of which, though it may not have been possible to anticipate, served as a small springboard toward the upcoming political disruptions that would shatter the band and have repercussions for years to come.

The first, most obvious, difference was that Scratch performances were usually held in public spaces, among the people, not on tiny stages in small rooms in dim or non-existent light in front of a handful of aficionados. That entire esoteric atmosphere, that implied aura of the "difficult to access," the "necessary to seek out" was dispensed with from the get-go. Scratch events were held in village greens, on the streets, in the daylight, enacted with the fervent—arguably naïve—desire to merge with the day-to-day goings on of "normal" citizens. There had been inchings toward this sort of environment in projects like Prévost's "Silver Pyramid," which was sometimes performed in public gallery settings and involved as many players from among a given crowd as chose to participate. Still, a Scratch performance must have had something of a "coming out into the sun" aspect to it for the AMM musicians, a direct aesthetic relationship with the everyday world instead of the hermetic near-secrecy to which they'd been accustomed. They would assemble outdoors, interact with whoever passed by and wished to play (a far cry from yelling at would-be participants in the audience at AMM shows to shut up) and in general partake of an atmosphere that was as playful as it was intellectual. Part of that, necessarily, was encountering the reactions of people who weren't in the locale explicitly to see and hear Scratch Orchestra activities. Scratch events didn't have public antagonism as a goal and indeed were quite open to the idea of a give and take with any onlookers who peered in. But it came as no surprise that the majority of the reactions thus encountered were of the bewildered, occasionally even hostile variety, the music's "point"(or that of whatever activity in which members were currently engaged, by no means always "musical") being entirely opaque to the average citizen. This disjunction with the real world was like a small pebble in Rowe's shoe, and later Cardew's, always slightly rankling and ultimately festering into something larger.

Ideally, the Scratch Orchestra would have achieved a unique musical/cultural synthesis, a seamless interweaving of advanced aesthetic ideas with an awareness of the concerns of middle and working class England. However, just as those "advanced" ideas included notions that were childlike in their simplicity—often a beautiful thing—so did many of their political conceptions, particularly involving the psychology of group action and organization. At heart was the conflict within the ensemble between what might be called the libertarian or anarchic faction and the authoritarian one, albeit a benevolent authoritarianism of the left.

There were valid points on both sides. Though largely brought to fruition by Cardew, the pervasive concept in the minds of most of the members was that any event or happening was to be entirely unregulated, the structure being determined by the participants, either sketched out beforehand or on the fly. People could bring exercises culled from their "scratch books" which would be acted upon or not, by themselves or whichever local citizens happened by and decided to take part. The whole notion was obviously very innocent and naïve in a way, though very much a part of the zeitgeist. After all, they were only creating art events—many of these actions would contain no recognizable musical component—and these events might be imagined expansively enough to allow for even negative reactions of passersby so long as things didn't escalate to physical levels. They would instigate a direction but once set in motion, whatever happened, happened and would be considered a viable part of the actualization of the idea. If a Scratch group arrived in a busy train station, carrying instructions on how many paces to walk in which direction and what small action to take upon arrival at a given point, and if no one outside of the "performers" ever realized that anything of an aesthetic nature was occurring, that was fine. The daily actions of that public would nonetheless have been subtly tinged by Scratch activity. There was an underlying confidence that whatever eventuated, things would tend to work out for the best, likely better and certainly more unexpected (and, after all, wasn't that one of the points?) than if matters were more rigidly planned. There was indeed much discussion about a desired "invisibility" of performance, a complete-as-possible integration into the community, an extension of the closeted aspect of a typical AMM concert where sublimation into the room or immediate environment was a goal. Guerrilla sub-groups could pile into an old delivery truck, descend on a school playground full of kids, and do as much of a performance as they could (whether or not the local citizenry could distinguish it as such) before being chased away by teachers. At the other extreme, there were events like one at a parish church in Wales where Tilbury, manning the organ, performed note-perfect renditions of Romantic classics like Ketèlbey's "In a Monastery Garden" or "In a Persian Marketplace" while orchestra members accompanied with bird whistles and Scratch sounds. Rowe remembers a congregation member saying, "I've never heard anything so beautiful."

Though it's by no means certain that many of the Scratch members thought of it in these terms, there's more than a little similarity between such ideas in the aesthetic arena and equivalent anarcho-libertarian models in the political one. In its purest form, individuals deal with other individuals without coercion, allowing trends, groups, etc. to emerge without conscious planning, often taking forms undreamt of by the participants.

On the other hand, you had persons like Rowe and Cardew who were becoming increasingly suspicious of "non-functional" art, viewing it more as the pastime of well-to-do students who, while nodding toward their less wealthy comrades, really preferred to operate at a remove, not deigning to get their hands dirty, and unwilling to communicate with the working class in terms they could understand and enjoy. At best, they were providing light amusement to the masses, not coming close to actually alleviating their condition or steering them down the morally proper political path (as they perceived it). And if they wouldn't see this self-evident fact for themselves, then someone would just have to take charge to orient matters appropriately.

Though the salient elements of what would become a pitched battle manifested almost immediately, there was no outright explosion for a good while. During 1969, the Scratch Orchestra functioned quite happily in its more libertarian guise. Cardew, having learned well from Cage, arrived at a similar, Zen-like point of stasis. John Tilbury, an original Scratch member, summed it up as "the virtuosity of restraint," while AMM had already internalized the Zhuang Zhou epigram, "What is it about uselessness that causes you such distress?" and Cardew had, in "Tiger's Mind," included the ancient Chinese line, "Sitting here, filled with emotions, why should I trouble to play? A breeze will come and sweep the strings." It was the spirit of the times and even if, in the real world, it was ultimately unsustainable, with Scratch the stance held up for a surprisingly long stretch. But eventually the realities of operating such a relatively large group of people and juggling the assorted bureaucratic duties involved served to create, in the minds of a number of its members, the necessity of establishing a center, which inevitably moved matters toward "leaders," a concept anathema to many on the more anarchic fringe of the group.

I think it's fair to say that Cornelius was more informed than other people, though if he was in the center, it was more through skill and talent than bossiness. He saw the need for a fairly strong center that the peripheral parts could engage with. Having an agenda for the evening, for example. They [the performances] were enormously elaborate conceits.

If you're playing "The Great Learning," for example, say with the core of only 30 people, there are 20 who want to do "The Great Learning" but there are 10 others who actually, yeah, we wouldn't mind that but really want to do this other stuff. They might well do that while "The Great Learning" is going on, develop a sub-group which would do a completely different concert on the edge of the stage with completely different material. The Slippery Merchants[77] would be such a group. Not troublemakers, but agitators.

It's almost like in any larger society you get groups who don't want to engage in what others are doing. So they do something on the side without being disruptive or without meaning to be disruptive. So you might actually have concerts where you could have five or six things going on. Eddie and I, sometimes, for various reasons, didn't make the rehearsals, but you want to be in the performance. So we'd go and do something called "Restaurant Music." We would just plant ourselves somewhere in the space and play, like, versions of "Moonlight in Vermont," you know? But it would be highly fragmented. Then you might get the

Slippery Merchants doing "1000 Activities." But the main ensemble might be doing a Skempton piece.[78]

Rowe took part in virtually every Scratch action while Prévost was a less regular contributor, a small oddity given his communitarian concerns of that time and later; possibly he thought some of the activities too "arty" and out of touch. If so, such an opinion ironically presaged that of Rowe and Cardew.

---

77   A subset of the Scratch Orchestra that often included Bryn Harris, Catherine Morley, Hugh Shrapnel, Dave Jackman, and others.

78   Although some might envision these sorts of goings on as a kind of Henry Brant spectacle, the fact was that, even if the works in play themselves contained some degree of compositional aspect, the juxtaposition of forces and hence the actual integration of sounds and activities was entirely improvised, the results unpredictable.

As with any well-intentioned but loosely structured gambit, there were times when everyone was on the same page, everything coalesced, and all felt similarly about how to approach a project. Early in its existence, the Scratch Orchestra could actually achieve its libertarian/communitarian ideal. Ultimately, however, it was a precarious balance subject to the insecurities and irrationalities of the people involved. Almost inevitably, a cult of personality was formed, and Scratch had Cardew ready and not entirely unwilling to assume the role of leader, albeit with the able assistance and influence of Rowe at his side.

On a purely practical level, Cardew was the one who got things done, the one who dealt with the technicalities and red tape that allowed events to occur at all.

> *Poor Cornelius! He'd contact the BBC, he'd organize a contract for payment of the orchestra, he'd get the programmes done, he'd write all the people. You had to write letters in those days! Post them! No photocopying. He'd do all that, he'd be interviewed, he'd go on the BBC and then when it's time to do the rehearsals, having got this opportunity together for people, he'd be endlessly sniped at by this hard line [the anarcho-libertarian faction]. He was always incredibly charming but I can't believe he didn't go home wanting to strangle the cat!*

Although Cardew had not been particularly political in his early career, neither as expressed in his work nor personal life, there had been since "Treatise" an implicit quality that one could analogize with communist theory, that of an action being centrally organized yet allowing for an extremely democratic response. Similarly in text-oriented pieces like "The Great Learning," the relationships between groups of performers were roughly pre-ordained though allowing for some amount of freedom of expression. One can imagine the Scratch Orchestra, in Cardew's mind, becoming a form of notation itself, the "notes" consisting of a community of individuals, their interaction with each other and their surrounding environment and citizens, the ideas of freedom, collaboration, cooperation, responsibility, etc. But he also may have thought of himself as the guiding force, the paternal philosopher-king. He'd of course been immersed for several years in an entirely anarcho-libertarian situation, AMM, a unit requiring no such control. By simple virtue of greater numbers, of a far more complex mix of personalities, as well as extensive interaction with the public (and all the necessary dealings with the bureaucracy that entailed), he doubtless felt that someone needed to grasp the reins.

Even if one accepts these issues as necessities that required action, one can at the same time understand how they could be seen as analogous to various collectivist psychologies that had arisen earlier in the century where "those who knew" exercised dominion, benevolent or otherwise, over "those who needed to be shown the way."[79]

Rowe had a strong hand in this. His fascination with all things Chinese had been brewing for several years at this point, at least since the advent of "Treatise" whose iconography bore some tenuous relation to Chinese calligraphy as a non-phonetic "alphabet." Via Gurdjieff, he had read Joseph Needham's *Science and Civilisation in China* which conjectured about the role of sound in early Chinese societies, for example discerning the psycholo-

---

79   Letters expressing concern over the course the orchestra appeared to be taking were sent to Cardew. One, signed "Dave 28.7.71 (David Smith?), lists six points of contention, two of which read:

2) I really object to any notion of a "correct line" of action or whatever. I thought one of the prime reasons for being in this orchestra was to get away from all that kind of stuff. It's more than a little strange to hear people, in the name of "historical necessity" & all the rest, suggesting how to write, sculpt, paint, play, think or live.

5) Down the centuries artists of all types have been used, not always successfully, by kings, princes, priests, rich idiots, fascists & other assorted morons. By now I think some of us have had enough & we've take our freedom.

gy of an opposing army by flute sounds that emanated from an encampment. Needham was also among the first Western scholars to evince a high regard for not only the accomplishments of Chinese science but also for the manner in which credit for their discoveries was diffused into the general populace rather than being attributed to single, "heroic" individuals. Partly as a result of a general disgust and disdain for Western culture, Rowe had turned to both the history and ongoing struggle of the people of China as a source of hope, including what had transpired there since the 1920s.[80]

Not that he was alone. A willfully ignorant veneration of Mao Zedong had been occurring in beat and hippie circles for a while, turning him into a pop icon alongside Che Guevara (via Warhol, among others), with only the fuzziest, most generalized understanding—often filtered through apologist leftist media which would brook not the slightest criticism of their "leaders"—of what had actually occurred, and was still occurring, in China. The West was vile, ran the story; Mao epitomized the anti-West stance (Stalin having gone irretrievably past the point where adherence to him could remain tenable for all but the most diehard), therefore he was good.

In fairness, the degree of horror, mass starvation, and murder that had taken place under Mao's rule, an estimated 45 million starved or beaten to death between 1958 and 1962 alone, didn't really trickle down into the public consciousness until the 70s, but the overall shape of the catastrophe was known to those who took the time to actually study the matter. It seems even the Beatles understood the nature of things when they sang in "Revolution" in 1968:

----

80   Additionally, several years spent working in ad agencies where his jobs included the manipulation and falsification of images designed to subliminally influence the buying compulsions of the public, particularly the emphasis on concealed phallic imagery and many other sexist strategies, had nurtured in Rowe an evermore severe contempt for the commercial, and hence capitalist, sphere of activity.

But if you go carrying pictures of Chairman Mao
You ain't gonna make it with anyone anyhow.

Central to cultural Maoism was the idea embodied in the "barefoot doctor," the breaking down of elite classes in the belief that the working class was every bit as capable of doing the same quality of work in jobs previously sequestered for the wealthy. In many ways, the Scratch Orchestra typified this ideal, encouraging "non-musicians" to become orchestra members, for their compositional ideas to stand side by side with those of more established artists like Cardew (though, interestingly, he didn't volunteer to leave the contemporary classical scene completely during this entire period). Indeed, being untainted by an upper class upbringing, their work should be purer and more meaningful to the lives of their fellow comrades in labor.

While this policy had proven disastrous when instituted in China in highly technical fields (as when skilled surgeons were ousted as class betrayers and replaced by clueless medical students, with predictably horrific results), in the realm of art, one could imagine a certain amount of invigoration injected into a sterile field, not dissimilar to what punk accomplished in rock a few years hence.

But—and it was a big but—commensurate with the breakdown of elitism was the obligation to produce work that was capable of being enjoyed by the common man, not the abstract stuff geared toward that selfsame elite from which they'd only just disassociated. And beyond mere enjoyment, the music should be morally pure, leading its audience toward a more enlightened path. There sits a mighty big rub.

When AMM performed in small rooms or clubs, some percentage of the audience was always receptive to the music; they'd not be there otherwise. By virtue of conducting most performances in public spaces, Scratch members could hardly avoid the knowledge that the overwhelming majority of people who paid any attention at all were bored or derisive, if not irritated outright. Well, there was clearly a problem here for those with the developing ideology of Cardew or Rowe. These were the very people for whom one should be playing and composing yet here they were, snickering, sneering, or yawning.

> *En route to a [Scratch] concert at the Portsmouth School of Art, we encountered some shipyard workers on strike in Southampton. I think we realized we had nothing to offer these workers. We're cultural workers, artists, and that, I think, became the crucial point where we started thinking about what kind of music we could make that was actually relevant. I think even to this day, it's something we still haven't solved. Mao was kind of the concentrated essence of that aspiration at that time. Whether it was a romanticization of what the Chinese were doing, I'm not sure. But I think we understood what the basic aspirations were.*

It was a problem facing many serious, left-leaning musicians around this time. If one was holding Maoism or almost any other collectivist politics as an ideal, it was difficult to ignore the fact that any remotely modern music (in a 20th century, European respect) was entirely banned in China, considered a symptom of bourgeois moral depravity. Composer/pianist Frederic Rzewski, who since 1967 had been performing with the improvising ensemble Musica Elettronica Viva, tried to straddle the fence a bit, first incorporating aspects of minimalism with politically charged texts ("Coming Together," "Attica"), then eventually composing neo-romantic piano works liberally dashed with modernist technical innovations, using folk themes or worker's songs as a foundation ("¡El Pueblo Unido Jamas Sera Vencido!," "Four North American Ballads," etc.). While it's easy to understand the reluctance of some musicians to *completely* cast off their prior learning and cultural habits, Rowe after all had essentially done just that during AMM's formation. Even though that was on an aesthetic, not political, front, his sense of absoluteness, of being willing to "drop everything," came to the fore.

Cardew, while always "of the left," still had something of a hands-off attitude with regard to the interaction of explicit political ideas and art, preferring to attack the matter obliquely in terms of structure and the philosophical systems implied therein. Rowe was just as drastic and forthright as he'd been in 1965 when he vowed never to play a standard note on the guitar again, even to the point of breaking that vow. As far as he was concerned, this was the new order, pure and simple. He began to harangue virtually anyone within earshot of his revelation, including especially his comrades in AMM. While Prévost and Gare, sympathetic though they were to leftist concerns in general, didn't buy Rowe's Maoist pitch, in Cardew he found fertile ground for conversion. Cardew respected Rowe enormously as a musician, thinker, and friend. Over long discussions with Cardew, he convinced his older companion of the essential correctness of the idea, that the music they'd been involved with for the previous few years was actually serving the cause of the bourgeoisie, not the working class, and that it needed to be fundamentally redirected toward explicitly serving the aspirations and moral character of the working class.

The psychological basis of this severe change in character and outlook on the part of Rowe is difficult to fathom. Krystyna, thinking about it decades later, surmised that it may have to do with paternal issues: Rowe never having known his father and being on a kind of search for a substitute figure, Mao fitting the bill while able to be integrated into ongoing aesthetic concerns. It seems clear that, whatever the ultimate origins, his proselytizing bore overt similarities to religious evangelicalism, just as it has for thousands of people for whom politics adopts all the characteristics of religious belief. All questioning was anathema, any doubts were thought-crimes: "There is only one lie; there is only one truth." Rowe adopted this attitude with a vengeance, alienating many a former friend.

The eventual demise of the Scratch Orchestra ultimately derived from the irreconcilable split between those who were disinclined to accept any manner of guidance "from above," who essentially felt as though they were being treated like children, and those who insisted on a stricter organization, a well-oiled machine that could better serve the needs of the working class. In other words, to do what they deemed morally correct.

Things rarely work out so neatly, with clearly defined edges. Within AMM, matters moved apace, the ethos of free improvisation still holding the day. Long simmering tensions still arose, however, especially between Rowe and Prévost. Since the late 60s, Prévost had occasionally taken the time to actually write down his complaints regarding Rowe in letter form. Often these would be concerned with musical issues; Rowe was playing too loudly and dominating the group, for example. This would be accompanied by actual cassette recordings of performances to document this "truth."[81] Rowe recalls another that stemmed from an offhand remark he made about Sigmund Freud that somehow upset Prévost enough to pen a missive. But as insular and self-contained as these problems were, and as isolated from external concerns as they may have wished to be, here and there the outside world and its political issues were burrowing into AMM. Cardew, for example, would interject a snatch of worker's song on piano (or an Irish tune as noted above, obliquely referencing IRA concerns) or Rowe might consciously attune his shortwave to Radio Tirana, catch a Chinese communist oration, or play a bit of the Yellow River Concerto from his tape recorder. While tolerated—after all, wasn't anything fair game?—Prévost and Gare couldn't help but see that an agenda was being none-too-subtly pushed and indeed, they were correct. Rowe remembered, "I think I was making such heavy statements which, by implication, were anti- what Lou and Eddie stood for." Rowe and Cardew began to badger Prévost and Gare[82] to accede to their understanding of this newly discovered

---

81   See the interview (Appendix A) with Prévost conducted by Trevor Taylor from "The Improvising Percussionist," *Drums and Percussion*, April 1974: Among other matters, Prévost expresses some concern over the "danger of being engulfed by electronic music" as well as some misgivings about contact mics, saying, "I was not able to control what was going on."

82   Hobbs having moved on due to an increased desire to focus on his

purpose of music in the world, insisting that AMM subordinate itself to the interest of the People's cause, but the percussionist and saxophonist would have none of it. Gare recalled:

> He [Rowe] could be very arrogant and critical of anyone that did not go along with his current ideas, and on occasions a very tedious companion when he would insist on spelling out the merits of his way of doing things as opposed to any other. We tolerated this and took this as being part of Keith's character...When he became deeply involved with revolutionary politics, following the theories of Chairman Mao in particular, it was a different level of commitment for him. This caused him great difficulty in trying to accommodate these ideas within the free flowing nature of the music, and his playing became very hesitant and a weak shadow of what it had been.

But by early 1972, the fundamental disagreements about the purpose of their music had reached the point where any quartet performance had become virtually impossible. Rowe and Cardew in fact became increasingly disinterested in creating any music whatsoever at the shows, becoming far more likely to engage in discussions of a political nature with the audience. The clear implication was one of an accusatory stance directed at Gare and Prévost for not being so inclined. Sometimes Cardew would show up for a gig but Rowe, in character with his normal mode of operation, would simply not attend. There were previous agreements in place for upcoming concerts however, ones that in good conscience couldn't just be ignored. So in February of that year, the AMM tour through Holland turned out to consist of two duos. Oddly, Prévost and Gare had begun to create free improvisation of a character only marginally removed from what could be heard elsewhere from the London and European free schools (albeit

---

own work as well as, interestingly, a certain amount of dissatisfaction with what he perceived as the "mystical" aspects of "Silver Pyramid," which he was often performing.

with lessons learned from seven years of AMM), while Rowe and Cardew performed a kind of socialist radio theater trying, with varying degrees of success, to somehow merge Marxist and Maoist thought with abstract art, an uncomfortable mix at best.[83]

> *Cor and I would do a festival at somewhere like Den Haag*
> *or Rotterdam and we'd play in the middle of the afternoon*
> *to, like, an FMP jazz audience and completely piss them off.*

Prévost in particular was entirely exasperated with this change in direction and on that tour, which turned out to be the final such for this incarnation of AMM, spent much of the drive to and from ports and cities absolutely reaming Rowe on political and aesthetic grounds. Although it wasn't documented in recordings and no reviews mention it, Prévost believed that the kind of playing he became engaged in with Gare was something that had been brewing within AMM for some amount of time. [84]

----

83   Evan Parker recalled that during this period, a couple of concerts were performed with a quartet that included Cardew, Rowe himself playing "Lou Gare's part," and drummer Dennis Smith in the Prévost role. At the same time, he would play in a quartet with Prévost, Gare, and Paul Lytton.

84   The two releases documenting the Gare/Prévost duo, *AMM at the Roundhouse* from August 22, 1972 (originally issued on Incus, reissued on CD by Anomalous Records in 2002) and *AMM To Hear and Back Again*, made up of performances from June 1973, November 1974, and April 1975 (issued on Matchless in 1994), provide a reasonable snapshot of the music the pair had migrated toward. A review in the *Sunday Evening Advertiser* of a Gare/Prévost concert that took place on June 4, 1972 would seem to indicate that the transition from AMM music as it had been practiced previously and the kind of music represented in subsequent recordings by the duo may have been a gradual one, as the writer notes that Prévost "experimented with various forms of banging, tapping and scraping, using the floor, drum stands and anything else that came to hand" while also advising the audience, "Just listen to the silence." Given the work of the previous seven years, however, the overwhelming first impression is how close to free jazz the playing is, how full it is of the very sort of approach which had been jettisoned earlier. The Roundhouse recording is to be sure an extremely strong one of the type, and *utilizes* more space between sounds than a typical freely improvised performance from the period (as well as an impressive array of extended techniques), but its essential structure is one of call and response and much of the instrumental work on the part of both musicians is

We didn't change direction then—more consolidated the way we were going—we gained a kind of urgency. The direction changed before Cardew and Rowe left. They weren't really interested in playing. I became very aware of the direction I wanted to go. The other two decided to drop out and it really took the brakes off.[85]

Independent of political issues, Prévost found that his own musical approach was changing as well, recalling in 1983 that "my drumming became more obviously drumming too"[86] around that time.

Martin Davidson, in a review for *Melody Maker* dated March 25,

---

clearly jazz-derived. It's difficult to listen to this session without wondering if this music had been pent up for years or if the extreme antagonism toward Rowe and Cardew led to a rejection of the earlier more purely experimentalist music they espoused, along with the more recent, expressly political variety. The Matchless disc begins with "Unity First," the most recent piece on the album (4/1/75) and, oddly, it's the most conservative from either recording, a relaxed jaunt through territory similar to that covered by, for example, AACM musicians since the late 60s. The bulk of the release, "To Hear" and "Back Again" (11/30/74), is only slightly edgier, bearing strong affinity to the classic 1967 John Coltrane/Rashied Ali session, *Interstellar Space*. Again, much of the music is first rate, but at the same time it's so conceptually distant from AMM's 1965-71 work as to imply a rejection of at least several of its principles— this despite the retention of the name, AMM. In a review written for *Jazz and Blues* (May 1973), Martin Davidson noted, "Today they [AMM] work mainly as a duo of Lou Gare, playing tenor saxophone in a refreshing style that comes out of Rollins (with a few much older phrases thrown in), and Eddie Prévost, drumming on a conventional jazz kit in a style that has certain similarities with Sonny Murray and with the free Max Roach...Their music is vaguely reminiscent of that of Ayler and Murray, except that they do not use tunes as a springboard." The pair also began to participate with musicians more firmly based in the free jazz realm. One such, listed as "Groupe A.A.M." [!], in Brussels on October 28, 1973, included Gare and Prévost with Marcio Mattos, Marc Meggido, and Derek Bailey. It should be noted, however, that Prévost continued to mount performances of his "Spirals," an entirely more abstract piece, through at least 1973. See Appendix B for a fuller fleshing out of Prévost's general view of his musical situation as of 1974.

85   Eddie Prévost, *Melody Maker*, 12/30/1972.

86   *New Perspectives*, 1983.

1972, describes an AMM concert (no date listed) that began with just Gare and Prévost, then included Cardew (arriving on stage after Gare had graciously dusted the piano keyboard). No mention is made of Rowe.[87] He had, apparently, just "walked away" from the group. At the time, AMM, some six years old, simply wasn't so much of a concern for him and could be easily discarded; it was something readily dropped, the ongoing political battle in the Scratch Orchestra having become much more of an important matter. The other members of AMM were caught in the web of his general societal critique, and for him the group had become irrelevant.

In the ensuing year, Rowe and Cardew played occasionally as a duo,[88] refining their politically oriented music and delving ever deeper into the reasons behind their own art. Evan Parker sat in with them on occasion, not having a clear idea which of the duos was "AMM" or if both were. Apparently, they would still make use of Cardew's graphic notation now and then as Parker recalled asking him how he was to interpret a circle. Cardew responded, "I don't know, ask Keith. He's good with these things." Prévost and Gare didn't intentionally choose to bill themselves as "AMM," but every time they'd get a gig or a review, they were referred to as such and eventually gave up and accepted the name.

*

On May 22, 1972, Music Now presented a major concert at Royal

---

87   On March 26 of that year, AMM joined with Gunter Hampel's band (including Jeanne Lee, Perry Robinson, Evan Parker, Alexander von Schlippenbach, Günter Christmann, and Buschi Niebergall) for a concert in Frankfurt, explicitly signaling their willingness to engage in free jazz, an idea they'd specifically eschewed seven years before. There is virtually nothing of the "AMM concept" of the previous seven years to be heard here.

88   Cassettes of some of the Rowe/Cardew performances exist and are evaluated by John Tilbury in his Cardew biography. They've never been publically released and I haven't had the opportunity to hear them.

Albert Hall as part of a series of events that included performances by the Scratch Orchestra, the Composer's Pool, and the Promenade Theatre Orchestra.[89] This evening also included the premiere British concert of John Cage and David Tudor. The program was in two parts, the first a simultaneous presentation of Tudor's "Rainforest" and Cage's "Mureau," the second also a simultaneous reading, this time of Tudor's "Untitled" and Cage's "Mesostics re: Merce Cunningham." The event received a good amount of pre-concert publicity, notably in *Microphone* magazine.

This publication had been begun by Nigel Rollings and Brian Eley in early 1972 and lasted for seven issues. "Magazine" may be stretching the term, as it was stapled paper ranging from four to twelve pages. By the second issue, it had taken on the subtitle, *New Music in London*, exchanging that in issue #4 for *New Music in Britain*. Its first issue included Steve Reich's essay, "Music as A Gradual Process," Hugh Davies' "Future Developments in Electronic Music" (including a graphic score by Laurie Scott-Baker which looks very "'Treatise'-ian" in form), as well as various concert listings, including one for AMM on February 18 where only Prévost and Cardew are mentioned.

The second issue immediately established a give and take within the musical community as Evan Parker responded to Reich's essay with a forceful volley against "process" as defined by Reich and in favor of "group improvisation," ending with the epigram, "No composers—no leaders—no hierarchy." This view, in turn, was countered by Michael Nyman who, in passing, touches on a number of concerns embroiling the members of AMM with regard to issues of leadership and hierarchy. He wrote:

> You are what you feel; performing in "Drumming" I felt in no way inferior (hierarchically or otherwise) except for

---

89   The Promenade Theatre Orchestra was an offshoot of the Scratch Orchestra, founded by John White and including among its members Christopher Hobbs and Hugh Shrapnel.

the fact that my drumming technique was not as sound as X or Y's. Ironically, because of the nature of Reich's musical processes you were able to "escape" without much difficulty from the music, while still playing, leaving you free to be more yourself than in any other music, while still contributing to it which flowed on regardless.[90]

Microphone magazine #4 (May 1972) had featured several articles on Cage in anticipation of the concert event, a major occurrence for London's avant-garde. The following issue, June 1972, was devoted largely to percussionists (Paul Lytton, Tony Oxley, Frank Perry, and others) but also featured a "review" of the Cage/Tudor performance by Rowe. In reality it was not a review at all, rather a polemical attack on the very premises of Cagean music and philosophy. Subtitled, "Music and Literature for Whom?," it led off with a quotation from Mao:

> In the world today all Culture and art and Literature are geared to definite political lines. There is in fact no such thing as art for Art's sake, art that stands above classes, art that is detached from or independent of politics.

> CHAIRMAN MAO

It continues:

> Often the basis for John Cage's work is the philosophy of "chance"—"random procedures." For the most part these Ideas developed from the ancient Chinese Book, the I CHING. These Ideas were very much in evidence at the Royal Albert Hall concert, Cage's low mumbling overlaying David Tudor's "Rainforest" and in the second half "Untitled" was, as it started in the programme, his latest

---

90   Cardew worked with various "minimalist" composers during these years and, in fact, appears on the Deutsche Grammophone recording of Reich's "Drumming," recorded in January 1974.

attempt to free the English language from syntax. In a late night television programme Cage stated that the reason why China was able to develop from a backward country to the most hopeful for the future was because of the lack of syntax in the Chinese language. Suggesting therefore that it was not the 30 years of bitter struggle under the leadership of the communist party that liberated the Chinese people, but something peculiar about their language. By standing truth on its head in this way, the only effect Cage can have is to attempt to liquidate the flames of struggle in the world. Cage feels that we are living in a rational-irrational situation, that he can perfectly well do something unnecessary, frivolous, he can be grand one moment and idiotic the next, and there's no reason why he shouldn't.

By peddling this nonsense Cage is upholding the line of the "Bourgeois individualist" that everything is subject to "personal opinion" that there are no facts, that it's fine to leave everything to "chance," that there are no definite scientific methods for solving problems. Cage's line both in his writing and music helps to sow confusion and promote disunity, and in doing so definitely support the most oppressive class in the world's history—U.S. Imperialism. The facts of history show that when the people organise under the Revolutionary leadership every miracle can be performed.

The outlook for Cage and the Imperialist Class reeling from one defeat to another both economically and politically is very dark. Whilst the outlook for the world's people is extremely bright, they are growing from strength to strength,

"Revolution is the main trend in the world today"
–CHAIRMAN MAO

Clearly, the intent of the article wasn't to critique the music, which is barely mentioned at all, but more to utilize the magazine as a soapbox from which to proselytize for his Maoist beliefs, conveniently skewering a hero of the avant-garde as an unwitting bourgeois tool in the process. As with much doctrinaire, rigidly leftist thought, politics is the be-all and end-all of human action. Everything is a problem that can be solved with the appropriate political action, a means toward or an avenue away from a solution to that problem. "Art for art's sake" or the mere contemplation of the nature of reality, of randomness, and found beauty was no longer permissible. While AMM had always sought to incorporate the entirety of the available world in which they were embedded into their art, this approach was now too general, not specifically committed to the improvement of life for the working class. Rowe's writing style is both florid and disdainful. He's not only challenging one of the 20th century's most prominent icons (all well and good), he's doing so in a hubristic manner that offers absolutely no possibility of any notion that there might be anything to discuss, that there could be the slightest fissure in his own premises. As was (and is) not uncommon in politically extreme thought, his words take on the zeal of the religious fanatic: "If you do things my way, every miracle can be achieved."

Taken piece by piece, many of the statements are at least defensible if not more or less obvious. It's the ruthlessly posited, no-contrary-opinions-allowed stance that sticks in the craw. One can easily imagine hearing a similar diatribe listing many of society's ills that would generally be acknowledged as accurate and then listening aghast as the author posits salvation through Jesus Christ as the only solution. It's this rigidity of focus, this lack of understanding (at least as far as is evinced in the article) of the enormous complexity of the problem, that baffles and irritates, although one could charitably apply that same simplistically hopeful outlook to a vast number of self-styled revolutionaries.

The following issue of *Microphone*, #6, July 1972 (the next to last edition before it ceased publication, as it happened) contained three letters in response including one from Prévost:

Dear Microphone,

The fundamental error in Keith Rowe's so-called review of the recent John Cage/David Tudor concert is that he confuses random and chance methodology with "laissez-aller" and "laissez-faire." Unfortunately and predictably, Rowe's brand of philosophy is unable to cope satisfactorily with such phenomena (which is indicative of its underlying sterility), except by quoting Cage out of context and using political diatribes.

Whether or not one appreciates or enjoys Cage's music or the colour of his politics, it cannot be disputed that his work has had a great effect upon music and upon how people generally view things. And its influence clearly percolates through to many people and spheres of life who may not even be aware of him. When you come down to it, it is this power to influence which Rowe dislikes.

As for service to the people, that is something which cannot yet, in Maoist terms at any rate, be attributed to any musician—alive or dead—so why pick on John Cage? I suggest that if "serving the people" is so important to Keith and his musical colleagues (namely Cornelius Cardew and the Scratch Orchestra) then they really must make their own musical actions speak louder than their words.

Prévost shows a broader and more deeply considered understanding of the percolative effects of aesthetic ideas, hinting at their often subconscious seepage into unpredictable areas of culture and politics. He makes the acute observation that perhaps there exists a certain jealousy on Rowe's part as to the extent of influence Cage has had on cultural life in the world. More trenchantly, Prévost challenges Rowe and Cardew to put up or shut up and to make their own work in the Scratch Orchestra live up to Rowe's expressed standards.[91]

Perhaps unfortunately, though inevitably, that challenge was taken up.

*

By the late 60s, a feeling of restlessness had crept into Rowe with regard to his marriage to Krystyna. While always remaining amicable, he came to think that the basis of their relationship derived more from a desire on her part to "get back" at her parents, especially her father-in-law for whom Rowe was drastically *persona non grata*. While she was sticking her fingers up to them, for Rowe there was also the aspect of combating class strictures, of "stealing" someone from the (at least purportedly) upper class. Eventually, the perceived lack of any firmer foundation than that, plus a mutual respect and admiration, proved to be too tenuous. There was no "other woman" on his part, just an anxiousness that reached a level where, in retrospect confusedly, he felt he had to leave.

Rowe moved into a London house that was in fact a kind of Buddhist sanctuary, presided over by a monk named Sangharakshita. Residents came and went in almost transient fashion, generally numbering a half dozen or so at a time. At one point in 1969 a couple returned from a pilgrimage to India, one of them named Carol Bell. They were already having marital difficulties and in short order she began a relationship with Rowe.

Though their time together was to last for several years, it was

---

91   In notes for a lecture, dated January 1973, Prévost, while discussing AMM and its approach to music creation, makes no mention of the specifics of the recent schism although he does reflect, "So maybe there is a lot to be said for something which says nothing. But no-one could work believing that he says nothing. And likewise, AMM believe that its music is relevant but we refuse to project a specific meaning onto our work."

a rocky affair. They had two daughters, Karen and Josie, born in 1970 and 1973 respectively. But their living circumstances were drab and relatively penurious. By late 1972, Rowe had virtually given up creating any music at all and had thrown himself into the service of the British Communist party. Though never an actual member, he was extremely active for a year or so, but would soon become disabused of his enchantment. Carol, meanwhile, would grow increasingly committed to Party life, creating ever-rising tension between the two.

Looking back, Rowe believed she tended toward the strongest male in a given situation which happened to be himself in the sanctuary but would be others later on, including higher ups in the party. She eventually married John Buckle, the General Secretary of the Revolutionary Communist Party of Britain (Marxist-Leninist).

Among Party members, there existed the real belief that fascism, explicit fascism not just a rightward drift, could actually gain power in Britain at that time and that it was one of the Party's primary duties to forestall this event. To that end, it would instruct its members or functionaries on where in England to move, focusing on particular hotbeds of proto-fascist activity. In early 1973, instructions were handed down to the couple with their young children to pack up and move to Leicester, where such activity was perceived to be brewing. Rowe gave away to friends all his paintings, all his books, put his AMM guitar in Cardew's cupboard, and the family took off for the north.[92]

Within a few days, he was scanning the local paper for a job. Leicester was a center of printing works and he had some minimal experience in the field so he applied as an operator of a Rotoprint R95 machine, a device he'd seen working but hadn't a clue as to how to operate. He nonetheless called and informed the plant manager that he was an old hand at R95s and got the

---

92   For quite some time, Rowe consciously kept only as many possessions as would fit into a car.

job. That Monday, he was confronted with four huge presses, told where to find his rags and ink, and instructed to get moving. Happily, there was a co-worker in whom he confided the desperateness of his situation who gave him some basic pointers, and in a few days he had gotten the hang of it.

Throughout this period, he was becoming more and more disillusioned with the Party on various grounds, including aesthetic ones, even though their position was essentially the same one that he had recently been championing. Cardew had renounced and even denounced his prior work, including "Treatise," as examples of decadent individualism and elitist art, moving on to explicitly political song forms. Rowe, as it turned out, could never quite make that strong a commitment, regardless of how much posturing on precisely that point he'd been doing in the prior couple of years within AMM and the Scratch Orchestra.

> If you talked to the comrades, abstraction was bourgeois individualism. I'd sit in these cultural meetings and they'd talk about Pollock or Rothko in a way which I couldn't tolerate. I'd still love those paintings...There would be these debates about improvisation, for instance. The party line was that improvisation was bourgeois individualism, drawing attention to the self, all that stuff. I just couldn't go with that. The political party would say that the cultural wing I was working in was independent, but they'd want editorial control over anything we did or said. In the end, I said either we're a democratic unit or we're a unit of the party; you can't have it both ways. And I fell out over that, over a point of principle. The party, I thought, just has to be honest and it wasn't.

He began to recognize that elites tended to form in even the most ostensibly egalitarian of organizations.

> It was the way they treated us at the time. Like, for example, I'd leave work on Friday afternoon or Saturday lunch-

time and I'd walk home and suddenly one of my "comrades"
would appear and say, "We want you to drive to London, to
take comrade so-and-so to London. It's not exactly a safe
house but one of their houses where they'd have meetings."
They said, "Wait until the comrade's meeting is finished,
then drive him home." And I'll be there all Saturday night,
all Sunday and then someone would appear on Sunday eve-
ning, saying, "OK, drive your comrade back." And I'd have
to go to work Monday morning.

Still he wavered, remaining convinced of the overall rightness
and importance of the cause and feeling that the Party had
indeed helped stall and even suppress the fascist movement in
Leicester. But the sense of being abused, of being utilized in a
manner no different than an archetypal capitalist wage slave,
strengthened over the months. He was working at the printing
plant one day after having received some particularly galling
instructions, fuming about it and paying less than appropriate
attention to the machinery with which he was engaged.

I took off the side panel of the machine to adjust the chains
inside it and stuck my thumb in the chain drive and, ouch!
really, really hurt. Chewed the top of my thumb down to the
bone. One of the guys took me in his car to the hospital and
I was in the waiting room. The specialist comes in and says,
"Ah, do you work at the so-and-so press?" And I said, "No, I
work at this other one." He says, "Oh, normally that injury
goes with this particular machine…" He says, "Unfortunate-
ly, I can't see you for an hour or two because there's been
this motorway accident, but I'll give you some pain killers."
So I sat in the waiting room with my thumb going throb,
throb; your whole consciousness goes to this one finger.
There's luck in that though, because in the early evening,
I got to see this surgical specialist guy who says, "OK, well
what we usually do is take it off to the nearest knuckle
and you'll recover quickly." And I say, "No, no, I'm a guitar
player, you can't do that!" And he says, "Well, that's all I can

do. That's the practice here." He went away and came back and says, "If you're willing to wait a few hours, there's an organ player who's also a surgeon who's coming in later this evening and he says he'll spend some time patching up your thumb because, as a musician, he appreciates your situation." So fine, I sit another four or five hours for this Welsh guy to come in and we talked about the organ and Bach and music while he very, very patiently took all the splinters of bone out of the top of my thumb. He said saving my nail was really important and he thought he could do that. He did a tuck and fold, sewed it up underneath, and I went back to work the next morning.

The upshot was a flattened, splayed thumb, one lacking a significant number of nerve endings and only about 50% useful.

Marriage still foundering, the couple returned to London in April 1974.[93] While in Leicester, Rowe had learned that a governmental organization, the Inner London Education Authority, was starting a program for "Media Resource Officers," basically people with arts degrees who would work in schools or other educational environments, counseling on usage of various media skills including video and the emerging field of computers. The program was connected to every school in London so the opportunities for work were wide-ranging and long lasting as well as socially worthwhile and inherently interesting to Rowe. He stayed in that program until the late 80s.

I worked in an anti-discrimination unit in South London, called the Industrial Language Unit. I worked on the images of black people, sometimes teaching camera operators how to film people without discriminating against them. For example, how to capture the image of somebody who is massively overweight without discriminating against them. Or gay men. But especially black people, because of

---

93   They broke up later that year, Carol Bell taking custody of his daughters.

the camera technology in those days that was driven by automatic focusing and light control, black people against a white background often came out as blobs. Whereas you could see the personalities and features of white people, black people didn't have that privilege. If you're politically conscious of what the issue is, you're able to work the technology to get around it. I did that work, with a 15-month training course, video camera operator course, remote learning course, and then went out to work. I got to work in psychiatric hospitals in the psychodrama department, working a camera. I worked in art schools in Central London on the issue of: Was the male gaze different from the female gaze? Was the female nude painted by a female inherently different from one painted by a male? Worked for housing departments on not discriminating on housing for black clients. Worked in an AIDS hospice in London, the Lighthouse. It was very painful, videoing the very last days of mostly men, appallingly thin, very gracefully dying. Because they had very strong hearts, they were 25-26 and would really take a long time. I was videoing them, almost like a video diary for their partners, so they'd have a memory. So I did that job from '74 right up through the 80s, though much of it was part-time, because I'd go on tour, etc. But we got to the point where Thatcher had closed those units down in the late 80s. I was really privileged to have the space and time to work on those issues.

Cardew had in the meantime taken the logical step of joining a musical group dedicated to the promulgation of socialist songs, People's Liberation Music (PLM). Despite having quit Party activities as such, Rowe remained entirely sympathetic to its essential goals and joined the band immediately upon his return to London, becoming a frequent participant over the next several years. Formed in December 1972 by John Tilbury, bassist Laurie Baker,[94] and keyboardist John Marcangelo, PLM was designed as

---

94   Laurie Scott Baker, Australian by birth, had been in England since

an adjunct service for various leftist and workers' causes. From 1974 to 1976, this was Rowe's only musical outlet. It's more than a little strange to see him in photographs, sitting among the other musicians, guitar on knee in the orthodox position. Odder still to hear him gamely strumming along with tunes like, "Smash! Smash! Smash the Social Contract!"

> The proper music for human beings is not the music of the spheres, or birdsong, or the sound of a steam engine, but the dynamic combination of rhythm and melody (which certainly may refer to all these other things) that produces a physical-emotional response in a social context. Only on that foundation of such a response can the mind be stimulated in a meaningful way.[95]

> *When I came back, I was trying to square the music with the social issues. I can put the music aside for a year or so but then I get frustrated. Plus there was a need for a revolutionary, socialist music at the point because there were a lot of street demonstrations. There was a real crunch between the fascists and anti-fascists. The right-to-workers, the Asian woman workers from the film factories. So I picked up the guitar again and began playing it in the regular way.*

In fairness, one shouldn't judge PLM only as a musical group. It served a purely functional role as cheerleader and sloganeer for

---

1965 and had been long involved in performances of Cardew's music and was very familiar with AMM since their beginning. In 1970, Rowe approached Baker about putting together a band with the proposed name, JAMM, that is, a jazz version of AMM. This ensemble, consisting of Rowe, Baker, Gare, and Prévost, would act as an "afternoon tea" ensemble within Scratch events. It served a specific role in the Scratch context, a contrasting focal point within a given day's activity, and wouldn't have ever been considered as something to pursue outside, on its own merits.

95   Cornelius Cardew, quoted by Adrian Jack, *Music & Musicians*, The Group Scene, March 1972.

dozens of rallies, protests, and strikers' marches, often blending "classic" songs from the Brecht/Weill songbook, Hanns Eisler, and others with original work which, in truth, didn't live up to its predecessors. But it was never intended to be recorded or to be listened to out of context. Were their lyrics, to be generous, naïve? Of course. But they were "made to order" for the events in which they participated, the musical equivalent of banners and posters, with about the same degree of subtlety. Many of the words, in fact, were written by Party officials who had little or no sense of song form and were set to music by Cardew and others as best they could. Even so, themes that Cardew would develop in his solo piano music of the same period (in many cases very similar to those of Rzewski) can be heard beneath the stridently declaimed lyrics and, in and of themselves, they're often quite beautiful in the judgment of this writer, although the general opinion with the experimental community seems to be that they're hopelessly reactionary.[96]

They often played to crowds perched atop a large flatbed truck, rigged with a generator and amplifiers, a vehicle that could serve more than one purpose:

It was amazing to play on a truck going down Oxford

------

96   As of 2016, two recordings had been issued of PLM proper (they also appear on the Impetus release, *The Cornelius Cardew Memorial Concert*, IMP 28294, 1985). The performances range from ragged to surprisingly slick, although the association of several of the members with the London production of "Hair" and consequent access to decent recording equipment might account for the latter. Rowe can be heard strumming away beneath a number of songs, buttressing the awkward, sloganeering nature of the lyrics, propelling the march along. As far as the group is concerned, their attempt at a hit pop song, "Mr. Media Man," stands out for its catchiness (Rowe is not present on this re-cording), but with regard to Rowe's own music, easily his most surprising play-ing is heard on "Golden Mountain in Beijing" (available on *Consciously*, Music Now, MNCD009, 2007). A traditional Tibetan melody, arranged by Rowe, Baker, and Marcangelo, finds a pure and idyllic Rowe, utilizing a wah-wah pedal no less, soloing in tempo and in tune over the accompaniment. It's actually a very touching performance, all the more so when considered in the broad context of his life up to this point.

Street with the music reverberating off the buildings and trying to contrive the truck being "stuck" against the railings of Hyde Park so the march could go past us and we could play for everyone entering Hyde Park with the police attempting to ensure that this didn't happen.[97]

Not surprisingly, the crowds they often played for vastly exceeded the number of people who had ever heard (or likely even heard *of*) AMM or the Scratch Orchestra. Protest rallies would often draw thousands of supporters (as well as antagonists) who by and large enjoyed the simple, driving, folk song-y pieces and nodded in agreement along with the vacuous, if well-intentioned, lyrics.

> The musicians union would actually give us money to hire a lorry and we'd sling a generator up on it and run cables off it. A drum kit in the back, driving through lousy areas, being attacked by people. There'd be like 2,000 people at the demonstration with PLM in the middle playing Eisler, Kurt Weill, etc. People really supported us. There might have been 100,000 at the demonstration in Trafalgar Square.[98]

It was on one of these occasions that Fred Frith first heard Rowe perform:

> The first time I saw him play, he was playing revolutionary songs, during that period of composer Cornelius Cardew's life when he'd abandoned all improvising as not being "politically correct." They were playing left wing songs and I was disappointed because I was expecting to see this guitarist everyone had been telling me about, and

---

97   Laurie Baker, 2007.

98   Ibid.

he was playing C, F and G. It *was* a bit strange, but not in the way I was expecting![99]

While Cardew thought of PLM as a temporary, ad hoc ensemble and would devote a good deal of time to his more purely, and romantically, classical reinvigorations of folk and workers' songs, this was essentially the entirety of the music Rowe took part in for two years after he joined in 1974. AMM was gone as far as he was concerned[100] and he'd painted himself into an ideological corner with regard to his earlier admired avant-garde composers, causing that potential path to be at least temporarily blocked. For the first year or so of his participation in PLM he was totally committed to its function as well as to his cog-like role in its operation. In addition to his duty as guitarist, he produced much of the graphic material the group used to publicize events, from leaflets to posters.

A *de rigueur* position in the British left of the 70s was a pro-IRA stance, not one of the safest platforms to publicly promote, a reality that was hammered home in late 1976 during a PLM tour of Ireland. During the course of their existence, PLM had become known as individuals to many a political personage, some of whom, like Peter Hain, would go on to positions of prominence in the Irish government. Another such was Maire Drumm, a well-known protest organizer and fan of the band. While they were in Cork, word came that she'd taken ill and been brought to hospital wherein two men disguised as doctors gained entry and shot her dead. There was a wake and funeral scheduled for several days later and the band was asked to go and perform, as it was imagined to be something she'd have liked. Extensive search-oriented

---

99   Interview with Dan Warburton, *Paris Transatlantic*, March 1998.

100   For Rowe, AMM must first always consist of more than two people and secondly, two of those people must be Prévost and himself. As mentioned earlier, Prévost and Gare came to refer to their duo as AMM, though Rowe believes it should have been more properly called AMM II, indicating a subset of the true ensemble.

delays at the Northern Ireland border at the hands of the British Police resulted in PLM's arriving too late for the funeral but, true to custom, there was a memorial singing and drinking party to which they were escorted at the Andersontown Social Club. This was located in a kind of bunker in the middle of a huge, drab concrete housing project. They were told to drive up and, as quickly as possible, get out their gear and hustle inside because of the high possibility of snipers in the area. They did so, and played to a large crowd of Republicans and the extended family of Maire Drumm. Suddenly, in burst seven or eight British soldiers wearing Irish fatigues, acting in an extremely abusive manner, knocking over tables and beer, pushing people up against the wall with their shields and generally behaving brutishly. Then they approached the bandstand.

> *They didn't recognize us. But they recognized our accents when we started talking. They began shouting in these odd-sounding fake Irish accents, "Who the fuck are you?" "What the fuck are you doing here? "The only fucking way that you could get here is through these fucking people…" you know, that kind of conversation. So Cornelius told them that we were playing music. I remember we were actually playing a piece called "The Lid of Me Granny's Bin," a piece from The Troubles. They basically retired with a kind of, "OK, we'll sort you out later, we'll see about you."*

So PLM finished its performance then ran through the reverse procedure they had done when entering the club, hastening their equipment out the door, into the van and took off with a couple of escorts who were apparently armed. They hadn't gone a half-mile when suddenly, bright searchlights blazed on their van. Saracen armored vehicles came racing alongside them and they were forced to the side of the road, against a wall. Soldiers streamed out of the armored cars, herded the van's occupants at gunpoint and marched them into a large nearby military complex that was entirely surrounded by razor wire (except for a helipad on its roof, the only safe way in and out of the area for the British police). They were told they'd be undergoing interrogation. Hurriedly conferring with each other in the few seconds before apprehension, the detainees came up with a rather naïve plan to more or less stick with the truth but enhance it a bit.

> *So they're asking Cornelius, "What do you do?" And he says he's a professor of composition at the Royal Academy. This was obviously met with an incredible amount of derision. But the Irish accents were beginning to fade and it was getting more British, from around Yorkshire or something. "You fucking cunt, you bastards, you pisser!" That sort of thing, pretty rough. They were poking and pushing us against the wall. I remember a machine gun being pressed into my armpit. Being pretty brutal. I'm not being tortured but it's not pleasant. You realize that you really shouldn't walk or go to the toilet or show them your back because they just might shoot you in the back. It was a very, extremely macho kind of culture, pretty sick characters.*

The soldiers returned to the interrogation rooms, apparently having had some communication via telex about Cardew and learning that he was considered something of a hot potato possibly due to his familial lineage. Rowe recalls having the distinct impression that they had been given the message that it was better to leave these particular feathers unruffled. Having been thus deprived of an evening's fun, the disgruntled soldiers loaded the musicians back in the van saying, "Don't think this is the end" and then, more chillingly, "Remember the Miami Show Band." The previous year, that group, a popular Irish cabaret band that played for pro-IRA causes, was stopped by members of the UVF (Ulster Volunteer Force), a paramilitary loyalist organization. Two UVF personnel were attempting to surreptitiously place a bomb in the group's van when it exploded prematurely killing them. Their comrades opened fire on the musicians, killing three of the band members.

> *So they threatened that for us, that they'd put a bomb in*

the van and that we should just drive and if we got out
of the vehicle, they would shoot us. The only choice you
have is to keep driving and hope that they haven't done so,
which they hadn't. So we're driving down the road, fairly
confident that we're all right and then we're stopped by
the English Army, the "good" army, just a few minutes later.
This time Brigid winds down the window and she's just had
enough. She gives them a tongue lashing, launching into
them. We're saying, "Brigid, Brigid, put a sock in it!" She's
invited to step out of the vehicle once again. And we're
saying, "Oh, come on, we've just spent five hours in the
bloody police station, give us a break." And they checked
that and they're about to allow us to go on our way when
a very small car drives right through the checkpoint and
they proceed to shoot the shit out of the back of this car
because it had gone through the roadblock. The guy in the
car probably didn't realize it. I think he's killed, yeah. We
found out later a young banker or something was killed.
Brutal, brutal.

Though PLM would return to play in Ireland, that was the last
such tour Rowe took part in. He continued performing with them
but his interest in that sort of music and explicit politics was
waning.

By '76, I'd completely returned after three or four years of
disruption in my head about social events and qualities and
came back to where I'm normally at. It's kind of interesting
to be in that position, because when I pick up a newspaper
or watch TV and see very extreme actions taking place, I'm
not saying I condone them, I'm not saying I can understand
them, but this [Al Qaeda executions in the early 00s]—and
I've never, obviously, been in such an extreme position as
considering cutting someone's head off—but I do kind of
understand something of that position, of how it makes you
blind. I feel a very important quote is one from this New
York detective, the one who defeated the mafia in Manhat-

tan. He said, when he was asked what he had learned from the experience, it was "not to hate your enemy because it makes you blind." And I think that's what happened to me.

By 1976, for Rowe's part, the tensions between him and Prévost had essentially evaporated. As far as he was concerned, certain events had transpired but they should be able to move past that and continue on. He didn't feel the need to apologize for his actions, perhaps no more so than he would have thought to explain a particularly discordant or awkward passage during an AMM performance. It happened; it's over; what's next? As events many years later would indicate, Prévost, though keeping his lid clamped at the time, appeared to have never quite reconciled himself to Rowe's actions but was willing to make accommodations for the time being. One surmises that he also had begun to tire of the jazz-based improvisation he and Gare had been creating and looked forward to a renewed delving into the abstract, the air having been cleared.

Rowe had gone and heard the Prévost/Gare duo and thought their music was very good, very sensitive, though it never, to him, was AMM music no matter that they'd retained the name. For Rowe the concept "AMM" necessitated the "chemical reaction" between him and Eddie. Without that, the tension required to reach the deeper levels of acoustic aesthesia was impossible. By late 1975 or early '76, he sat in with the duo on occasion on an impromptu basis, though Gare wasn't convinced he could simply "show up" and automatically return to the level of playing they'd achieved seven or eight years earlier.

By the end of '76 though, they had actually agreed to reform as a quartet, Cardew newly, if tentatively in tow, a decision which seemed solid enough that Rowe designed a postcard exclaiming, within a starburst balloon, "AMM—Together Again." They never actually held a performance however, only getting as far as printing that card before Gare suddenly up and decided to go off and live in Devon, disrupting the logistics of the group.

Shortly thereafter, Cardew apparently rethought the notion of dipping his toes back into abstraction and returned full-bore to a political program.

That left Rowe and Prévost, rarely playing, muddling along as a duo.

c.1947, a student in the Plymouth Public School System

TOP: c. 1952, with classmates
BOTTOM: c. 1957, at Plymouth Art School (Rowe third from left in rear)

c. 1955

This startling form of "art" is evidently fascinating the bystanders, or perhaps they are just as intrigued by the antics and ultra-Bohemian garb of the "artists." This almost-Parisian scene, in Plymouth City Centre today, was just one facet of Plymouth and Devonport Technical College students' Rag Week activities. (See Page Three.)

c. 1958, Rag Week at Plymouth Art School, Rowe in derby

237

c. 1959, Mike Westbrook band
TOP PHOTO: l. to r.: Stan Willis, Ron Hills, Westbrook, Graham Russell, Dave Webb
BOTTOM PHOTO: l. to r.: Terry Lidiard, Rowe, Malcolm Le Grice

28	BERKELEY SQUARE	£40
*29	INGRES AND BATHSHEBEE (Print)	£5
*30	YOUNG WOMAN (Print)	£5
*31	TWO WOMEN (Print)	£5
32	DRAWING	£15
33	DRAWING	£10
34	DRAWING	£10
35	DRAWING	N.F.S
36	DRAWING	N.F.S

* Unframed prints £3 each

Underhill (Plymouth) Ltd., Printers. Works: Rogers Street

CITY ART GALLERY, PLYMOUTH

PLYMOUTH PAINTERS

4

TONY COMMON
BOB HARRISON
KEITH ROWE
MIKE WESTBROOK

4th to 21st APRIL, 1963

CATALOGUE

All works in oil unless otherwise stated

TONY COMMON, born Indian Queens, Cornwall, 1940. Studied at Plymouth College of Art. Now working in London and making a film.

1	THE LINE	£50
2	STIRLING MOSS	£50
3	FILM	£50
4	IMAGES IN THE WALL	£50
5	THINGS AND IMAGES (I)	£50
6	THINGS AND IMAGES (II)	£50

BOB HARRISON, born Devonport 1939. Studied at Plymouth College of Art and London College of Printing. Now working in a London Printing House.

7	YELLOW LANDSCAPE	£10
8	ROMANTIC LANDSCAPE	£20
9	THE MOON	£15
10	WEST HOE	£20
11	THE SUN (on aluminium)	£10
12	RETURN TO PLYMOUTH	N.F.S
13	THE FINAL SCENE	£20

KEITH ROWE, born Plymouth 1940. Studied at Plymouth College of Art. Now working in London. Jazz guitarist.

14	LOVERS	£60
15	CHURCH WITH RED WINDOW	£50
16	CHURCH WITH ANGELS AND STARS	£50
17	SMALL CHURCH	£53
18	LONG LOVERS AND VIEW FROM WINDOW	£60
19	PORTRAIT OF AN ANGEL	£30
20	WOMAN	£50
21	ELLA AND OSCAR	N.F.S
22	LIFE	N.F.S
23	JAZZ	N.F.S

MICHAEL WESTBROOK, born High Wycombe 1936, but has lived in Devon since 1940. Studied at Plymouth College of Art. Now married and living in London. Leads own jazz group.

24	THE RIDER	£40
25	THE RED SAIL	£30
26	SERPENTINE	£60
27	APPLE TREES	£30

1963, catalogue of painting exhibition

c. 1964, TOP PHOTO: l. to r.: Rowe, Mike Osborne, Lou Gare.
BOTTOM PHOTO: Rowe, Osborne

c. 1964, Rowe while with Westbrook

Sheaff Rowe Prevost Steve Lacy (Amm with steve lacy?)
(white coats are Ammi 'uniform' slaughter house ware)

TOP: 1966, AMM at Royal College of Art
BOTTOM: 1966, AMM. l. to r.: Rowe, Cornelius Cardew, Gare, Eddie Prévost

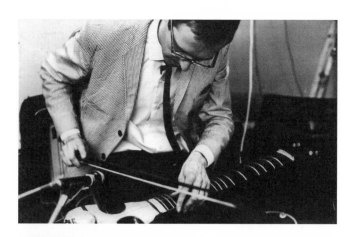

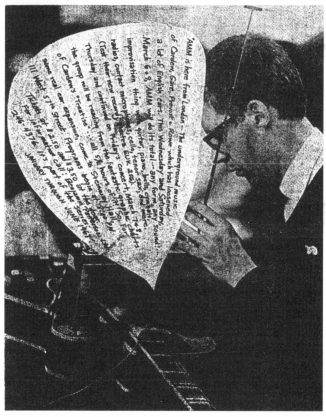

TOP: c. 1966, at the Indian Art Institute
BOTTOM: Photo from *Village Voice,* March 7, 1968, on the occasion of AMM's first US visit

1977, Rowe, Cardew

c. 1979, photos from newspaper article on music therapy
Liam Genocky on the left in bottom photograph

TOP: c. 1981, in performance
BOTTOM: Early 80s, in performance

AMM, c. 1987, l. to r.: Rohan de Saram, Prévost,
Gare, Rowe, John Tilbury

Early 90s, in performance

2014, Nantes, France. During rehearsal with Christian Wolff and Tilbury
as part of the Wolff's 80th birthday celebration

Chapter 7

After the political and musical turbulence of the early and mid-70s, Rowe's life settled into something of a routine as much of his time was spent working at an increasingly responsible position in the occupational therapy world. He had a handful of brief romantic relationships but lived alone, devoting more energy to his daily job than to any musical investigations. For a couple of years, virtually his only outlet in that regard was as a result of the rapprochement with Prévost.

They played sporadically as a duo, garnering the odd gig here and there, attempting the possibly insoluble task of translating AMM music into something that could be manifested by only two musicians, a tough enough problem as such but made far more so by their intermediate work (PLM and AMM II) which didn't offer obvious pathways between any desirable goal and where they had found themselves situated. Rowe's conservative playing with PLM might have had the effect of opening him up to a somewhat more melodic and, ironically, individualistic approach to the guitar, not the most fertile ground for cultivating AMM music. It certainly caused him to at least temporarily put on the back burner the basic principles he'd established some ten to twelve years prior. He now often held his instrument in the orthodox position and would not be actively loath to tune it on occasion though a brief mention of the pair in a festival review of an event at Hammersmith Town Hall by Karl Dallas cites Rowe "doing unspeakable things to his guitar" as well as Prévost "sawing at his cymbals with a bow" indicating that, at least as far as instrumental attack, the duo was maintaining a certain amount of "tradition." More oddly, they found themselves on occasion playing compositions.

Cardew continued on in PLM as well as writing his own works for solo piano in the socialist-realist style (such as "Thälmann Variations"), though Rzewski's music in the same vein gained far greater public visibility. Having rejected the temptation to rejoin AMM in 1976, his later work seemed to be at least partially concerned with attempting to bridge that gap and, toward the end of his life, he'd once again consider a reunion.[101]

Before there was any documentation of the Rowe/Prévost duo, however, another opportunity availed itself. In 1978, Trevor Watts, one of the founding members of the Spontaneous Music Ensemble, the improvising group begun in 1966 which, while retaining a goodly amount of jazz-based elements, was otherwise as close in conception to AMM as any in England at the time, invited Rowe to play with his band, The Universal Group, which included musicians such as pianist Howard Riley and bassists Harry Miller and Barry Guy. Though Rowe only participated in a handful of concerts with that particular line-up, Watts thought he would be a good fit in another of his working ensembles, Amalgam, and asked him to join in early 1979.[102] While Amalgam, as its name implies, had incorporated any number of different

---

101   An undated concert flier announces a quintet show with Cardew, Rowe, Prévost, Marcio Mattos and another indecipherable name, though Rowe cannot recall exactly when it occurred.

102   As well, in Rowe's day job he often found himself working alongside Liam Genocky, Amalgam's drummer. The two would offer therapeutic sessions to seniors and other individuals in recovery institutions via percussion sessions. An article in the March 9, 1980 edition of the *Sunday Mirror*, titled "Bashing Way to Get Well" includes a photo of the pair doing just that with several middle-aged women. Genocky made regular appearances at the time on *Top of the Pops* as a member of Gerry Rafferty's band whose "Baker Street" was a huge hit, so his showing up in group homes like this one was something of an event.

approaches in its music since its formation in the late 60s, a decade on it tended toward a kind of harsh, aggressive jazz-rock of a general type that had become relatively popular in the wake of Ornette Coleman's electric Prime Time band. Watts was excited to have him as part of the group, though the invitation carried a strange odor as far as Rowe was concerned. Watts was quite knowledgeable about AMM and Rowe's contributions thereof yet wanted him to play far more conservatively in Amalgam, in the vein of James Blood Ulmer perhaps. He may have been aware of Rowe's work with PLM and felt that, if anything, an approach such as his would steer him into more creative streams but Rowe, already struggling to venture back into experimental music via the duo with Prévost, didn't take it as such and was somewhat miffed at being asked to play in what he felt, ironically given his activity in the early 70s, was an essentially reactionary fashion. As well, to the extent that the music bore the influence of punk rock (or "punk jazz" à la the nascent No New York scene), this came in the wake of Cardew's incendiary article, "Is Punk Rock Fascist?" from a couple of years prior[103], something that may have still resonated for Rowe. Still, it was an outlet for playing so he accepted, at the same time crafting an especially devious way to both satisfy Watts' demands and to create a meta-commentary on the music. He strolled into a local musical instrument establishment, bought a couple of "how to" books (*Improvised Rock Guitar* and *20 Great Rock Guitar Licks*), dutifully learned the bland, clichéd sequences contained therein and regurgitated them in performance with Amalgam, albeit slightly camouflaged and played more roughly than presumably intended. Just as he had done with AMM, hearkening back to what he had learned studying Gurdjieff, Rowe felt no need to inform Watts or the other musicians of what he was in fact doing.

The riff-oriented nature of his conception is immediately clear on the opening track of Amalgam's 4-LP set, *Wipe Out*. A three-note descending sequence is brutally hammered out throughout

---

103   *Nua-Chultúr*, July 27, 1977.

the entire piece, fuzz-drenched and redolent of recent punk. It achieves a kind of classic, hyper-concentrated minimalism reminiscent of Tony Conrad a decade or more prior, while at the same time the group as a whole prefigures Last Exit from a few years hence. (In a review of a live show, Ken Ansell referred to Rowe's playing in Amalgam as "claustrophobically repetitive," an accurate assessment.) Later on in the cut, Rowe drops the fuzz and articulates some ringing variations on the same theme (with a surprisingly Coryell-like tone) before viciously dropping back into the sludge. His playing manages to be both awful in a show-offy, macho fashion and fascinating for its sheer ostentatiousness and car-wreck aspect. Several times he launches into rapid fire picking, the kind of playing that doubtless would wow the odd refugee from a prog-metal show but it's all surface, all pose. On many of the pieces, Watts appears to be employing a kind of harmolodic approach, all instruments "soloing" all the time, though Rowe could be said more accurately to be comping or riffing continuously. On others, the band sounds like a fragmented version of the music Arthur Blythe was creating around the same period, except that the drumming tends decidedly toward the leaden. To be sure, when called upon to do so, Rowe plays the thematic material, often in tandem with Watts, in a clean and entirely satisfactory manner. Though he probably never mentioned the specifics of his sly attack, Rowe felt that, overall, his fellow musicians weren't very fond of it, bassist Colin McKenzie apparently being particularly baffled at just what it was that he was supposed to be contributing. One can easily understand why, McKenzie having taken on the Jamaaladeen Tacuma role, unspooling heady and complex jazz-funk bass flurries all over the place whilst Rowe more or less repeated simple figures without cease. All told, it's one of the odder chapters in Rowe's career, difficult to listen to in light of prior and subsequent developments, a little as though Rothko was constrained to produce imitation Warhols. The group played a decent number of concerts and festivals over the year Rowe was a member, usually a couple a month, and since he was otherwise working a regular job, it provided a means to maintain his presence on the music scene. Eventually, however, it became clear that the direction Watts wanted to travel was increasingly at odds with the music Rowe was beginning to reform with Prévost and the two agreed to part company. As a perverse justification for the effect of Rowe's strategy in Amalgam, one need look no further than Barry McRae's review of *Wipe Out*:

> ...it is perhaps Rowe whose playing surprises most. The man once concerned with AMM's "search for sound" here produces music that is genuinely personal and full of heart. On *Wipe Out* it is rock orientated, on *Outgoing Situation* he produces a guitar ostinato like a drone, while on *Homecoming* he almost adopts the flow of the saxophone. On *War Dance* he even takes over the responsibilities of the absent bass player, serving the group before considerations of self-aggrandizement.

The mind reels.

One might accept Rowe's approach as a unique and mischievous way to subvert what he felt to be ill-informed expectations, putting aside for the time being the sort of music he'd create if things were totally up to him, adopting the meta-role of purveyor of banal guitarisms for a retrograde musical conception. But things apparently weren't so simple. There was no particular reason to expect that those same forms would be used when he returned to AMM music or that he'd play traditionally in any manner whatsoever given the opportunity to reunite with Prévost. But to a large extent, that's exactly what occurred, making the subsequent album an even stranger item in the Rowe discography, perhaps the strangest.

Over the course of the 70s, ECM Records, founded in 1969 by Manfred Eicher, had risen from a small, independently produced label specializing in the further reaches of the European and American jazz avant-garde to a thriving concern, distributed worldwide by Polydor, and sporting some of the bigger names in the field, though issuing music that was generally much less abstract in nature than had been the case originally. Steve Lake, an Englishman and writer, had done liner notes for the label and was gradually being given other responsibilities including scouting out music for potential release, either on ECM or its sister label JAPO which issued slightly more adventurous fare. He'd been an admirer of AMM, had owned and enjoyed *AMMMusic* and had taped AMM performances off BBC radio when he was a youngster. He knew Prévost and Gare, having seen and appreciated their duo in action during Rowe's time with PLM. In 1978, Prévost wrote him, offering ECM a licensing deal on the Elektra sessions, though Lake suggested he contact Chris Cutler at Recommended Records instead, which Prévost eventually did. But Lake had heard that Prévost and Rowe were working together once again and was a huge fan of the current incarnation of Amalgam so, without ever actually hearing the pair, he offered a studio session in Ludwigsburg, Germany which took place in December 1979, resulting in the album, *It had been an ordinary enough day in Pueblo, Colorado.*

The project got off to an inauspicious beginning as British Airways lost all of Rowe's and Prévost's equipment and took more than a day to recover it, reducing the time available in the studio. Lake recounts an interesting anecdote, indicating that Rowe's political sympathies and their inherent crudeness hadn't entirely changed:

> Keith and I almost immediately had an argument. On the way to the session I'd just been reading a newspaper article about the Dalai Lama, who interested me a lot in 1979. I mentioned this at dinner and Rowe went off the deep end, loudly arguing *in favor* of the Chinese invasion and occupation of Tibet! When I've read occasional interviews with Keith since then he's always sweepingly dismissive of some nation (the French can't play jazz) or idiom or music *in total* and it seems in character with that first impression, and I've sometimes thought, yeah, it figures: the guy who said that the Tibetan monks and

nuns were asking for it. They were very good haters, the Cardew clique, and some of their followers still are.

The music produced that day remains singular in AMM's discography, certainly the least representative recording of their work and as fate would have it due to the label's prominence, by far the best-selling, as many as 50,000 by Rowe's estimate. In a decided break from past practices, the two had been working through pieces that were essentially pre-plotted if not precisely composed. "Radio Activity" had been performed by them on several occasions prior, including once on BBC radio, and was constructed in a set sequence of events. Heard on its face, especially if one had knowledge of previous AMM music, it's something of a shock. The first couple of minutes might have come as a welcome indication that Rowe and Prévost were "back in the fold," a low guitar drone accompanied by ethereal stroked metal and clatter with a radio capture bleeding in around the edges—classic AMM. Suddenly, however, there's a smooth, sustained guitar on top of things that sounds like nothing other than Robert Fripp in full Frippertronics mode. It's tonal, quasi-virtuosic, and disconcerting, to say the least, though not too dissimilar to his playing on the Tibetan piece from the PLM session a few years earlier. Clearly, the guitar is in the upright position and being attacked "normally." In fact, for this date, largely recorded in real time save for an edit here and there (including a snatch of disco-y radio considered too prosaic for inclusion in the session!), Rowe utilized two guitars, sometimes both flat, sometimes played as heard here and often engaged simultaneously. It's the *language* employed that's disorienting, the phrasing having become more standardized, more subject to external conventions; one usually knows with some degree of certitude what's coming next. Prévost, on this piece, is actually much more in tune with AMM logic although he too is on occasion more overtly reactive than had been the case previously. When, some nine minutes in, Rowe rips off a Sharrock-ian flurry, Prévost immediately switches to drum set and, in the spirit of "traditional" free jazz improvisation, joins in for a sparring match. This section in particular, though it might easily fit in with the sort of avant-jazz/

rock melding that was beginning to take place around the globe (in downtown New York City, especially), seems so utterly in opposition to the principles vigorously and explicitly espoused during AMM proper's tenure as to leave one shaking one's head. There's no reticence, no care in sound placement; everything is garish and obvious, potential pathways being shut down left and right. After the fine and serendipitous radio capture that served to impart the title to the album, Prévost's small metallic tinkling is offset by some echo-y twanging, again both overly smooth and gestural. Then comes possibly the most bizarre segment. In the final moments of the 18-minute track, Rowe strums a gentle, slightly funky, entirely melodic, and pretty little motif, something that wouldn't be out of place over the closing credits of a contemporaneous, saccharine, romantic television comedy.

The explanation, at least partial, of the strangeness of this piece lies in the fact that it was indeed pre-assembled and in a vaguely programmatic manner at that. Likely more at the hands of Rowe than Prévost, "Radio Activity" was intended as a mini-history of AMM from 1965 to 1978, including specific events such as the US tours (echoes of Hendrix?) and the disparate paths taken by it members subsequent to the 1972 break-up. Thus the "Fripp-like" guitar near the beginning is intended to represent the cello, always the quintessential AMM instrument to Rowe, in all its Romantic splendor. Admittedly, drawing further direct parallels is no easy task (perhaps the closing, pretty chords are a reference to the "café music" he and Prévost once undertook during Scratch events) and one tends, if anything, to hear echoes of his 70s activity with PLM and Amalgam more than other sources. It seems clear that Rowe hadn't entirely worked out how to free himself of the strictures he'd imposed on both his playing and his musical philosophy over the previous six or seven years. [104]

---

[104]   This desire to recapitulate his own or AMM's prior history would ecur over the years up through the live solo concert from September 2007 issued on ErstLive and beyond, including the 50th anniversary reunion concerts in 2015 inHuddersfield and at Café Oto, London.

The four tracks on Side Two muddy the water even further. "Convergence," an improvisation, opens with strummed guitar that recalls flamenco motifs and brushed drums before settling into much the same spiky playing, albeit augmented by wah-wah (!), as heard in the middle of "Radio Activity." It's very call and response in nature, Prévost sounding more than a little like Barry Altschul to Rowe's...Michael Gregory Jackson? The piece could almost have been lifted from a routine post-Loft Jazz session. "Kline," again improvised, though the title seems to have come from Rowe, is quite similar in general attack except that it's softer—a balladic version of the prior track. Rowe squeezes out plaintive, ringing tones, referencing blues forms though in a very clean, English manner that indeed recalls Frith's work from his solo album on Caroline, recorded in 1974, making for a disjointed boomerang feel. Prévost gets a feature (can one even imagine using such a term in relation to an AMM musician a decade before?) on "Spittlefields' Slide," drumming for all he's worth in standard post-Roach avant style, Rowe gamely scratching and plucking away behind. It might be the most distressing cut here, not that it's bad playing in and of itself—it's not—but that it sounds so entirely banal in the context of what was being played in 1979, so utterly without any kind of conception, just thoughtless, rote musicianship, something one would have thought they'd left well behind in 1965. Rowe's "For A," a composition of his that he would record at least twice more, is a programmatic piece relating to an ex-girlfriend and attempting to limn various aspects of her character, the difficulties they experienced, etc. Nonetheless, aside from a repeating guitar vibrato throughout, it's essentially Rowe wailing away with a fuzz-toned axe and Prévost providing various percussive accents. In other words, more quasi-jazz rockish noodling. Apart from the first couple of minutes on the album, a blindfolded listener would have been hard pressed to identify the musicians here as the same ones who were partially responsible for *AMMMusic*, and that's not to their advantage.[105]

---

105   Although Graham Collier would nominate it as Jazz Album of the Year in *Gay News*.

Even hearing *Pueblo* in the most favorable light, there is certainly a great deal of doubt, here in December of 1979, as to what the future of AMM would be, both members making far more reference to their recent musical output than to that prior to 1972. It's almost as if all the grime and sludge from the previous eight years had to be scoured out and regurgitated; a 45-minute belch. Rowe would later say (*The Wire*, 1995), "I'd looked into the chasm and seen what the alternative was; it gave me an even stronger belief in the AMM process." If so, it was a process that took quite a while to work its way through his system.

*

A bit before the JAPO album was recorded, Prévost and Rowe asked John Tilbury to become a permanent member of AMM, thereby creating the core group that would last for almost a quarter century.[106] They'd known him since 1965 from his participation in Cardew performances, had worked closely with him in the Scratch Orchestra, and had invited him to sit in with AMM on occasions when Cardew was unable to make the gig. Rowe and Tilbury, in fact, had played two or three times as a duo in 1976-77 at a small theatre in London during which Rowe recalls that the music created was more closely related to that from the late 60s than what he was concurrently producing either with Amalgam or Prévost (though, unfortunately, no known recordings exist). Tilbury could have been included in the session that became *Pueblo*, but both Rowe and Prévost felt it necessary to document the stage of AMM where they were a two-person unit, hence the name "AMM III" (the Prévost/Gare duo having been, in Rowe's understanding of the nomenclature if not their own, AMM II). Although Tilbury was a known quantity, his inclusion created a fundamentally different AMM than had previously existed. With regard to the issue immediately at hand, he clearly served to expand the musical possibilities far beyond merely increasing the number of musicians from two to three. Whereas

106   Their first concert as a trio was in November 1979.

AMM II was to some degree necessarily polar in nature (Rowe and Prévost), the new AMM possessed triangular coordinates, its depth more a cubing of potentialities than a mere additive function. One can sense a tripodal aspect, an extremely solid and fertile *grounding*, based on the inherent musical qualities of each member. This rootedness is the essential reason one often thinks of this grouping as the "classical" stage of AMM. They operated in a subset of the infinite possibilities of the 1965-72 ensemble; "anything" might still be possible, but it was a somewhat smaller, more refined anything than had existed before, due not only to the number of musicians but the particular combination of musical personalities. Though Tilbury might occasionally wander away from the pianistic, he was essentially the "piano player" (prepared or otherwise), generally the tonal center of the trio, providing an essential lyricism, however tenuous, which could anchor the more extreme explorations of Rowe and Prévost (a function certainly doable by Rowe via drones or Prévost via cymbal bowings, for example, as well, but more routinely handled by Tilbury). While his touch and attack on the keyboard was somewhat similar to Cardew's[107]—more sensitive, arguably—his activity during performance would not normally encompass also negotiating radios, a cello, an accordion, electronics, percussion, etc. The music could not be as *diffuse* as heard on *The Crypt*, not as richly chaotic, but it could become more *concentrated*, more able to be focused on identifiable areas of sound which, in turn, could produce a music just as new and fertile, but more subtly contained and contoured. While still far more present relative to most improvising groups, there was a lesser sense of not knowing who was responsible for a given sound. Rowe, Prévost, and Tilbury tended toward the occupation of more distinct areas: the strings/electronics, the percussive, and the pianistic.

Additionally, Tilbury was by necessity further removed from the concerns that spurred the group at its inception, ideas that had become less radical (if still rarely practiced outside of AMM) over

---

107   Tilbury was himself, of course, strongly influenced by Cardew. He

the intervening fifteen years. He had made something of a name for himself as an interpreter of contemporary scores, having recorded Cage's "Sonatas and Interludes for Prepared Piano," for example, in 1974 so AMM wasn't ever the be-all and end-all for him that it had been for Rowe (prior to 1972, at any rate) and Prévost; he was less *devoted* to the concept, however enthusiastic he might be about it, a subtle difference in the group's make-up that could have both salutary and negative impact. Recorded evidence would have to wait a few years, however.[108]

In the meantime, Chris Cutler's Recommended Records did indeed release *The Crypt* in 1981, bringing AMM's music to a somewhat wider, though still tiny, audience including, one assumes, some listeners intrigued by what they heard on the JAPO recording. Though in reality likely the result of having arbitrarily consulted a given record store owner (or employee)—which was how such lists were often assembled—the August 22, 1981 issue of *Melody Maker*, in its "Charts" section, which had Electric Light Orchestra's *Time* in the #1 Album slot and Foreigner's *Urgent* topping out the Heavy Metal category, included the following Top Ten Independent albums listing:

> #1 AMM – Music at the Crypt
> #2 De Tian – Two Spires

wrote in 1983: "I first met Cardew at the Dartington Summer School in August 1959 when we were both 23 years of age. He had a project in mind, a concert of experimental music for one and two pianos (music by Americans Cage, Feldman, and Wolff, and by Cardew himself), and asked me to be the other pianist… Those floating, sourceless sounds, which he played with an unerring sense of timing and artistry that was convincing as it was unconventional, evoked an emotional response quite unlike any other I had experienced listening to music, and which was intensified by Cardew's profound identification with Feldman's work." [*Contact*, Spring 1983]

108   Intriguingly, in a letter from Rowe (addressee unknown) dated April 24, 1981, referring to a proposed AMM performance two months hence, he writes, "With regard to Treatise we are looking at the possibility of concerts with Rohan de Saram cello, and maybe Cardew himself, at the end of this year, early next."

#3 You're Not Moving the Way You're Suppose To
– The Homosexuals
#4 Corrected Slogans – Art and Language
#5 Present Themselves – The Dave and Phil Duo
#6 Dog Photos – Laughing Hands
#7 Smiley Smile – Beach Boys
#8 Sort Of – Slapp Happy and Faust
#9 Negativland – Negativland
#10 Rags – Lindsay Cooper

*

In November of 1981, Rowe met Stephanie Evans who was working in the Industrial Language unit of the same organization as he. They'd sat in on a few meetings, felt an attraction, and soon began to see each other. Rowe, true to form, downplayed his musical career, enough that Stephanie only vaguely knew it existed. A month later, when Cardew met his death at the hands of a hit and run driver,[109] she was shocked at how much renown this close friend and associate of Rowe's apparently had.

They soon moved in together, making for a relatively stable financial situation. AMM had maintained its policy of never soliciting for gigs which, combined with their almost negligible appeal and affinity with the musical scene, meant long periods between performances. Rowe, now over 40, settled into something of a workaday existence, always (as ever) thinking about aesthetic ideas, rarely having the occasion to actualize them.[110]

*

109   Rowe remains uncommitted as to whether or not the incident was accidental or intentional, the latter possibility as payback for Cardew's political activism.

110   Tilbury made a living as a teacher as well as performer of contemporary classical repertoire. Prévost had a couple of actual jobs, such as laborer on

The issuance of *The Crypt* in the summer of 1981 provided a brief flash of recognition, partly due to the general shock that the music had been recorded thirteen years prior and remained all but unlistenable to ears ostensibly attuned to free music, leavened perhaps, by the nagging sense that those listeners might be missing something. It garnered numerous appreciative reviews, though given its age, many seemed to regard it as something of a closed chapter, a reminder of how bracing and original music could be in 1968 with little thought that the creators of same might still be practicing their art.

In 1982, Hannah Charlton, in *Collusion* magazine, published likely the first thorough history of AMM, based on research and interviews conducted by herself and David Toop in 1980-81. It's no puff piece, containing strong opinions, sometimes questioning ones:

> AMM music is often referred to as being ego-less, which, by comparison with virtuoso, solo front line playing, it was. But, in contradiction, individual egos, still strong, were consumed into a group ego, which became arrogant and exclusive. Cornelius referred to it later as something similar to a secret society. Although the philosophy of AMM music was open, idealistic, pointing the way to a potentially better society, in practice the group was closed to outsiders, and admitted only the influence it wished.

Charlton gets at one peripheral reason for the group's lack of acceptance at the time: "AMM music is, to a large extent, a model of the 60s—the opening up, the general euphoria of the possibility of change, 'doing your own thing' in anything from an utterly flamboyant to an introverted, mystical way." In an era dominated

---

the motorway, but by and large depended on his wife for support, choosing to live as an undistracted musician. *"As a consequence, I think Eddie went through a period of having to be very, very careful with money, a level of poverty that most people in the arts would be very surprised that someone as important as Eddie would have been subject to. He had several kids as well."*

politically by a resurgence of conservatism in the US and England with a concomitant return to traditionalism in jazz and glossy ephemera in rock, AMM was less *au courant* than ever outside of a tiny contingent of admirers. Much the same could be said about a good portion of post-abstract visual art and post-serialist music that came of age in the 60s but would only gain wider general recognition in the 90s from minimalist art and sculpture to Fluxus and Fluxus-inspired music and performance. It was easier, in the 80s, to look back at those movements as self-indulgent or overly arcane instead of attempting to grapple with the issues they raised, which remained as thorny as ever.

Rowe, quite possibly as a partial result of his current on-the-job responsibilities, is quoted as observing:

> *I've come to understand the therapeutic aspect of AMM music: we were not very outward people in the conventional sense, quite quiet, probably suppressed a lot of things and the music is like a ventilator, a way of working things out.*

Indeed, the Dutch pianist/composer Misha Mengelberg remarks, "…it [AMM] was really a *monologue interieur.*"

Charlton casts the revitalization of AMM as a project involving some degree of almost religious fervor, Rowe coming across as its chief proselytizer, concluding:

> There is about it, the sense of a crusading mission, or bringing the achievements of the group to those unfortunate enough to have missed AMM's most creative period.

One of the regrettable results of such an article, admirable as it is in many respects, was to cast AMM as a relic of the past—those strange days of the 60s, a group that, even if it continues to exist in reality, is from here on in to be considered something of an anachronism.

Perhaps the single most frustrating gap in recorded documentation of AMM is the more than two years between the December 1979 *Pueblo* date and the concert recording from The Great Hall in London on February 20, 1982, issued as Disc Two of the *Laminal* 30th anniversary retrospective in 1996. The aesthetic distance between this recording and the one on JAPO is enormous and, despite Rowe's assertion that the music he'd created in duo with Tilbury in the late 70s wasn't so far afield from "traditional" AMM music, one would still like to have had some interim examples to hear whether two parallel—though widely differing—paths were being traveled or if one stance suddenly gave way to another. Whatever the case, "The Great Hall" marks a welcome return to the general sound-world that had been abandoned a decade before and in fact stands as one of the early high points in this trio's oeuvre.

It takes a while to get there, though. At the onset, Prévost's drumming veers toward the bombastic, all thunder and bravado, while Rowe rumbles quite noisily alongside and Tilbury struggles to insert some pounding at a sufficient volume level so as to be heard at all. At times it rises to the level of the sublime chaos of *The Crypt* but it seems to arrive there only through the application of intentional sonic force as opposed to a more natural welling up of tension-fraught elements. Rowe's electronics are positively brutal during this segment, anticipating the open-circuit work of years hence (Voice Crack, etc.). There's an early, wonderful moment when a fuzz-drenched throb is suddenly accompanied by a radio capture of a disco beat at almost the same tempo. Shortly afterwards, the ensemble subsides into an area that would come to be emblematic of the trio, a desolate but endlessly fascinating plain where elements occur with an apparent randomness that's undergirded by a conceptual root system which imparts its own subterranean logic. Tilbury engages in the soft, gamelan-via-Cage approach to the keyboard that became one of his trademarks, Prévost switches to smaller percussive objects, deploying their sounds with care and an exquisite ear toward timbre and Rowe lurks behind, growling here and there, tingeing the environment with washes of tone and the odd harsh spike. The remainder of the first half of the concert fluctuates between what one might think of as "mature" AMM and a music wherein the struggle to slough off some of the previous decade's skin can still be heard, though certainly to a far lesser extent than on *Pueblo*, making it all the more aggravating, as a listener, to have no material from the intervening years for comparison. Around the 25-minute mark, the concert really lifts off, beginning with Rowe's shuddering, entirely atonal guitar that is perfectly set against a rapid, steady percussive tapping, augmented by an utterly inappropriate (and, therefore, excellent) capture of "Love Me Do" and, later, "Heat Wave." It's an astonishing several minutes of work, utterly abrasive in one respect, sugar-coated (the pop songs) in another, with several additional elements careening throughout—a conglomerate in the geological sense, as dense and complex as stone.

The second track finds AMM back in the kind of agitated state they occupied near the beginning of the first cut, Prévost flailing away, Tilbury hopping distractedly in the upper ranges of the piano, Rowe bowing either his guitar or perhaps a cello. Moments like these find the group at its closest approach to the European free improvisation that had matured in the years since AMM's initial breakup. Less care is given to the placement of sounds; there's more of an "anything goes" feel, though not starting from nothing. Ten or so minutes in, AMM, as was its wont, subsides into a quieter, drone-based section, all bowed sounds and effervescent percussion. Gradually, this drone begins to seethe, first with Tilbury's gentle arpeggios, then with a combined assault from cymbals and guitar, still on a relatively low flame, but combusting steadily for a bit before crumbling into a disjointed section where the piano and trap set vie for attention, Rowe setting up several grinding hums beneath. A brief episodic period— Tilbury isolated with some lovely playing, then Rowe yawping and introducing a leaden rhythm followed by a propeller-driven thrum, each event seeming to occur in a separate space, as though occurring in some large cavern where the principals are remote from one another, making contact only via sound. The aura is alien, dark, and vaguely threatening—claustrophobically oppressive. All of a sudden, through the metallic haze, a woman's voice appears. She's robotically reciting numbers in sets of five, in German. "Sieben, fünf, fünf, sechs, neun," "Acht, viur, sieben, acht, acht," etc. She does so steadily, chillingly, at a regular pace, sounding at once machine-like and disturbingly sensual. Rowe, whose short-wave radio was responsible for the introduction of this element, had no idea what it was.[111] But it fit so well, so perfectly, that he let it continue throughout the remainder of the concert, some ten minutes, the group responding by generating music equally disturbing and disorienting. The result was the kind of moment only possible with musicians dedicated to using whatever occurred with no preconceptions and incorporating it into their aesthetic as an element every bit as legitimate as those they'd created themselves. The sheer serendipity of such a capture would never have happened had a more constrictive philosophy been in place.

In late 2007, Rowe said, looking back at the trio version of AMM:

> *It's something I've been aware of for years and years, was imagining what it would be like to be a classical player, to be in a string quartet. That your performance is all plotted out, years ahead, centuries ahead, that you had this very fixed kind of material and when you sat down to play, you could play it creatively or in a mechanical way, lifeless. Or you could go beyond the notes and express something, bring the piece to life. How you would get your experiences of being in the 20th century through something that was entirely fixed.*

---

111   He would later be told that he'd intercepted a coded transmission from East Germany, then still behind the Iron Curtain, a common method of communicating to the West. Indeed, such transmissions were collected by certain sound-miners and issued, among other places, in the late 90s as The Conet Project.

But, given that material, you somehow made comments about contemporary society, yourself, what you believe in. And of course, I've never had that experience but I could imagine how those issues worked. Increasingly, during that period, I began to think of AMM as the nearest I would get to this kind of classical situation. Because in a way, I have an idea of how John is going to sound and what the range is. In the early days of improvisation, that would have been taken as a kind of criticism, you know, if you knew someone's sound palette that would be taken as criticism. Cornelius' playing, you could say was more open than John's. For Eddie, it was the same thing. Partly it comes from the maturity in Eddie's playing, the comparatively flashier playing—Eddie was never "flashy," but the kind of playing that could be confused for flashy technique, which we all have done when we were younger, I think in our mature years Eddie stripped that away to the bare bones. In all our cases, it was outside of AMM that our techniques were very different. I was much more expansive outside than inside. I think for all of us, this was a similar experience, of this kind of classicism in the form, the knowability of it. Yet at the same time, allowing the music to have a profound effect and feeling.

If you were to look at the classical form, the sonata, that form is very recognizable. I think that arc is AMM's version of the sonata form. The other thing that happened in the very early days of AMM, there was a much more strident defense of the word, "improvisation." In order to gain a distinct view of what improvisation was, we made very determined [choices], full of revolutionary zeal, of the difference between improvisation and composition. I think it was the entirely correct thing to do, to make a bedrock set of foundations for the belief in improvisation, its character, not having it confused with anything else. But now in 2007, having established pretty firmly what improvisation is, I think a lot of us can see improvisation as a form of composition, because when AMM sat down to play, it wasn't actually completely free. Our original notion that "any sound was possible" is no longer true because there's a whole raft of stuff that is not possible. In fact, you could say we're hemmed in by all the things that are not possible to do. Then it becomes compositional. There's an early recognition of that in an interview with Cornelius where he says, "Well, we're composed. We have arms and legs and walk into a session composed." [referring to Rowe's own comment, cited earlier] I think we can be freer in expressing that thought now.

Matchless Recordings was initiated in 1983, a collective endeavor though largely under Prévost's administration, designed around AMM and related music. During the 80s, only three recordings of AMM proper would be released: *Generative Themes* from December of 1982,[112] *Combine + Laminates* from May of 1984 (both with the trio) and *The Inexhaustible Document* from January of 1987 (with cellist Rohan de Saram). Additionally, AMM appeared on Tom Phillips' *Irma* (May 1988), and Rowe and Prévost made up half of the Supersession quartet who issued a recording from September 1984.[113]

Generalizing about the music with such a small sampling is a hazardous affair, though in that AMM maintained their tradition of not soliciting gigs and combined with their rather enormous lack of acceptance, this handful of recordings is likely more representative than one might at first think. There is, over the course of the decade, a certain directionality to be discerned; not a smooth line by any means, but a tendency toward the more serene and contemplative. In a word, toward a kind of classicism.

―――――――

112   The 1994 CD reissue appended 31 minutes from an April 24, 1983 concert in Zagreb.

113   During the 80s, Prévost continued to lead more free jazz-oriented bands and released several recordings on Matchless. Given AMM's original precepts, it's slightly jarring to see group names like the Eddie Prévost Band or the Eddie Prévost Quartet.

Though AMM now had an outlet for issuing recordings in Matchless (distributed in the US by the New Music Distribution Service, the principal such organization), they received little press, played seldom, and most importantly, their music had almost nothing to do with any contemporary strain. They were too cerebral and "unemotional" to appeal to most fans of European free improvisation as represented by Brötzmann, Han Bennink, etc. (much less to those brought up on the post-Coltrane American variety), too roughhewn and improv-centered for the modern classical audience, which was going through the maturation and homogenization of minimalism, as well as a spurt of neo-Romanticism when not still absorbed by post-serialism. The latter area might be where they fit in if at all, though only insofar as that territory overlapped with the music and ideas of the four "members" of the New York School and their sympathizers.

At least on Rowe's part, there was something of a push to place AMM in the context of a contemporary classical ensemble, one that both performed modern repertoire with an emphasis on graph-oriented or other non-notated work (consciously extending the tradition of pre-political Cardew), and that improvised as well. It was also at about this point that they began a practice of spending an entire day at a location, dividing time between performance and "instruction." In February 1982, for example, they appeared at Goldsmith's College and offered individual classes in the morning:

(a) Prepared piano (with particular reference to the music of John Cage) – John Tilbury

(b) Percussion techniques – The drum as sound box – Bowed cymbals – Eddie Prévost

(c) The guitar – from single line instrument to orchestral sound source. Preparation and amplification – Keith Rowe

In the afternoon:

> History of AMM's development from 1965 to present, its particularly integrated form of music. Use of transistor radio, its changing role between the periods 1965-72 and 1977 to the present.

> Discussion of AMM's aim to supersede established ways of making music in order to develop a new and more satisfying basis for a musical life.

> Practical music making session.

> Examination of group attitudes and dynamics. Instrumental techniques used in contemporary improvisation.

Then, an evening performance.

It's interesting that this aspect of AMM's social interaction with their audience is not dissimilar from that of the AACM and similar organizations that looked beyond purely musical matters, considering music as a tool toward other goals in addition to an *objet d'art*. At the Cardew Memorial Concert in May of 1982,[114] AMM again acted both as a repertoire ensemble and an improvising group and it was a guise they'd adopt for much of the next two decades, going so far as to print a repertory list for distribution to potential concert venues, much as a nascent string trio might do.

Throughout the 80s, AMM took part in performances of work by other composers. Cardew was, of course, represented, not only with "Treatise" (or selected pages thereof) but with various earlier pieces as well such as "The Great Learning," as were Christian Wolff ("For 5 or 10 People," "Prose Collection," "Edges," the latter

---

114   Rowe also initiated a memorial event to mark the first anniversary of Cardew's death in December 1982, inviting former Scratch Orchestra members to gather for "an informal evening in which music will feature."

written originally for AMM), Feldman ("The King of Denmark"), Earle Brown ("December, 1952," "Four Systems"), Cage ("Variations I–III"), Toshi Ichiyanagi ("Sapporo"), and Howard Skempton ("For Strings..."). These concerts would often involve musicians from the classical world like clarinetist Ian Mitchell, violinist Alexander Balanescu, and, later, cellist Rohan de Saram. Some would also be asked to participate as members of AMM in fully improvised concerts. These associations were largely at Rowe's urging and resulted in a growing tension between him and Prévost, who still showed more affinity toward jazz-based forms. Decades later, amidst a flurry of harsh e-mails around the time of AMM's second dissolution in 2004, he'd accuse Rowe of fawning toward such musicians in a pathetic attempt to gain their approval, as though validation was needed from some kind of authority figures. What Rowe looked at as a natural progression, Prévost seems to have regarded as an unwanted distancing from more vital, perhaps more communitarian music. In an address from around 1985 titled "Improvisation: Music for an Occasion," Prévost argues for methods of getting through to younger listeners the ideals of improvisational music, presumably via speaking in a language they're capable of understanding and can relate in some fashion to music of which they're already aware; Rowe's flirtation with the abstract end of contemporary classical music would hardly qualify.

> It is the case that I was uneasy with the direction Keith seemed intent on taking AMM at that time. Apart from the "new" musicians there was a suggestion we wore black polo-neck shirts and that I should be named "Edwin" on publicity material. These were, I think, perhaps symptoms of a desire for a professional (as well as an aesthetic) identity shifting away from the scruffy boots and beards of many of our contemporaries. I was uneasy but didn't have strong arguments against these ploys. I agreed in the most part with Keith's analysis. This was, I suppose, that we were not working in a milieu that seemed suitable or particularly sympathetic to what we

were doing. In effect the "music world" of the time was either the informal world of "improv" which was based upon mutual back-scratching or the more formal world which (at that time) still embraced what one might call "modernism." Evan and Derek seemed to work this "improv" network to substantial advantage in terms of connections. We perhaps because of the time lost during the early schism were effectively outside of this loop. On the other hand the more "formal" music promoting structures were more interested in our connection with Cardew. Hence, perhaps, Keith's strategy.[115]

...I think within AMM, the three of us perform it ["Treatise"] in quite different ways. I would say of Eddie that it's like a love-hate relationship. On one level he clearly has enormous respect for the piece. Without any question Eddie endeavors to uphold the beauty of the graphics and the ingenuity and the planning and the cunning. It's not coded in an obvious way but there is something running through it, though I'm damned if any of us can find it! Maybe if one knew Wittgenstein's work enough maybe one could actually decode it and work with that. On one level Eddie has tremendous respect for that. On the other hand, I never get the feeling that he's happy performing it. He loves to have it in front of him to respond to when the notion grabs him. But you really feel he wouldn't go out of his way to perform it, although he would be happy to partake in performance of it. I think his playing is quite subtly altered by the score; he would perhaps see it as a restraining element on his playing.[116]

That pull, more on Prévost's part but not entirely without some vestigial appeal for Rowe, toward more jazz-based improvisation

---

115   Prévost, 2016.

116   Mouldycliff, 1995.

in the wake of Amalgam and the JAPO recording, was still somewhat strong in the early 80s. In 1980, after AMM had become a trio, the pair joined Evan Parker and Barry Guy in a quartet that adopted the unfortunate moniker, Supersession.[117] Only one recording emerged from this grouping and that not until 1988 (from a 1984 session), but the music represents, at least as far as the AMM members are concerned, yet another odd step backward—though listened to through the ears of one unaware of their music from the prior two decades, there's certainly a level of visceral excitement achieved.

Prévost's liner notes are slightly defensive, clearly aware of the conceptual discrepancy between this music and, not only AMM but also the experimental art with which it had affiliated, arguing that "all alienation strategies and all avant-gardes become exhausted." He takes a shot at members of the Scratch Orchestra (unnamed but clearly indicated) who abandoned that group's ultra-democratic approach for the security of academe. Prévost seems to exempt free improvisation alone from his withering gaze, no longer distinguishing between the kind of improv developed by AMM and that evolving from what came to be called European Free improvisation (EFI).[118]

As such, we have two aspects from which to consider the resultant music, at least as represented by the Matchless recording. To the AMM aficionado, the differences are stark. A dozen years on, trombonist Radu Malfatti would refer to EFI as "too gabby," and that description applies here in spades. The four musicians

---

117   In fairness, one might hope they intended the dictionary meaning of the act of superseding or of having been superseded, not the crass commercialism of the "super-" prefix...or perhaps they were using archly dual reasoning.

118   Shorthand terms such as this and eai (electro-acoustic improvisation, often lower-cased to imply a quieter nature) are not meant to be exclusive or terribly exact. Rather, they are convenient terms for generally referring to a given area, understanding that any boundaries, to the extent they exist at all, are exceedingly fuzzy.

engage in unceasing interplay, a conversation where listening takes a back seat to asserting, often in the most forceful, insistent manner possible. Granted, that very glossolaliac, four-part exchange is capable, as with any good example of EFI, of reaching its own dizzying, euphoric heights and there are several occasions where it does so here. For a fan of Parker and Guy, "Supersession" was undoubtedly an exciting release, Rowe and Prévost (especially the former) providing sonic colors not normally associated with the pair. But to the listener schooled in AMM, the after-effect is like having indulged in an overly rich, nutritionally vacant meal—one feels a bit queasy and fundamentally unsated, having digested little if any actual substance. There's no sense of the music having emerged from the room in which it was created, no connection to the world outside.

Rowe, more than 20 years later, was surprisingly wistful about its potential:

> *I was actually disappointed it never really developed in any way; it got kind of marooned. I wish it had continued so that we would have broken through where we were. I think I could truly say that Eddie and I probably caused no excitement whatsoever in the [free improvisation] community! If it was done now, it would be a major event. But in those times—I'm not sobbing, but I think discrimination against AMM was pretty thorough. Evan always—always—was highly respectful and never badmouthed AMM period. Other people, like Mike Cooper, were always respectful. The remarkable thing was that Derek's book on improvisation actually didn't mention AMM, except in the reprinted version where Eddie's asked to write a half page.*

Within AMM proper, however (again, at least as far as can be determined from released recordings), while there was always a push and pull to be experienced, Rowe's preferred direction seemed to be getting the upper hand. *Generative Themes*, a studio recording created on December 11 and 12, 1982, was the record-listening public's first taste of non-duo AMM to appear since *The Crypt* from 1968. At its onset, it actually hearkens back to *AMMMusic* in overall tone, the radio captures floating atop an acidic drone for the first several minutes, Tilbury's presence heard only (one guesses) in percussive, gong-like patterns derived from the prepared piano, eventually incorporating rhythmic sequences, with roots in Cage's "Sonatas and Interludes" (and, through them, with allusions to Southeast Asian music). These initial minutes alone enact a mini-journey from AMM-past to AMM-future.

There remain clear perturbations in the flow, however—AMM dealing with the various issues that grew from their continuing involvement in projects like Supersession. The second track commences with Rowe's clattering guitar, objects such as rulers and files being thwacked and reverberating, feedback in force. Prévost returns to the drum kit, bashing away as though in consort with the EFI crowd. Tilbury, however, remains Tilbury: a mediating figure, tossing consonant arpeggios into the mix, having the effect of corroding the more abrasive elements, framing them as tendrils unfurling from his stalwart stalk. It's already clear, at this early point in the trio's tenure, how fundamentally Tilbury has changed AMM. He's more "fully formed" at this stage in his career (45 years old) than Cardew was while with the group. The range of possibilities open to the group may have lessened in a sense, but a cohesiveness, a permeating sense of sheer, glorious musicality was attained in exchange. For his part, Rowe often seems more at ease working with single, sparse ideas and allowing them to gestate, initiating a rough hum for instance, and letting it hover as a hazy ground for more raucous exchanges between his partners, nudging it along only occasionally.

There's still more of a call and response approach in effect than one might have expected (or desired, if one knew AMM's earlier work). When Tilbury begins to pound the keyboard (generally his least effective gambit), Prévost responds in kind with a barrage of heavy drumming. The ethic of the original AMM, to insert sounds laminally, in a more complex and organic manner, gets lost at times like this; the improvisation assumes an air of forced "automaticism": he did this, I must do that, something very typical of EFI.

Radio reappears prominently at the beginning of the third track, snippets of conversation grounded by Prévost's deft tom-tom work and Rowe's bowed guitar. They've seesawed back into a more forward-looking attack, the contributions more amorphous, the blending of sound more natural. Here, when an abrasive element surfaces, as when Prévost loudly rubs one of his drumheads, it's allowed to stand on its own, not overtly commented upon or slavishly accompanied. The music becomes roiling and disturbed via an accumulation of detail, at least for a while. Soon, however, the fourth track begins with a "loud section" much like the one in the prior cut, except that here Rowe's a more out-front participant, skronking away for all he's worth. While it's somewhat more satisfying than before, as it varies substantially within the basic approach, there remains the nagging sense of banal group "interaction" rather than serendipitous confluence.

The CD reissue of *Generative Themes* (1994) took advantage of the medium's increased length and appended a live set, or portion thereof, from the Zagreb Biennale held on April 24, 1983. Initially, we hear a similar dialog between Tilbury and Prévost, fairly active and chattering. Interestingly, Rowe confines himself to distant feedback moans, well in the background, sounds providing no clear reference to those produced by his cohorts, simply existing on the fringes of the same space. Eventually, however, it's his sounds that seem to draw down the activity as though these animated but constrained conversationalists gradually become aware of a larger world outside their immediate concerns. It's a lovely moment, serving to widen the music, allowing it to splay out into a number of areas rather than being restricted to one or two. One notices that the sections of silence or near silence, once so much a part of early AMM, have disappeared as well as extended long sounds or drones. Since there was, of course, no "reindoctrination" of Tilbury, no rehashing of the ideas developed in 1965, it might be expected that his addition would necessarily mean that certain approaches would not, for him, be part of his second nature as they were for members of the original quintet. Indeed, years later, Rowe would comment that he was unsure whether or not Tilbury ever really grasped the nature of AMM, without by any means gainsaying the profundity or beauty of his contributions. AMM had morphed into a different creature in several respects. On the one hand, they still stood almost entirely apart from other improvised music of the day; their conception remained more extreme than that of perhaps any other improvising ensemble. But it may not have been as extreme, as "pure," as that of AMM from 1966-71. One has the impression that this sat well with Prévost but less so with Rowe who would continually push and nudge things, as much as he was able, on the one hand toward the music created by the group of *The Crypt*, on the other toward more contemporary classical concerns. There's a disjointedness in the Zagreb performance that, for all its individual strengths, results in a less organic, protean whole than was achieved 15 years earlier, despite that session's enormous fluctuation in volume, attack, etc. While of a roughly similar sound-world as the music from its first seven years, the addition of Tilbury has clearly enabled the creation of a unique music, unique both with regard to the history of AMM and with respect to almost anything else being dreamed of in the early 80s. This "apartness" is striking. One might have guessed that in the ensuing 16 years between *AMMMusic* and the 1982 London concert, some number of musicians would have struck out along similar pathways, but finding examples of such is difficult.

Around this time, Rowe had formed a short-lived guitar quartet, his first stab at tangentially emulating the balance he heard in string quartets. It was called Magnetic Attractions and included the Canadian Rene Lussier (suggested by Fred Frith[119]), Raymond Boni from France, and Pierre Urban (Charles Aznavour's guitarist) and performed at a few jazz festivals, often playing set pieces.

---

119   Frith on the problematic relationship between his music and Rowe's,

from a private correspondence in 2003: Part of the problem of perception of our relationship is based on the fact that until the last few years I have been much better known as a guitar player than Keith, so many assumed he had been influenced by me. That's sad, of course, but the subsequent move to establish him as the pioneer he undoubtedly is has sometimes rubbed off on me in a negative way, the implication being that somehow I was ripping him off and taking the credit that should have been his. Given our totally different interests and ways of working this is a bit silly, but we both have to live with it.

AMM's first LP definitely had a big impact, specifically in its lack of emphasis on "technique" and "self-expression." The suggestively descriptive titles situated the listener in a hypothetical movie scenario, which I found curiously ambivalent, and no doubt ironic, given the anti-narrative position of the group. I heard it, however, in the same general period that I heard a lot of other experimental music for the first time, and I would say that reading Cage's *Silence* and hearing Berio's "Visage" were more important to me in many ways. It was in any case all new and exotic, and I was making up for lost time, voraciously soaking up every conceivable strand of activity in the contemporary music world without much discrimination, and without having a very clear idea about aesthetic difference between different protagonists. Having said that I was aware of Cardew and his political ideas from the late 60s on, and I then associated AMM entirely (and erroneously) with him. Anyway, AMM's LP was just one of many important records in my collection in 1969, I didn't see them play, and I didn't listen to the music from a technical perspective at all, so Keith Rowe as a "guitarist" just didn't register.

Keith (who I also met for the first time in 1971 at the notorious "songs" gig) [sic—perhaps a PLM affair from a couple years later?] was the opposite [from Derek Bailey] as far as I was concerned—not only a Southerner but part of a group which seemed to be totally self-sufficient and self-absorbed, with a lot of ideological baggage tending towards the idea that only they were following the true path. I think that missionary zeal is still an aura that AMM carries, and is quite obvious in Eddie Prévost's book. These are serious people on a serious mission and with serious self-regard. On the couple of occasions I met Keith over the course of the 70s our relationship was friendly but a bit stiff. That has changed now, but that may be to do with the fact that he is established as the key figure that he is. There must definitely have been some resentment on his part before that, however, reluctant he was to express it.

[On any influence of Rowe on *Guitar Solos*] Sadly not. From my point of view, if I'd really been aware of Keith's guitar playing when I made that record it's unthinkable that the record would have sounded the way it does. After all, the technical innovations implicit in *Guitar Solos* concern the use of a pick-up at the wrong end of the neck, with the instrument played in the conventional position for the most part, and with the idea that I could separate the instrument into a large number of sound sources which can be recorded on separate tracks. This ented playing, we see that Rowe was as yet not averse to expanding the varieties of styles to which he was open. No recordings, to the best of the author's knowledge, exist.

AMM's first live set as a trio to be issued, *Combine + Laminates*, was recorded during their second US tour, at the Arts Club in Chicago on May 25, 1984 and appeared originally as an LP on Pogus Records.

With only scant recorded evidence available, it's difficult to say with any assurance, but in comparison with "Generative Themes," one can discern both a conceptual inching forward as well as an enduring tendency to fall back into the more individualized playing of the previous few years. It's tempting to hear Rowe as trying to rein in this backsliding, as at the beginning of the performance where he again remains resolutely in the background while Tilbury and Prévost tussle out front. But if that strategy was indeed attempted in the first few minutes, he shortly initiates his own agitated scrabbling with frantic bowing operations that sound not at all dissimilar to garden-variety free improv emanating from contemporaneous English and European practitioners. Tilbury is especially active, even florid; one has the impression that he's as yet reluctant to fully inject the lessons learned from Cage and Feldman into AMM. Happily, Rowe's introduction of a radio capture, a romantic song with a male vocal and chorus, serves to bring matters into stasis. The effect is almost alchemical, as though once the element is proffered, Prévost and Tilbury simply cannot continue their interplay. Unsurprisingly, the music takes on a far greater depth and mystery; one does in fact think of the Rauschenberg's Combines alluded to in the album's title with their extreme opposition of vigorously paint-

---

direction was dictated by my having worked for the first time in a multi-track studio in 1973, and by my obsession with amplifying the notes that I could hear being generated to the left of my left hand. The techniques I use with this extra pick-up are as far as I know unique to me—I don't know of anyone else who was pursued this direction since I started experimenting in 1969.

ed surface and serene, everyday objects, each given equivalent psychic weight. This is one of the "problems" (more like, joys) in AMM listening—that the portions making up a performance can't really be judged in isolation from that which precedes or follows. This static section might be deemed perfectly fine on its own but, in relation to the earlier, more overt interplay, it carries an additional layer—lamina—of profundity. Still, these few minutes allow one to observe clear intimations of AMM's more mature subsequent work (even if, ironically, they refer back to several of their initial premises), when the concern with sound placement, timbre adjustment, and psychological reticence comes to the fore. When the volume swells here, it grows from what has been previously seeded, not as some ordained point to be aimed toward.

Rowe's splotches are particularly "ugly" during this part of the session, vicious clunks and echoing, Pollock-esque splatters that stand in forthright opposition to what Prévost refers to in the liner notes as the art of "the neo-classicists and their technocratic offspring." After Rowe immortalizes San Francisco Giant Chili Davis in another radio grab, Tilbury emerges with some scintillating work in the upper reaches of the keyboard, the kind of music with which it's very difficult to engage in conversation, resulting in a fascinatingly disjointed interplay between the three. In a sense, it's more atomized than that heard at the concert's outset, less give and take, therefore richer and, as appropriate, more stratified—three layers to hear *through*, each of which refracting the other. The listener is less spoon-fed, required to work on a more active interpretation of what he hears, and is much the better for it.

They close with a protracted, and magnificent, quiet drone, an apparently bleak soundscape strewn, on closer inspection, with all manner of beautiful detritus, from piano interior tolling to shards of Tina Turner. It's a classic example of this trio at their finest. Indeed, the performance can be heard as a recapitulation of what they (Rowe and Prévost, especially) had gone through in the prior decade, something Rowe referred to in an interview in 1983:

That coming back is rather like Picasso's life, where he con-
tinually does drawings which relate to each other all the way
through, and they're recognizably Picasso's drawings, and
they're rather like some kind of springboard or some stan-
dard you can relate other things to, and from which other
things can develop. And I suppose it's almost like Mondrian's
way of gradually, almost imperceptibly, developing to an
abstraction from a very regular form at the beginning, very
naturalistic and representational. And in a sense it's proba-
bly something like the AMM development too, that it comes
from a representative form, and gradually develops into this
so-called abstract form. And what's interesting, I think, is the
length of time it's taken us to do it the second time around as
opposed to the first time around.[120]

When Matchless reissued *Combine + Laminates* as a CD in 1995,
a performance of "Treatise" from the same concert was appended. The difference in approach is immediately apparent,
most notably in Tilbury's prepared piano playing that not only
clearly refers to Cage but is also, presumably insofar as he was
elucidating the source, far more spacious than that heard in the
improvisation. Overall, there's a decidedly more "classical" feel to
the music; one can easily imagine that certain constraints are in
play although, true to the premises implicit in its score, these so-
called constraints serve to open up the musicians to areas they'd
likely not have explored otherwise. The delicacy with which
AMM translates this section of "Treatise" is fraught with tension,
as though they're tiptoeing from symbol to symbol, trying not to
upset the entirety of the structure erected up to that point. It's a
stunning, beautifully-controlled event, surely one of the strongest
(partial) interpretations of "Treatise" on record.

The contrast between the two pieces on *Combine + Laminates +
Treatise '84* is emblematic of the bifurcation of AMM as improvising ensemble and, increasingly, a group steering toward a

---

120   *Perspectives of New Music*, Vol. 21, No. ½ (Autumn 1982–Summer 1983.

more classical conception, a direction largely at Rowe's behest. Between having garnered virtually no acceptance from the avant-jazz community and his deepening fascination with the work of the classical experimentalists of the New York School and afterward, Rowe felt that AMM's best fit was in the latter world.

As mentioned earlier, Rowe had never been particularly comfortable with the notion of AMM consisting of as few as three members, thinking the number five to be ideal. Partially as an occasional antidote to this, the idea of guest musicians was a popular one and given Rowe's concern as to AMM's place in the contemporary musical milieu, his tendency was to invite people from non-improvising backgrounds. This was also based in his belief, certainly more often right than not, that improvisers would inevitably bring along conceptual baggage from that world which, especially on what might be a one-off occasion, would be impossible to shed. AMM had gone through this molting stage in 1965 through 1966 and there was no need to revisit those problems. Evan Parker was always an exception to this rule, the one musician from the improvising world Rowe felt had enough of an affinity to AMM's ideas to be able to seamlessly enter into the music.[121]

The clarinetist Ian Mitchell, who had premiered Cardew's "Mountain" for solo bass clarinet, was one such; a second was the cellist Rohan de Saram. Rowe had encountered de Saram while working on videotapes for his day job in a London studio building. He heard the beautiful sounds of strings echoing through the corridors, investigated and discovered a practice session of the Arditti String Quartet, perhaps the leading performers of contemporary music for the format. He introduced himself to de Saram and discovered a formidable intellect interested in learning about im-

---

121   Hugh Davies, who had a foot in both the classical and improv camps, played with the trio on at least one occasion in the early 80s. Years later, after Davies' death, Rowe would remark that he was the one improvising musician he regretted not having been able to work with more often in the AMM context. Another person who Rowe thought might have made an intriguing fit was Luc Ferrari (!).

provisation. Given his prodigious musical talent and the fact that Rowe had always considered the cello to be the quintessential AMM instrument, it was natural for him to extend the invitation to participate with AMM.

The only official recording with the augmented trio of AMM and de Saram, released as *The Inexhaustible Document*, took place on January 10, 1987 at Union Chapel, London and was the first publicly-available documentation of AMM since *Combine + Laminates* from almost three years earlier. Ascribing the general tone to either de Saram's presence or simply the evolution that had occurred in the intervening years is only a guess, but the maturity encountered here, the extraordinary pacing, the subtle fluctuations of volume and texture, make this the re-formed AMM's most accomplished and probing recording up to this date, if anything justifying Rowe's intuition about whom to ask in. For a few years, de Saram was a semi-regular member of AMM, playing as often as his increasingly busy schedule with the Arditti Quartet would permit.

de Saram's presence is clearly heard from the start. He concentrates, as near as the listener can ascertain, on what might loosely be described as extended techniques within a relatively conservative modern classical form—that is, odd bowings, high pizzicato (perhaps below the bridge), etc. but nothing so outré as bowing the body of the cello, scraping the floor with the point and so on. In fact, for much of the recording he plays in quasi-tonal fashion, an echo of Tilbury when the latter is in Feldman-mode. Perhaps the expansion to a quartet is responsible, but this session has a far greater group feeling throughout than much of the previous work from this decade. Prévost largely contains himself to low, rumbling rolls, resonant taps, small percussion, and bowed and scraped surfaces while Rowe is content to provide deep throbs and distant rasps. Associative vestiges of jazz or EFI-based free improvisation seem to have been finally and completely expunged from their system. After seven or eight years, AMM had attained the heights of control/unfettered freedom that they had occupied at the time of *The Crypt*, even as they were oriented in a different direction. Not that there didn't exist bumps in the road ahead.[122]

Tom Phillip's opera, *Irma*, dates from 1969 and had had a long performance history in addition to having been previously recorded on the Obscure record label by an ensemble under the direction of Gavin Bryars. On the Matchless recording from 1988, AMM (the trio) is the central instrumental element, augmented by Ian Mitchell (clarinets), and Lol Coxhill (soprano saxophone, vocals), in addition to vocalists Elise Lorraine, Phil Minton, Birte Pederson, and Phillips. Both Rowe and Tilbury manipulate radios (Rowe also plays cellos) that provide welcome and often humorous counterpoint (as when "Song Sung Blue" appears) to the arch, declamatory vocals. Otherwise AMM's own sounds are embedded enough within the contest so as to make it next to impossible to parse out any shifts or evolution of the trio.

Whatever its success as a musical work, the participation of AMM in *Irma* was yet another step in the direction of the avant-classical and away from EFI—again, more a Rowe-weighted path than Prévost. In the 1983 *New Perspectives* interview, Rowe had stated:

> So that's what we're looking at now, where AMM fits in that much larger thing, and probably too in a way that it does adopt many of the ideas of Varèse, Cowell, Cage, Ives...

To which Prévost responded with great perspicacity:

> I'd like to shift the emphasis slightly, because I've got an idea you're putting forward an idea which indicates a

---

122   Two unreleased recordings of AMM plus de Saram exist, one recorded on March 1, 1987 in London and the other from January, 1988, recorded at the BBC Maida Vale studio, also in London. Both attain similar aesthetic probity as heard in *The Inexhaustible Document* and make one wish that the association had been more ongoing.

kind of sympathetic development; with the Americans, I'm sure that's true to a certain extent, but I think even the American stuff was a response to, and some of the European experience that we're part of was a response to—if you transfer the serialists' mentality to the rest of the way of life in Europe, which you can with some reasonable justification—a response to the feeling of alienation with the forms which that represents. The high-rise blocks for instance—a very structured way of organizing people. Even the Welfare State, which was a marvelous thing when it began, began from an organizational, paternalistic point of view rather than looking at people as separate entities. People were seen en masse. And I think a lot of improvisation was a kind of response to that dehumanising aspect of life. And that's the link I would put into it, and I think it's just one of the recurring moments, if you like, that you can see if you look at the whole history of jazz; you can say it gets sharper where there are things to react against of that kind. And I sense that in the 60s there was a general reaction against those kinds of forms which were quite alienating, and one obviously picked up with the Americans and saw them as kindred spirits who were likewise responding.

Rowe, as he often would in subsequent years, had already begun to think of his and AMM's work as part of a larger, ongoing stream, one that is more particularly art-based, to the relative (not complete) exclusion of extra-aesthetic concerns, while Prévost is insistent at relating their music more directly to societal issues. At the same time, Prévost maintains more of a libertarian approach to these problems, expressing opposition to thinking of people as groups rather than as individuals, than did Rowe during his Maoist phase and possibly still up to this date. Rowe would, over the course of time, come around more to Prévost's point of view on specifically political matters, but the amount of stress he placed on AMM's place in the "canon," a position derived somewhat by similar thoughts on the part of painters he admired like Rothko,

Guston, and Twombly, and a "classical" canon at that, remained something of a sticking point between he and Prévost. It wasn't that Prévost objected to such work—musical, visual, or otherwise—just that it wasn't what AMM was about.

The 1980s were an era in American and British politics and culture dominated by Reagan, Thatcher, and a tidal wave of conservatism in mass art culture—from the resurgence of bop-based forms in jazz at the expense of post-AACM music to the championing of the "New Romanticism" in classical music (Corigliano, Del Tredici, Bolcom, MacMillan, etc.), as well as the degradation of Minimalism (which, recall, had been promoted by Cardew and Tilbury in the past) into a form that was anything but minimalistic, increasingly catering to the general public as well as the official aesthetic establishment. The experimental art that had flowered in the early 60s in music, the visual arts, and in between (Fluxus) became commonly seen as self-indulgent, overly arcane, and effete. Many of the individuals still actively pursuing ideas developed at that time had retreated into academe, still perhaps producing vital work but isolated from any kind of creative community beyond the ivied walls. Among musicians out "in the world," those who continued to mine the rich lode of ideas—still largely untapped—that had been exposed in the 60s were few and far between. More from the *New Perspectives* interview:

> EP: What's certainly perplexing is that really, apart from Musica Elettronica Viva[123], there have been very few manifestations of the kind of group which uses, to use Evan Parker's term, a "laminal" approach; layered textures. In the European free jazz side there's still been this emphasis on individual statements in juxtaposition to each other....I mean, why don't we have lots of imitators?

---

123   Rowe, while possibly allowing that MEV utilized a "laminal" attack, would not include them among musicians who otherwise understood the fundamental approach of AMM to music.

KR: So possibly one of the answers is that if you go and look at a lot of free improvisation groups you can see the system in the music, even if it's relatively arbitrary—whereas I think AMM is so intuitive and so non-systematic that it's very hard to copy, and Eddie made the point the other day that because AMM is such an individual contribution, based around the notions of the individual deciding for himself what he's doing, that if you go and copy that you immediately take away its most essential feature...It's much more difficult. I mean when you get those very long suspended near-silences which are very, very delicately balanced, it's very hard to re-create that. I mean, it's hard enough for us to be able to get to those optimum situations.

EP: "OK, Bud, like that bit, keep it in for the next set."

KR: "Can you do that again?" (Laughter) And I think when you're playing with prepared instruments too, instruments which you've actually built up, then they become quite unreliable.

EP: Like that piece that you made on the duo record. That particular weighting of the ruler where you've got it oscillating [a metal ruler inserted between the guitar strings and then set rocking to and fro]. I've heard you do it again, but it's extraordinarily difficult to get the same feel.

KR: Of course, one wouldn't attempt to get it...I mean, ultimately all music is non-repeatable. So I think AMM is really much more...the *essence* of AMM is much more a recognition of the differences in performance. Was it Horowitz who said that getting the right notes ought to be secondary to getting the feeling? I think we obviously extend out from that...I think it started off by being a re-action to the situation we found ourselves in, but I think now it's become much more a confirmation of the other musics that are around us and have been going on before. I think we now feel quite a lot of unity with someone like Horowitz playing the Liszt B sonata or something like that; we recognize that in there are the same kind of aspirations; with Beethoven or with iso-rhythmic motets; AMM is part of musical history too.

One doubts whether Prévost shared Rowe's notion of the particular lineage into which he was attempting to insert AMM.

In any event, throughout the decade (and into the 90s), AMM often gave "repertoire concerts," almost always with a true AMM performance as a component. The following program from a 1986 date in Istanbul (with Ian Mitchell along) is typical, as is the inclusion of a piece by a local composer:

K. Stockhausen	Intensity
C. Wolff	Clarinet Work
C. Cardew	Ode Machine II
Îlhan Usmanbaş	Cîzgîler
C. Cardew	Treatise Percussion Solo
C. Cardew	Solo with Accompaniment
AMM	Improvisation

Little by little, matters began to improve at least as far as the printed media were concerned. Magazines devoting themselves to aspects of experimental music started to appear such as *Option*, *The Wire*, and *Avant*, periodicals with reasonably large circulations and distributive networks with enough reach to enable their placement on racks in metropolitan areas throughout the US and Europe. These magazines were often staffed by at least a few writers who were aware of AMM and who provided the occasional feature or review—an invaluable source of publicity simply to get knowledge of the ensemble out into a public arena. While there had been the odd younger band that acknowledged AMM as a source of inspiration, such as the American trio Borbetomagus (Jim Sauter and Don Dietrich - saxophones, Donald Miller - guitar, active since the late 70s), there was a tendency to concentrate on a single aspect of the AMM experience. In the case of Borbetomagus, their brutalist, balls-to-the-wall approach seemed more a superficial reaction to the cacophonous sections of work like *The Crypt* than to any deep understanding of AMM's underlying aesthetic. The Bohman Brothers, in England, were a closer approximation.

In a more general sense, ideas were gradually coalescing that may have had AMM as one of many possible roots, and which were more accommodating to that aesthetic. To take a single example, in 1986 the Swiss drummer Gunter Müller had formed, with Jacques Widmer and Andres Bosshard, the trio Nachtluft, which used percussion, electronics, computers, and cassette manipulation in a freely improvised, non-jazz derived manner. Müller wouldn't actually hear AMM until 1992, but by the mid-80s had already intuited that a similar attack was becoming increasingly valid:

> We never played on ordinary stages but in rooms [with] the audience standing or better, moving between us. We distinguished certain parts that could include highly active and sometimes rhythmic sections from parts we called, "Klangbaustelle" (sound construction piece) creating rather static atmospheres often merging with the real sounds of the site [where] we were playing. We switched from a Klangbaustelle to an active part of several minutes and perhaps switched back to a Klangbaustelle again and of course everything was improvised. Later on, mainly when playing special sites [such] as a quarry or a dam or in a special architecture, we combined these two forms more and more; we used to call this "konzertante Klangbaustelle." This was happening in a time of rather strict rules, what was allowed and what was condemned by the scene, mainly by other musicians and writers. It was still the time of a more masculine power playing, the faster

the better, the time when the audience automatically was clapping after a sweating solo was finished. As I said, we had from time to time sections of power playing or more rock-like stuff, but we were concentrating on a collective and not on a soloistic improvisation.[124]

Bit by bit, the fringes of the musical world were beginning to catch on not just to AMM but also to the fundamental sense of their philosophy, their aesthesia.

*

Around the same time, the late 80s, something crystallized in AMM.

By and large, it's a fact of human existence that as people age they settle into habits, become comfortable at what they do, lose something of the desire to push and prod at things. In artists, especially musicians, the examples are endless. Take almost any example of a creative musician and chances are he made his most significant, strongest contribution while in his twenties or thirties, not necessarily losing ability afterwards but treading on paths already well-worn, elaborating on earlier discoveries but generally settling into what might uncharitably be called a "rut," a routine. There are exceptions, of course, but they only prove the rule. AMM, as a trio, continued to create very beautiful music up through Rowe's departure in 2004, work that stood apart from almost anything else being conceived during that time and which, as represented on albums or in live performance, still had great power and depth. However, all three members were in their 50s by 1990 and, as a group, one began to pick up a certain typical kind of arc, a familiar structure in their music. On a broad scale, this might take the form of a soft-loud-soft curve, a natural enough strategy given their fundamental desire to emerge from the room and recede back into it. But by this point, that became

---

124   Müller, 2008.

almost second nature, something they knew *how* to do, a kind of fallback position that could become something of a crutch. This is by no means meant to suggest any waning of their individual abilities; quite the contrary, if anything. But as extraordinary as, say, Tilbury's touch on the keyboard was, or Prévost's ability with bowed metal, or Rowe's summoning of complex drones, they more and more tended to be put into service toward an architecture that gave them no particular problems. They knew how to produce a successful event. But Rowe felt that could be a problem in itself. The early idea of the "value of failure" (Beckett's, "Fail again. Fail better.") seemed to have gotten lost.

The emergence of the CD as the principal medium for recordings, of several well-distributed magazines in part devoted to experimental music and the appearance of specialty record shops in large cities similarly oriented meant that, for many listeners, this stage of AMM was their initial taste. AMM released several recordings created in the 90s, all of them powerful, mature statements. Apart from *The Nameless Uncarved Block* (from a concert at the Swiss Taktlos Festival, 1990) that featured the short-lived re-emergence of Lou Gare as a member, they are all trio sessions, all live events: *Newfoundland* (1992), *AMM Live in Allentown USA* (1994), *From a Strange Place* (1995), *Before driving to the chapel we took coffee with Rick and Jennifer Reed* (1996), and one side of an LP shared with Merzbow, *For Ute* (in Vienna, 1999). While each is excellent in its own right, and stands apart and arguably above most other improvised music being produced during that time, there is a kind of classicism, if not a complacency, that can be heard to have set in. The "AMM arc" is readily discerned. Rowe was aware, in most cases, how the performance would go, where it would end up. And even if the journey was beautiful, insightful, probing, there was a nagging feeling that he was missing some essential element of extreme importance to his own nature. He needed to look inward.

Back in December of 1978, during the period he was playing as a duo with Prévost, Rowe recorded solo for the first time, at the age of 38. He chose a piece that was also included on the JAPO album, *For A*.[125]

As in the JAPO version, a seesawing, repeated rhythmic figure underlies what's essentially "soloing," in a style that recalls Henry Kaiser from around the same period. Clearly, this fits in with the "working through the previous decade" aesthetic that marked the late 70s and early 80s. By 1989, things had become quite a bit more focused.

Rowe wasn't entirely keen to produce a solo recording and, indeed, had to be badgered into doing it by Prévost. Its title taken from a line by Cardew, "Musicality is a dimension of perfectly ordinary reality," the album (*A Dimension of Perfectly Ordinary Reality*, 1990) is a major statement by Rowe and points the way toward his music for the next decade and beyond. The four photographs adorning the CD booklet emphasize, in grainy black and white, the corporeality of his aesthetic: the metal, wood and plastic, the files, springs, washers, paper clips, buttons, and screws scavenged from the workaday world, not to mention the rough wood on which these items and the electronics are resting. It includes a piece by Cardew, "Ode Machine No. 2," and one by Chicago-based composer Frank Abbinanti, "City Music," as well as two lengthy improvisations by Rowe. The first of these, "Untitled," is a 24-minute performance that evinces numerous things, not the least of which was how readily he could deliver an extraordinarily rich and dense piece of music left entirely to his own devices (which were many). He had begun to think of his guitar as a kind of microclimate, using timbral variety to create specific environments wherein sounds could "evolve," though this evolution could be disrupted by unexpected events (mutations).

Immediately, one hears abstracted electronics and a radio conversation involving the dangers of cholesterol. Both the radio and some small mechanical device set to beat against one of the

---

125   It appeared on the album *Guitar Solos 3* (Red Records, RED-008) in

guitar strings serve to create a kind of continuo, a surface upon which to elaborate. As with any good modern painting, it's not a "background," and one can hear it as equally important to the more forceful, even strident elements one might otherwise hear as foregrounded. All of these sounds are in flux, emerging or receding via Rowe's control of the volume pedal, an essential tool in not only his music, but in most electro-acoustic improvisation generally, a device which enables a "walking through" sensibility, an ambling quality that not only allows for forward motion but for doubling back and standing still. Rowe's attack on his strings is fairly violent, very active, and scrabbling, but utterly without the jazz-rock references that similar attacks would have produced a decade prior. There's a far greater cognizance of the overall architecture of the piece, a sense of where a given set of sounds is leading, of how it fits into the whole, what its role is in shoring up the entire structure. It's a subtle distinction, but whereas in much quasi-similar music one hears a clear episodic quality, of one event or set of ideas following another, in Rowe's strongest works those "scenes" are subsumed into the whole. He has integrated Feldman's later career notion, derived from the close observation of patterns in Turkish rugs, of considering sequential sounds in relation to only those immediately adjacent while at the same time having the intuition of how they will combine on a far larger scale. One *can* hear episodes if one chooses to concentrate on that aspect, but the psychological drive imposed by Rowe onto the music compels one not to. The sense of the *expansiveness* of the work permeates; one can feel the presence of a larger creature beyond the given several seconds, much like standing at the artist's preferred 18-inch mark when contemplating a late Rothko. So when the pop song appears some 14 minutes in, it's noted mentally as an event but it's just as quickly integrated into the work as a whole, achieving parity with the co-synchronous scrapes and drones. In a solo context, one is much more aware of how crucially important choice is to Rowe

1979, along with tracks by Henry Kaiser, Chip Handy, Peter Cusack, Fred Frith, Eugene Chadbourne, Davey Williams, and Akira Iijima.

and this music generally. When (if) to introduce an element, at what volume, with what texture or timbre, for how long, which other ongoing elements to maintain—an enormous number of considerations to take into account and, with near instantaneousness, make a decision on and, of course, to acknowledge that decision and move on—all the while being very conscious of the kind of mannerisms any human is likely to fall into and, as far as one is capable, attempting to avoid them. When a popular and arguably quite catchy song like T Rex's "Bang a Gong" surfaces, for instance, how much presence do you allow? How long should it linger? Rowe typically will offer just a taste, cutting it off (often brutally) just the moment before it threatens to dominate the listener's psyche and thus the performance. On the other hand, when he serendipitously happens upon a detached (and therefore all the more horrific) discussion on decapitation and questions about how long or if one retains consciousness in such a situation, he might allow it to unspool a while longer, his accompanying music thus acquiring a much more forbidding aspect. As well, it might be a loaded signal, as apparently here, to appropriately end the performance.

Rowe's performance of Cardew's "Ode Machine No. 2," a piece he'd played often since its composition in the late 60s as part of "The Great Learning," is entirely more severe. The score consists simply of lines, variously jagged or wavy, over a Chinese text. Rowe sticks entirely to bowed guitar, referencing Chinese stringed instruments such as the erhu, while enunciating the text in an eerie, hollow manner, the barely decipherable phrases given something of a Chinese inflection. *In toto*, it sounds remarkably akin to Harry Partch's setting of the poems of Li Po for voice and adapted viola. The other composition is by Chicago-based composer Frank Abbinanti, "City Music," written specifically for Rowe, designed in part to evoke the essence of certain metropolises and broken into sections distinguishing "known" and "unknown" sounds. It begins with an extremely heavy, almost viscous, flutter of some flat metal—a large, steel ruler, probably—set between the guitar strings, a trademark

Rowe-ian sound. Soon, two intermingling radio sources are heard: a talk station and one playing Indian or Pakistani music. One pauses to note how often one hears music from the sub-continent arising from Rowe's radios. It makes sense, of course, given the large ethnicity present in and around London and serves to establish a wonderful link to a specific and pervasive aspect of the exterior world, injecting as well, particularly for the English listener, a reminder of the ongoing tension that existed and exists between the dominant white culture and the increasingly present immigrant one. In 1989, the post-modern collage aesthetic in modern music was in full swing, as popularized by John Zorn and others, but whereas the inclusion of snippets of pop culture served only, at best, dual purposes there— the appreciation of the music itself and/or the arch, knowing irony as to its placement in an ostensibly avant-garde piece of music—with Rowe, it acquires an added, more fundamentally human and important role: a small window out of the studio, into the complicated, troubled world. Much of Rowe's attack on the Abbinanti work is harsh, viciously plucking and hitting his strings in between shortwave feedback, chatter, a swatch of ragtime piano, and the ongoing Asian songs. It's a very gritty, rumbling, uncompromising performance, limning out an area he'd often return to, an anti-respite to his quieter, more softly droning explorations.

The final track, an improvisation titled "'73," is a wonderful illustration of a concept certainly engaged in by AMM (and others) previously but developed quite a bit by Rowe in upcoming years: an anti-episodic performance wherein the listener can't rightly opine about a given brief section as to whether it's "good" or "bad," whether or not it works, but rather must integrate the entire work in his/her consciousness, retaining memories of each portion and understanding how they relate to one another, what their role is in the overarching narrative. Here, after a short, morose bowed section, Rowe launches into a seesaw kind of attack that, truth be told, sounds like nothing so much as the piece, "No Birds" on Fred Frith's solo recording from 1974. But Rowe swiftly begins deconstructing it, isolating component parts, lowering the pitch in one area while roughly maintaining the original rhythm, allowing alien elements to seep in and corrode the overly glossy line. He's clearly commenting on that initial attack, unearthing yet another vestige of those fallow several years only to at least attempt to bury it once more. Nine minutes in, it's history. But rather than really butcher it, he's allowed it to sublimate, to open out into an airier, sparser locale where guitar-events can sprout unobstructed. It's as though he's acknowledging, "I had to go through that to get here, so as relatively banal as that may have sounded, it was necessary." There are even a few lucid plucks of the guitar, hanging in space, anticipating Taku Sugimoto a decade hence. One imagines reading a large painting; on the left, the vibrant sheen of a Rosenquist assemblage of colorful objects, gradually giving way to a near-vacant, though rich field à la Barnett Newman, becoming somewhat more rigorous and subtly structured toward the conclusion (Agnes Martin?) as Rowe appends a page or so from "Treatise."

Approaching 50, having participated with AMM in creating some of the most trenchant music of the preceding 25 years and finally casting out of his system the psychological dregs accumulated during the 70s, he was clearly finding his own deep voice.

Chapter 8

As the 80s wound down, American jazz bifurcated into the "new traditionalist" branch, surfing along atop the general cultural conservatism embodied in the Reagan era while, at the same time, the stalwarts from the free scene—now entering middle age and, in most cases, finding their creative juices evaporating— tended to revisit earlier ideas; by the end of the decade it was becoming increasingly difficult to distinguish between the essentially reactionary character of a Wynton Marsalis and that of a David Murray, regardless of superficial differences. In New York, an offshoot of the boho fringe of the downtown loft jazz period bore unlikely fruit with the emergence of a number of largely white, upper-middle class, highly educated musicians who arrived on the scene with the inquisitive boomer's immense, if often skin-deep, knowledge of music from every genre and geographical area, a situation that had become possible for the first time in the 60s and 70s via the profusion of recorded media. This was epitomized by John Zorn, and for a period of time his creations and that of related others seemed to revitalize the improvisatory landscape, offering a collage aesthetic that assigned equal value to Ornette Coleman, Charles Ives, surf guitar music, Ennio Morricone, thrash, and Balinese gamelan, among thousands of potential sources. Despite attaining relatively high popularity, much of this music proved to possess more surface appeal and shock value than substance and, as with much post-AACM jazz, eventually tended toward rote standardization and institutionalization.

In the classical field, the vibrant promise of the so-called min-imalists who came of age in the 60s had matured and ossified into an ever-increasing blandness, enshrined in the temples of upper-class aesthetes desperate for "serious" music with a patina of hipness that could be easily digested—a thirst most composers in that area were only too happy to slake. Alongside them were the New Romanticists, attempting to assure listeners that con-temporary music could remain tuneful *and* modern, often failing at both. The deaths of Morton Feldman in 1987 and John Cage in 1992 served (as is often morbidly the case) to push their work somewhat more into the public consciousness as record labels be-latedly began issuing their music in greater quantities, with wider distribution, on compact discs capable of holding pieces of longer duration. A label like "Hat" and its branches (hatOLOGY, hat [now] ART, etc.), by virtue of already having been something of the standard bearer for avant-garde jazz, particularly that of Euro-pean origin, doubtless served to introduce a rather large group of listeners, including many jazz fans, to a good portion of post-1950 contemporary music when they began to issue works of the New York School and others. Many of those listeners, sensing the diminution of creativity and new ideas on the American end of things (as well as being spurred on by musicians/promoters like Zorn), began turning their ears toward an area that had received short shrift in the US in prior decades: European free improvisa-tion. One began to see names like Derek Bailey, Evan Parker, Peter Brötzmann, etc. showing up with some regularity in print maga-zines as well as performing in New York establishments like the Knitting Factory and elsewhere in the United States.

As has always been the case, art that had once been considered oddball and fringe suddenly found itself occupying something of a favored position, albeit on the far sidelines of popular culture.

All this activity had virtually no musical impact on AMM and only gradually did it result in any wider appreciation or understand-ing. Referencing Cage's oft-quoted remark on there being "just the right amount" of suffering in the world, Rowe opined, when asked in 1991 if he felt overlooked, "Maybe I've had just the right amount of attention."[126]

*

Keith and Stephanie had their first child, Clement, in 1986, their second, Barnaby (named in honor of jazz guitarist Barney Kessel) in 1988. They were residing in London, each maintaining decent enough jobs at first but also becoming increasingly dissatisfied with political trends in Britain under Thatcher. By the early 90s, although AMM continued to make narrow and fragile inroads into the consciousness of a smattering of music listeners and musicians, work for the group remained sporadic to say the least: one or two concerts per year, the rare tour. Rowe might not see Prévost or Tilbury for months at a time. Given the cultural and political situation including increased violence in their neighborhood and some recent job instability, the couple figured that Rowe could just as easily not perform in France as not perform in England (his last paying gig there had been a year prior) and that Stephanie could earn a good living as an English instructor, so they made the leap, emigrating to Nantes in 1992. Rowe's brother George lived in Northern France and they had visited during summer vacations, enjoying the political ambiance, finding it more socialized than the current scene in England, and, as Rowe put it, "better traffic, better wine, better food, and good coffee." Seeing Ali Akbar Khan and Tal Farlow in the space of a couple of weeks shortly after moving sealed the deal.

In 1994 they purchased a structure in the village of Vallet, about 10 kilometers east of Nantes. It was a *cellier*, an old stone house formerly used to process the Muscadet grapes from the surround-

---

126   Rowe, in a 1991 interview with Gino Robair, portions of which were published in *Option* magazine, hazarded a guess as to one of the reasons of AMM's lack of recognition, even relative to other European improvisers: whereas, at base, their underlying influences were African (via jazz, for the most part), AMM's were more Chinese in their premises, possibly less palatable to Western intellects.

ing vineyard, a square building about 15 by 15 meters with a very high ceiling, built in the early 1800s. There were several such structures in and around the vast vineyards, none of which had ever been converted into living spaces (the very idea was a source of much mirth and bafflement on the part of local residents). But this unusual British pair tore up the floor, had radiant heating installed, and added an extension of several bedrooms to one side of the structure, creating a unique and comfortable home on a quiet road, with a fine English garden looking out onto acres of grape-vines. The quiet and solitude would suit Rowe very well—his daily dog walks with their yellow lab, Maddy becoming his "workshop" wherein ideas would be developed, premises questioned.

He became more and more absorbed in European classical music, citing Purcell's "Chaconne in G Minor" as his favorite piece of music in 1991. Mahler as well, with his seamless integration and development of thematic material proved "heavily influential" at this time. More and more consciously, he began to think about aesthetic links, progressing from, say, Ives to Rossolo to Duchamp to Varese to Cowell to Cage, Tudor, Wolff, and into AMM and his own contributions therein. Rowe also began to concentrate on projects apart from AMM. On the heels of the solo recording on Matchless, he thought more about performing on his own, able via technological innovations to more easily create full environments in which to experiment. At the same time, perhaps to counter the abundance of means now available, he would introduce strictures into his performances—curbs that would force him to re-imagine the capabilities of his instrument. For instance, he might do a concert wherein he'd restrict himself to only "string sounds." How, then, to incorporate the radio? Could he view his metal coils as strings, thereby approaching them in a different manner? He would often include work by Cardew, Skempton ("Waves, Seagulls, Shingles"), and others into his solo shows alongside improvised sections. Rowe even began to "compose" pieces after a fashion, for example "Pollock," which took tracings from details of Pollock's paintings as scores for groups of musicians, performed around that time by Chris Burn's ensemble and a decade or so later, by Zeitkratzer.[127] He began using field recordings and constructing works around them, pieces like "Frogs," where violent guitar noise mixed with the local amphibian population; nothing New Age about it, more trying to come to grips, to balance between his creation and the creatures.

AMM, on the rare occasions it would play and/or record, was slowly edging into a more pristine territory, a quieter realm where Tilbury's tendencies to evoke late Feldman combined with Rowe's increasing interest in almost evanescing his sound into the room, working toward becoming an empty canvas on which the ideas of others could be imbued.[128] Yet this transition, judging by recorded evidence, was still a work in progress. The first section of *The Nameless Uncarved Block*, recorded at the Taktlos

---

127   *In forging a correlation between the different kinds of dribbles and splashes and effects that are on the painting to particular sounds, there seemed to me tbe certain splashes which reminded me or recalled certain artists rather than representing sounds for particular instruments. For example, there would be particular splashes which would remind me, say, of John Tilbury. So what I did was to devise a grid in which I took a piece of A3 [paper] and divided it so that there were nine horizontal strips on the piece of paper. Each of those strips represents a minute because it is a practical length. My experience of reading graphic scores is that something like the long end of an A3 piece of paper is about a minute's worth of activity. Therefore the piece is nine minutes, read in the traditional way top left to bottom right. Then what I did was to take the most obvious kind of musical profile they have in Western music, which I suppose would be quite quiet at the beginning, fairly inventive in the middle, very active three quarters of the way through, and becoming quite quiet again at the end. Very much a kind of familiar High Arts-like form. The splashes themselves were quite literally transposed from reproductions of Pollock's paintings and laboriously copied onto acetate using a Rotring pen or something like that, and then photocopied. From that I was able to make a correlation between the kind of splashes and the shapes that you found on the paper with particular people I wanted to work with. So therefore what I actually did in devising a nine minute page for John Tilbury was to collect all the splashes and things that reminded me of him and his instrument and basically just trace them down, hoping that there would be something of the feeling of both, and that there might be some kind of fidelity if the person knew <u>how</u> to play them.* [Mouldycliff, 1995]

128   An idea that would continue to preoccupy him into the next decade the canvas needed to be there for the painting to exist but the viewer remains all but incognizant of its presence. Placing himself in that role was very appealing for this musician who began his career as a rhythm guitarist, an accompanist.

Festival in Basel and Zurich in 1990 with Lou Gare back for his brief return stint, begins as an exercise in softness, as though all four musicians are playing their instruments with feathers. But soon enough, Gare's presence, clearly still somewhat in thrall to his free jazz-related development of the 70s, stirs Prévost into some corresponding thrashing as things heat up to a boil similar to what had often been the case in the prior decade. Still, the overall trend was to downplay these routine kinds of outbursts, to funnel the music along less recognizable, more abstract paths.

The next release, *Newfoundland*, recorded on July 2, 1992 in St. John's, Newfoundland, points much more strongly toward future developments by AMM, and Rowe in particular. An almost 77-minute performance, it reaches new levels of spareness at the same time as it inflates the perceived sonic space into an enormous volume within which to operate, an area with only scattered material objects but vast amounts of air. Tilbury seems to be the instigator here, early on staking out delicate ground on prepared piano, again recalling the gamelan-inspired work of early Cage. Rowe has removed almost every trace of gesture from his playing, bowing the thinnest shavings of sound as from a metal lathe while Prévost concentrates on deep, tonal thuds; the combination of textures and timbres in the opening minutes is a perfect example of three distinct, piquant flavors melting into a broth that has its own unexpected and rich character. The performance has something of an A-B-A-B-A structure in terms of its dynamics—the opening, unsettled calm giving way, some twelve minutes in, to a full-on storm. Even here, though, with Prévost using his full kit, Tilbury plumbing the roiling depths of his keyboard, and Rowe generating harsh yawps, there's a strong sense of control in play. The ecstatic abandon heard in *The Crypt*, where the music is a fraction of an inch from careening entirely out of control, is absent here. There's a confidence at hand; the band knows what they can do and, if the details remain a surprise, the envelope within which they occur has been demarcated. This is both a strength in terms of a kind of classical form and perhaps a limitation insofar as degree of danger is concerned. *Newfound-*

land represents something of a high-water mark for the trio thus far: it's a perfectly balanced construction, expertly laid out, an extraordinary fabric. However, it may also be seen as representative of the kind of "beautiful rut" with which Rowe became increasingly concerned.

After an extended section of medium-cool agitation which has served to push out the potential exploratory space, to scrape away barriers, to scour clean the surrounding acreage, AMM settles into the sublime, a lengthy inhabitation of the almost-not-there, an utterly abstract soundscape of alien beauty. Whereas in the more aggressive tracts of its work, they might no longer be able to scale quite the giddy heights they had as a youthful ensemble, these more pensive, thoughtful moments benefit just as much by the maturity, restraint, and, especially via Tilbury, pure sensuality of touch now present. They glide into it imperceptibly—suddenly you're in a different space, spare but very alive. Rowe remains very much in the wings, mechanical in his rumbles, the hidden industrial core of this new world. Tilbury's gong-like chimes, like exotic hanging fruit, are offset by Prévost's bowed scrapes, the fauna scrabbling for sustenance. The sheer *landscape* aspect is overwhelming; the listener really feels transported to some spacious, infinitely rich environment, having the sense that there's even more occurring momentarily outside the range of his hearing. Things dwindle down to a point where individual sounds stand out like sparks in an enormous darkness; they're embedded in the previously-created space, not isolated on a stage—it's a very magical sensation. Rowe's sigh-filled bowing at around the 50-minute mark is a swatch of unexpected, ethereal beauty. When he slowly allows a radio feed to enter the mix—a newscast of sports results—it sounds entirely natural, an organic part of the matrix, simply a hitherto unseen thread, as are Tilbury's almost bluesy, romantic chords at the one-hour point, which Rowe quickly counters with some especially cantankerous guitar shards imparting the opposite feel.

The ensuing chaotic several minutes thus acquire a different flavor as they've grown from unique soil. One gets the sensation of encroaching on a small city, having just spent weeks in largely uninhabited terrain. AMM offers a taste of this then turns away, back toward the openness, the empty space.

We're fortunate to have two documents recorded ten days apart during AMM's 1994 tour of the United States, serving to illustrate how temporally-adjacent performances could vary widely in content and quality.

Live in Allentown USA, recorded at the Muhlenberg College Arts Center Recital Hall on April 24, is a massively cohesive, elastic, pulsating, and alive document. Tilbury's clarion piano opens, soon wedded with rich gongs and harsh guitar gashes. The rapid coalescence of these three disparate sonic elements is a marvel to hear; one gets the sense of three strands of paint being swirled, retaining their individual character even as complex patterns emerge in which that character is entirely subsumed. From that point, the ebb and flow of the dynamics possesses a tidal sense of naturalness, eddies roiled here, breeze-lapped tide pools languishing there. One has the sense that it's Prévost occupying the middle ground, willing to bend toward either the delicacy of Tilbury or the unrelenting, though often quiet, sandpaper grit of Rowe. The music attenuates to a spidery thinness only to erupt time and again, as though the barest strand contains extraordinarily compressed information, seeds waiting for the proper moment to germinate. That "kernelization," that packing of metaphorical DNA folded and refolded, is one of the key aspects of mature AMM and was rarely more clearly evidenced than here.

Recorded only a week and a half later in New York, "Contextual," released on the 1996 *Laminal* 30th anniversary, three-disc set, shows how perilous the balance could be between "success" and "failure," to the extent those terms have meaning in this music. The elements are obviously identical but everything sounds more brittle, shallower. Prévost spends a good deal of time on the traps, the piano lacks resonance, and Rowe's guitar treatments seem unfocussed. All of these are subjective judgments, to be sure, but whereas in *Live in Allentown USA*, virtually each morsel of sound contributes in an often ineffable manner to the whole, here there's more a sense of desperation, of tossing ideas out to see if they'll stick, and they generally don't. It's entropic, but of a ragged sort, chunks falling off rather than a graceful erosion. Rowe often spoke of a certain amount of dissatisfaction with late AMM in the sense that it became almost too easy to create a "good" performance, that over the years it had become something the trio could do, to some extent, without batting a lash. He felt duty-bound, by virtue of the philosophy developed in 1965, to insert "stumbling blocks" when he felt this was occurring, to create aural obstructions that would force his partners out of what he considered a routine kind of improvisation. These actions might well result in a "failed" performance on a given occasion, but Rowe thought that was far more valuable than just another deemed success. Perhaps that notion was in play here.

This touches on an oft-considered controversial approach of Rowe's that would reappear in coming years, so it's worth going into a bit. One of the fundamentals of the AMM philosophy was that there be no discussion of intent prior to a performance (or afterward, generally, apart from whether it was worthwhile to possibly issue as a recording). As time went on this became largely impractical in any case as the three core members didn't see each other often, though Rowe, by his move to France, had become more isolated from Prévost and Tilbury than they were from each other. But the point was that the music be as entirely fresh and unprogrammed as possible, so there would never be any back and forth on the order of, "Why don't we try this?" or "I was thinking of going somewhere along these lines." This by no means, of course, precludes the individual members thinking of such approaches themselves. Indeed, if not explicitly stated, it could be easily inferred that there was an expectation that the musicians would in fact *constantly* be thinking of new strategies, different attacks, and oblique ways of approaching problems. The potential benefits, as well as huge complications, are clear:

you're introducing a strategy that your companions will necessarily react to (to the extent they're aware of its presence), even if they've no idea as to its specifics, while at the same time, *you'll* be responding to ideas emanating from them. The explosion of possibilities in the aesthetic matrix could be rapid, large, and invigorating. Or daunting. Rowe took this philosophy to heart and would ruminate over certain ideas, problems he thought AMM was encountering, new uses for instruments, different directions the group might take, and would freely introduce them in performance. He wouldn't expect that they'd automatically be accepted by any means, but the ideas would exist in AMM's conceptual field for a certain time, to be reacted to or not. He fully expected the same to be coming from Prévost's direction, perhaps less so from Tilbury.

Presumably, this give and take did occur for some period of time—but over the years, little by little, a kind of complacency was setting in, Rowe felt—a reluctance to continue to push the envelope regardless of how far they'd already extended it. There was an increased sense of safety and comfort in AMM's concerts, no matter how much the average audience might have still regarded them as all but unlistenable.

Posing problems, attempting to solve them, often failing but in the failing discovering previously unknown options or potential paths—this was how Rowe thought AMM should be operating. Too, one had to deal with liking or not what one's companions were doing at a given moment. Rowe always felt that if, say, Prévost played something that he found "wrong," that was his own problem, not Eddie's. It was what Eddie felt was proper or meaningful at the time and Rowe had to accommodate it, understand it. This attitude, as it turned out, was not always mutually held.

In many ways, *Before driving to the chapel we took coffee with Rick and Jennifer Reed* might be the fullest recorded statement of the Rowe/Prévost/Tilbury incarnation of AMM. Performed at Rice University in Houston, Texas on April 19, 1996, the concert, though a single improvisation of over 64 minutes, is divided into tracks on the Matchless release as 1) Musette, 2) Vivace, 3) Toccata, 4) Intermezzo, 5) Aria, 6) Ballade, and 7) Recitativo/Coda. These allusions don't appear to be entirely tongue-in-cheek. At the beginning, the twining bows of Rowe and Prévost form a sinuous, luxurious undercurrent for Tilbury's delicate prepared piano. Toward the section's end, the drones acquire a brooding character and Rowe introduces some harsh, though fairly quiet, attacks—those disruptions he so reveled in. Tilbury maintains a kind of dreaminess, forming a delicious dialectic with Rowe, the music's path splitting, marking out huge swathes of territory between them. This could well be an example of Rowe's occasional practice of "listening by not listening." That is, he knows the general area that Tilbury is occupying and places his sounds athwart but doesn't need to "hear" each sequence of piano notes to react to them. Prévost enters closer to Rowe, with abstract clatter even as Tilbury's playing grows ever more ethereal, acquiring a kind of ghostly music-box aspect.

"Toccata" opens as Prévost seats himself at the drum kit, producing relatively conversational sounds, staying with high-pitched tones, while Rowe's scrabbling becomes furious, both all but drowning out Tilbury who also finds himself near the uppermost regions of the (unprepared) piano. It's very nervous music, like water dancing on a sizzling pan, and is the one point in this performance that still harkens back to the earlier, free jazz issues the group had in the 80s. Tilbury eventually responds in kind, sounding a bit like Charlemagne Palestine, pounding the keyboard with force, working his way toward its lower depths. It's perhaps the least successful "section" of this concert, the one where the listener senses the trio more or less treading water, but it seems to serve to get that conception out of their system and allow for the beauty of what follows.

This begins, in the "Intermezzo," with Tilbury playing brief, upward-running arpeggios, mid-range, again with preparations. From hereon in, the performance bends toward the piano, almost as though the sheer beauty of his touch becomes impossible to resist. Rowe, for his part, gradually recedes, anticipating his desire to "be the canvas" from a few years hence. Prévost, as well, reins in any too-active tendencies, the pair deferring to the nearly magisterial quality of the piano. The music flattens out, splaying like a delta, single drum and metal taps, a radio conversation, and the thoroughgoing, gentle but insistent piano. As in "Newfoundland," *air* begins to be created, vast stretches of space within which the music attains a three-dimensionality that's palpable, intimating a fourth. Rowe and Prévost create high, piercing tomes, presumably with bows, extending the piano arpeggios like clouds going from cumulus to cirrus, wisping away, accompanied by the faint voice of Billie Holiday singing, "Our Love Is Here to Stay" which, appropriately, begins the "Aria" portion. This combination: ultra-high bowed metal, spare, gorgeous droplets of notes from Tilbury and Holiday is absolutely exquisite, held for several minutes until it attenuates into vapor.

A whistling sound (a recorder?), strident and clear, announces the "Ballade," Prévost quietly rumbling, the radio switching to faraway slide guitar, Tilbury unearthing lovely clusters of notes, jumbled like sliced samples of gamelan. Rowe aggresses somewhat here with low growls and twangs, though he keeps the volume level down, integrating perfectly and helping accomplish one of those slow, brewing *stews* of sound, far more dense than one would think possible from a trio, thick and viscous. Tilbury also aims low, his pummeled keys counterpointing the garbled radio talk. The music once again starts to expand, Prévost on mallets and toms, fomenting a story, "Is this the beginning or is this the end?" emerging through the miasma, but the boiling point is kept tantalizingly out of reach, the flame reduced to a simmer, underlined by a burbling, super-low drone from Rowe. This whole track is superbly contained; not constricted, but not allowed to overflow as may well have happened in the past, the musicians willing to investigate that enormous tract of sound just below the transition from heated to aboil.

The "Recitativo/Coda," as had long since become something of a tradition, is calm and peaceful, AMM seeking to return the sound to the room as it was before they began to play, a relaxed deflation of the previous 50 or so minutes, a breathing out. Tilbury returns to the territory from whence he began the set, bell-like couplets now carrying a tinge of the evening angelus from a rural church. His unerring sense of note placement has rarely been in such clear evidence as here; one has the impression that Rowe and Prévost are reluctant to intrude, offering only the slightest of comments. Prévost soon introduces some extraordinary low, bowed moans, the perfect foil, the earth beneath the cantabile, while Rowe contributes disembodied, quiet strums and drones, perhaps a gentle reminder of the highway just beyond this bucolic scene.

For all its disc-specific division into parts, *Before driving to the chapel we took coffee with Rick and Jennifer Reed* (surely one of the *great* album titles) is a remarkably complete, entirely cohesive performance, the hour-plus elapsing in what seems to be half that time, the multiple connections becoming quite apparent in retrospect. This may represent the AMM trio at its height.

The Autumn, 1997 issue of *Avant* (with *The Wire*, at the time one of the two most highly distributed periodicals devoted, to some degree, to new music) was a "Guitar Special" and there, nestled in amongst more prominent luminaries like John McLaughlin, John Scofield, John Abercrombie, and Derek Bailey, was one Keith Rowe. Trevor Taylor conducted an interview that allowed Rowe to muse at reasonable depth and which provides a decent snapshot of his state of mind in 1997. While giving a brief account of the whys and wherefores of AMM, he touches on its relation, or lack of, with jazz:

> But I would argue that all of that music [jazz] looks back, and there appears very little of it has moved forward since 1965. A few perhaps, but as a piece of construct, I don't think it's much different, and for AMM we wanted to decon-

struct the music and then reconstruct it with extra agendas. Although we were inspired by jazz musicians, largely musicians like John Coltrane and Louis Armstrong who had such an individual voice and managed to leave their mark, but I think in jazz that process has largely stopped for the moment. It seems to me to be consolidating what it has done, making it very neat and correct.

In his mid-fifties, one has the clear sense of a man looking back at his work and trying to understand it within a continuum, to create a kind of narrative where his music, much like that of AMM in a room/context, emerges from a culture, carrying with it many influences but remaining true to itself. Rowe makes a rare reference to Cecil Taylor, remarking of his mid-60s music that he was "listening to what Cecil Taylor was doing and trying to use it on my instrument," adding, "Surely that's the way most instrumentalists actually move on. It's not just listening to people on their own instrument, it's looking at a painting or listening to a poem."

He discusses current goings on, including his graphic score, "Pollock," his participation in one of Butch Morris' conductions,[129] and the nascent Music In Movement Electronic Orchestra (MIMEO), "a project with a lot of young and unknown musicians, and many of them work with ambient music."

Rowe expresses dissatisfaction with the French improvising scene, mentioning its bureaucratic and incestuous nature (a system where friends give each other gigs that count toward a state pension but stifles, in his mind, creativity and chance-taking):

---

129   "Conduction #60, The Ploughing Season," performed at the Nickelsdorf Festival on August 21, 1996. With an ensemble consisting of: Joëlle Leandre, Matthias Bauer (basses), John Russell, Stephan Wittwer, Keith Rowe (guitars), Martin Schütz, Tom Cora (celli), Carlos Zingaro, Phil Durrant (violins), Otomo Yoshihide (turntables), Helge Hinteregger (electronics), Oren Marshall (tuba), Hans Koch, Ernesto Molinar (bass clarinets), Luc Ex (electric bass). This was Rowe's first contact with Yoshihide. Rowe, in 1997, also was a part of Conductions #81 through 87 in England.

Unfortunately, I feel that most of the music[ians] in France playing in my kind of field are total crap...culturally lazy. I just don't think they have that hard edge they have in Britain, the USA or Germany, where the musicians struggle a lot more. Here it is much more like a career! A lot of young musicians won't play with established musicians because they are career musicians. They are just getting a tick on a card to end up with a state pension. I support the idea but the music that comes out of it is absolutely awful. I have never heard such bad music.

It's a fairly cranky performance, evincing someone in a degree of discomfort with his current situation, itching to expand. Asked about Pat Metheny, who had recently recorded with Derek Bailey (*The Sign of 4*), he mentions his disinterest in the "petty digital scramble" (a phrase from Roland Barthes describing certain harpsichordists), and cites the story of a Russian filmmaker turning down a chance to make a film in Hollywood: "When the money runs out, the shame remains." Asked if there were any contemporary guitarists he admired, Rowe responds,

Not particularly. My greatest hero would be Ramon Montoya who only has an hour's worth of music, recorded around 1936. He plus Julian Bream were relevant. Those two plus Reinhardt and some other jazz guitar players I have mentioned.

Still, at the conclusion of the interview, he appears positive about the potential of MIMEO especially with its imaginative and inclusive use of electronics and sourcing. When Rowe mentions using a fragment from the Spice Girls, he again quotes Cage's line on suffering: "I think the Spice Girls are part of that!"

I am continually astounded by the enthusiasm and range, especially from younger players, rock, jazz, contemporary new music and ambient for "our music" and at festivals the sense of community is fantastic. It's like meeting old friends

over and over again, some one has known for over thirty years or more, others for just one day.

At fifty-seven, one can clearly read a strong desire to be reinvigorated and challenged by a new generation of musicians, those who cut their cultural teeth on AMM, among other music. By extension, a growing dissatisfaction with many of his contemporaries can also be felt, an unease at any complacency, even from those he generally admired.

American alto saxophonist Jeffrey Morgan was already in his early 40s when he and Rowe recorded *Dial: Log-Rhythm* in October 1997, so he wasn't *so* young, but the recording represents an early attempt on Rowe's part to come to grips with the saxophone as such, something he would return to with a kind of nagging tenacity over the next couple of decades. It's an odd entry in Rowe's discography, not the least because it was his first full-length release outside of AMM since his 1989 solo disc, something which might have been an event of sorts. Instead, we have an oil-and-water collaboration that doesn't work very well on its own merits but more, gives the impression of a one-off occurrence that adds little to Rowe's oeuvre in terms of conception, except in that general sense of dealing with the saxophone itself. At best, it offers a glimpse of where his own playing was focused, a location that might become clearer with "harsh," from a couple of years hence, as here, he remains in something of a post-Bailey mode.

Rowe did appear, in the mid-90s, to be briefly attempting some kind of reconciliation with jazz; perhaps the invitations from Morris (a large portion of his ensembles were culled from avant-jazz players) and the interaction earlier in the decade with more jazz-friendly guitarists like Frith and Hans Reichel had caused him to wonder whether a re-evaluation was in order. Tackling the saxophone would have been as aggressive a course as was possible to take. Unlike brass instruments, it's all but impossible to remove from the saxophone its jazz "baggage," the human cry that's so essential to that art form but which tends to be distracting and beside the point in post-AMM music. Even so, one might have expected Rowe to work with someone on the order of Evan Parker, someone familiar with AMM (including having guested with them) as a springboard from which to investigate possibilities, to move outward. Instead, we have Morgan, a very "saxophonic" player, working in a style very commonly heard in avant-jazz environs since at least the early days of Roscoe Mitchell and Anthony Braxton.

On the opening, 20-minute track, "Addition," if Morgan is listening at all (to Rowe, to the room), it's not apparent, as he reels off an endless series of high-pitched squeals and chirps. Rowe gamely attempts to engage, strangely adopting a kind of call and response approach, something anathema in AMM, for the first half of the piece. He eventually introduces the radio, perhaps in an attempt to nudge Morgan off point, which works after a fashion, the saxophonist softening his attack a bit, allowing a cubic centimeter or two of air into his playing, Rowe contributing a lovely, high scrim of sine-like waves, interspersed with harsher explosions. On subsequent cuts, like "Savannah Heat," Morgan reins in his free jazz tendencies, but the overall result is still an uneasy mix, the music lacking a real sense of purpose.

In 1997, Rowe was bristling with ideas, not fully formed, and clearly needed aesthetic stimulation that he wasn't receiving from his colleagues in AMM or from the "traditional," jazz-derived free improvisation scene in Europe. One path toward a solution was the ensemble MIMEO.

MIMEO was the brainchild of three promoters on the European music scene: Peter Van Bergan (Den Haag), Gerlinde Koschik (Wuppertal), and Hans Falb (Nickelsdorf) who thought it would make sense for some senior musicians to work with a group of younger electronic musicians and to rotate between festivals. They chose George Lewis and Rowe, but the former couldn't make the dates. Rowe took the opportunity and what was intended to be a one-off situation turned into an ongoing, if sporadic, enterprise. The initial three events were unwieldy affairs, the group consisting of about twelve musicians at Nickelsdorf, six at Wuppertal due to budgetary issues, and then a larger ensemble at Den Haag, though for some reason without Rowe. But the musicians had a generally positive feeling about the potential for the group, so they maintained contact. Due to their geographical scattering around Europe, Rowe would often comment that it was an ensemble that would have been absolutely impossible pre-email.[130]

Asked by Phil Mouldycliff whether or not communication on stage differed between AMM and MIMEO, Rowe responded:

> *For me personally, it doesn't. I approach it exactly the same way. It's a complicated issue...I mean communication with-*

---

130   MIMEO's first recording, released in 1999 on Perdition Plastics contains extracts from all three initial performances. The musicians are Rowe, Peter Rehberg, Richard Barrett, Gert-Jan Prins, Jérôme Noetinger, Cor Fuhler, Christian Fennesz, Justin Bennett, Thomas Lehn, Phil Durrant, and Yannis Kyriakides. By 1998's *Electric Chair + Table*, Rafael Toral, Kaffe Matthews, and Markus Wettstein had been added, replacing Barrett, Bennett, and Kyriakides. Kevin Drumm and Marcus Schmickler appear on 2001's *The Hands of Caravaggio,* while Fennesz is absent. The line-up remains fairly steady after that point, Fennesz returning, up through 2009's *Wigry*, released in 2011 by Bôłt and Monotype—the most recent recording by the ensemble at the time of this book's publication.

That sort of communication leads to things happening, which otherwise just wouldn't happen if it was letters or phone calls. In the old days it used to take ages to get things done...but I think for a lot of us who weren't so well connected, the e-mail has become a real revolution, allowing us to get things together that we wouldn't have been able to do five, six, ten years ago. I think MIMEO is a case in point.

What initially attracted me to MIMEO was that this was a huge "found object." I haven't ever chosen a single person in the group. Marcus Schmickler for example, wasn't in the original edition, but was in the Cologne series because Felix Klopotek at the Stadtgarten said that "he's really fantastic" and that he had to have him in there. Somewhere else we played, they wanted Jérôme Noetinger to be in it. Suggestions have come mainly from promoters, so the selections haven't been made in terms of instruments. [Mouldycliff, 2004]

*in AMM is more or less possible. If you choose to, you can
influence what's going on to a much greater degree than in
MIMEO. So in AMM you can actually change the direction
of the way a piece is developing, very radically and very
easily with no problem whatsoever. In MIMEO "turning
an oil tanker" doesn't begin to describe it (laughs). Like
in AMM if you stop playing totally for an hour it would be
noticeable whereas in MIMEO if you stopped playing for an
hour, no one would notice. So I think in a way, clearly one's
relationship to what's going on, is different. I don't think I
approach it any differently except that I know that in MIM-
EO I can do almost nothing. It's quite nice being able to sit
there for ages and ages just fiddling about until you feel
you have something you want to contribute.*

Largely due to a combination of economics and individual com-
mitments of group members, MIMEO only performed less than
twenty times, though their realization of Rowe's "The Hands of
Caravaggio" in Bologna in 2001 would have repercussions on the
fate of AMM (discussed next chapter). One recording, though it
did not appear until 2007, is worth discussing here as an example of one of the most thorough integrations of visual art and
musical ideas in Rowe's oeuvre, something he'd been considering
for quite a while, including in the late 90s.

*That whole kind of "response" stuff, I've never, never liked...
though at various times I've done it. Increasingly as the
years have gone on, I've got to the point where I now
actively don't like it at all. It seems very primitive to me...
artistically very obvious. So I wanted to produce something
that didn't have that...call and response. I knew that Cy
Twombly often drew with his wrong hand, blindfolded, rubbing paint directly onto the canvas with his hands so that
when he removed the blindfold..."voilà...that's it." I felt that
there was something we could do a MIMEO version of, with
each person away from all the others in different times
and spaces. During the month of March 2004 I invited the*

eleven of us to each create a sixty-minute CD-R, that would then be stacked/layered on top of one another to produce a single master-copy, which would be released without any of us having heard it. The idea then is to find someone to release it without having heard it...so that maybe you don't get to really hear it until the CD comes out. It could be awful...or it could be incredible. This is where it's important that everyone pays attention to what Cy Twombly is about...that is, thinking about what the others might be doing without actually knowing and laying down something that they are very proud of. Hopefully people will produce about two minutes of material in total, spaced out over the hour. When these are stacked together, hopefully there will still be a lot of "space." So the appreciation here is...what are we dealing with? If we are thinking of Cy Twombly, we have to make a "triangularization" between three things... between what you do, what the others might possibly be doing, and what the Cy Twombly painting indicates to you. So, the only "known" in that is the Twombly painting... which actually has loads and loads of space in it! So what does that tell us...it tells us we shouldn't do very much. It shouldn't have a thick texture...it's not a Jackson Pollock or a Rothko! It's the "blindfoldedness" and the "non-listeningness" that seem to me to work together. If we do our jobs correctly and do what we're supposed to do, it will have that "uncatchability" of eleven minds.[131]

The project took a while to be realized, the collection of individual contributions (eventually totally about five minutes per musician, spread as intuited over an hour) being completed in 2006. Marcus Schmickler then mastered them as received, without listening. Richard Pinnell agreed to issue the results on his Cathnor label without any prior listening. In fact, he went down to a local record store and purchased a copy himself, taking it home, unwrapping it, and hearing it for the first time. It was called *sight*,

131   Ibid.

a double pun on both Twombly's name (Cy T) and the sense he did without on occasion; the title was embossed on a pure black sleeve. It's a remarkable recording, very sparse—the performers restrained themselves admirably, no automatic assumption by any means, given the general vociferousness of several—the listener tasked with creating patterns and structures for himself, investing happenstance overlaps or contingencies with meaning, always a fascinating experience.

The *sight* project was indicative of the sort of thing Rowe always had brewing, ideas that required more than AMM to actualize.

Chapter 9

Earlier this year I did a small number of solo concerts in a straight row, and over a matter of three or four days I said everything I wanted to say. So that when I came to one particular night in Derby, I remember going on and I just sat in front of the instrument and asked the question, "Right anybody, what do I do now?" Quite literally, I performed while holding a running commentary, stopping sometimes midway through a piece to discuss the decisions that I felt able (or unable) to make. Obviously it's very difficult, you can't always have such an intimate relationship with your audience. Sometimes you just have to look as if you know what you're doing. (laughs)[132]

AMM fractured for the second, and seemingly final, time in the spring of 2004, but the seeds for the disjuncture had been planted much earlier.

I first encountered Keith in the fall of 2000, at a performance in Boston, also my first opportunity of having the privilege to see AMM in concert. I'd driven up with Jon Abbey, who had already met Keith in 1998[133] and established a personal and professional

---

132   Mouldycliff, 1995.

133   Rowe recounts his introduction to Abbey while at a music festival in

relationship with him, having just that summer released *The World Turned Upside Down*, a seminal recording by Rowe, Gunter Müller, and Taku Sugimoto on his label, Erstwhile Records. The Boston show was stunning, Rowe in particular contributing elements both extremely reticent and hugely rich that impressed me deeply. Afterwards, I was introduced to him and we talked for a half-hour or so in the vacated auditorium seats. My main recollection was his concern that AMM's music was becoming too routine, that it was now far too easy, given the abilities of the three members and their long-term relationship and sensibilities, to create a "good" concert. This disturbed him greatly. He mentioned that he'd taken to introducing "stumbling blocks," awkward offerings on his part that would disrupt a flow that he thought was in danger of becoming pat, forcing (as it were) Prévost and Tilbury to deal with an ill-placed or "improper" element, at the risk of, in one sense anyway, destroying the event. "I often find failure much more rewarding than success," he said.

This is hardly an unknown sentiment, of course. Even if rarely stated so boldly, it has many precedents, in Beckett and others. Cage had discussed the need for failure as well but, like many concepts generated by the 20th century avant-garde, the notion was more often paid lip service rather than adhered to, including by most musicians involved in this area of music. But it was something that, however belatedly, struck a chord and caused me to look at his work, and AMM (and much else) in a different light. That whole idea of expecting each performance to somehow be "great" (after all, you paid money to be there!), something that's very much ingrained in the vast majority of listeners, was laid bare as an absurdity, all the more so with regard to a music that purported to be improvisatory, explorative, and adventurous. One expects the musicians to make a concerted effort toward the

———————

Wels, Austria in 1999. Watching a performance in which a guitarist was using a handheld fan on a horizontal guitar, he heard a voice in his ear mischievously asking, "Mr. Rowe, have you ever thought about using a fan?"

realization of some idea (or, perhaps, to act in opposition to that notion or even to consider it irrelevant), but *that* is where whatever "success" to be had would lie; if things occasionally come together into a transcendent whole, great, but it's senseless to expect that every time out, given the experimental nature of the work. The feeling certainly fed in, however, to Rowe's growing restlessness in AMM, combined with his increasing exposure to, and aesthetic collaboration with, many other musicians who had absorbed AMM's lessons and, in certain respects, moved on from there. As well, it contributed toward his use of "strategies" during AMM performances, ideas he'd develop while in Vallet, walking the dog, which he'd introduce without, naturally, informing Prévost or Tilbury, some of which would eventually annoy them enough to take action.

> *If you were to look at the classical form, the sonata, that form is very recognizable. I think that arc is AMM's version of the sonata form. The other thing that happened in the very early days of AMM, there was a much more strident defense of the word "improvisation." In order to gain a distinct view of what improvisation was, we made very determined, full of revolutionary zeal, of the difference between improvisation and composition. I think it was entirely the correct thing to do, to make a bedrock set of foundations for the belief in improvisation, its character, not having it confused with anything else. But now in 2007, having established pretty firmly what improvisation is, I think a lot of us can see improvisation as a form of composition because when AMM sat down to play, it wasn't actually completely free. Our original notion that "any sound was possible" is no longer true because there's a whole raft of stuff that is not possible. In fact, you could say that we are hemmed in by all the things that are not possible to do. Then it becomes compositional.*

Speaking of his work with Toshimaru Nakamura, specifically the *Weather Sky* recording on Erstwhile, Rowe said:

I thought, yeah, I've probably been wanting to make this music for years, but even in AMM there isn't that patience. You'd think there would be. If you were going to appraise AMM, one of the things you would say is that compared to all the other music around, AMM was extremely patient music making but when I hear Toshi, no it wasn't! All this reinforces the idea that, for me, AMM is a particular classical form. I was becoming aware of AMM's limitations, that it wasn't actually free to do whatever.[134]

In years to come, Rowe would often opine that *The Crypt* was AMM's freest, most probative, and beautiful recorded work and, thinking back on his state of mind, one feels that this appreciation of that "point," reached early on, must have been gnawing at him. The Rowe/Tilbury/Prévost trio was classical in an intended and successful sense, but it had, in the process, left something behind: an openness to a larger infinity of possibilities, so to speak, something that for Rowe was most closely approached in the incarnation of the ensemble from its conception, through the late 60s, when the members were far less aware of the possibilities and limitations. I'm not sure that Prévost would agree, or more, that he'd think in those terms at all, of there having been a "high-water mark," rather than experiencing and transmitting the music as it came, without regard to consciously positioning it in any historical continuum.

Several developments in Rowe's psyche seem salient: his extensive interaction with non-AMM musicians, his growing appreciation of where (if anywhere) his work stood in relation to the Western "classical" continuum, and his, it might be said, *more* steadfast commitment to the fundamental principles of AMM, which could well

---

134   Rowe's collaborations with Nakamura resulted in some of his most wonderful and satisfying work, including two releases on Erstwhile, the above-mentioned *Weather Sky* and *between* (2006), as well as countless concert performances. In one instance, where they were surprised by a promoter's insistence they play two sets instead of their standard single set, the second part consisted of Toshi giving Keith a haircut.

include the introduction of ideas not conducive to an easy outcome, difficult and obstreperous notions that might perplex or aggravate his cohorts. Let's look at this latter element first.

It wasn't an "official" AMM dictum during the formation of its tenets in 1965, but Rowe had carried (at least) one aspect further than most of the musicians involved, certainly in a manner different from Prévost and Tilbury: he only *played* music in performance. Not only did he never practice; any ideas that occurred to him—and ideas surface with some regularity in Rowe's head—were not tested except in live conditions, in front of an audience, with other musicians when not playing solo.[135] Prévost had, in interviews and elsewhere, extolled the virtues of practicing, and clearly Tilbury emerged from a classical milieu where practice was a given, although not necessarily "practicing" improvisation. Prévost was, and is, a master technician and doubtless could have been a pre-eminent free jazz drummer were he so inclined.[136]

One has a strong sense indeed that there was always some degree of pull in that direction, which once upon a time formed one of the central, beautiful nodes of tension between he and Rowe, with Tilbury eventually becoming a kind of ameliorating force or, more accurately, a third ideational node. Rowe, to a large extent, was explicitly anti-technique in the Duchampian, found object

---

135   A small example: During the morning before a solo performance in New York City in the late oughts, Keith came along as I did some grocery shopping. At one point he noticed on display a kind of battery-operated tooth polisher. It seemed interesting, so he made the purchase. That evening, it took its place among the various items on his tabletop. Several minutes into the performance he picked it up, turning it on for the first time, and brought it close to his guitar, causing a massive yawp of feedback. He gently replaced it on the table. About twenty minutes later, he returned to it, holding it at a three or four foot distance from his guitar, the feedback becoming modified into a resonant, deep hum that integrated seamlessly with the other various ongoing sounds.

136   Readers are urged to hear his extraordinary 20-minute solo performance on the duo recording with Alexander von Schlippenbach, *Blackheath* (Matchless, 2008). It both incorporates lessons learned from AMM and is presented in a manner that would have made Max Roach proud.

sense, although inevitably his mastery of choice and placement can be said to be another, broader example of technique or virtuosity. He would often site David Tudor's realization of Cage's "Variations IV" as one of his favorite performances ever, which can be heard as an epitome of this sort of non-technique technique. But his method was always more cerebral, more idea-oriented. This was something that chafed at Prévost's more organic, visceral sensibility (despite his own occasional forays into the field, as far back as *Silver Pyramid*), an approach that he'd criticize as deriving overly much from the art school mentality, again serving, within AMM, as a delicious point of tension, a feedback loop of aesthetic antagonism that propelled the ensemble's music into great, mysterious depths. Rowe's embrace of various electronic devices and the remoteness they arguably implied could also have been a sore point, something he understood.[137]

> *It's an old argument, and every arena probably has the same thing. In the development of the gun, in the Middle East, you had these men who were like samurai who grew up using these sabers from Egypt and they were real masters. They developed the skill from childhood. Then these African guys bought guns from the British and the ones who had spent years honing their skills became, understandably, very grieved. They would say something like, "A woman could pick up one of those things and bang! kill you! That's not right!" And it's really sad and I do understand the position, but that's the reality, they've invented these things and it's true, a woman can pick one up and point it at you and pull the trigger and with all that skill that you've honed, with that blade with four million layers folded in, it doesn't matter.*

137   Rowe would come late to actually using a computer as part of his set-up, not doing so until the middle of the 2000s and, even so, found that he derived far more substance from holding a contact mic to its surface and amplifying the mechanical sounds therein than from any software applications. The laptop only lasted a short time as part of his palette.

Since AMM began, it was a principle of Rowe's, and presumably most, if not all, members that, as he put it, "If Eddie does something that I don't like, it's *my* problem, not his. *I* have to figure out how to incorporate his sound into my conception of where the group sound is."[138] By extension, the same principle applies not only to a given sound or set of sounds that one might conjure up during an improvisation, but a wider, more general set of ideas that might have been thought of between performances that seem, to him, capable of fomenting some exciting interaction, upsetting the equilibrium, etc. When introduced, these ideas might be pointedly strategic (as in "The Hands of Caravaggio"), more general, or even arcane (listening by not listening). Often they were borrowed from the visual arts: trying to fill the role of the canvas beneath a painting, trying to replicate the tinge a Rothko imparts to a room, trying to evoke Twombly's apparent randomness. Whatever his ideas at a particular event, these were, it almost goes without saying, kept to himself, not discussed with Prévost and Tilbury any more than he would clue them in on a specific sound he was intending to introduce. This seemed to be the obvious way to operate and, more, he assumed that his ensemble mates could (and would) well be doing the same thing, thereby opening a vast matrix of possibilities wherein competing

---

138   In fairness, Rowe himself could be inconsistent in his own reactions when placed in a similar circumstance by musicians with whom he was performing or recording. When compiling the recordings with Radu Malfatti for what eventually became *Φ* (Erstwhile 060-3), the agenda was in three parts: an improvised set, a composition by each musician, and two compositions by other musicians. For the latter, Rowe selected a piece by Cardew, "Solo with Accompaniment," while Malfatti chose Jürg Frey's "Exact Dimension Without Insistence," the score for which demands that the guitarist cleanly pluck a clear b-flat eleven times over the course of some 20 minutes. Rowe was annoyed in that Malfatti knew very well he didn't carry a tuned guitar and, moreover, didn't play it in the "classical" sense required by the piece, didn't even carry a standard plectrum in his arsenal. It took him quite a while to accommodate himself to this, eventually finding a pigeon feather in the street outside of Christoph Amann's studio and, after several hours, managing a single acceptable note, which was reused for each required presence over the piece's duration. But he was unhappy about being "forced" into such a situation One can imagine the mischievous Malfatti's delight.

(or cooperating) strategies would vie with each other, accommodating or resisting as their proponents felt appropriate. It would keep the music invigorating and open-ended.

However, as mentioned above, he was acutely aware of the tendency for any long-term creative venture, no matter how strongly premised, to develop its own kind of ruts, beautiful though those ruts might be. With AMM, most serious listeners had long since sensed a kind of AMM-arc: a very quiet beginning, a gradual crescendo, perhaps two, a diminuendo back into silence. Within that there was a reasonable amount of variation and, to be sure, that model provided a great deal of extraordinary music, but it's not difficult to see how, stepping back, a certain kind of sameness, a structural comfort zone, had developed, a model had formed and become a limitation—one could do "this," but one daren't do "that" lest the arc would be interrupted and the set might "fail."

> I mean often there have been times when I haven't liked what's been done, but that's my problem! My view has always been that if someone is doing something within the group that I'm uncomfortable with, then I have to find a way to make sense of it, to reconcile it with what I'm doing. Over the years I've made sense of it in terms of the word, "juxtaposition." I never felt we all had to be doing the same thing. For me it's always more interesting looking at objects on a shelf—they're just there! I wanted the music to be like that, not even "artistically" arranged, just an extension of reality with no central interest, totally flat on the level of creativity. From my perspective, the "art" of the music was somehow to produce music that was poised, that had an emotional response, that had significance, without intentionally conveying meaning. I think in the very early years it was much more about "playing in a space," but it became more political at some point, the "playing" became "performing" and the "space" was replaced by a politically charged "environment." Performing, for me, definitely has

*more intentionality and projection than playing. I think
with environment, we were more conscious about what was
going on around us in a specifically political way. I think of
late, AMM has definitely become more stylistic, partly to do
with the way John plays, maybe some kind of narrowing of
the language, to the point where it could be a fair observation to say that it's become fixed...I think we've probably
got to the point where we have to decide whether or not it
should be allowed to ossify into a highly predictable sound
world with an identifiable style and repertoire. Maybe it's
appropriate that AMM should be like that in its old age,
but I'm not convinced it should be! I think of it as my role
in AMM to add an edge to what goes on. But then again,
maybe there's a place in improvisation for a trio that makes
exquisitely beautiful music precisely and without wastage
and almost no experimenting in the broader sense.*[139]

In the spring of 2002, I attended the Musique Action festival in
Vand'oeuvre France, near Nancy. Several pages from "Treatise"[140]
were scheduled to be performed by an ensemble made up of
AMM, Formanex (Julien Ottavi, Christophe Havard, Anthony
Taillard and Emmanuel Leduc) with the late Laurent Dailleau on
theremin and John White on electric keyboards, the latter having
played on some of its earliest performances.

The first 20 or so minutes of the set were quite attractive, subtle in the manner one had come to expect. As I recall, Formanex
and Dailleau began, the music gradually segueing to AMM, then
all together, keeping the volume level quite low and creating
wonderfully complex relationships, timbral contrasts, etc. It was
quite satisfying, just the sort of thing that had begun to disgrun-

---

139   Mouldycliff, 2004.

140   Rowe feels that each page of this score should, ideally, take 8-10 minutes to "read" and that recordings or performances that purport to play all 193
pages in less than two and a half hours, as in the hat ART release realized by an
Art Lange-led ensemble, are absurd and have entirely missed the point.

tle Rowe. White was seated mid-stage, between Formanex on his right and AMM on his left. I don't remember if he had contributed to the first section or not but, if so, he blended in finely.

Suddenly, from at least one of his devices (something like a cheap Casio mini-keyboard, I believe), came a sequence of the most banal, crass, and "inappropriate" sounds one could imagine: sheep baaing, babies crying, gunshots, and more, each more awful than the previous, entirely and disrespectfully disrupting the exquisitely balanced mood in a pointedly show-off-y manner. I sat there appalled by the wretchedness of what was transpiring, the ruination of what had been, prior to White's entrance, such an enthralling experience.

And yet…

Something gnawed at me. There *had* to be some sort of rationale in play, I thought. Still, as the performance tortuously wound its way to its conclusion, I writhed in my seat. When it was over, I sought out Rowe and asked him what that was all about. He explained that he thought that most readings of "Treatise" were approached with too great a sense of reverence, so he had asked White to inject sounds "that one would simply never hear in a "serious" performance."[141]

This triggered an unusual reaction in me, one that would recur many times in subsequent years listening to Rowe's work: A qualitative reappraisal of my initial impression based on coming

---

141   I hadn't realized at the time that White had operated along similar lines as early as the mid-60s! Rowe on White's readings of "Treatise": "...he has deliberately calculated to do the opposite of what you might conventionally expect; long lines would be treated as very short plucked sounds, for example... In a way, performing indeterminate scores relies on that [strategic undermining] but also opens out a set of possibilities which can lead into complex areas, where the black areas or marks are treated perversely and the white spaces, that is the page, or even the fabric of the paper itself becomes a subject of focus; then you get very strange relationships indeed." [Mouldycliff, 1995]

to know additional information that was unavailable before or during the first hearing. This opened fascinating areas not necessarily even intended by the (in these cases) musicians, often initiated by the (here) listener, even if such ideas had been in mass circulation at least since "4'33"." Problems of identity—what *is* the work? Does its nature (or quality) change depending on what you know? In some ways, it's a variant on the ancient "ship of Theseus" problem, where the dissembled boat, its component parts having been removed little by little over the years until nothing of the original craft remains—is it the same boat? What does "same" mean? More, and more to the point of the above instance, had someone been discreetly collecting the discarded pieces and reassembling them, after a complete overhaul—which vessel is the "real" Argo? Which performance was the "real" one that day: the cringe-inducing one or that in which White's contribution was placed in a larger, more completely understood context? Among other places, this idea will recur with Rowe's introduction of European classical themes and forms into his solo improvisations beginning later in the decade.

Now, Rowe may have felt that his companions in AMM "should" be operating along the same lines (or at least Prévost; as mentioned, Rowe has remarked that he's not sure if Tilbury ever *really* understood the essential premises of AMM, not through any fault of his own but simply by virtue of not having been involved in the specific gestalt of its inception), but he was surely not so innocent as to ignore the likelihood that they weren't. For Prévost, aside from the inherent value or lack of same therein "art school" strategies, there was also the sense that by initiating them, Rowe might be imposing a subtle form of coercion on the others. The experience of "The Hands of Caravaggio," both in actuality and in misinterpretation on my part, is a good case in point.

MIMEO, Rowe has mentioned, could not have existed prior to the advent of e-mail, its ten to twelve members scattered throughout Europe, each with involvement in his or her own music and other musical collaborations. Opportunities to perform were quite rare; at this writing, in 2016, those instances might still number less than two score since the group's birth in 1997. So as to avoid the unfortunate tendency, with so many musicians manning such powerful equipment, of disintegrating into a loud, formless morass—a constant hazard—MIMEO generally adopted a format wherein one member sketched out a plan of attack for a given performance, a composition if you will.

In the early years of the new century, Rowe was fascinated by the recent (1990-93) discovery, in the dining room of an Irish monastery, of a hitherto unknown painting by Caravaggio, always an important artist for him, which depicted the taking of Christ. In addition to various states of awareness on the part of the characters represented, there emerged from the shadows of the canvas a number of beautifully expressive hands forming an absorbing and complex dance. As ever conflating painting and music, Rowe conceived of a project for MIMEO and John Tilbury in which the musicians would assume the roles of characters in the painting. Moreover, they would act as the "orchestra" for two pianos, a kind of 21st century double piano concerto, with at least one of the pianists in the role of Christ, having to hold his own against an electronic scourge. One has to wonder whether this may have been, in part, a kind of subconscious dramatization of the conflicts, largely unspoken at this point, occurring in AMM.

The concert was set for Bologna, Italy in May 2001. As it happened, only one piano was available so Rowe adjusted the plan, asking Cor Fuhler to operate inside the piano while Tilbury played the keyboard. This is where the misinterpretation on my part enters the picture, a mistake that may have had reverberations later on vis-à-vis Tilbury's relationship to Rowe and subsequent siding with Prévost when the second AMM split occurred. Discussing his ideas for the piece with Rowe shortly afterward, I had the following impression: knowing Tilbury's "typical" contributions on piano, as beautiful as they were (the Feldmanesque sequence of seven or eight rising notes, for instance, something that any AMM devotee would immediately recognize), he asked

Fuhler to listen for those same events and, when heard, to block them by damping the piano strings in one way or another, "forcing" Tilbury to seek alternatives, pathways he would otherwise not have taken, avoiding those gorgeous routines. This turned out not to have been the case, although I didn't realize it until after I had published a review at Bagatellen[142] stating the above. The reality was that no such instruction had been given. Rather, Rowe had known, simply by virtue of Fuhler being inside the piano, that Fuhler would necessarily impede some of Tilbury's figures and was content to leave that to chance.[143]

Tilbury, upon reading my inaccurate description, was incensed, bristling at this apparent coercive action on Rowe's part, taking it upon himself to negate whatever spontaneous contributions the pianist had decided to make at the time. But let's say that it had been the case, that Rowe had intended just such strictures. Would such a strategy have crossed a line? Is there a substantial difference between formulating a pre-performance plan that would shape the subsequent improvisation in a way unknown to (at least one of) the participants and doing so, via his own sound activity, during a performance? Was part of Tilbury's reaction a reluctance to acknowledge that, the same as anyone, his improvisations over time began to fit comfortably within a given area? Surely he realized this, though perhaps, it would be impolite to have it pointed out overtly. (Is this more offensive in the context of British musicians than, say, Americans? Different cultural mores might apply.) But, adhering to the AMM premise of the basic newness and apartness of each event, one could also view it as an earnest effort to knock him out of a (perceived) rut, to, out of love and respect, jostle him away from a natural kind of complacency, one that affects the vast majority of musicians, however

---

142   Bagatellen was a website begun by Derek Taylor, Alan Jones, Jason Bivins, Nathaniel Catchpole, and myself as a discussion point for matters related to electro-acoustic improvisation and related music and art.

143   See further discussion below, relating to Prévost's critique of the event.

much they may strive to avoid it. Rowe, as mentioned above, had taken to doing something similar when he thought AMM's music was becoming too pat as well, injecting some disruptive noise if things were becoming too routinely ethereal (perhaps taking a cue from John White re: "Treatise" readings) or, the reverse, if the music was approaching a quasi-free jazz freneticism, receding into a featureless and quiet hum, acting as a sound-sucking vortex, absorbing the excesses. Ideally, of course, the other members would be operating on the same wavelength, resulting in a wonderfully complex fabric of give and take with unpredictable results. In Rowe's view, however, this seemed to increasingly not be the case and perhaps he felt incumbent to take matters into his own hands, so to speak, hence risking the ire of the persons being unwittingly "manipulated." Prévost had always had some misgivings about this aspect of Rowe, complaining for example of his use of amplification to sometimes drown out he and Tilbury, thus "imposing his will" on them. Rowe, commenting on AMM procedure in 2004, shortly after leaving the ensemble, said:

> One of the early purposes of AMM was to develop a music that was probably based more on "trust" than "genre." If you think of a jazz or pop group, you agree which genre you are going to move in and this provides the primary point of departure. Because AMM was formed at a time when there wasn't a genre for that music, I suppose like any other group under those sorts of conditions, trust was what it was based on. After the initial period of being very analytical we converted that trust into a way in which we would work anyway and, bizarrely, on one level, we decided not to talk about or discuss the music and let it take care of itself. The history has been that you haven't commented in any depth on past performances, there wouldn't be any detailed picking apart of individuals' contributions, which is different from other groups I have been in where there has been a specific expectation of the way you would play. Clearly, of you don't have a genre/style agenda, what that meant was that over the years the members move off

into different stylistic areas. One of the very early state-
ments for AMM, written I think by Victor Schonfield, was
that "AMM has the ability to emit all sounds." I think that
it was important that there were no limits to what could
come out. So for me, for instance, the sound source could
be a symphony being played on the radio or a German
"number calling" station; it could be virtually anything.
The issue then is exactly how you control "that" in the
context of what is going on around you. So for me it was
the implicit/explicit agreement, I think, that we wouldn't
comment on each other's work. That we would do what we
felt was needed under the circumstances at each moment
of performance, using all our available skills, to make our
contributions work within the totality of the space. Why it's
difficult to talk about now is because Eddie seems to have
published a fairly comprehensive and critical view of my
way of working. For me, it breaks something that is funda-
mentally "AMM," that notion of tolerance about what other
people in the group do.[144]

A more subtle "strategy" was something superficially described
as "not listening" on Rowe's part which, possibly given fuel by
such incidents as occurred or didn't in "Hands of Caravaggio,"
led Tilbury and Prévost to later attack Rowe for his aloofness,
arrogance, etc. Of course, what was meant by the phrase was the
attempt to integrate more fully than ever the sounds being created by his companions (and himself) into the totality of the room,
to give them (only) equal weight, no more than anything else that
might be occurring therein or, perhaps more importantly, happening in the world at large, that greater "room."

It might be worth noting that the whole concept of "the room" for
Rowe went far beyond the walls that happened to be surrounding
him, though the actual sonic content of a given space, in a Cagean
sense, was always crucially important. What had occurred in the

---

144   Mouldycliff.

world that day or in recent times, what he'd experienced himself, what all his friends had undergone, what he'd eaten—anything at all. As he'd been famously quoted, there were always several dozen things he'd be thinking about as his hand first descended toward the guitar, all of which might be brought to bear during the performance. What Tilbury or Prévost would be doing were two elements, but their place in Rowe's consciousness might or mightn't be paramount—he *heard* them, in other words, but he didn't feel compelled to react *only* to them.

All of these issues and more besides were simmering then and some had been on the burner for a very long time. Another matter that, for Prévost in any case, likely exacerbated the situation was Rowe's increasing amount of non-AMM performances and recordings, especially his association with the American label, Erstwhile, run by Jon Abbey.

Abbey, a music fan and former writer for *Time* magazine, had begun the label in 1998 for the expressed purpose of documenting music that *he* wanted to hear that wasn't readily available. A long-time admirer of AMM, he met Rowe in Vienna in 1999 while attending a festival curated by Otomo Yoshihide, titled Mottomo Otomo. Aggressively opinionated by nature, he badgered Rowe with ideas for recordings, including a duo with Jim O'Rourke, but something else eventuated...

Let's back up a bit. Around 1997, Rowe heard a piece of music on the house PA system at an event organized by the young Nantes-based electronic musician, Julien Ottavi. It was from a record called *Opposite* on the short-lived hatNoir label (a subsidiary of hat ART), played by the Japanese guitarist, Taku Sugimoto. Its extreme sparseness and simplicity struck Rowe with enormous force. Amidst the gabble of free improvisation at the time (including, still, occasional eruptions within AMM), it was a beacon of rigor, reticence, and clarity. It was also his introduction to that Japanese scene, sometimes referred to as "onkyo," which dwelt in areas of severe quietude, with long stretches of minimal activity (in reality, at least in part urged in that direction by the small, thin-walled rooms available for playing in Tokyo). He would soon come to meet and perform with others in that circle, including Yoshihide, Toshimaru Nakamura, Sachiko M,[145] and many more.

In 1999, at Instants Chavirés (a new music venue located in the Parisian banlieue of Montreuil), he was able to perform in a trio with Sugimoto and the Swiss drummer and electronicist Günter Müller; Müller's late 80s ensemble Nachtluft, as previously mentioned, was one of the first groups to clearly sport an AMM influence. The recording, through a series of mishaps, essentially fell into Abbey's lap and was issued as Erstwhile 005 in 2000 titled, *The World Turned Upside Down.*

Listening to it more than ten years later, it does less to presage Rowe's work in upcoming years than to open up a range of other possibilities in electro-acoustic improvisation—not that this was the only example, but it was a prominent one, with Rowe's imprimatur—including the more tonal and pulse-oriented ranges explored by Müller and affiliated musicians. For Rowe, it was more of a portal into, specifically, the world of the Japanese improvisers and, within that, the discovery of his aesthetic brother, Toshi Nakamura.

Several of the key Tokyo-based musicians had been involved in a severe paring down of their sound, reducing the material resources employed to a bare-bones level, then seeing how much of interest and beauty remained to be extracted. The ensemble I.S.O. (Otomo, Sachiko M, and Yoshimitsu Ichiraku) was one of the first working groups to deeply investigate this area but Sachiko M on her own and Nakamura were the two who stood out in this regard. Sachiko, a "non-musician" who had been a member of Otomo's formidable Ground-Zero ensemble in the mid-90s, used a sampler—ubiquitous in that decade—but empty of any samples, utilizing only those sounds capable of being evoked from

---

145   Given name, Matsubara.

the instrument's basic electronics: sine waves, static tones, etc., wielding them with knife-edge precision and, most importantly, patience, allowing those "unvarying" tones (but endlessly varying if the listener simply moved her head) to linger for extended periods of time. Similarly, Nakamura took a portable mixing board and, essentially, ran the outputs back into the input slots, creating feedback loops that generated an immense garden of sound, not always controllable. He too was often content to reside in a single wash of tones for lengthy stretches, providing the listeners time to discern the multitude of details within for themselves.

This approach struck a strong chord in Rowe, both the paring away of clutter and the complex stasis of the sound. As he had been working with the idea of becoming akin to the canvas in a painting—unremarked upon but essential to the actuality of the work—so they might be likened to the sand in a Japanese rock garden. The sand accommodates the beautifully placed rocks more than it reacts to them. It acknowledges its essential separateness even as it admits to sharing the same space. The awareness of this fact was becoming more and more crucial to Rowe's conception, an idea antithetical to Prévost's communitarian spirit. As said, this may always have been the case to an extent and, indeed, it can be argued that this contrast provided one of the basic nodes of tension that enabled AMM to attain such richness. But it came more to the fore as Rowe continued to push in that direction (and others) while Prévost, I think it can be fairly argued, "settled in" to more of a routine form of improvisation. This is not to belittle his work, of course—it remained very impressive—just to acknowledge the tendency, with age, to become comfortable in one's habits and, perhaps, more bound by them. Rowe is unusual in that regard, in consistently searching out new ideas, making *himself* uncomfortable, continuing to resolutely question premises.

Prévost, as evidenced by many of his side projects, notably AMM II with Gare but also in the workshop groups he organized, retained an abiding love for the rich organicism of free jazz. It would clearly surface on occasion with AMM, to these ears an incongruous sound for the most part. But Rowe's response was more expansive and, one would think, more in keeping with the original premises of the ensemble. As mentioned, he felt the obligation not to criticize the contribution of others but to figure out how to embrace it. Prévost seems, to an increasing degree, to have had much more difficulty with this, at least as time went on, if not early in the group's existence, though Rowe recounts that there were arguments along these lines throughout AMM's history. Prévost took it personally which, in keeping with the communitarian ethic, perhaps made sense: he was intensely involved in the social interaction and internal cooperation while Rowe was stepping back and observing the scene, the performance, in a wider context. Neither was right or wrong, obviously, but the strain was beginning to tell.

Prévost was always a writer; Rowe was not. In the years prior to compact discs and the internet, they would happily give the occasional interview but those opportunities were scant. To the extent there were records of the philosophy behind AMM music, they were largely encapsulated in essays by Prévost, some of which were published, many not.[146] Prévost was also the principal force in the operation of Matchless Records that was almost exclusively the source of AMM and AMM-related projects for the world at large. The advent of CDs and, by the early 90s, the somewhat increased exposure to the public via magazines such as *Option*, *Avant* or, ultimately, *The Wire*, helped get Rowe's own ideas to the public but the internet had a far larger effect. Rowe was much less reserved in open conversation or written dialog than Prévost, indeed was voluble and always willing to discuss the most arcane matters for the asking. As well, he was genial and as interested in the opinions of his fellow conversationalists or posters as in expounding on his own. He adapted quickly to the on-line world whereas Prévost was more reticent. All of

---

146   This writer hopes that one day Prévost will see fit to publish these tracts as the ones I've read have been extremely rewarding.

this, over the course of time but certainly by 2000 or so, led to a situation, unintentional though it might have been, of Rowe having become the de facto spokesman for AMM as well as the *éminence grise* of the burgeoning eai scene, unfair though this certainly was. He became the focal point, the go-to reference, aided no doubt by his increasingly wide range of activity with younger musicians from Japan, Europe, Australia and the US, including extensive touring. This, one suspects, could not have sat well with Prévost, especially insomuch as many of the ideas being espoused by Rowe were not shared by him and might be interpreted as "AMM" rather than "Rowe."

There was also the increasing influence of Abbey via Erstwhile, which had become by the early 2000s more or less Rowe's label of choice for his major work outside of AMM. Abbey took on a much more active role as producer than many in the field, rarely being very interested in functioning musical units, preferring to suggest new groupings of musicians that he thought would work, often involving meetings of people who had never before played together. In fact, he had proposed a recording of AMM with Christian Wolff but couldn't get an agreement by Prévost to allow any such session—unfortunately it never occurred—to come out on Erstwhile as opposed to Matchless. He also had recognized the pull of the free jazz sensibility in Prévost and wondered, during a particularly awkward and poorly produced concert at Bard College in 2002, how a duo with Rowe and Tilbury would sound. Abbey actually raised the possibility in conversation immediately after the show, Rowe placing a quieting finger over his lips, indicating that it wasn't the proper time, then and there post-concert in a student center, to discuss such a venture. To be sure, it was treading on delicate ground.

Abbey was opinionated and not shy about expressing his views. Worse still, he was American and easily fit into certain European views of the typical American character—brash, aggressive, forward. Prévost already had misgivings about so much of

Rowe's recorded work appearing outside of Matchless, though he couldn't issue a huge amount of material himself and, in any case, wasn't very convinced as to its worth. Still, any sort of "control" of the AMM legacy was clearly slipping away. Abbey's idea of a Rowe/Tilbury duo, as enticing as that might be to many a listener, could fairly be viewed as a cutting out of Prévost, a statement saying, "Perhaps more could be achieved without you," a provocative, not to say offensive notion. The idea clearly appealed to Rowe, however, and eventually a deal was negotiated (with Prévost's blessing) and a recording session arranged to take place in January 2003 in Vand'oeuvre, France, in the theater used for the annual Musique Actuelle Festival.

I wrote of the event for the Bagatellen website and reproduce it here:

*

I should begin, I suppose, with a few caveats. One, I'm a good friend of Jon Abbey, the owner/producer of Erstwhile Records and was fortunate enough to be in attendance with him at this session. Two, I've gotten to know Keith Rowe quite well over the last few years and am currently working closely with him on his biography. For that matter, though I had only met Tilbury fleetingly prior to this date, I came to like him very much personally and recently published a profile of him for The Wire, generating a tiny swirl of controversy.

Despite having known each other since the mid 60s and having been together in AMM since 1981, this is the first time the two had performed, much less recorded, as a duo[147] ("Except," as Keith mischievously remarked, "when Eddie stops playing.") The event almost didn't occur. Three days prior to the recording,

---

147   In fact, they had played together as a duo a handful of times in the mid-70s, unfortunately never recorded.

Tilbury's 95-year old mother, Doris, had a stroke. She died the next evening and Tilbury, understanding the lengths that had been gone to arrange the date, originally scheduled for two days, agreed (insisted, in fact) to come down from England to France for a single day of recording. This was accomplished in the same Vand'oeuvre theater, and with the same rented piano, that AMM had recorded *Fine* two years before. At dinner the evening before the session, Tilbury asked Rowe if he had any ideas for the next day. Keith replied no, that he thought when John touched the piano he'd actually be using, the ideas would flow. At the session, aside from the two participants and the recording engineer, Jon and I were the only ones at hand; a very special day.

They created five pieces over the course of about three hours of playing, three of which were selected for this two-disc set. Tilbury warmed up by playing some Chopin, a little Schoenberg (a quote from which he interjected into the proceedings, much to Rowe's amusement, in one of the improvisations not used for the final release) and a few English folk songs. The first piece on *Duos for Doris*, was also the first performed, a 70-minute construction of immense range and depth. Tilbury begins by rubbing a drumstick on the brass inner frame of the piano, treating it as purely percussion for the first six or seven minutes. Rowe, as has been more and more the case in recent years, is very much content to provide a "canvas" for his collaborator's activity (though not necessarily a featureless one by any means), positioning his music as an element as integral as it might be unnoticed. He arranges laminae of drone-like sounds, with low, middle and high tones of varying and complementary textures. The swelling nature of these drones creates a highly dramatic sense of anticipation, one deeply rewarded when Tilbury finally enters from the keyboard with several low, pulsing chords. The release that occurs about fifteen minutes in, when the improvisation seems to acquire a life of its own, is one of several extraordinary moments to be found here. The music is redolent with emotion, giving lie to the charges of aridity and stoicism often leveled at musicians such as these. Granted, knowledge of the immediate and tragic events surrounding Tilbury's personal life may have played into my perceptions, but it seemed (and does still seem) clear the emotional depths he plumbed. Some of his playing will be recognizable in general type by listeners familiar with his work in AMM, other aspects find him exploring entirely new territory (a judgment rendered not only by myself, but Rowe as well). The piece quiets down noticeably for fifteen or so minutes, remaining fascinating in a rustling, chittering way, before building to great intensity at about the 40-minute mark. In fact, the volume level rises enough, Tilbury pounding the keyboard with fury, that some distortion sets in for a minute, although nothing that detracts from the force of the music. He builds to it with piercing chords, struck in a slow but nearly regular pattern that generate a huge amount of psychic pressure, accompanied by screeching metallicisms from Rowe, before the inevitable explosion. A series of funereal chords from Tilbury lead to contrastingly bright, Feldmanesque arpeggios, ushering in a kind of entropic process, the two musicians scraping and plucking in a dark, cavernous space for quite some time, almost to the point of a-musical activity. But in the last few minutes, Tilbury finds an amazingly delicate, single note "melody," more like some faint, ghostly chorale, with which he brings the piece to a close over the poignant, Rowe-generated sounds of a distant propeller plane and what briefly sounds for all the world like an EKG monitor. Here, as everywhere else on this release, Tilbury's incredible sense of touch and of pure note placement is beautifully apparent; always fluid, always the slightest bit off the cadence.

This second piece begins with the sound of birds over a faded, swing-era jazz recording. Tilbury quickly emulates the birdsong, trilling in the upper register. Rowe utilizes the radio more often on this track than elsewhere, though it rarely appears with clarity, instead appearing buried under distortion and static. Tilbury has placed nails, dowels and metallic balls on his strings, generating gamelan-like sounds from his keyboard when he's not attacking the piano's body with drumstick or fist. Rowe is operating at least four or five levels of sound here but all occupying such distinct zones that it's difficult to comprehend them at the same time; different listenings almost necessarily cause one to concentrate on different aspects. Here as elsewhere, especially in the album's closing moments, Rowe employs a tactic that might be initially irritating but, I think, serves a meta-purpose: when things get a little too beautiful, a bit too smooth, he will cause some rude noise to erupt. The crinkling of a scrub pad on the guitar strings or the harsh buzz of one of his many small fans will interrupt the sonic bliss, reminding the listener of the real world, one in which any thoughts of a peaceful heaven might be as ultimately meaningless as they are understandably desirable. There's some remarkably anguished playing by both musicians about 20 minutes in, Tilbury eliciting frantic sounding yelps and Rowe ripping brutal, strangled roars from his machine. Eventually, a deep, throbbing drone develops. When it gradually peaks and begins to dissipate, Rowe conjures up a surprisingly (for him) rhythmic little motif, a casual thump accompanied by a metallic swish, boom-shee-boom, a beguiling nubbin that jauntily carries the next several minutes of the improvisation. This gets subsumed beneath a billowing hum as the music enters a cloud-like steady-state feel for a while, Tilbury casting about as though swimming through darkness, seeking elusive shards of light. Toward the end, Tilbury floats to the depths of the keyboard, phrasing the dark chords with more a sense of acceptance than surrender.

The final piece, in some ways the most moving, is in two distinct parts, each of equal length. Tilbury plays two high notes off a chord that sounds almost as though lifted from a processional while Rowe maintains a steady white noise pattern that feels subtly ominous. There's very much a dark and light sensation here, the piano striving to remain optimistic, even rosy, the electronics steadfastly insisting that there is no way out, threatening each dreamy Feldmanesque arpeggio with a deluge of feedback. After a brief pause, Tilbury stands and begins to stroke one of the piano strings between his fingers, eliciting an extraordinary, ghostly tone. One by one, he fashions a simple, lovely melody with these coaxings, just on the edge of audibility. Ever so subtly, he transfers this ethereal song to the upper reaches of the keyboard, a single note threnody heartbreaking in its purity. It's difficult to imagine any other companion not letting this hymn stand on its own and gleam but Rowe just will not allow this illusion to remain untouched by reality. He scrapes and rubs his devices, quietly enough not to totally interfere, but with enough presence to make his point. It's a tough lesson, and one that many listeners may actually object to, but that's one of Rowe's great strengths: No easy answers.

Duos for Doris captures two musicians of immense intelligence, probity, and aesthetic rigor at heights arguably unscaled by either. It's as powerful a performance as I've ever heard.[148]

*

How much this event, the performance, and subsequent recording (which was widely regarded in the AMM-aware community as a signal achievement) contributed to Prévost's simmering animosity and resentment is impossible to say with certainty but it surely carried a good deal of weight. Tilbury as well, both in reaction to strategies imputed to be in effect in "The Hands of Caravaggio" and to comments such as my own above theorizing one of Rowe's roles as a counterweight when the music drifted toward the conventionally "beautiful," later expressed displeasure with what he viewed as manipulation and control freakery. Where the line between "controlling" and influencing was drawn seems to have been the object of significantly different points of view. Had Tilbury heard a typical "Rowe-ism" and said, "Well, I know where this is going, let me put an end to that right now," Rowe would not have objected:

> *No, of course not! There are scores and scores of occasions*

---

148   For Rowe's comments on the recording, see: http://www.erstwhilerecords.com/catalog/030.html

when John has done something completely surprising and outstanding. For example, we were doing a concert in Sapporo, Eddie and I walked on stage and began playing. After about five or six minutes, there's no John Tilbury. I think we were both thinking the same thought: I hope he's not been ill in the toilet. We became slightly concerned. It was like 20 minutes but it seems like an age. Then through the dark of the audience, you see this stooped figure walking through the chairs and tables in this raincoat with the collar turned up, very Brecht, and then he sits at the piano, hunched over making these very strange sounds. Fantastic!

In the spring of 2004, Eddie Prévost (using his given name, Edwin, as he did for written work) published a collection of essays titled *Minute Particulars*[149][150] in which, among other things, he presents his views on recent trends in contemporary music and improvisation and how those trends size up against his commitment to communitarian music and ethics. In his introduction, he stresses this stance, calling for artists to "look beyond the idea of 'art for art's sake' and sense that in all creative activity there is a reflection—and at times an inspiration—of a wider civil society." Before going into the arguments he sets against his long-time ensemble mate, it needs to be mentioned that, according to Rowe, Prévost never once advised Rowe of the nature or content of what he intended to publish. Presumably, there was some period of time, a year or two, perhaps more, when they were performing together with AMM at the same time as these essays were being written. Rowe's first awareness of the existence of the book was when he received a telephone call from an Italian journalist asking for his reaction to what Prévost had written about him; he had no idea what the caller was referring to. As he would later say, "...if he came up to me in May 2004, put his hand on my

---

149   Copula, 2004.

150   "He who would do good to another must do it in Minute Particulars." From "Jerusalem" (1804-1808) by William Blake.

shoulder and said, 'Look, I've published this book, it's out in the world. There's quite a lot in it that you'll take exception to. I'm really sorry, I had to do it, there was no other way. I really had to get it out of my system. There's a lot you'll be irritated by but let's see if we can work through it.' I probably wouldn't have left." But the sense of betrayal he felt at having played, talked, and dined with Prévost in the interim, while all this was going on, was powerful enough for Rowe to consider it impossible to continue the partnership, hence his self-removal from AMM. As to Prévost's motives for approaching the matter in this fashion, I will say more after analyzing the content at issue.[151]

Early on, in the essay titled, "Music as a Site for Social Existence," Prévost begins to establish his targets, adopting a slightly tendentious tone. After tracing the claim that "sounds exist in their own right" (at possible variance with the title of his earlier book, *No Sound Is Innocent*) to Cage via Varèse, he writes:

> Improvised music as a setting of communitarian art form is receding. It is not retreating from this position. It is being pushed.[152]

and

> Some sort of permanent change (for change's sake?) has become a necessary totem for this activity. New music dare not stand still. This seems to me to be as much to keep curators happy as to keep work fresh. But fresh for what? For I can see little evidence of any socio-political agenda, other than a reinforcement for the priority of a

---

151   Over the years, Prévost had, in letter form, expressed his disagreements with various aspects of Rowe's approaches many times, dating back to the late-60s. He would even send cassettes of performances, offering them as proof that Rowe was overly dominating, playing too loud, etc. They would also stray into more personal matters. So the general notion that Prévost had relatively deep issues with Rowe's music and/or behavior was by no means unknown to Rowe.

152   *Minute Particulars*, p.10.

market economy, in which the parts are variously con-
tending and consuming.[153]

Thus Prévost begins to frame his aesthetic adversaries as representative of an encroaching (if not already present) individualist
ethic, self-centered, and at least relatively heedless of the idea of
an art embedded in and beholden to society. The next section,
"On Idiom-discourse, diversity and the potential for repres-
sion" focuses on two guitarists, Derek Bailey and Rowe, and the
problems which arise, in Prévost's opinion, as a result of their
insistence on, in Bailey's case, terming his work "non-idiomatic
improvising," and in Rowe's, of "not listening" (discussed in a
later essay). He's fairly gentle with Bailey, offering the common
critique of the idea of "non-idiomatic," reasonably wondering
whether any such terminology carries meaning and observing
that experienced listeners will often be able to determine that
a given piece is improvised, indicating that there may well be
something idiomatic about that music. He then, perhaps, gets in a
preliminary jab when, after positing that the act of "writing tends
to be the most coherent way to create a logical construct," he
says, "In music-making, maybe relevant ideas only come through
the actual practices."

He briefly discusses Rowe's purported contention against the notion "that dialogue has any (conscious?) place within his music."
He contends that Rowe prefers "musical co-existence" as opposed to actively engaging with his playing partners, their relation signified by "spatial position" rather than interpersonal relationship or communication. Later in the essay, he seems to relate
this stance to glorification of the individual at the expense of the
collective, though no names are mentioned. Here, Prévost appears to be warping Rowe's notion of "listening by not listening,"
a Buddhist-derived idea, with willful distancing and personal
isolationism. Rowe has commented upon the essential impossi-
bility of really, deeply communicating with other individuals and

153   Ibid. p. 11.

bristles at the facile sort of "interaction" found in any number of free jazz or other improvised ensembles wherein one hears the banal "he played this so I'll play that" kind of call and response over and over again. Additionally, one of the guiding principles of AMM music is that it arises from the situation at hand, from the room and that "an AMM concert begins fifteen minutes before the first sounds are played," implying (if not overtly stating) that the entirety of the situation, or as much of it as can be gleaned by the performer, is the "partner," the collaborator with whom one is interacting, not merely the individuals happening to be sharing the stage. Contrary to any idea that he's exempting himself from the proceedings or placing himself on any kind of pedestal, he's actually immersing himself more deeply into the reality of the moment. If he's relegating his playing companions to a status they consider lowly or impersonal, who is more concerned with their individuality?

"The Almost Unintended Consequences of Indeterminacy" traces the influence of Cage and others down through Cardew (specifically, "Treatise") and contemporary improvisation. Prévost makes several astute observations questioning the depth to which current musicians come to grips (or not) with Cage's ideas. He concludes with comments about the quieter areas of improvisation often, with some lack of clarity, corralled under the catchall term, "reductionism," an area for which he has no great fondness, citing one possible root in the silences created during AMM performances but claiming a distinction insofar as these were context-driven whereas modern musicians, it is implied, arrive at their quietude without having the "proper" understanding or preparation.[154] Prévost then makes a rather startling leap, introducing a perceived hierarchy limned with explicitly religious references: "...if Radu Malfatti is indeed the Pope of reduction-

---

154   This is, doubtless, an accurate observation in many cases, akin to the free jazz musician who immediately leaps into full-blown late Coltrane-isms without having followed a similar path to arrive there. But, of course, it's also an extreme generalization that would time and again be gainsaid by given musi-

ist music, then Keith Rowe is its Jesus Christ." He continues, "Although at the moment [presumably around 2003] even the messiah himself seems currently to be somewhat in thrall to the theology of reductionism."

Leaving aside his problems with this area of music, Prévost's affixing of religious titles to Malfatti and Rowe certainly carries along with it, to the modern secular mind, the stench of blind adherence on the part of listeners as well as self-delusion and self-aggrandizement on the part of the named pair. It feels like an almost involuntary burst of rancor born of, one imagines, years of brewing enmity and resentment. On a purely personal level, it's not difficult to understand how painful a stab this was to Rowe. "The Rhetoric of Compassion Couched in the Sounds of Destruction" concerns the idea of extra-aesthetic aspects embedded in art, whether it's worthwhile or counterproductive to allude to, for example, real world tragedies in a work of art. Prévost rightly asserts that this can often act, to the audience, as a substitute for actually effecting change—a vicarious thrill to provide the ersatz sensation of experiencing something apart from the (in this case) music, allowing a kind of superiority/complacency. He seems, however, to countenance only these two poles—either one alludes ineffectually to some external matter, however abstractly, or one doesn't, that it's somehow immoral to make reference to an ill without (at the very time) performing some more direct action to correct it. It's odd to proscribe art from this in-between aspect where, one presumes, there would be no problem with having a conversation about a given issue in lieu of hastening to physically do something about it. In any case, Prévost devotes the second half of the essay to Rowe's solo release, *harsh,* (Prévost

---

cians who are quite well aware of these matters. It also maintains a notion that comes increasingly under question by, among many others, Cage—that there is some vital distinction between "professional" and "amateur" artists won by dint of hard work as opposed to natural affinity and openness. Presumably, under this mode, a self-described "non-musician" like Sachiko M would not be credited with having produced deep and meaningful music, something that Rowe, for one, would argue against.

omits the comma from the title), citing it as an example of a failed attempt to inject social concerns into an aesthetic work.

Rowe's conception of the performance, as is often the case, contains multiple levels of reference. The first, pedestrianly enough, was the simple fact that it was extremely cold, near freezing, in the garage in which he was performing in Köln on November 30, 1999—harsh conditions indeed by typical musical performance standards. But Rowe had enough sensitivity to understand that whatever discomfort he was undergoing sitting there, it paled next to that experienced daily by billions in the world. He naturally took that as the "subject" of his improvisation, not dissimilar to the manner he'd generally imbue his playing with various aspects of the "greater room," abstracted though they might be. As Prévost notes, the music itself isn't particularly harsh by AMM's or Rowe's standards; in fact, arguably, the degree of "harshness" is in inverse order to that implied by the three track titles, "Quite", "Very", and "Extremely", perhaps indicative of a wry commentary on his own temporary pains. This mode of operation couldn't have been news to Prévost. Indeed, and rather ironically, it was Rowe and Cardew pushing this idea to the extreme in the early 70s, squeezing out the aesthetics in favor of the political, that caused Prévost (and Gare) to bristle enough that AMM disbanded for the first time. Again, one may well agree with Prévost's basic premise, that mere allusion in art to serious social issues acts as a sedative on the audience, enabling the *feeling* of having done something rather than the actual doing of something, but any number of musicians could be found "guilty" of this. He singled out Rowe and, as well, didn't bother to talk to him about it, eschewing the possibility of garnering some explanations or counter-arguments. How simple to have asked, "Keith, what were your ideas and concerns during the concert that came to be, in its CD release, called, "Harsh,"?

The affair surrounding MIMEO's performance, with John Tilbury, of the Rowe-conceived, "The Hands of Caravaggio" is the subject of the chapter titled, "Simulacrum? - a case study." Prévost, who hadn't attended the concert from which the recording was drawn, relies on a piece written by Tilbury for the Erstwhile site, a thoughtful work conveying the pianist's trepidation at the venture (the massed electronics vis-à-vis the piano) as well as, possibly, the misapprehension of Rowe's motives due to the reading of my own mistaken notions of the work as outlined above. Rowe's description of his conception of the work (in 2007):

> The whole piece would start for who would make very long sounds with his ebow. That was designed. What I said to the whole group about that, including John and Cor, was that the piano was dreaming the history of the piano. It was dreaming about something it could never do, make long sounds, but Cor Fuhler would do so with the ebows. But what I didn't want was a MIMEO...starting the concert in a MIMEO way, like the Grand Prix, where everyone shoots away from the starting line and it becomes a dog's dinner in seconds. I wanted the start to get really into the space, to think about it. So I had the idea for a very gentle start, very quiet, everyone thinking about it and feeling the space. Then this history of the piano. Then John would join in and play whatever he wanted. Then gradually, we'd come out of those long sounds and begin to encroach on the piano. This was based on the painting, an act of betrayal. At the center of the story is that in MIMEO there were two violins in the line-up with Kaffe Matthews and Phil Durrant and you'd see these acoustic instruments being subverted by the electronics. This is all in the program notes. The acoustic piano is then in a battle situation, fighting for its survival. There's no real ending where the piano's crushed, but it's definitely encroached upon—the parallels with the taking of Christ. The other thing was that the temple guards in the painting are pretty ignorant people; they have no idea what's going on. So I actually didn't tell the whole story to everyone so some people didn't have the whole idea of what's going on. I told John more than anyone! I don't think he realized that. So Kevin Drumm

was in complete ignorance of what was going on; he was a temple guard. (laughs)

I have no idea where [your idea] of the damping comes from. Maybe your thoughts come from this: What I probably said to you was that realizing there might be two pianos there'd be no issues. But with one piano there might be a problem. What I wanted then was that a thin edge of the wedge for the piano in the 20th century goes back before Cage to Cowell. That's the thin edge of the wedge. So that's what Cor was representing, this decline of the piano. So that's what Cor would be doing in limiting where John could play his notes. But knowing that John is an incredibly skilled performer, that he could see the strings which were available to him. So his possibilities were definitely being limited but not in a way that was antagonistic or offensive. There are constraints and he'd have to use his skills in dealing with it which I didn't think would be a problem.

I could see that it could turn difficult depending on the mindset of John. There were a whole number of unfortunate things. For one, it's in Bologna. The guy who organizes the concert was Massimo, who's a huge fan of John's. John brings his wife Janice and I think, "John is at the piano in a public concert in Bologna, with his wife in the audience," and he wasn't able to do his usual John Tilbury stuff. If I'm going to put it crudely, I think his ego gets the better of him. I think he felt snubbed. He issues a statement which has some surprising elements which makes a kind of case and Eddie jumps on that statement because it satisfies a whole number of things. So he's got John Tilbury as one witness but completely ignores Cor Fuhler at the other end of the piano. He uses Alvin Curran's ear witness account which seems to come from the wrong part of the concert. Whatever. But I think it's brilliant because I felt a sense of betrayal from John and Eddie so it goes right back to the painting!

Prévost, again without taken the simple precaution of consulting with the work's organizer (Rowe), any of the participants apart from Tilbury, label owner Jon Abbey, or mixing/mastering engineer Marcus Schmickler, chooses to view things in the worst possible light, positing that Tilbury had been "inveigled into a situation," an act that "borders upon cultural exploitation and possibly sadism." It says something about his predisposition toward Rowe that he seemed so willing to jump to the extreme, malign end of things without taking the common courtesy of routine fact checking.

He also relies on the testimony, largely negative, of the composer Alvin Curran, who interpreted the work as a kind of "ritual slaughter" in which the pianist "was overwhelmed, trampled on, and finally murdered," though he acknowledges that he left before the work's conclusion. From the recollection of others, including an audience recording of the concert made by Lukaz Zagoričnik, it's likely that Curran actually attended a rehearsal event that occurred the afternoon previous to the recording, a wilder affair. But even if not, the complex arrangement of the speakers more or less ensured that the only area from which to gain a balanced appreciation of the many elements involved was near the middle of the room, a fact which Cor Fuhler, who was in that space, verified, also saying that the resultant recording, on Erstwhile, matched his memories of the event. Prévost nonetheless takes the CD to task, claiming that there's been a "technological revision, to make the recording acceptable to the public." Curran, writing about the disc version, seems baffled by the difference between it and his memories of the event, wondering if he's been "completely inveigled" and "Is this CD a hoax?," never questioning either his location in the room or whether in fact he might be misremembering which event he actually attended. Neither he nor, more importantly, Prévost opted to merely talk to Schmickler, who was in MIMEO apart from being responsible for the mixing and mastering. Prévost writes:

> Given that struggle and obliteration seem to have been
> a significant (and intentional?) part of the musical

agenda and of the concert, it is curious that evidence of this rather uneven conflict was not translated onto the CD. And, given that some of those present at the concert do not recognize the CD as representing or supporting their memories of the event, it has all the hallmarks of, if not a cover-up, then at least a re-configuring of history. For what we have left of the actual event are the fading memories of the concert and the recording as an aide memoire. Given the time-honoured insecurity of reminiscences, which version in the fullness of time is likely to be taken as the truth?[155]

Certainly a fair question, though leaving open the implication that only those consulted by Prévost have correct reminiscences. It's hard to avoid the observation that, were he interested in fairness, it would have been supremely easy to get Rowe's opinion of the affair, not to mention those of Abbey, Schmickler, Fuhler, etc.

Next, Prévost sets his sights on Rowe's remarks about "not listening,"as written in his notes for the *Duos for Doris* recording with Tilbury. At this point, it becomes hard not to perceive a willful misreading or at least misunderstanding about Rowe's meaning. Rowe is clearly reacting to the all-too-common situation in so-called free improvisation where one encounters variations on call and response, where the music is "conversational." Rowe had often decried the notion that you could really, deeply communicate with someone on that level and so, to at least some extent, he attempts to eschew it, choosing to embed his sound contributions in the world at large, not only the space in which he and others are performing (where they will become, in his perception, elements no more or less important than any others) but in matters of history, aesthesia, politics, and so on—things he has been thinking about while not on stage. Prévost clearly understands this idea, of course, early on citing Tilbury's method of improvisation as being "informed by listening to everything

---

155   *Minute Particulars*, p. 80.

(both on and off stage) that is going on" but insists on denying this approach to Rowe, whom he has preconfigured as a selfish individualist. Granted, Prévost's ideas about communitarian improvisation are different from Rowe's and I've no doubt he took exception to the latter's wonderful phrase, "visceral chic" in describing the common substitution of forced energy and angst for deep musical content but he would also have realized how the tension between the pair, exemplified in this and other differences of approach, was one of the salient foundations of AMM's success. Rowe's then-current desire for "obmutescense" (muteness)[156]—of trying to be like the canvas beneath a painting, necessary but not apparent—is taken by Prévost to be antagonistic and adversarial, self-centered and possessive. "Music...is not painting," writes Prévost, knowing full well that for Rowe, music *is* painting. But rather than deal with that, to recognize *that* assumption as part of the community that must be negotiated, he attacks it in principle, snidely relegating the attitude to "hermetically sealed apartments, in which communication occurs more through the intercom (or, more likely, the internet), rather than through direct and responsive human connectivity." All, of course, without contacting the object of his scorn and, perhaps, gaining a fuller understanding.

Among a collection of other essays appended at the end of the book, Prévost includes a previously unpublished appreciation of *Duos for Doris*, written in 2003. It's very sympathetic and admiring, though he gets in a few jibes at Rowe for his "marauding self-assertiveness...on AMM's 'The Crypt' or his own 'Harsh' [sic]." He obviously understands that much of the beauty of this recording derives from just the kind of interplay, here between Rowe and Tilbury, that he derides elsewhere: Rowe's skepticism, his "air of irritability, of menace and foreboding," all of which create a dialectic between his insistence on a grimmer reality and Tilbury's heavenly, ethereal thoughts. It's more than a little

---

156   Rowe savors a remark by the French Baroque painter Nicolas Poussin: "I who make a profession of mute things."

baffling that Prévost can't (or, at least, doesn't) extend this line of thought into the other areas he's criticized.[157]

In any case, leaving aside judgments on the rightness of this or that argument, the vindictive tone taken surely pierced Rowe's person. That and, as discussed, the disappointment of Prévost not having mentioned that these assaults were in progress, much less talking with the object of his attack, was enough for Rowe to decide that he could no longer have any professional association with Prévost, such a longtime friend and collaborator, and hence with AMM. One is forced to wonder whether this result was the one anticipated by Prévost, whether this wasn't a passive/aggressive method of forcing the issue, of easing Rowe from the ensemble. It's difficult to think of another reason for springing this on a longtime friend.[158]

---

157   There exists a recording of an AMM concert performance in Glasgow on June 28, 1997 wherein one could get a sense of Rowe being what Prévost might consider overbearing. Much of the first half of the set is dominated by Rowe in terms of volume and presence, with both guitar-generated sounds and radio grabs. Although the music eventually resolves into more of an equilibrium (and beautifully so), it's not difficult to imagine that, in this instance, his companions might have felt themselves being corralled into a certain kind of enclosure.

158   Over the years, of course, I have attempted to document Prévost's side of the argument regarding the whys and wherefores of publishing *Minute Particulars* without in any way apprising Rowe. As the book was begun shortly before the 2004 break-up, there was an understandable reluctance on his part to be involved with someone who might be "taking sides" against him (I had only met him a couple of times and then only superficially). There was a brief thaw around 2006 when we spoke over the telephone and he graciously sent me some burns of early AMM performances. After the episode outlined in the following footnote, communication again ceased. Despite several attempts, this remained the state of affairs until the AMM 50th anniversary celebration in Huddersfield, England in November 2015, whereupon we spent a great deal of time engaged in extremely pleasant conversation. Thus heartened, I initiated another e-mail dialogue, covering various issues and gradually getting to the nub of the matter as of August 2016, after which I once again heard no more from him. As of the end of 2016, the deadline for submitting this manuscript for publication, Prévost has regrettably declined to continue, other than to say that he understood what the reaction would be when he published *Minute Particulars*.

And so Rowe's relationship with AMM came to an end. Prévost and Tilbury would continue to perform and record as AMM, often with guests, although in Rowe's mind "AMM" had two basic prerequisites: that it contain at least three members and that two of those had to be himself and Prévost. He thought that the post-Rowe grouping should properly be called AMM IV, AMM II having been the Prévost/Gare duo and AMM III his own with Prévost. E-mails were exchanged, some of them much nastier than anything printed publicly; it was clear no fences were to be mended anytime soon. [159] Tilbury sided with Prévost during this ordeal—apart from his frustration and anger with Rowe, he and Prévost both lived in London and were close friends on a day-to-day basis—though largely without the percussionist's degree of malice. For political reasons, largely having to do with the ongoing invasion of Iraq, Tilbury had refused to travel to the US and wished to have as little to do as possible with American-funded

---

I do have one idea, a particularly devious one given Prévost's belief about, and antagonism toward, Rowe's ostensible use of hidden, coercive strategies within AMM and elsewhere (as thought to have occurred in *The Hands of Caravaggio*), that his fellow musicians should be able to cope with any "obstructions" he throws their way, and, given AMM's longstanding erasure of any distinction between their music and "real life," perhaps Prévost thought of his own verbal attacks as similar "stumbling blocks," in life instead of on stage—things Rowe would just have to deal with, unpleasant as he might find them.

159   In late 2006, a flurry of e-mails erupted that were at first centered around a proposal by Eric Lanzillotta for his label, Anomalous Records, to release the pre-AMM, November 1965 acetate recording and the March 1966 AMM concert at the Royal College of Art in a newly re-mastered boxed set. Rowe was in favor of the idea while Prévost had reservations, preferring to release any such material on Matchless, if at all. Rowe, at this point, did not wish to be further associated with Matchless and had already objected to the recent (2005) release of *Apogee* which he claimed to have preferred remain unreleased. This resulted in a lengthy e-mail from Prévost (the other recipients were Lou Gare, Lawrence Sheaff, and Lanzillotta) detailing a litany of complaints against Rowe, many of a very personal nature, including charges that Rowe "manoeuvered" both Sheaff and Gare out of AMM and a certainty that he was next on the chopping block had Rowe not left on his own. The specificity of the charges aside (some of which Rowe acknowledged, some he didn't), the intensity of the exchange leaves little doubt that at this point in time, emotions were still running quite high. As of 2016, these recordings remain unreleased.

companies, including record labels like Erstwhile, which was publishing more and more of Rowe's work. In 2010, following the death of Rowe's mother, Tilbury thought it appropriate to renew contact, given the circumstances with regard to his own mother just prior to the *Duos for Doris* recording, and offer a rapprochement. The pair played a concert at Instants Chavirés in Montreuil, just outside of Paris, that December (released on Potlatch Records as *E.E. Tension and Circumstances* in 2011) and would continue to perform together on occasion thereafter.

It's an arguable point that, while this was a wrenching decision on a personal level (severing a long-term relationship that had produced much astounding and profound music), Rowe's own art may have been better served outside of AMM which, as we have seen, had become to an extent somewhat stultifying to him. Its dissolution, as far as he was concerned, freed him to expand into areas that, despite its ostensible premises, were not possible within the mature AMM trio formation. He could freely abandon anything he perceived as a crutch, re-evaluate his guitar, decompose it (literally), and work with an extraordinarily wide range of aesthetic companions, venturing into unknown area after unknown area.

He could also begin to investigate and utilize the continuum in which he'd for a long time come to perceive himself as a component, that of the Western classical tradition, something that caused friction within AMM. Like painters he admired such as Rothko and Twombly, he knew the tradition in which he was necessarily embedded and, without making any qualitative assessment of his own contributions, knew that they had to be placed in relation to music from (at least) Renaissance chorales through David Tudor. It caused him some distress that musicians with whom he would perform, especially younger ones, seemed to have little awareness of this, somehow assuming they existed in an aesthetic vacuum.

In the mid 2000s, on a visit to New York City, Rowe was invited by saxophonist/electronicist James Fei to give a class at the Columbia University Computer Music Studio on West 125th St., among other things a marvelous storage space for some of the earliest synthesizers and other electronic instruments. In front of a group of twenty or so students, Rowe announced that, before beginning his talk, he'd like to play a piece of music. I imagine that, like myself, the students anticipated either a selection of his own work or, possibly, that of a contemporary master of the electro-acoustic tradition. Instead, what issued from the speakers was a mellifluous stream of Baroque music, a motet by the French composer Jean-Joseph de Mondonville. The students looked puzzled. He let it play for about ten minutes before switching off the machine, turning to the class and asking, "OK. What is the question?" If the class was puzzled before, they were uncomfortably so now. Rowe simply sat facing them and, after a minute or so, repeated his query. "What is the question?" One or two of the students sheepishly ventured a guess, many of the rest doubtless wondering what this old guy was going on about and what it had to do with electronic music. Rowe sat for another few minutes, calmly observing the class. Finally, he said, "The question is: 'How can I, as a contemporary electronic musician, achieve the level of probity heard in that work by Mondonville?'"

From the expression on their faces, I had the impression that the very idea of probity struck them as hopelessly old-fashioned, not something to which they'd ever given any particular thought. As well, the idea that they were in some kind of lineage, that they should consider themselves to be part of a continuum, was hierarchical and confining. Extending from the realization by the founding members of AMM, way back in 1965, that they were young, white Britons, not black Americans, and it therefore made no sense to try to reproduce what those admired musicians had done, Rowe was increasingly cognizant that he arose from a European musical tradition and not only did it make no sense to deny or hide the fact, it required, in his mind, that he familiarize himself as deeply as possible with that tradition, that he understand its structures, its meaning and its relationship to the world surrounding it.

One manifestation of this concern with the continuum between the European classical tradition and his own music can be heard in several recordings created using Rowe's ideas just before the dissolution of AMM.[160]

The first recording made under Rowe's name that had something of an overt conceptual reference to classical was *cloud*, credited to "4g," shorthand for "Four Gentlemen of the Guitar." The release was comprised of three pieces from three dates: May 23, May 30 and June 7, 2004, and the gentlemen apart from Rowe were Christian Fennesz, Oren Ambarchi, and Toshimaru Nakamura. While each of the first three used electronics or computers in addition to their guitars, Nakamura, despite the group's moniker, stuck to his no-input mixing board. More importantly, this ensemble continued an obsession of Rowe's that had manifested first in the early 80s (the quartet with Rene Lussier, Raymond Boni, and Pierre Urban) and would continue long after this date, that of the guitar quartet as a contemporary version of the classic string quartet, with himself and Nakamura in the violin roles, Fennesz as viola and Ambarchi as cello. More, by choosing

---

160   Three recordings from the festivals held in Cologne and Berlin in May 2004, co-curated by Rowe and Abbey, were also released by Erstwhile under the ErstLive imprint, a quartet with Toshimaru Nakamura, Marcus Schmickler, and Thomas Lehn, a duo with Burkhard Beins, and a quartet with Sachiko M, Nakamura, and Otomo Yoshihide. These were purely improvisational meetings, not "projects" of Rowe's. To the extent discernible, however, he seems to have proceeded musically without any break from his previous explorations, despite the emotional weight and sorrow involved in the AMM break-up which, to use an obvious analogy, was much like a divorce between a long-sparring couple. Indeed, in the range shown from the collaboration with Beins (rich, noisy, external world-referencing—it was in part a reaction to local discomfort and rudeness, more to the current state of the world re: the US invasion of Iraq, a subject caught in some of the radio grabs and indirectly, though sublimely so, in the capture of Dusty Springfield singing, "Son of a Preacher Man") to that with the Japanese trio (infinitely subtle, evinced by Rowe's cover image for the eventual release—ErstLive 005—a series of roughly-torn squares of watercolor paper, an homage to Josef Albers). John Tilbury was originally scheduled to participate in the Berlin portion of the festival but pulled out at least partially as an adjunct to his boycotting of the US due to the Iraq conflict, here citing his reluctance to accept US-derived money in payment.

these particular musicians, he was, in a way, able to approximate aspects of the 19th century Romantic music for strings that he so loved (Brahms, in particular), as well as those characteristics laced with a sense of tragedy unique to the following century as heard in composers such as Shostakovich. Ambarchi and Fennesz, though veterans of the free improvisatory world, each possessed a very melodic sensibility and had released music with a certain amount of pop cachet; they could be more or less counted on to provide relatively tonal, if not quite melodic elements, even though the performances were always improvised. Nakamura, whose instrument of choice was quite difficult to control at all, was something of a wild card. This enabled Rowe to sit in the balance, as it were, to add a bit of weight to one side or the other, trying to approximate, in homage, the essentials of the string quartets he so loved. And whereas the earlier attempts in this format involved players of a more gestural bent, there was only a modicum of this approach to be found here, mostly in the gently plucked tones from Ambarchi, allowing an oblique reference to the tradition couched in a very contemporary sound field.

Another oblique example, unrecorded, involved an intriguing quartet which went by the name [N:Q] and often, as on the release *November Quebec* (2006), consisted of sounds only generated by radios, here manipulated by Rowe, Julien Ottavi, Will Guthrie, and Emmanuel Leduc. On one concert occasion, Rowe had noticed that a Brahms work was to be played on the local radio station at a given hour, so instructions were given that the musicians were to begin generating sounds from areas between receptive stations, in places of static and interference and, very gradually over the course of the set, drift toward the frequency that would elicit the Brahms work from the depths of abstraction. This, and the subsequent inclusion of samples from various Western classical compositions, is a significant step away from pure improvisation, very different in kind from the random radio captures he'd been working with for decades. The strong sense of intentionality that emerged was somewhat disorienting to long time listeners and, to some, troubling.

At home, Rowe immersed himself in the European classical music tradition. Visiting him there, one rarely if ever heard music from the contemporary improvisational field. Instead, there was Purcell, Haydn, Dvořák, motets, and masses, as well as the occasional bit of classic jazz (guitarist Johnny Smith was a consistent favorite) or non-Western classical music like Nusrat Fateh Ali Khan. On one occasion, virtually upon arrival, I was pulled in, Rowe exclaiming, "You have to listen to this! If I were 'in charge,' I'd gather up all these musicians I know and play with, lock them in a room for six months, and make them listen to nothing but this." He proceeded to put Brahms' "String Sextet" on the CD player and became quite rapturous as we listened, sighing, "Ah, listen to that!" He was genuinely aggrieved that, by his reckoning, improvising musicians tended to know next to nothing about their own musical history, about the music that, in one sense or another, laid the groundwork for their own art. He was no less severe about the listening audience, frequently complaining that they weren't understanding "obvious elements" contained in his own performances, for example not recognizing that beneath his concert at The Stone in New York City, on the 10th anniversary of 9/11, lay buried the same compositional structure that Shostakovich had used in his Eighth String Quartet, which contained references to the bombing of Dresden in World War II. He thought it should somehow be clear to any intelligent listener.

> In the final analysis, I'm a white European. I come from a poor background, but I'm a white European. I'm not an intellectual exactly, but I'm from that class of thinkers and had a classical arts education. Therefore I know about Giotto, about Hildegard von Bingen. I'm very conscious of the baggage I'm carrying. It's like playing multi-dimensional chess; it's quite difficult.

> For years and years I've been imagining what it would be like to be a classical player, to be in a string quartet. That your performance is all plotted out, years ahead, centuries ahead, that you had this very fixed kind of material and

when you sat down to play, you could play it creatively
or in a mechanical way, lifeless. Or you could go beyond
the notes and express something, bring the piece to life.
How you get your experiences of being in the 20th century
through something that was entirely fixed. But, given that
material, you somehow made comments about contempo-
rary society, yourself, what you believe in. And, of course,
I've never had that experience, but I could imagine how
those issues worked. Increasingly, during that period, I
began to think of AMM as the nearest I would get to this
kind of classical situation. Because in a way, I have an idea
of how John is going to sound and what the range is. In the
early days of improvisation, that would have been taken
as some kind of criticism, you know, if you knew someone's
sound palette that would be taken as criticism. Cornelius'
playing, you could say was more open than John's. For Ed-
die, it was the same thing...In all our cases, it was outside of
AMM that our techniques were very different. I was much
more expansive outside than inside. I think for all of us, this
was a similar experience, of this kind of classicism in the
form—the knowability of it.

This burden of understanding can be heard in a number of
Rowe's works at this time. Granted, there had always been an
enormous amount of *thought* involved in his improvisations,
consideration for matters well beyond those normally deemed
apropos, including an awareness, somehow to be transmuted
into the music, of events occurring in the world, outside of the
performance space, but equally, if not more so, as important
as any art being created that day. Making the audience directly
aware of such elements without simply being didactic about it
was another matter, however, though Rowe would sometimes
seem baffled as to how difficult these things were to discern
during a performance or recording. For instance, when he played
in Tokyo in 2008 as part of the AMPLIFY: light festival organized
by Abbey, he was very conscious of being the only non-Japanese
musician present, and felt it necessary to foreground his own

traditions. For the first time, he introduced pre-chosen musical samples from that tradition to be inserted at certain points during his solo performance. These were clear enough and, to one used to his work, somewhat startling in context, very different from a piece of the classical repertoire that might be randomly grabbed from a radio. But there were subtler matters afoot. During a section in which one hears a baroque oboe concerto, there's also some hard-edged, scratching sound. To understand at first blush, as became apparent much later when discussing the matter with Rowe, that he was (in a way that had something to do with his concerns as expressed in the Columbia University classroom) attempting to parallel the grace, line, and fundamental beauty of the oboe with a contact mic drawn along his table, is a great deal to ask. But a sufficiently attuned listener, Rowe felt, should have been able to ascertain that. More, he had an inscribed steel ruler flat on the table in front of his guitar. As he, in his mind, "advanced" through the centuries, giving examples and commenting on the foundations of the music that would lead into the 20th century, to Cage, AMM, and his own work, he would drag the contact mic over the ruler's grooves, having mapped a calendar of sorts onto its length measurements, moving slowly up this alternate time field. This too, should somehow be recognized by those in attendance, people who not only had no idea of the general notion behind his set but who couldn't possibly see that there was a ruler there to begin with, much less that it had morphed into a century-spanning calendar. Rowe spoke about this and surrounding issues at some length shortly after the solo concert in Tokyo, much of it while watching a video of the event, sometimes in a very free-associative manner:

> *Just recently, in Oslo, playing in the Sonja Henie Museum, there's a photo of Tilbury and I holding a banner that says, "Make the Past Serve the Present." I think that's something that runs through our culture. Like Rothko always trying to make the past serve the present, Greek mythology, etc. Even the solo thing in Japan, there are concrete things in there that have to do with the past serving the present. There's*

an imitation of the banjo, representing the American tour, for example. The solo ends with Dido and Aeneas; it ends with death. Going against God. That's making art, trying to become eternal, resisting loss. Dido screams, "Remember me!" It's what Simon Schama writes about, or Julian Bell. The earliest drawings, when the seamen went to sea and they'd trace their profile on the wall by candlelight so that if they never came back, their loved ones would have this image, a way of preserving the person. If we try to preserve our image, we're breaking the Second Commandment. There's this idea of going back, or reinvestigating something old. It's partly while on holiday in Italy, seeing the Lorenzo Lotto paintings and talking to Walter Zaletti about classical guitar and wanting to do a project with him, working the classical guitar into what I'm doing. This little guitar I have now [gets his practice guitar neck]...it's so cute! So that, this is a classical guitar and that is the image of the Spanish classical guitar, but when it's on the table it's hidden from me, which I like. On the website it says, "This is not for making music." (laughs) It's acoustic, I've put a pick-up on it and changed it. The sounds aren't particularly guitar-ish! But there's something there, something very ethnic about it.

On one level it [the solo set] obviously pulls together a huge amount of past music. It's enormously ambitious, maybe too ambitious, I might have tried to do too much. Whereas in the room, it was very much about being in the room—with Rothko, it feels to me that the layers of paint are layers of emotion, things that have never been seen. It's a feeling that whatever is there is the state of existence he feels is right. In this, what I'm trying to bring into the room in Tokyo is actually the fact of me, Keith Rowe, being in Tokyo, in this box, in the context of a Tokyo experience. And what I'm recognizing is that I'm not Japanese, I'm not from here, this is not my culture. I knew I'd do a solo and I had no idea what it would be. But after the first day, when I went back *to my room the day before the concert, I knew I wanted to make a statement about who I was, about my culture. I wanted to make a very clear template that I've come here, form this background. It seemed important. I wanted four pieces, for various reasons, pieces I really loved and that each of them were specific examples of something that was meaningful to me. I've used these before, once at Columbia, where I asked, what is profound meaning in digital media?*

When the solo starts, what's important to me are the moments of silence after the sounds. I think it's very clearly articulated there. The first oboe piece is also an articulation of a version of silence. What I think I've always been doing is making silence audible. So when the oboe is playing, that's a version of silence, but he's making it audible. My commentary after the piece is to play softly with something which I've thrown away—the Brillo pad—very quietly, something from my past which I've given myself permission to use again. Now I hear it used grossly [by others], so I want to bring it back and reuse it in a sensitive way.

The thing is, I live with these pieces, they're my life and a lot of it is beyond words. I think what I wouldn't want is people listening to it thinking that it's all arbitrary; it's not. I make mistakes and judge things incorrectly but generally it's okay. It's not entirely planned either, though, it's that twilight area. It's about having intentions, it's a painterly process. But keeping it raw, I like. It's actually quite worked-out, but you wouldn't know that unless you were told. I knew that I would bring in some radio, but not so much. It has something to do with sonata form, you know where the "exciting" bit is about three quarters through. I thought I'd bring in the radio around there. I was being a bit snotty there, if I'm being honest. I'm sort of saying that there's this beautiful stuff, but in our world we go for this crappy, impure, distorted music, so they're not clear images. All the pieces are from around the 1730s; I wanted pieces that have survived...the Purcell is even older, like 1690. They've existed for three centuries and they have this status in my culture, whereas the pop songs don't, they're peripheral. It's snotty!

See that plastic box is from the very early 60s, maybe '65. So I'm beginning to select the...[classical piece starts] It's louder there. It's more reticent on the recording. I try to keep absolutely still. That movement there is a ruler, for it's to do with the passage of time, counting. I make these clicks, maybe 500 of them. The fan is a reference to something going around, the passage of time. Now the Mondonville. All harsh sounding after it. Now the clean guitar sound. That passage of time is sometimes very violent. That ruler is a real old technique. There's always this kind of racket music just before the purity. The next piece is about the revolution. Whatever is new, still gets absorbed into the tradition. These horns, this is Rameau, were utterly revolutionary to do. Of course, we don't hear the revolution anymore. Being novel, being new is not important. What's important is having the passion. With the Duchamp urinal, no matter how revolutionary we thought it was at the time, at some point it gets subsumed into the history of art. This piece of music is a reminder of that. All of these sounds are foreshadowing the end, the Dido, I know it's coming. It's about death. It goes away and comes back. What I'm saying with this death motif going, is that that's what will become of our music, and us all, in 100 years probably. There are so many ideas flying around of what to do or not to do...I think I'm just working with six or seven: the passage of time, sensitivity, profundity, silence...more old techniques. You try to keep it as fresh as you can. Early on the fans were cocktail mixers, the first whizzing things. They shouldn't be a fetish. It's hard to know how Western European art ideas resonate with a Japanese audience. Here, I wanted it to just be lost, very uncoordinated, very before the Dido. So I take sounds I've never made before, mix them with sounds I have made before—long sounds, short sounds, a real mix-up. No central theme but it would be very active. A confirmation of sonata form, still not being afraid, being completely unabashed. It's a tricky thing, using absolutely in-your-face techniques from a long way back; it's about freedom. I wanted this part [the Dido] to be clear, so I did nothing...that descending motif. I'm totally immobilized by it for a little while. She says, "No trouble." "Remember me!" "Forget my face." She's basically saying, "Don't worry." These notes are like going into a grave, digging a hole, things going into the earth. For me, this is like all humanity, like fascist soldiers in a hole, Iraqi soldiers, Vietnam, hearing this sound [helicopters] coming toward them. Then just cut off.

When Michael Graubert talked about Dido and Aeneas, he thought it was the high point of English music. It was actually written to be performed by schoolgirls. So I wanted to raise those issues. Lester Bowie would talk about his grandmother. I wanted to say, as someone who's been involved in music for a very long time, that people should feel freer to investigate these areas. I think there's a broader path. I wanted to let it be known that these four pieces of music weren't little trickeries, they were very serious works of art that meant a lot to me, that posed and solved problems. When I arrived in Tokyo, I didn't really have many ideas. It came from being there. I think it had been building up in me. Being in an art gallery and seeing a Rembrandt or a De Kooning, the freedom there. Or Guston—doing abstract painting really well, then having the freedom to go and paint cigarettes!

Shortly before this, in 2007, Rowe created something else that involved a different mode of operation and was, as well, something of a defining moment, even a magnum opus of his up until that point: *The Room*. It's a crystallization of everything Rowe was about at the time, a dark and brooding modern tone poem of sorts, imbued with thoughts of Cardew, and bathed in the aura of Rothko. Rowe did two paintings for the exterior and interior of the CD package, each taking up three "panels," both identical in form though differing in coloration. The outer cover can be read as a conventional, if almost featureless landscape: a blue (sky) upper half and a green (grass) lower, almost bisected by a thickish black line (it sits just below the midway point). The paint is applied smoothly though not without grain and there's a touch of unevenness where the colors meet the black line. It's subtly disturbing. The blue is solid top to bottom, giving no hint of atmosphere, and the green is likewise flat enough to remove any notion of depth. More, they look as if painted over a black ground, imparting a leaden appearance that belies any comfort offered by a landscape effect. It's as though Cardew's "Treatise" has been boiled down, the calligraphics reduced to the dense line, widening its existent "spine." Opening the case, we see roughly the same construct except the colors have changed from blue and green to a hellish dark red on top and an even grimmer reddish black below: the colors of a cancerous tumor. The brushwork is more painterly than before, the areas abutting the central black line more irregular; indeed, a hint of the lighter upper portion is seen below the line, giving some sense of depth, of a distant mirage. I'm reminded of an infernal, bleak setting from a Cormac McCarthy novel. There's an overall sense of sootiness, stifling air, and an unforgiving harshness. The music lives up to this.

Instead of being an improvised performance as such, *The Room* was constructed over time in Rowe's home, resulting in a work that was often very densely layered as well as being almost claustrophobically "close" to the ear of the listener, who feels almost as though miniaturized and caught on his table, running between guitar parts, electronic components, files, springs, and other Rowe-ian detritus. While many of the individual elements are recognizable to anyone familiar with his work, there's a throughgoing sense of dread, bitterness, and acknowledgment of the bleak realities of existence. The music is steady-state for the most part, not the scattered, intermittent sounds that would have been heard in the few years immediately hence (as on *contact with Sachiko M*), but each layer is dark, industrial, spiky with static, or sluggishly oozing. It's rather like listening to a melting nuclear plant, with all the multiple threats that event implies. If it's Rothko, one is tempted to think of his suicide. Through the dismal throb, erratic bleeps are heard, power surges sizzle in the murk. Its push is unrelenting, inexorable in its painful slowness. Some twenty minutes in there's an interlude of sorts, the layers falling out, replaced by hollow bangs, pops, slides along strings, and more ghostly scurrying—small creatures occupying an abandoned space. Their life is brutal, though, clawing and aggressive, spasmodic. When the onslaught resumes, it's with an increased intensity and heat, boiling up, cracking through walls; there are portions extreme enough to be physically difficult to bear, the sounds lacerating one's ears. A break occurs a few minutes before the work's conclusion, followed immediately by a new kind of sound-set, something that seems culled from the outside world; you can just discern voices buried deep in the mix, possible aircraft sounds, flutters that seem derived somehow from a "room" in which there's more air, some light. It's just a glimpse, though, and as it builds to a roar it's abruptly cut short.

The Room was one of Rowe's most fully-realized and powerful statements to date, the essence of which would resonate in his thinking for a long while, ultimately resulting in the release of *The Room Extended* in 2016.

Over the years, Rowe continued to engage with an increasingly wide range of musicians[161], generally younger (sometimes quite a bit), many coming from a different lineage in the contemporary tradition with approaches that offered a challenge to Rowe's way

---

161   Among many other interests, he continued to work with saxophonists despite his misgivings about the instrument with regard to the difficulty of removing itself from all the jazz historical "baggage" which seemed to be a virtually inevitable accompaniment (unlike brass instruments which possessed the quality of, if approached with this in mind, to more easily shed their past). The recordings that resulted were of variable quality but occasionally, as with

of handling matters. Amusingly, they'd sometimes find themselves having arrived at the same location via different routes. A case in point was Graham Lambkin, who performed with Rowe for the first time at a concert in New York City in January of 2013. Lambkin had achieved some recognition with the ensemble Shadow Ring in the 1990s, a group that blended murky rock with spoken word and noise, becoming somewhat popular on the outer extremes of the college alternative rock circuit. AMM had been an early influence: "one of the groups that gave us license to just do what we wanted, regardless of whether it fitted with convention or employed 'accepted' techniques, and did so from a very English standpoint, which held great appeal."[162] After the group's disbanding in 2003, he had begun to release music under his own name, notably *Salmon Run* on his own label Kye in 2007, a recording that raised considerable interest in the new music/improv listening community, including Rowe, eventually resulting in the issuance of several collaborations with electronicist Jason Lescalleet on Erstwhile, the same label where a predominance of Rowe material had seen the light of day during the previous decade. Jon Abbey scheduled them to perform together at a small festival he organized in New York City (a series of rotating duos involving Rowe, Lambkin, Michael Pisaro,[163] and Christian Wolff). Never having played together before, each gave much consideration as to how they would engage the other and, rather

---

his project with Swedish saxophonist Martin Küchen, *The Bakery* (2016), the results yielded fascinating and tasty fruit.

162   From Lambkin's notes to the release on the Erstwhile site.

163   Rowe would continue to play with Pisaro in various configurations, both in improvised sets and more defined ones, including an idea of Rowe's titled "The Venerable Bede," based on a parable which goes: *The present life of man, O king, seems to me, in comparison of that time which is unknown to us, like to the swift flight of a sparrow through the room wherein you sit at supper in winter, with your commanders and ministers, and a good fire in the midst, whilst the storms of rain and snow prevail abroad; the sparrow, I say, flying in at one door, and immediately out at another, whilst he is within, is safe from the wintry storm; but after a short space of fair weather, he immediately vanishes out of your sight, into the dark*

miraculously (though each knew the other routinely engaged in visual art), came up independently with the same unexpected answer: they would bring art materials, the concert consisting of the sounds (via contact mics) made while creating works of art: drawing, scissor cutting, adhesive tape pulling, paper tearing, measuring, etc. It was an amazing set, just the soft (slightly amplified) sounds of activity with pens and paper, each working on their own "project," sometimes borrowing items from one another, calmly going about their concentrated business, a set unlike anything I had previously witnessed. A few days later, Rowe travelled up the Hudson (recording various train sounds as he went) to Lambkin's home in Poughkeepsie NY where they recorded another session, using the same approach while realizing pieces from Cardew's Schooltime Compositions. It was subsequently released as *Making A.*[164]

Another major collaborative partnership, one that continues through 2018, is with the Norwegian video artist Kjell Bjørgeengen. Bjørgeengen concentrated on creating abstract, often black and white videos involving white noise and flicker; sometimes the flickers created the illusion, in the eyes of the viewer, of phantom colors. Working with Rowe, they developed a complex interactive system, a mutual feedback loop of sorts where Rowe, using a contact mic/mini-camera apparatus, would pass the

_____

winter from which he had emerged. So this life of man appears for a short space, but of what went before, or what is to follow, we are utterly ignorant. This was recorded in May 2016 for a 2017 release on Erstwhile Records and was also performed at the Sanatorium of Sound Festival in Sokołowsko, Poland in August, 2016.

164   Any remotely comprehensive listing of the musicians and other collaborators that Rowe has worked with, and continues to work with, would be lengthy and cumbersome. Suffice it to say that he was always open to such situations, ranging from small ensembles to larger ones where he might himself be only a tiny component, as in several conductions led by Butch Morris. Often enough, he would anticipate going in that nothing much was going to come of it, that his approach and that of the musician(s) involved were unlikely to yield much of value, but he would do his best nonetheless. For a fuller understanding, please refer to the discography/videography.

device over a screen of video feed, generating sounds depending on the patterns it was reading. These sounds, in turn, would generate new video patterns in Bjørgeengen's equipment. Clearly, this sort of constant, near instantaneous interaction created a system always on the fringes of any kind of control. It also, on Rowe's part, "de-gesturalized" his contributions even further. He had once mentioned with pleasure, after a tour with Toshi Nakamura earlier in the decade, that he had reached a point where he could do a concert without physically touching his guitar. Here, the "touch" was physical but arguably more remote than an engagement of electro-magnetic fields—a contact mic on a video screen. Taking in a performance, such as one I witnessed at Phill Niblock's Experimental Intermedia loft around 2009, the viewer/listener has the clear impression of a third presence in the room, one that even overshadows the human performers who often seem more like sentries or, perhaps more aptly, *herders* of the sounds and sights. It was disorienting, slightly chilling, and oddly exciting all at once.

Rowe's collaboration with Bjørgeengen eventually merged into that with Tilbury and the three performed as a trio often[165], Norway being relatively lavish with its arts funding. A tangible result of this was a 4-disc recording of a 2014 event issued on the Norwegian Sofa label titled, *enough still not to know*[166] (2015). Though originally conceived to accompany the video work of Bjørgeengen, the audio portion stands entirely well on its own, indeed serves as an extension of and elaboration on the music recorded more than a decade prior and issued as *Duos for Doris*. A comparison of the two reveals the distance both men had traveled in the intervening years.

Before the set had found a publisher, Rowe was casting about in

---

165   See video excerpts from 2013 performances listed in the discography/videography.

166   A phrase from Beckett's "Worstward Ho."

search of a title for the set. One option was, "Late Music." Though not used finally, this grim and realistic assessment of music by, at the time of recording, a 74- and 78-year old is an apt encapsulation of the session. Arguably enhanced by the spare, near-black box in which the discs arrived (in fact, video stills from Bjørgeengen), the pervading sense is one of a clear-headed acknowledgment of how things are near the end of one's life, with fleeting rays of hope and beauty amidst a more dispassionate assessment of one's contributions and the general state of things, including , as alluded to in the title, not knowing. Rowe's contributions are sparer, more fragmentary, and, in a positive sense, more a-musical than perhaps anything he'd previously done. Beckett comes to mind, but stripped of whatever remnants of Romanticism still clung to that writer's frame. As had at least recently been the case, he incorporates specific thoughts and memories into the music, writing in the accompanying booklet:

> "Unexpected music for the occasion" might be a Purcellian way to describe the task before us, to produce music for an installation, a music which might disturb the normal relation between sound and image, an opportunity to explore a non-linear relationship with our material, we sit staring [at] the higher and lower range of frequencies, I'll explore in the third section, the lower end.

> Over and over, with significant consistency John's piano resonates, it's incredible, calculating the distance, a crystallization of the silence, finding ways to not play and create form.

> My ever-present list of concerns, flashes in and out of focus, a single mood, degrees of opacity, disclosure and withdrawal, seduction and rejection, accident and controlled, classical answering, delayed perception, absorption, unknowable, on and on, the list is long.

> I attempt to emit a single sound with exquisite care, with

degrees of self-consciousness, and reflect on its construction, hoping to avoid the danger of effect over evidence.

The sheer scale, at around 224 minutes, renders the work difficult, if not impossible, to take in at once. One alternates, perhaps, between total immersion—imagining oneself at the event, including (if one had some prior knowledge of Bjørgeengen's work) picturing the videography and listening in the background—and allowing the music to serve as an uncomfortable but telling soundtrack to one's daily life. Sometimes Tilbury's playing is impossible not to isolate; it's so extraordinary, often quite different from anything previously recorded, so incredibly attuned to the environment, so perfect in touch and placement as to leave one somewhat dumbfounded. But the music is all the richer when both are perceived equally, even (especially!) when Rowe is all but silent. The resoluteness, the clarity of focus, and the pure musicality of both artists is in full effect throughout, making "enough still not to know" the defining example of their work in this listener's opinion. Late music indeed, difficult to face but ever so true.

*

In the summer of 2015, the director of the Huddersfield Contemporary Music Festival, Graham McKenzie, sent e-mails to Rowe, Prévost, and Tilbury proposing a reuniting of the trio in honor of the 50th anniversary of AMM for a performance at the festival that November. Rowe was immediately enthusiastic but Prévost expressed some misgivings. First, he was put off that the suggestion should come from a promoter, not originating as an idea of the three principals. More, he wanted to ensure that, if he agreed to the event, that it was understood to be a one-off, that Rowe shouldn't expect to be brought back in as a regular member of AMM. His tone, if not his words, expressed the clear notion that he'd just as soon Rowe didn't accept the invitation. Given this sentiment, Rowe was unsure how to respond, but eventually decided to put his best foot forward and accept the proposal, hoping for some degree of reconciliation.

As it happened, things turned out excellently. Prévost was giving a talk on aspects of AMM philosophy when Rowe and Stephanie arrived at the venue, discreetly seating themselves in the rear of the room. When the lecture was concluded, the once antagonistic pair met and warmth immediately pervaded the atmosphere. Despite essentially having not seen each other in over ten years, it seemed more like it had been a few weeks. As near as one could tell, Prévost displayed not the slightest bit of animosity and, indeed, was effusive in his good humor to everyone around. There was a welcome air of "let bygones be bygones" and to pick up and go on from here.

As could be reasonably expected, the concert was a rather tentative affair, more a matter of establishing re-acquaintance than pushing matters, the trio very respectful of each others space, keeping matters on a low simmer throughout. But the extra-musical satisfaction and pleasure of seeing Rowe and Prévost interacting once again as friends more than outweighed any purely musical judgments. The aftermath at a local bar was just as joyous. The sense of a massive weight having been lifted off their shoulders was palpable.

Things went well enough that it turned out not to be a one-time event after all. A concert was held at Café Oto in London the next month, at Église Saint Merrie in Paris in April, 2016 and in Budapest in the fall of that year. As of this writing, there is at least one pending show in Japan on the schedule. In some manner or form, AMM, 50 years on, continues.

*

Visiting Keith and Stephanie at their home in Vallet in the summer of 2014, I noticed a small tremor in his right hand. It seemed to manifest when the hand was idle but not when engaged in some activity. I didn't mention it and Keith proffered no explanation. In November, I returned to Vallet to witness a two-day celebration of Christian Wolff's 80th birthday. Rowe, Wolff, and John

Tilbury would take part in concert events along with Onsemble, a group of young musicians organized by Julien Ottavi. It was an extraordinary few days; I felt awash in the history of 20th century music, Wolff regaling us with story after story. At one point Wolff addressed the hand tremors directly and Rowe confirmed that he had been getting opinions on the condition and that it might well be a form of Parkinson's disease. During the ensuing months, this diagnosis was verified and he began taking medication. The symptoms, the shaking of the right hand, didn't noticeably intensify in the months to come and as of August 2016, when I spent several days in Rowe's company at the Sanatorium of Sound music festival in Sokołowsko, Poland, it still appeared to be of approximately the same strength and didn't appreciably interfere with his music making.

Over approximately this same time span, Rowe was working on a project that had obsessed him for quite a while, titled *The Room Extended*. As with *The Room*, this was constructed at home, over a period of three years. When it was ultimately released, in December 2016, the cover image was a MRI head scan of himself, bearing the identifier CHARTERS ROWE KEITH, M 74, DOB: 16 mar 1940. True to form, there was no obfuscation of reality.

The work lasts over four hours and is spread over four CDs. Originally, Rowe had wanted the music issued on an audio DVD for two reasons: firstly, to obviously make for an uninterrupted listening experience but secondly, for the listener to hear the work via as generic a device as might be possible in 2016: a TV or computer as opposed to a (potentially) high-end stereo system. Economic imperatives prevailed, however: audio DVDs cut down possible sales to a significant degree. The CD package is in black, the above-cited scan in black and white, centrally located in a black field. The back cover and two interior panels contain similarly situated color scans, offering top-down views of Rowe's brain. The discs are printed in flat colors of yellow, red, green, and blue, recalling the colors often used by Rowe in his paintings, each lying on black as his paintings were often bordered by thick, black lines.

Rowe's workspace is in a loft on one side of the main room in his Vallet home, over the kitchen and looking out onto the living area, where he has a table upon which sits the current incarnation of his guitar, various electronic devices, and other sound-producing detritus, not dissimilar from his standard table array in performance. Especially given the title of the work, much less his lifelong preoccupation with one's general awareness of one's surroundings while creating, it's not difficult to imagine him there, acting as a kind of *sponge*, absorbing sounds from the air around him, both physical and cultural, allowing it to flow through him, achieving equal standing with the impulses traveling from his brain through to his hands. The first sound heard is a field of static, but already one possessing depth and, within a second or so, showing multiple layers. Indeed, throughout the recording there are almost always four or five or more strata in place, enough that multiple listenings still reveal previously undetected components; in the first couple of minutes, for instance, disembodied voices are barely perceptible through the haze, hum, and guitar skitterings. That's another notable element: the foregrounding of overtly guitar-like sounds, from plucked strings to single, violent thrashes like the one occurring almost four minutes in. Similar to those voices, one can barely pick out the glimmer of orchestral strings, just for a moment, the slightest hint of things to come.

At the ten-minute mark, the strings clearly appear, signaling a meta-motif that will recur throughout *The Room Extended*. Rowe layers string portions from various sources atop one another, but one that breaks through for several moments, from both its orchestral competitors and some rather wrenching and furious scratching and torqueing from Rowe, is the theme from Wagner's *Tristan und Isolde*, which he'd been dwelling on for years and which will appear multiple times in this work. Perhaps surprisingly, many of the themes that Rowe would listen to over and over again as well as discuss with friends at the slightest provocation during the previous decade, were pieces of music that one might describe as Romantic; if not technically so, certainly with a profound sense of melody and emotion. The Wagner, the opening notes of Shostakovich's String Quartet No. 15 (Borodin Quartet version), the Mondonville motet, Brahms' String Sextet, the death scene from Purcell's *Dido and Aeneas* (heard starkly here, much later).

Being so accustomed to hearing Rowe in improvisatory situations, it's often necessary to remind oneself that *The Room Extended* is a thought-out construct. As had been the case for several years at this point, the introduction of Western classical themes, intentionally chosen, not merely snatched from the ambient airwaves, still stands out in some relief by virtue of the listener *knowing* of their intentionality. It's not always comfortable. But it's also not quite as frequent as the first impression might lead one to believe. When present, the motifs are generally but one element among many, if a salient and perhaps over-intrusive one. And yet...this is "the room," this is one element that filters through with some regularity. It's an honest appraisal of what exists in that space, over that span of time.

I suspect that there's also a great deal of recapitulation occurring, revisiting points in Rowe's career, unearthing a signpost now and then and throwing it into the mix. It's not obvious, however. In fact, one of the fascinating aspects of *The Room Extended* is how little of it sounds explicitly "Rowe-ian," even to listeners who know his music thoroughly. At numerous points, lines of attack appear that sound nothing like his previous music. There's a tiny, two-note, early synth kind of sound that pops up a few times which seems familiar, for instance. But there's so much more, including buried sections derived from tapes of his own work dating back to the mid 60s. A section with scattered applause that lasts impossibly long, drowned amidst scratches, burbles, and odd percussive sounds is like nothing heard in his work before. And we're still not quite halfway through the first hour. The realization grows, and continues through the piece's entirety, that he somehow never allows the interest to flag, that the *truthfulness*, for lack of a better term, of what he's been experiencing over several years, sitting at his table, the things he's contemplated having imbued the space, is so on point, so abstractly vivid, that the listener is immersed into a quite believable reality.

The Western classical fragments hover ghostlike, descending into the space periodically, disappearing. And not just Western. Fifteen minutes into Disc 2, a radio capture of what sounds like Egyptian popular music (Mohammed Abdel Wahab?) enters the ambiance, a string section supporting a female singer, intertwining with rich cellos from a Western source, each soon wending their way through a thicket of metallic crunching, deep electronic pulses and sizzling static. Later what might possibly be a sarangi is heard amidst a Romantic swelling of strings. A knotty cello line blends with a choir, a keening violin surge, Rowe afflicting his guitar string with some rough-edged object, all sifted through some sonic colander, leading to Dido's lament, "When I am laid in earth…" Death is always present. So many layers, so many possible relationships left to the listener to parse, to read differently each time through. *Tristan und Isolde* is never far away, a tacit presence that flickers in every so often. There's a tension achieved between succumbing to the easy temptation of identifying elements as they pass versus simply letting the sounds wash over you, relying on your subconscious to find patterns, to create any kind of narrative sense. Perhaps this is why Rowe wanted it to be playable on a DVD player through the TV, to lessen the likelihood of the listener concentrating overmuch, to allow the music to act like his beloved Rothkos and only tinge the atmosphere of these many, far-flung rooms. Indeed, among many other experiences on my part, hearing a choir coming from a source outside my own room, played over a computer by my partner in the adjacent room, was easily integrated into *The Room Extended*, felt entirely consistent with the present work, its apartness only ascertained upon removal of the headphones.

The segment of *Dido and Aeneas* heard toward the end of Disc 2 descends into a disturbing, almost rude area of brusque rubbing, a snatch of French pop, and other notably harsh sounds, the atmosphere thinned for a few minutes, the air somewhat miasmal, almost as if that death knell had, halfway through, been realized and one's consciousness is slipping away, materially, unbeautifully.

That sense of hard materiality permeates most of the third hour. The possible emoluments offered by the classical samples are nowhere to be found for over a half hour (and even then, the faded appearance of some Purcell—?—is fleeting), replaced by metallic clatter, grit-filled and mechanical, summoning images, perhaps, of Rowe's youthful toiling in the bowels of enormous aircraft carriers docked in Plymouth. The sound field is thinner, flickering out entirely at points, the atmosphere more severe, unforgiving, the sounds in stark relief, bearing few aesthetic pretensions. Matters "brighten" only past the 50-minute mark of this disc, when a bubbling, somewhat aqueous section emerges, offering a possible hint of rebirth, perhaps via the reappearance at the conclusion of this section of the earlier Egyptian music ,which itself, combined with the frequent Arabic music heard during the final quarter of the work, might portend the changing demographics in Europe, the possibly transient nature of Western culture, and the emergence of an increasingly Islamic one—an inevitable shifting away from the values inherent in the Western classical music heard elsewhere and here, at the very end of the disc, some dark, deep strings meshed with the Arabic popular song.

The first fifteen or so minutes of the final disc, out of its 70, continue in the spartan vein established earlier but then things become dense and rich once again, the hums multiplying and spreading in tonality, glimmers of orchestral music seeping in from the side, static stretching across the aural space. The guitar itself is more prominent now, whether it's the fluttering of buffeted strings, the soft siren of an e-bow, or the occasional harsh pluck. There's a disquieting near-silence; there may be faint footfalls, hard to say. When sound returns, we're in an adjacent space to the sparse one we thought we'd left, one laced with slender buzzes, very distant strains of some unidentifiable music, similarly indistinct voices, and foreground clatter. It's alien, almost insectile, as though the room is being viewed from a crack in the floor. From that small crevice, we again emerge into the world of Arabic pop music, but the surrounding abstractions are more strident now, more intrusive, and even threatening, some of the tones taking on the character of coded military signals. Back and forth between the full and the spare, reluctant but pushing forward, indecisive in a profound sense. Ringing bell tones, artificial-sounding birds on an interminable loop, recalling the "banal" sounds John White would instigate during performances of "Treatise"—a world turned upside down.

54 minutes in, beneath an intense electric whine, like a heightened flat-line signal from a hospital vital signs monitor, a bar or two of mournful cello from Wagner is heard, but abruptly severed. For several minutes, it hums from several sources, in the darkness with isolated guitar scrapes and rustles. An Arabic singer appears, male, intoning "Allah o Akbar" amidst a steadily increasing welter of words—German, French, Portuguese—and static, ultimately joined by baroque cello, that quintessential AMM instrument. The lines multiply—voices, other music, throbbing electronics, petty digital scrambling, a lute, a news report on a violent protest in Ankara against US policy in Syria, a rock beat, string sections of six or eight different works overlaid, tear gas, water cannons, and pepper spray in China. In the density of all those elements that inhabit this room, an alarmed Spanish voice is cut off mid-sentence.

Appendix A

An interview with Eddie Prévost conducted by percussionist
Trevor Taylor and published in *Drums & Percussion* magazine,
August 1974. The interview not only gives an excellent overview
of Prévost's thinking at the time but also provides glimmers of
the issues with Rowe that would surface later. The text went a bit
beyond the bottom of the copy of the interview from which I did
my transcription, hence several ellipses which are noted.

*

**Trevor Taylor: Don't you find that the kind of music you play
requires more of a varied percussion set-up offering more
possibilities, rather than a drum kit which is designed basically for specific kinds of music?**

Eddie Prévost: I think that one is likely to go full circle eventually. I have used a lot of extraneous percussion and other sound
producing equipment but the realisation that there are limitless
possibilities could make you go mad! So I think that what happened a few years ago was that I became aware that limitations
were very useful things to press yourself against. And that you
can probably get more by consciously confining yourself to a
limited amount of instrumentation than if you go on changing.
It's a question of assimilation. It was also (if albeit unconscious)
a rejection of the "throw away" syndrome. There is perhaps an

awful tendency to go onto new things just for novelty's sake. It is easy to create a mystique and there is an element of deception in this—perhaps self-deception—the Emperor's new clothes.

Most musical instruments have had hundreds of years to evolve, the violin for instance has become a very efficient means of producing sound. Now a yoghurt cup hasn't had too much time to evolve as a musical instrument—it is therefore not surprising that it is somewhat limited to play. And the electronic thing has not yet evolved sufficiently (in my opinion) for it to allow the player to be as subtle, versatile and as dexterous as he can be with more conventional instruments.

I agree that electronics are limited at present in terms of musical application but surely the future offers wonderful possibilities?

Yes I'm sure you're right. Electronics have enormous potential but at the moment they are still very much toys. What worries me is that it seems as if we are in danger of being engulfed by pure electronic music which I think would be a pity. Let us have it by all means but also let us keep the beauty and that sense of immediacy that comes with the physical feel of acoustic music. I think that this was one of the reasons why AMM began to revert to the use of more predominantly acoustic instruments. Because we became aware that what you hear at a live performance is a very different experience from what you hear over the radio and on records. There are a number of reasons for this but most of us hear more music via the loudspeaker than we do live—which means that we are becoming used to electronic music without realising it. Make no mistake about it—anything that comes through a speaker is electronic! As a result many people are literally disappointed when the live music does not match the "processed" version! Really they ought to discern that the two are totally different things.

Tell me how you started to play?

Well, it was in the Boy Scouts. And I got interested in jazz of all kinds at about the age of 12.

Were you influenced particularly by the drummers, or just the music in general?

The music in general. I never really listened to the drummers to the exclusion of all else. I think I've only really liked drummers when they energise or really contribute to the group. I don't particularly like soloists. I admired Art Blakey probably more than any other drummer because he energises his groups so much.

It's funny. I never really thought of Blakey as that much of an influence, but Tony Oxley, Paul Lytton, Frank Perry and now you, have all cited him individually above anyone else.

For me it was because he inspires groups and gets the best out of his players, and this is a characteristic I try to emulate.

So what drummers did you like from then on?

Well, like all the kids I went through a "skin deep" stage and then I remember that I liked the Chico Hamilton Band. But I must admit that there has never really been a drummer who I've attempted to imitate—and I don't think you should play that way, not even in the early stages.

Yes, but surely it's very unusual for a musician not to have been influenced in the early stages?

Obviously I must have been influenced—I didn't live entirely in a vacuum, but I didn't have many opportunities to be influenced! I came from a very poor background. I hadn't a record player—no money to go to concerts. And, as far as playing trad was concerned I was just trying to make it work rather than copying what I'd heard others doing. At first I didn't even know the names of most of the tunes but I just found out what to do instinctively.

Did you develop to modern jazz from this?

Yes, I got interested in more complicated things as I became capable of handling them.

You had plenty of people to play with at this time?

Not as many as I would have liked but around 18 I formed a modern jazz quartet playing East Coast style material, and then later I formed another band that eventually included Lou Gare which must have been about 12 years ago.

So this was way before meeting Cardew etc.?

Yes it was a kind of hard bop band and I suppose that Rollins was a definite influence on Lou, as Blakey must be on me. Lou was also playing with the Westbrook band which, although very early, had Surman and Mike Osborne and also the guitarist, Keith Rowe.

So you all really came from a jazz background?

Us three yes—and Lawrence Sheaff who joined soon after. But Cornelius and the other musicians associated with AMM, Christopher Hobbs and Christian Woolf [sic], had no jazz influences at all.

So in fact AMM has definitely been the mainstay of your career, so far?

Yes it started in 1965. So I've been playing non-time music longer than time music now.

When AMM first started playing in a total improvisation context who else was doing this at the time?

Well, there wasn't anybody apart from say John Stevens and Peter Lemer, although their music was different from ours. I seem to remember that an American pianist called Bob James had a trio that was doing similar things but that is all I can recall. And, at that time Lou and Keith were getting a hard time from the Westbrook band; it was quite sad.

Simply because of their musical ideas?

I suppose so. They wouldn't even talk to them! Keith would never get a solo. I suppose they felt that they couldn't trust him!

Who was Keith influenced by?

I don't know really. I don't think there was ever any direct influences except that Keith was very interested in painting and I suppose he always thought that painting was always ahead of music. I think you can see that there are parallels between music now and painting twenty years ago or more.

Free improvisation came very naturally to the group did it?

I don't know about naturally.

You didn't actually have a discussion and decide not to play pieces any longer?

No, but the fact is that as individuals we didn't fit in anywhere else meant we just had no reason not to do what we wanted. It made the personal bond between us greater. In fact we used to meet at first once a week and just talk about things.

So how did Cardew get involved, considering he was the only one without a jazz heritage?

Well I think it had always been a lifelong ambition of his to play in a jazz band and we were the next best thing! Apart from that, at the time he was working on "Treatise" which as you know is a graphic score and I think he had been long aware that the composer had a diminishing role, or whose role was no longer to determine exactly what was to be played and that idea, plus hearing us at the Royal College of Art one day, did it, and he became one of the group.

I've got an old record of AMM on Elektra which, apart from your Incus EP appears to be one of the few recordings the group has made. Could you explain how that came about?

There are others, including a limited edition—very limited—about six copies of a pre-Cardew AMM. The other is on Mainstream. The Elektra record was organised by four guys—John Hopkins, Ron Atkins (who writes jazz for the Guardian), Alan Becket and Peter Jenner who got together to form a record label called DNA for putting out new music and I think the first and only production was us; they sold the idea to Elektra via Joe Boyd who was the early manager of Pink Floyd. On the first recording session the engineers were completely at sea. They assumed that we would play instruments in conventional ways. But we moved about a bit and they couldn't understand it at all. That was in 1966 I think.

Were you put into a drum booth?

They tried to. Anyway at this time and encouraged by Keith (…) and wasn't always using the drums in a normal way.

On the record sleeve it states that one of the band's aims in playing music is to find out why you want to play. Is that still relevant?

Yes I think it is. To follow on from that I think that if you ever found out what it was all about you'd give up.

Considering the lack of work, how has AMM survived?

Well it *is* survival rather than anything else but we have always put the music first, therefore it has never actually been dependent upon the market for its existence. Most of AMM's playing has in fact been done in private but most of our income has come from abroad. You get good money compared to England. We also went to America twice, first in '68 and played in New York and then in Buffalo, which came about through Cornelius who had some kind of a fellowship there. In 1971 we did a much wider tour of America and Canada.

Did working with Cardew involve you with the contemporary classical world more? Isn't that a contradiction of terms?

Yes a little. Of course he had worked with Stockhausen etc.—although Cornelius was always reticent about his "straight" connections. Gradually though, we became aware of other things. In America we came into contact with quite a lot of avant-garde musicians.

Did the group ever play notated pieces?

Only graphic and indeterminate pieces. Cornelius still being a composer would often want to involve us in playing pieces and he began to realise that he needed people like us who were prepared to go out on a limb as opposed to being told exactly what to do. We were all involved in the first complete performance of "Treatise" at the Commonwealth Institute in '66 and a few other pieces of La Monte Young and Christian Woolf [sic]. As time went on we realised that there was really no point in being involved with these things—and anyway we would start to disregard them.

What relevance would you give this type of notation?

I think they are useful introductions to improvisations especially for musicians who have always played compositions. It gives them some kind of framework to start from. Although I think most composers with any integrity realise that it is only a stepping stone; that a graphic score cannot be a definite statement, in a world that is supposed to accept Einstein's view of the universe making definite statements, especially in music seems a dubious business anyway.

Stockhausen is perhaps interesting when you consider he still writes music that has only verbal instructions but at the same time writes totally composed pieces like Mantra?

I'm not convinced about his interest in improvisation. Even in his so-called free pieces he controls the players very rigidly. In some of the verbal pieces which you would expect to have quite a range of interpretation, I understand that he often tells players that they're doing it wrong!

Have you heard Percussionist [sic] Jean Pierre Drouet's playing on the new Stockhausen recordings of the group improvisations Aus Den Sieben Tagen?

No. Actually I hear very little music other than my own—unless it's on the same bill. Intellectually, it's philosophy that interests me, whereas I like music from a practical point of view because I can contribute and take part in it.

Did you ever study music at all?

Not in any academic way. I was taught a little of drumming when I was a teenager. I've never found anything that music teachers had to say about music to be particularly appropriate to what I wanted to do. I have learnt much more from people who have never picked an instrument up in their lives.

You said earlier that you used contact mikes etc. before reverting back to acoustic sound. Was this only because of a desire to make the music more subtle?

Yes, contact mikes are very unsubtle. I was not able to control what was going on.

I'm finding that a lot of these problems can with sufficient development be overcome. Don't you envisage using contact mikes and electronics again or would philosophical considerations rule them out?

Well, I think that now I am a lot less interested in sound production. The physical means of making music seem less important now than the how and the why. I wouldn't rule out the possibility of using electronics, but it's just a minor consideration. The dominant motivation of my playing is to be making music with other people. This may seem strange seeing that I am best known for working with only a few people, especially Lou Gare. But, amongst other things I have a band which has been going for some time.

What's the line-up of the band?

Lou and Geoff Hawkins on tenor saxophones, Gerry Gold on trumpet and Marc Meggido and Marcio Mattos on double basses and me.

Does the fact that you've basically played with a limited number of musicians worry you in any way?

Well that's actually not true but I think one of the reasons AMM stayed together for so long is that we defined a particular area of sound and it became very difficult when other people came into the group because these areas would become diffuse. It seems to me that you need a lot of time to work on all the different kinds of relationships that are inherent in a collective improvisation. Playing with many groups can easily be so very futile. It's important to concentrate upon how you are making music, rather than on what you are producing.

So the end result is not important?

You cannot split the means and the result. But if you can concentrate upon the ends it will be at the expense of the means. The process is the important thing to be concerned about. Naturally I want the music to be meaningful but it will only come out right is the process is working correctly.

Is there any point in recording this music?

I suppose there isn't. A recording—a recall device—is totally alien to what this music is about, although I suppose it could be instrumental in bringing people to the music.

What would you say it is all about?

I think it's probably about making people realise what they are; to trust their own experience.

If you say you are interested only in the process, is there any need for an audience for instance?

Yes, because they're a part of the process. As a player can participate in a piece by not playing, so the audience participate by listening, by giving the music their attention.

I know that you've worked with the same people for quite a time to build up a mutual direction. Don't you find that a rather safe idea in the sense that you know beforehand the various formats, whereas with working in a situation with many different people you have no real pre-conceived idea of the result, which can be more stimulating and therefore an interesting situation?

There are two assumptions in your question that I must first repudiate. Firstly, AMM has probably worked with more people than almost any other group. The old quartet conducted numerous workshops and sessions in the US, Canada, Germany, as well as at home. And Lou and I since 1972 have extended this by working with musicians and non-musicians in Norway and

Belgium besides still more people at home—including school children. But, we are not exactly noted for our zeal to get into every group in town, if that's what you mean. Following form that and to the second assumption, about different people being more stimulating—that is also part of the "throw away" syndrome. As I have indicated we have played with lots of people; sometimes it is stimulating and sometimes it is bloody hard work. It's working with people who have great strengths that is stimulating and seeing that I have been playing with Lou for about 12 years now indicates the strength I respect in his playing. But, some of the most stimulating players I have come across would not normally be called musicians!

Tell me about the reasons for making instruments?

I suppose that rather than making very many instruments I have been more interested in searching for sound itself. There's an innocent, if naïve, curiosity which makes you look at any object and ask yourself—what is its sound? And, if it has one how can I prise away its secret? Do I bow it, scrape it, amplify it—or kick it? In this way many odds and ends found their way, almost permanently, into my equipment. I still have a much battered tin-lid, after eight years. Biscuit tins are quite good. Yoghourt cups seem to have more potential than they actually have. Coffee tins are very good for rolling on resonant stages (Keith Rowe was a master of this particular art). Children's toys, pieces of glass—the list can be endless—and you can always play the stage itself. I have made a few things, consciously decided to build an instrument. Almost inevitably is was a drum. Inevitably because of the "area of sound" business we talked about earlier. An individual must be allowed to contribute and to know that his contribution is effective; although he is the one who must make most of the effort to see that it is. In AMM this grew into an unwritten law, which meant that I had no right to an area of sound that another player was effectively using—at least not without his implicit condonance. So I made a huge drum from a wine barrel—very conventional although very beautiful. Really it was the making of it that appealed to me most, although I have since derived much pleasure from its deep resonances. But it was Cornelius who played it most because it soon became, together with our two enormous home-made gongs, part of our mutual or collective playing areas. These together with whatever could be found within the playing environment, apart from our individual instruments, became common ground.

I have always been interested in how you actually play an instrument—we all were. And every member of AMM, past and present, has used a bow for instance, irrespective of what they played. Naturally percussion was uppermost in my thinking and the stick or beater came in for some scrutiny. Ultimately I produced a number of beaters which were either very difficult or even painful to play with. The most sophisticated one that I made I gave to Cornelius, who by the way is a most discriminating percussion player. Another had a handle made from the stem of a rose bush—thorns and all! I kept this one to myself—must be the masochist in me!

What is your attitude toward practising?

I practise regularly to keep myself fit and capable for playing—I also run five miles most days for the same reason. Improvisation implies being called upon to cope with what is demanded by the immediate situation; in other words it is about responses, and I wish to be able to respond as quickly and as finely as possible to these demands. This mean being awake and acutely aware of the music—listening and then responding. You need to be capable of doing what your responses indicate even though you may not be fully conscious of them. So I practise rolls, paradiddles for hands and feet, plus a few things of my won in a very disciplined manner to achieve the kind of control I want. When I play however then that is all left behind; not referred to consciously. The other point that I think is very important, is about practising too much. I never practise or run on a day that I am playing. There is an old boxing adage about not leaving all your strength in the gym; I think there's a lot of truth in that for musicians also.

Do you use the traditional military grip or the matched grip—and what about brushes?

I only use the matched grip. I changed from the military style soon after I left the Boy Scouts! There seems to me to be no reason why a beginner should ever be introduced to the military or so-called orthodox grip. Quite obviously it was devised for the marching side-drummer. You try playing a side drum on the hip with the matched grip. It's not only awkward (...) is the most passive hand, to develop so much easier.

I have not used brushes for years. The last pair I had, inherited from my murky jazz past, was last used with a contact microphone in a last ditch attempt to discover if they had any musical qualities at all—they hadn't—or I failed!

You're known as the composer of a piece called "Spirals." Could you tell me about it?

Well it's not really a composition in the normal sense. If anything it's just a jumping off point, albeit fairly sophisticated, for improvisation. The first performance was on June 15th 1966 at the Commonwealth Institute. The musicians were Keith Rowe, Christopher Hobbs, Lou, John Tilbury, Cornelius Cardew and myself. It seemed to work remarkably well but that was only because of the commitment of the people involved. "Spirals" is a conception which I suppose shows the other side of myself. The "free" musician wanting to concretise things—perhaps. But, over the years it has grown to reflect many of my ideas about improvisation and it even incorporated some of my non-musical interests—the etymology of the Hebrew language. An expanded version, written with funds provided by the Arts Council, believe it or not, was performed at the Roundhouse in March 1973. There were about forty musicians and I tried to make it meaningful in a visual way also. The players all wore robes of colours associated with their parts, and great spirals of light were projected onto the circular playing area. That apart, it is really an attempt to enumerate and classify and then enact all the constituent parts of an improvisation. The object being to get each player or group of players to concentrate upon one particular part, in the hope that all together we would create an improvisation that was complete. Let me give you a few examples of the parts. Players were asked to develop the ability to absorb all other influences, others to regulate the performance or to complete what they thought were incomplete statements and so on. In all there are 23 separate parts. It is really no different from any other improvisation in that it relies totally upon the commitment of the players. It's a work that does take quite a time to fully assimilate but only because most improvisers have some blind spots, an these we don't care to demonstrate. But I am hoping to work on the piece as a long term project; working on it over a long period of time with the same people before actually performing it. There are a few musicians who have expressed their interest in participating—but it does seem unlikely to occur with regular musicians because of the time factor. However, there is an enterprising art college that is thinking about asking me to do it with its students—so who knows?

Can you say how you actually play the drums? What about technique, tuning, cymbals etc?

I find it difficult to say precisely how or why I play the drums. Hopefully, most of this comes through the other questions I have tried to answer, but there is one thing I do feel certain of and that is that the instrument is an extension of me. And, I suppose, I am an enthusiastic and committed type—so I play that way. I take all that I know and dive in at the deep end—all or nothing! I would rather fail miserably than play safe. Like all men concerned with coming to terms with their environment, my technique and knowledge is a means of coping and to some extent controlling my world. I do not have an academic approach to music because that is anathema to me—analysis destroys music—synthesis is the way to new creation. I play because it is physically and emotionally important for me to do so and I hope that it may also be important for musicians I play with and to the listeners. I want to play as freely as I breathe or speak (people who know me might find that amusing, as I stammer!).

As regards things like tuning and the quality of cymbals etc., my attitude is firmly based upon compatibility and effectiveness in terms of collective playing and upon my own enjoyment of sound—and to what I can afford! The instrument is a means to an end, not an end in itself. What's the good of a beautiful drum kit if the drummer fails to play with the band? As you no doubt have observed, my equipment is pretty old but somehow I manage to keep it going. But if you know anyone who wants to give away a new set of drums.

Appendix B

Keith Rowe's notes to a performance of Cornelius Cardew's "Treatise," page 54, to be played on the 20th anniversary of his death. (presented as typed save for several insertions for clarity)

*

Cornelius Cardew died 13th Dec. 1981, twenty years later I decided to pay a personal homage to Cornelius during the year 2001. I would work my way through his 198 [sic] page graphic score Treatise, performing a few pages at every performance, for the most part integrating a page or two into an improvisation, at other times performing a selection of pages as on this recording performed as Treatise.

I formed an approach that allowed a range of different ways of dealing with how I performed the pages. These different approaches allowed extremely tight detailed renditions, all the way through to vague approximations, this might also include other approaches like retrograde inversions etc.

For this performance which took place in Austin, Texas on the occasion of Ricky Reed's birthday (09)? February 2001, for this evening I had decided to perform around 6 pages, I had started the year 2001 by performing page 1, and by mid February had reached page 54, I planned an approach that would see page 54 performed rather tightly, and the following pages successively loosened until the last page in this performance almost "abandoned" [the score].

The performance

The time indications that follow coincide with the time indications I've marked on the score

00:01 Page 54 the first thing we encounter is a number 2, for this performance this number will announce two aspects that will caricaturise this performance, firstly a "sweep of the strings" motif, from left to right. In some ways this sweep of the strings imitates a Koto, and refers [to] the influence of eastern ideas on Cornelius, and the way AMM had grappled with Chinese ideograms in order to have experience of a graphic language without for the most part a phonic indicator. We thought this might help dealing with Treatise.

The second aspect is a recognition of my reading the score from left to right.

00:40 thin motor sound at 00:56 changes direction and ends at 01:14

01:22 the second two sweeps for the second number 2, I regard the numbers throughout Treatise as a very different order of graphics to the squares circles shapes line etc. in that they are "near universals" we find them having specific functions in everyday life, money bus numbers etc. for this second number 2 I pronounce it with more insistence and depth as if it had built on the existence of the very first number 2. Ends at 1:42.

02:01 we encounter a five line stave I treat this as a continuum at 03:10 slightly higher sounds are added to indicate and recognise a very slight optical illusion of two invisible squares, which become more audible at 03:20 onwards as the "Tilbury motif"

this motif is a recording of a single note played on the piano by John Tilbury, and played in reverse (via loop station) this reversal represents history, (looking back) it comes from a comment John made while sitting at the piano, whenever he touches the keyboard history comes back at him, rather like Eliot when he writes when judging a living poet "you must set him among the dead" throughout these pages a square or significant right angle will trigger a "T motif."

At **04:07** the continuum becomes influenced by the "T" motif and adds a repeated reversal snatch of distortion of its own, in some respects recognising that the outer form of the five line stave continuum are right angles.

06:38 a wobble is introduced (Boss PS-5) to reflect the height of the stave and ends at 06:50

06:53 we encounter a number 1, a single sweep in the manner of the Koto sweeps, as you can detect up until now I have allowed these numbers a large degree of surrounding space, they become events and stand vertically, unpressured by a wish to move on. In a sense displaying their graphical difference and independence.

07:12 a single short vertical line and at 07:30 a development of that vertical single line, for this verticality I'm using a spring anchored at one end by the strings and standing vertically on the guitar pickup, for the single line the spring is sounded simply, for the vertical lines development (on its left it has a thinner pre echo and its main stem has grown a short five live stave) I in response to this elaborate the basic sound. Thickening its centre etc.

07:52 a number 1 is represented by a single sweep, something I should add here to explain why this number does not have the independence of the earlier numbers, often during performances of Treatise I've chosen to overlay aspects from other Cardew compositions into the way I view the pages, or graphic motifs. For this page I had decided to overlay the plus/minus (+-) aspects of his Solo with Accompaniment, found in the way the matrix works is that symbols are either attracted or rejected to each other, a symbol will adopt and become influenced by a neighbouring signs content and qualities, or on the contrary reject them. Rather like the ends of a magnet. Attraction/repulsion. In addition plus/minus acknowledges Cornelius' work and cross-fertilisation with Stockhausen.

07:52 [sic] the number 1's independence has been subsumed and overpowered by the larger neighbouring graphic at 08:12, this graphic is a development of the two earlier single vertical lines (07:12 and 07:30) a powerful attraction has linked these signs, in that they are related in a single development.

08:35 a number 1 is overpowered by both the larger number 5, and the strong graphic, what has happened is that after the number 1 is sounded, the powerful attraction of the larger number 5 sucks my attention across in its direction and rather [than] reading the graphic from left to right, the magnetic attraction is forcing me to read in a circular clockwise direction, reading the two small circles first then the quarter circle, the short line, the larger circle and finally the two small filled in circles. Here I should say how the circles are dealt with. In Cardew's Treatise hand book where he outlines the composition's earlier performances Cornelius refers to how John Cage employed a radio for the circles, the circle relating to a tuning dial perhaps? What becomes possible here is aspects of a performance based on historic principals [sic], in that one could adopt an earlier technique or approach [to] integrate into ones performance.

For this performance (and countless other performances) I've adopted Cage's use of the radio for the circles, reading the graphics in a clockwise direction the two small circles result in a country and western radio grab,

08:37 "even though we ain't got money"

08:55 "I'm so in love with you"

08:46 [sic] "chain of love"

08:50 quarter circle radio scan

09:03 Larger circle finds Lulu To Sir with Love

"But in my mind…
I know they will, will still live on and on
But how do you thank someone
Who has taken you from crayons to perfume?
It isn't easy but I'll try…"

09:38 death motif

I need to backtrack here to 09:03. Remember this performance is a personal tribute to a close friend and musical colleague, that this random grab of Lulu singing To Sir with Love is so strongly evocative of the period Cornelius was around the AMM, Lulu's recording was a prominent part of the musical landscape in 1967, but when the words pour out of the radio *"But how do you thank someone who has taken you from crayons to perfume?"* … how can this be? Here in an arbitrary twist of the radio dial a pop song appears to recognise how Cornelius influenced AMM's early development. *"how do you thank someone…from crayons to perfume…but I'll try"*

During the thirty seconds that this chance radio broadcast has its emotional impact on me I'm struggling to hold to my basic plan, I feel the need to comment on the violent means of Cornelius' death, I quickly decide to use the number 5 that is looming, as a violent interruption, guillotine like, to reflect the abruptness of Cornelius' passing, The first sweep of the number 5 at 09:38 becomes a death motif, I also notice that there are five graphic pieces of material that are between each of the number that has passed so far, I decide to revisit these graphics in an oblique and minimum manner. Working backwards,

09:38 first sweep of number 5 which should comment on the Lulu graphic but remains solemn

09:54 second sweep revisits the graphic between 07:52 and 08:35

10:00 third sweep graphic between 06:53 and 07:52

10:04 fourth sweep between 01:42 and 06:52

10:07 fifth sweep 00:25 and 01:22

10:13 the strong right angles evoke the "T" motif

11:08 the half circle introduces a snatch of radio, and again referring [to] the plus minus gauze I've overlaid on parts of the score, here the radio is repulsing the low note notation within its vicinity, and produces high sounds.

11:22 number 1, this sweep in order to balance the radios repulsing of the low note notation, the number 1 becomes attracted by the low note notation and gets treated likewise.

Also here I added an extra layer of influence from a Cardew composition, "The Tiger's Mind" in the way the low note notation affects the radio and number 1, the manner in which two independent aspects become affected by a third element.

Appendix C

Keith Rowe, painter in different media
by Lutz Eitel

I've never seen a Keith Rowe painting in the flesh. Since the cult of the original is only upheld by rich people who want to keep the meaning of the art they own to themselves, that of course shouldn't keep me from making them mine, gazing abstractedly at the work while following the scrape and rustle coming from my stereo speakers. The music sounds out on its own—the cover paintings seem to offer something of a background in place and time, part picture-book quaint Englishness, part American art between pop and colourfield. It was probably not from the pictures themselves, but through reading interviews with Rowe that I started picking up little messages from between that. I then wrote an article on the artist-curated gallery of his CD covers, reconstructing Rowe's development as a visual artist to satisfy my own curiosity...which has led to the unsuspected suggestion that my text be used to introduce a forthcoming exhibition, where it would have to face of a whole roomful of true Keith Rowe paintings. Just the imagination of those actually existing as objects in "real" life (scare quotes because it's only in a gallery) make my projected perceptions noticeably shift. What I wrote was largely concerned with iconography, which is the element that changes least in the transfer from object to illustration. Right now that won't help me much—because I'm staring at snapshots I have been sent, of the originals propped up on an easel hit by unflattering lamplight, their edges bent in those bulging lines only a cheap digital camera can draw. They look so fresh and uncontained, not at all like packages to recordings whose classical status is being cemented in canon decades after their first appearance. I suddenly have to really see them as paintings, not as clues to ideas behind the work. But how can I do that, when the music already is painting? I turn off Rowe's record The Room...*the music doesn't exactly help me build sentences anyway.*

Music seen as painting...the idea belongs to Rowe's own characterization of his practice. Here's what I found on that, excerpted from my earlier essay: In a 2001 interview for *Paris Transatlantic*, Rowe speaks of his outlook during the student days at Plymouth College of Art, where he was both educated in quasi-academic painting and encouraged to find his own voice: "I abandoned the canvas and worked on hardboard, using house paint from Woolworth's... In the end my paintings came down to about three colours, which they still are today, I guess. Postbox red. Stripes. Trying to get away from the aesthetics of taste, and from what you were supposed to do." In music he was still trying to emulate American jazz masters, and the lesson he took away from art school would prove crucial: "In the painting class I was finding out who I was, making the kind of paintings which were uniquely mine, in a way which was uniquely mine, but with the guitar I was just slavishly copying American guitar players. This was late 1950s, early 1960s."

If we now fast forward to the cover painting of a yellow truck that Rowe would do for the debut record of the improvisation group he co-founded, *AMMMusic* from 1966, this is hard to reconcile with such ambition of uniqueness—instead, the image also seems derived from distinctly American sources. Many stylistic traits could be found in the art of Roy Lichtenstein. One wouldn't call it a slavish copy, since the strong diagonal is completely unlike the American painter, there's more individuality to the line and Rowe makes no attempt to render his image iconic. Also, if Rowe was following that development since the end of the 1950s it would have been concurrent with Lichtenstein's. (And then I squint hard at the 1967 version of the painting for the new edition of the record on Elektra, which has a wider frame and a more slender black-and-yellow lorry on its white ground, and suddenly remember that Warhol's banana cover for The Velvet Underground was from the same year.) While during those times the impetus would have felt to come mainly from the US, such commonalities are no coincidence. It is not at all the point of the picture to express a uniquely individual artistic voice, but rather to use a popular pictorial language which makes for good communication. The image on the cover speaks immediately. I somehow think of it as "hitting the ground running": a big ebullient tour truck going straight to Mediterranean places where AMM would enjoy life in the sunset, play stadium shows like the big rock acts of the day and probably sell lots of merchandise. It is a very upbeat painting, and it sort of reads the pop agenda backwards. Where pop had taken the commercial image out of its context, rendering it more meaningful but useless, Rowe, like many a designer of the time, is re-appropriating the style for commercial product (with a fittingly ironic twist, since the music would not be expected to turn over large quantities).

A poster from the same era, which was later used for the release of a 1968 concert under the title *The Crypt*, shows how Rowe was repeating the same formal concerns. The composition shares the truck's forward thrust, even in an object that should be static, or maybe not even static, since the empty speech bubble coming from the transistor radio indicates silence (as owned by John Cage). The radio was one of the tools Rowe started to use at the time, his main instrument being a guitar laid flat on a table. This musical practice would appear much more radical than the painting and, interestingly, in its process much more informed by the history of visual art. Rowe remembers the creative breakthrough as a musician in a 2010 conversation with singer David Sylvian for *Bomb* magazine: "In the mid-1960s I regarded the electric guitar as an empty white canvas, an object to stare at and imagine: What can I do with this thing? It helped to look at cubist images of guitars and wonder how they would sound. My dissertation was on George Braque's guitars. The sense of liberation that emerged from detaching my grip on the instrument and abandoning its conventional technique was extraordinary. I directly applied the processes of the visual arts to this electric instrument: Pollock's when laying the guitar flat on its back and interacting with its surface; Duchamp's by using found objects such as knives, face fans and cocktail mixers to play it; Rauschenberg's when integrating a radio. Regarding playing as painting offered, almost immediately, a new language for the instrument."

Lying the guitar flat became a crucial act of liberation from the bodily aspect of the instrument (if not the most phallic then surely the most masturbatory of them all), and it offered limitless possibilities. Much of it was thematic: Rowe filled his guitar table with sound-making objects that he could choose for reasons outside of their musical properties; they would carry iconographical or psychological meaning. Most of all, though, playing became a gestural act in which the decision-making was close to visual art production—the main, and welcome, difference being that there was no commodity created through the act, but a sound that immediately vanished in time. (Rowe's perspective on contemporary art is mostly on the Americans, and on Pollock regarding gesture. Still let me add that in France in the early 1940s, Jean Fautrier also laid his canvas on a table or the floor, so he could build thick *hautes pâtes* of plaster paint with a palette knife. With those, he modelled pictures of the heads of prisoners shot by the Nazi occupying forces in France. Sometimes I find Rowe's approach closer to the concentrated work of the Frenchman, who used a much smaller amplitude of bodily movement, than to the no less deep but always sweeping gestures of Pollock.)

For the 2006 exhibition *Debris Field* at Bolton Museum and Art Gallery, Rowe transferred the guitar tables into visual art proper. He talks about that in a conversation with Richard Pinnell on the radio programme *Audition* from 14 May 2006: he made three reconstructions of historical guitar tables from the 1960s to the 1990s, building them in a rather generic fashion, so they would represent something typical of the times they represent. He fixed guitars and all appliances and gizmos to the boards and hung them on the wall. When you listen to the artist describing the implications of his work, the detail of reflection is quite fascinating. Every guitar embodies the artist's outlook of the times, every tool he uses to touch or circumvent touching the guitar brings its own set of connotations and every cable of the wiring makes its own psychological connections. The table arrangements do not follow the logic of building an instrument, rather everything is chosen for connotations or even aesthetics. The act of hanging the tables on the walls to Rowe is the closure of a circle which began when he first laid a guitar flat on its back.

It is important that these tables are reconstructions, not historical documents, so the work speaks of memory as Rowe intends... but, still, maybe the art context is so much more over-determined than even a complete chart of all connotations within the works could ever be; without having seen the pieces I still have to imagine that submitting them to a situation where they have no choice but be self-sufficient works of art might do them more harm than good. Let me quote the only review I found online, from one Kay Carson: "Musician Keith Rowe's *Guitar Retrospective* is a delightful piece designed to bring a wistful, nostalgic smile to the lips. Each of his three old instruments comes with its own scattered entourage, providing a social commentary of the era... This is a quirky and touching homage to his beloved discipline." That's (unintentionally) harsh, but not completely unfair, and especially the fact that one could listen to sound samples from the respective eras on headphones must have given this a touch of an improvised music hall of fame display...

Let me interrupt my earlier (by a couple of months) self here: measuring this exhibition I haven't seen against the one I've yet to see, in which there will be only one of those reconstructed tables on the wall, that from the 1960s, it's immediately obvious how much better the thing must work in a context where its main task is not to embody its creator's memory of what it once might have meant and add historical perspective, but to tell the viewer something about the artist, about how he is wired, making all art in the room resonate with imagined sound from that hollowbody on the wall. It puts the painterly practice of playing the guitar table into the visual art equation... As listeners, we would not really need to know about that practice at all, because it carries a baggage that rather spoils the idea of music as the pure medium whose condition all art aspires to. The practice has perhaps become most fruitful in Rowe's most ambitious project over the last years, The Room*:*

As a first realization of a long ongoing process, *The Room* is not just about spaces or more specifically a space of performance, it is also about the act of listening itself. In his *Audition* interview, Rowe explains how it can be important to not listen in a musical situation, a central aspect of his practice: "Not being afraid...not being dogmatic. Challenge the overemphasis of what listening is about. What does it mean? Listening can stop you from being in the room. Not listening in order to be in that place at that time." All the implications of this strategy would lead too far from a discussion of the artistic strategy; but it is interesting to keep in mind that Rowe made the recordings at home in his own room over a time, and that although he has engaged with the project for many years, the resulting tracks sound completely in the moment and allow for obviously spontaneous accidents.

In a post on the internet forum I Hate Music from 3 February 2009, Rowe speaks about the determinedness of every sound detail in his solo music, starting from an earlier recording: "Perhaps one might see a theme running through *Harsh* which was about the invisibility of harshness (sewn into our jeans trainers t-shirts etc TV quiz show colours...), *The Room* (traces and whispers of process are overtaken by blankness and silence, in these spaces important transactions take place, absorption of a single mood, a contemplative aura)... My inspiration for disguise is of course along with Duchamp, is Rothko, to what extent do the Seagram Murals leak information about the Laurentian library in Florence and Michelangelo?"

That last question goes back to Mark Rothko himself, who felt that impressions of Michelangelo's cramped vestibule, especially the blind, walled-up windows, were behind his Seagram murals, his darkest cycle before the Rothko Chapel. (The painter engaging with a room by listening to his memory of another room. Which of course is like an invitation to Rowe.) On 1 June 2007, some months after recording the music to The Room, *Rowe played Rothko Chapel and there used a catalogue essay by Barbara Novak and Brian O'Doherty on Rothko's dark paintings as a guideline for his own engagement with the space, keeping in mind the artist's legendary anxious stare at his own work (an attempt to discover the resonance of his paintings that often lasted unbroken over a considerable time, if it didn't fall flat altogether). Interpretative phrases extracted from the essay served Rowe as a score of sorts: "Faith vs void / experience of darkness...paradoxical insights / repainting / eyes become dark adapted / classical "answering" on opposing walls / disclosure and withdrawal..." (quote and all information from an e-mail by the artist). It is maybe not the score-like quality of these extractions from the text that most characterizes the strategy, instead the whole situation of an engagement with the room is like acting out a set of performance instructions that might carry the bottom line: within the chapel, play back the interpretation of the art to the art itself and explore the self-consciousness of the room (of the performer and of the open-minded listener within the space they help define).*

"What I do on guitar is itself a heavily disguised painting," Rowe puts it in that same e-mail, and one might wonder why he insists on calling his practice that, when it might more obviously be termed a kind of performance art. I think it is painting because all conceptual background feeds into an expression by gesture. Rowe's paintings on the other hand are in fact more driven by ideas than gestures; they add what can be expressed through imagery (iconography, but also the facts of it being a painting). This can take place on a quite hermetic meta-level beyond the unsuspecting viewer, or it can, when coupled with a piece of music, be an invitation to the listener to let thematic concerns in on the listening expe-

rience. The CD cover to The Room *on the outside shows a painting of a blue colour field separated by a black line from a green colour field beneath, an (empty) landscape (format) stretched over three fold-out panels. When you open the package, you get the same composition in dark Rothko reds, the darkly self-burning inside to the somewhat dim colour pastures (that have an amusingly ambiguous relation to the words of the title). If we take both paintings together with the title as part of the musical object, things start to become readable. The Rothko reference is obvious, his artistic involvement in a room brings a heavy baggage of discourse, and our knowledge of his frame of mind at the time of his Seagram paintings helps set a sombre mood which seems to relate to the starkness of the sounds on the CD. (Which is something I else might have tried to explain away: much avant-garde music would seem in a lousy mood to the naive ear, but as a connoisseur I neutralize that because it's art, I disconnect my listening from certain emotions... except when my kids are around and the passive-aggressive behaviour of the sounds can become intolerable.) The cover paintings open that whole discourse for the music, and it can become fruitful to follow the exercise and explore the connections between the room one is in/moves through for listening, the imaginary room the music was recorded in and one's memories or imaginations of the Rothko Chapel and the Laurentian library (and now I seem to suddenly remember how I was once herded through the Michelangelo vestibule: tourists spilling over the voluminous stairs whose swelling forms are shoeboxed into narrow confines, but our barely containable masses made them seem appropriate in proportion). These are paintings about how an abstract painting can be coded with distinct levels of meaning. Paintings with self-conscious brushstrokes trying out how it is to be colourfield paintings. Which, since there is no way to get rid of subtext anyway, makes them paintings pure and simple.*

The central piece of the exhibition that I have yet to see will be a four-metre-wide painting in black tones with an elongated white drip wiggling horizontally through it. I haven't a digital image of that one, but it is from the same series as the cover of the CD Contact *by Rowe and Sachiko M from 2009...which I quietly dropped in my essay on Rowe's art because I had no handle. I always see in it a sort of cartoon image of a sperm ghost taking flight (which means I win the Rorschach test, but do not have anything else to offer). When I give up and ask the artist what the hell it all means, he kindly suggests a few readings he does not at all place above anyone else's reading, because it is a painting and it will have to be seen. I'm struck by one suggestion he makes, though, that does seem more valuable to him than the others, where he sees the drip as "the architecture of a musical phrase, that Mozart and we (now) share this same exquisite architecture. I can read this drip as a phrase from the opening of the Adagio K488 (Curzon playing)." I frankly wouldn't be able to tell a drip by Curzon from a splash by Horowitz if it poked me in the eye, but the precision of the association does suggest something apart from synesthetic experience (at this cue, though, think of Rowe's duo with video artist Kjell Bjørgeengen, where both feed into each other's circuits—synesthetics inscribed into the schematic of their set-up, an exploration that avoids the esoteric tendencies of the genre). Rather, it is again about a gesture fixed in time and space, performed (by Mozart/ Curzon) in music, translated into objective form in the painting.*

And then there is that objective form resisting interpretation as the topic of another painting in the exhibition, The Unknown Object, *painted with hard edges despite its unknowability, and rendered unknowable by painting.*

(Lutz Eitel blogs at tonotfallasleep.blogspot.com.)

Appendix D

Blindfold test with Keith Rowe conducted by Dan Warburton, published in *The Wire*, issue 287, January 2008

*

RAMÓN MONTOYA "Fandango" (1936)
From *Grandes Figures Du Flamenco Vol. 5* (Le Chant Du Monde)

Flamenco...it's a world I know very little about. It's often said that Ramón was the greatest player who ever touched the instrument. Guitar in its purest form, I guess. We kind of know it yet we're continually surprised by how it moves along. The sense of Narrative is pretty strong.

How did you discover his work?

I knew [the music of] his nephew, Carlos, when I was about 18, maybe even younger, and I was impressed by the flashiness. You know, when you're young you like Salvador Dali, until you realise that it's too tricky, too flashy, too smoothed out—and you begin to like Picasso's ugly period. I think it was like that in a way. And then I read that his uncle Ramón was even better. It took me years to find a recording. For a long time there weren't any, until this French label brought them out. The way he touches the instrument...he's one of those players who couldn't play badly.

Like Johnny Smith, Jimmy Raney, Tal Farlow, Django Reinhardt. Players who had supremely good musical taste, who were supremely gifted. The other thing I've always admired about Ramón is that he only ever recorded an hour or so of material, in October 1936 or something.

So you think there are too many records around today?

I think we'd have to say yes and no, wouldn't we? And I think that puts us in a peculiar—in a positive sense—position. Improvisation is a continual work in progress; we never really reach a stage when the work is finished. It's a series of works. We think of compositions as finished works, but they change depending on different interpretations, whereas what we do as improvisers becomes fixed. So it's a peculiar state of affairs where the work in progress becomes fixed and the finished work becomes a work in progress. I think we ought to be a bit more careful about what we bring out, but on the other hand the things we might not consider as all that wonderful now may be the things that will survive. That's not for us to decide.

MIKE WESTBROOK CONCERT BAND "Sugar"
From *Release* (Deram, 1968)

(Listens to the piece in its entirety, smiling briefly during Mike Osborne's alto sax solo) You know, when I hear this it brings back feelings of exasperation. It really does. I just had to get away from it. I had huge respect for Mike, his integrity and his musicianship, but I had to get out. The rhythm is so…dumpety dump, you feel like there are big anchors holding it back. Osborne was the sharpest thing there.

Weren't the members of the Westbrook band open to influences from the freer stuff that was around at the time? What we have on disc sounds rather conservative nowadays, but he was, after all, quite tolerant of your own experimentation.

There were some open free jamming sessions back in late 1965, before this was recorded, and Mike came to a few of those. His earlier band was more adventurous. Less competent, perhaps, but I think Osborne and John Surman were always good. That's about when AMM was formed, and we had a more radical agenda. By the time this was recorded I'd stopped listening to this kind of stuff altogether, and I haven't listened to it since.

PINK FLOYD "Lucifer Sam"
From *The Piper At The Gates Of Dawn* (EMI, 1967)

This is the kind of stuff I never listen to. I kind of recognise it. I think I can guess what it is.

It's the first Pink Floyd album. They were AMM fans, so I've heard.

I think Syd Barrett probably was. We used to share the bill together, but only for a very short period. If you listen to "Flaming," the fourth track on this record, the first 30 seconds of it are supposed to be an imitation of AMM. Syd was in the studio when we recorded AMMmusic for Elektra, and one of the tracks there is called, "Later during a flaming Riviera sunset." I don't know if he chose the title "Flaming" as a deliberate homage or not. You know, in music there are often a whole set of *permissions* given... John Cage in a way gave us permission to do certain things with AMM. And in a way AMM gave Syd Barrett permission to do what he did. Because someone else had done it.

How were you received by the Swinging London public of the time?

People came along without any preconceptions, it was certainly more open then. But our involvement in that scene didn't last very long. We soon sensed it was going off in another direction. The experimental music of that time was a kind of laboratory for people to try stuff out which some pop musicians would later develop into product. When I listen to this that's what I hear—not overwhelmingly creative music, but music becoming a product.

In some of the AMM sessions we used popular music elements, like [the Velvet Underground's] "Sister Ray," through the radio. I would take the radio and an old Grundig tape recorder and make long kind of loops of things like "Ba ba ba ba Barbara Ann" and repeat them endlessly, as a kind of equivalent of the multiples you found in Pop Art at the time, a sonic version of what Warhol was doing with repeated images. It was loud, because there was also the "wall of sound" notion that came from Coltrane and, I suppose, Phil Spector, quite literally a wall of sound that [saxophonist] Lou [Gare] would try to penetrate.

Is there any truth to the rumour that you were invited to join Pink Floyd yourself after Barrett was kicked out?

No, that's total nonsense. I don't think there was the remotest possibility of that. Nice story though. But then again things were so open in those days that I suppose any young guitarist could easily have ended up playing in the Rolling Stones, or The Who.

EARLE BROWN "Octet I" (1953)
From *The New York School 2* (hatART, 1993)

The first thing I should say is if I don't like something, it's my problem. It's not the musicians who are making the music. It's their privilege to make that music, and if I can't connect with it for all kinds of reasons to do with having my nose so close to my own canvas, it's my problem. There are particular sounds and timbres in this that I find very difficult to listen to. What is it?

Earle Brown's "Octet I," a tape collage piece from 1953.

I'm a huge admirer of Earle Brown, the *Four Systems, December 52*. Did he make that piece himself? Maybe I'd prefer it if it wasn't played by Earle Brown. For me the great Cage pieces are played by David Tudor, not by Cage. I would say the two supreme recordings of last century are John Tilbury's [recording of Morton Feldman's] *For Bunita Marcus* and David Tudor's recording of Cage's *Variations II*, the one on Editions RZ. The tension, the touch, the timbre, everything...it's almost another world. When I listen to this there are a few things I find finicky. I think one of the difficulties with so-called abstract music is the difficulty one has with abstract painting, the problem of affectation. When you look at a de Kooning you don't have a feeling of affectation, whereas other lesser paintings you definitely do. Sometimes it's a question of over-stylisation, but the actual work becomes affected. Using a radio for example is more complex than we realize. It's not just a question of turning it on. There's the appropriateness of the context. It has to have meaning and yet be transparent. Just because you're using a hiss on the radio doesn't mean to say you shouldn't use it with the same exquisite care as if you were playing first violin in a Shostakovich string quartet. What we do now with clicks and hisses is just the latest episode in centuries of music.

Do you hear a lot of affectation in today's music?

Well, think of all the paintings that were made in 1960. There are a handful of really great ones, the rest are not so brilliant, and a lot of them are awful. Why shouldn't that also be the case in music?

AMM "At the Roundhouse" (1972)
(Anomalous, 2003)

There was quite a break in AMM at this time when Lou and Eddie [Prévost] did this together and Cornelius and I went of on our own. Unfortunately hardly any of it was recorded, though I think Eddie's got some cassettes that Stella [Cardew] recorded of a tour we did about this time. *(Listens)* I would say that for me personally this is definitely jazz, the whole way it works, the forward motion it has definitely comes form jazz. Going back to Tudor's recording of *Variations II*, the wonderful thing about it is that sense that events are events, one doesn't prescribe what the next one will be. Whereas this is not going to go anywhere else than where it goes.

I take it that there's little chance of an AMM reunion.

It's difficult to imagine. After what was said, a lot of it in emails between Eddie and myself after the book was published, I don't think there's any way I could entertain the possibility, to be honest. For me it's just a really sad episode. It's like losing two friends in one fell swoop, not to be able to perform in a group which was the closest thing I'll ever get to classical music, in a sense. The actual criticisms themselves, about playing too loud or too soft, or being a part of this or that, didn't bother me so much. I don't think I was that important to need skewering so securely. But I worked with Eddie for forty-something years, if he'd just approached me about it beforehand I could have coped with that. I'm really surprised he didn't show me a pre-publication manu-script and ask me for my reaction. I had to buy a copy myself, and I read his critique of my work with astonishment. If it had come from someone who didn't like our kind of music, it would have made sense. It has a kind of willingness not to know, not to see... the way he describes how [Rowe's 1999 solo album] *Harsh,* was made, the way he conflates suffering with harshness, there are endless conflations. "Sometimes I wouldn't listen" is conflated to "I never listen." The kind of stuff you get from a bad historian who's changing history to fit the prejudices. But as I said before Eddie has the absolute right to write the book he wants to write, he has the privilege of saying what he wants to say and think what he thinks. In AMM if I didn't like something Eddie was doing, that was my problem. Not Eddie's problem. I just think it should be the same the other way around.

HOWARD SKEMPTON "Surface Tension I" (1975)
From *Surface Tension* (Mode, 1998)

I think we can talk over it, can't we? I don't know what it is.

It's your former fellow footsoldier from the Scratch Orchestra, Howard Skempton, a piece written in 1975.

Is it? It's kind of...very filmic. Pattern music. I think the Scratch Orchestra was a wonderfully creative movement, which probably lasted just long enough, instead of going on too long, the way most of us do. I like the fact that there aren't many recordings of what we did, like leaving no trace, or a very faint trace of inspiration. In a way the Scratch Orchestra was something we couldn't possibly document. The orchestra itself was a kind of elaborate form of notation, and trying to notate notation itself is an impossible task. That's what I liked about the Scratch Orchestra, the fact that it couldn't be turned into a product—no-one could own it. It was fantastic to be in it—I did virtually every Scratch Orchestra performance except one or two. Pretty well every week, during its most intense period. The joy of being in such a creative group or people, the politics of it was very interesting. People being able to do what they wanted within a very Confucian kind of framework.

Is there still a political dimension to what you do today?

Yes, certainly. When I think of the projects I was involved in, like People's Liberation Music or Scratch Orchestra, it was appropriate to make a political statement that was very direct. But there's another kind of politics too, the AMM kind, which is kind of slow burning, whose influence is ultimately perhaps a lot deeper. The idea of tolerance, of working problems out in the music itself.

Is that also the case with MIMEO?

Not really. With MIMEO there's no manifesto in that sense, whereas AMM started off with a very specific set of ideas.

PLURAMON "Have You Seen"
From *Dreams Top Rock* (Karaoke Kalk, 2003)

(Smiles) I've got a pretty good idea who this is. I think Marcus [Schmickler aka Pluramon] is utterly remarkable. He's one of the very few people I know who has such a grasp of these different areas of music. Generally someone who's involved with popular music cannot play our music. I don't think Sonic Youth can play avant-garde music. They don't have a clue. Something which is difficult to find in pop music is the idea of the architecture of a phrase—that's what makes John Tilbury such a great performer, his understanding of the importance of a phrase. In the avant-garde there's music *in time* and music *as time*, and I don't think Pink Floyd, for example, knew what music as time was. It's to do with the architecture of a phrase, the actual weight of notes, how the surface tension between notes works.

TAKU SUGIMOTO "A Whispering Page"
From *Fragments of Paradise* (Test, 1997)

I love the waiting, the patience.

I remember you saying you enjoyed playing with Sugimoto because his ideas were so clear.

Yes, like the investigation of those very small acoustic beats you get when two pitches are ever so slightly apart. It's funny, I remember seeing Tal Farlow play here in Nantes about ten years ago, and he started playing some standards in the same way...just sat on the stool, chewing his lip, looking at the guitar, and then played these very broad abstractions which would coalesce into "Stella by Starlight" or something.

Does it make a difference knowing if the piece is improvised or composed? Most of Sugimoto's recent music is the latter.

Whatever you're playing you need precisely the same tools. If you have to wait four or five minutes to make your note, you still have to make it with exquisite care. You could argue that you actually load more consideration into that one note than you could if you were playing a hundred.

That reminds me of the instructions you devised for the members of MIMEO in the recording of *sight* [in which the musicians were invited to record five minutes of sound anywhere they liked onto a blank 60-minute CD-R working independently of each other]. When you finally heard the album, what was your reaction?

I was surprised how well it worked, and how closely it paralleled the emotion I felt in front of the Cy Twombly painting I saw in Houston. We're getting into a very difficult area here, listening as a function of memory. I think you can argue that in the *sight* project there *was* a form of listening taking place. Listening related to memory. At one point you can almost hear what I'd describe as a group lack of concentration! Which of course is impossible, given how it was constructed *(laughs)*.

The Lappetites "Disaster"
From *Before the Libretto* (Quecksilber, 2005)

Very carefully done, isn't it? I don't know it at all, but it's really beautiful. The care of the transitions, the way it moves, the layering and stacking. Who is it?

There is a MIMEO connection. It's Kaffe Matthews with Antye Greie, Ryoko Kuwajima and Eliane Radigue, aka The Lappetites.

Ah, I've heard a lot about this but never heard it! Beautiful piece of music.

You've recently taken to using laptop.

Yes, but not in the normal way. I suppose it comes from a quotation from Nicolas Poussin, the French painter from the 1650s, from one of his letters, "I who make a profession of mute things."

I like the idea of *de-muting* something. I use a telephone pickup coil on the mouse, and pick up the Bluetooth communication between that and the laptop, and where the motor is, where the laser reader is, basically picking up the circuit board, rather than stuff from the sound card. I use it as a sound source. It's a continuation of that Duchamp modernism, exploring the object.

MICHEL HENRITZI "Independence"
From *Keith Rowe Serves Imperialism* (wmo/r, 2007)

(After a minute or so of violent thudding) I find the actual strike rate more formulaic than creative. It's not something I feel attracted to. There must be a way of doing it that's more inventive. Oh, it's getting going quite nicely now. But I have no idea what it is.

Well, your name's part of the album title.

Oh, right, that one! I think I played it through once. The disc is better than the text, as I recall. Mattin did at least have the courtesy to email me in the afternoon before he released it *(laughs)* and told me what is was called and asked me if I'd be offended. I said I wouldn't be if it was intellectually coherent, but it wasn't. It's obviously a reference to Cornelius Cardew's *Stockhausen Serves Imperialism*—which Michel's never read. As far as I recall, Cornelius's arguments were, one, Stockhausen detached himself from the progressive avant-garde, two he actually changed his relationship with the performers in his compositions, and three, that he started talking mumbo jumbo *(laughs)*. I think there's a lot of mumbo jumbo in Henritzi's text. It's a shame it wasn't better translated.

I see it more as a shot aimed against your professional relationship with Jon Abbey and Erstwhile Records.

Yes, I think it was more to do with Mattin's or Henritzi's dislike or disapproval of Jon Abbey than it was to do with me. I think I got dragged into it. It's a shame, because if you want to do a homage to Derek Bailey and Masayaki Takayanagi—which is what this album is, by the way—you should leave it at that. But had it come out just as a CD without the silly-arsed title it probably wouldn't have got so much attention, would it?

WALTER & SABRINA "Archaeology Part 1"
From *Chioma Super/Normal The Dark Album* (Danny Dark, 2006)

This sounds quite old.

It came out last year, actually.

Sounds like it's referencing things from a long time ago. *(Listens carefully...Walter Cardew's spoken voice comes in after a couple of minutes.)* No, I just find it uninteresting. The music seems oddly dated, but I'm not sure whether that's not intentional. The words are...well, words. Words are not so reliable as music.

Reliable?

Music seems more true, more able to know things. I have a great deal of difficulty with words. Occasionally I'm gripped by them. The way Wittgenstein uses words, for example. But I often find it difficult to express myself with words. Music is more articulate than words. Words are the things politicians use.

That was Cornelius Cardew's son, Walter.

Was it? I was kind of shocked when I saw that photo of Walter in *The Wire*. I thought I'd better write to him to find out how he was.

LEONEL POWER "Credo" (ca. 1415)
From *The Old Hall Manuscript* (Virgin Classics, 1997)

Amazing, isn't it?

The playlist you sent in to *The Wire* a few months ago was

basically all classical music. Is that what you listen to most?

Yes, generally speaking. I'd probably have been better off today if you'd played Schubert and Haydn. I've been lucky this last couple of years, because I've had the privilege of seeing the Tallis Scholars live twice. Is this the Tallis Scholars?

The Hilliard Ensemble, actually.

I give no prominence at all to knowing what the piece is. You don't need to know who it is. The only thing that attracts me is the music itself.

Just as well because we don't know for sure who wrote many of the works in the Old Hall Manuscript. This is by Leonel Power.

Is it? It really doesn't matter who it is. When you walk into an art gallery, you approach a painting, it doesn't matter whether it was painted in the 12th century or the 20th—the painting itself is what matters, its quality, the way it's been put together. There is really no difference whether it's by Leonel Power or Peter Rehberg.

Postscript

September 11, 2017

Dear Brian,

Yes, we missed you both in Sokołowsko. We took the opportunity to remember you by eating the cake around about your birthday.

This year was interesting, with a shift towards political/environmental, away from straight musical performance. Julien's install piece sort of reflected this shift: a clod of earth, with copper and zinc plates, reacting to the changes in acidity (a 24-hour cycle) powered by photoelectric cells, producing a very slight minimal drone, with very small changes.

A complete absence of clunky free jazz.

John and I did a two-part set (in the cinema/theater). In the first part we placed ourselves out of sight of the audience, extreme left and right of the stage, and on the empty stage we placed various things: a table, a ladder, lamp, banana, three books. It looked like a staging for a play, starting in complete darkness, the stage gradually filled with bright light. Our incidental music would have normally accompanied the actors, but the actors never appear. This is incidental music for a play that never commences (clearly linked to *enough still not to know,* incidental music for a non-existent video installation). Second half, we moved just outside in the foyer where you might recall there is an old, broken piano. During the day, John and I talked about age, navigating ill health, the constrictions and physical stiffness and the effects of age. This broken piano becomes us: the Parkinson's, the loss of speech, the lack of control.

The star of the play is the piano. In the first half, we see the piano (us) as a young man, in control, with agility, etc. There is a point in the second half where the playing becomes crude, violent, ugly, lacking any sense of dignity, unlikable. The piano is shown a photo of himself as a young man and rails against his plight (the photo is a recording of Thurston Dart playing the clavichord). John hammers against this recorded inclusion but sometimes playing along with the recording, sometimes fighting violently against. We ended the play with the Lully 'Marche pour la Cérémonie des Turcs', a classic all's well that ends well.

Some people liked it, some hated it.

Working with John, oh! He is so open and creative.

Here in Clisson, things are going well. I feel fine, getting in a bike ride here and there, depressed at the state of things, Parkinson's getting its way bit by bit.

All the best,
Keith

Keith Rowe Discography/Videography

The following discography and videography is reasonably complete (though doubtless not entirely so) as of the end of 2016. It includes several unreleased recordings.

—1964–1965 Unreleased recording

The Mike Westbrook Band (likely personnel: Mike Westbrook, piano; John Surman, baritone saxophone, clarinet; Mike Osborne, alto saxophone; Lou Gare, tenor saxophone; Malcolm Griffiths, trombone; Henry Lowther, trumpet; Keith Rowe, guitar; Lawrence Sheaff, bass; Alan Jackson, drums)

—November, 1965 Unreleased recording, pre-AMM

Keith Rowe, guitar; Eddie Prévost, percussion; Lou Gare, tenor saxophone, violin; Lawrence Sheaff, bass; unknown pianist

—March 23, 1966 Unreleased concert recording

AMM: Rowe, Prévost, Cornelius Cardew, Gare, Sheaff

Royal College of Art

Note: a 6:24 excerpt of above concert was released as

part of Not Necessarily English Music by Leonardo Music Journal in 2001, curated by David Toop

—June 8 & 27, 1966

AMM: Rowe, Prévost, Cardew, Gare, Sheaff

AMMMusic
    Elektra (EUK-256, EUKS-7256), LP, 1967
    ReR (AMMCD), CD, 1989
    Black Truffle (BT018), LP, 2016

—April 20, 1967

AMM: Rowe, Prévost, Cardew, Gare, Sheaff

An Afflicted Man's Music Box
    United Diaries (UD 012), LP, 1982
    United Diaries/RRRecords (UDT 028), Cassette, 1987

    Recorded at the Commonwealth Institute

    Note: One AMM track included on compilation, about 14 minutes in length.

—June 12, 1968

AMM: Rowe, Prévost, Cardew, Gare, Christopher Hobbs

The Crypt
    Matchless (MR5), 2xLP, 1981, 1988
    Matchless (MRCD05), 2xCD, 1992

    Note: a 23:22 excerpt was released as one side of MEV/AMM – Live Electronic Improvised by Mainstream Records (MS-5002) in 1970, reissued on CD by Wergo (WER 6930-2) in 2009. This track was also released on the Earle Brown Contemporary Sound Series Vol. 1, Wergo (WER 6928 2), 3xCD, 2009.

—March 16, 1969 Unreleased concert recording

AMM: Rowe, Prévost, Cardew, Gare, Hobbs (?), Christian Wolff (?)

Recorded in London

—May 4, 1969

Music Now Ensemble: Prévost, Rowe, Cardew, Gare, Hobbs, John Tilbury, Gavin Bryars, Howard Skempton, Michael Parsons, and many others.

Silver Pyramid
Matchless (MRCD40), CD, 2001

—November 1, 1969

Scratch Orchestra (personnel unlisted)

London, 1969
Die Stadt (DS23), 10" vinyl, 1999

—December 16, 1969

AMM: Rowe, Prévost, Cardew, Gare, Hobbs

Laminal, Disc One: The Aarhus Sequence
Matchless (MRCD31), 3xCD, 1996

—1969

Laurie Scott Baker

Gracility

Musicnow (MNCD012), CD, 2009

Note: Rowe appears on tracks 1–10 in the "Gracility" portion of the compilation in a quartet with Baker, Derek Bailey, and Gavin Bryars.

—January 20, 1970 Unreleased concert recording

AMM: Rowe, Prévost, Cardew, Gare, (Hobbs?)

Recorded in London

—February 3, 1970 Unreleased concert recording

AMM: Rowe, Prévost, Cardew, Gare, (Hobbs?)

Recorded in London

—February 15 & 16, 1971

Cornelius Cardew/Scratch Orchestra

The Great Learning
Organ of Corti (21), CD, 2000

Note: No personnel is listed. Rowe is assumed to be present.

—March 26, 1972 Unreleased concert

AMM: Rowe, Prévost, Cardew, Gare with Gunter Hampel Group (Hampel, vibraphone, bass clarinet; Günter Christmann, trombone; Evan Parker, soprano and tenor saxophones; Perry Robinson, clarinet; Alexander von Schlippenbach, piano; Buschi Niebergall, bass; Jeanne Lee, voice)

Recorded in Frankfurt, Germany

—1973–1978

Cornelius Cardew/People's Liberation Music

We Only Want the Earth
        Musicnow (MNCDx004), CD, 2001

—1977

Cornelius Cardew/People's Liberation Music
        Consciously
        Musicnow (MNCD009), CD, 2006

—December, 1978

Keith Rowe

Guitar Solos 3
        Rift (RIFT 1), LP, 1979 (UK)
        Red Records (RED 008), LP, 1979 (US)

        Note: one track, "For A," 7:20. Other contributors: Henry Kaiser, Chip Handy, Peter Cusack, Fred Frith, Eugene Chadbourne, Davey Williams, Akira Iijima.

—April 23, 1979 Unreleased session

AMM III: Rowe, Prévost

        Recorded in London, BBC Studio

—November 2, 1979

Amalgam (Trevor Watts, soprano and alto saxophones; Rowe, guitar; Colin McKenzie, bass; Liam Genockey, drums)

Over the Rainbow

Arc Records (ARC 01), LP, 1979
FMR Records (FMRCD132-L0903), CD, 2003

—November, 1979

Amalgam (Watts, soprano and alto saxophones; Rowe, guitar; McKenzie, bass; George Lyle, bass; Genocky, drums)

Wipe Out
Impetus Records (IMP 47901), 4xLP, 1979
FMR Records (FMRCD111-L0203), 3xCD, 2007

—December, 1979

AMM III: Rowe, Prévost

It Had Been An Ordinary Enough Day in Pueblo, Colorado
JAPO Records (JAPO 60031), LP, 1980
JAPO/ECM Records (JAPO 60031/843 206-2), CD, 1991

—1980 Unreleased session

Supersession (Rowe, Prévost, Evan Parker, tenor and soprano saxophones, Barry Guy, bass)
Recorded in, London, BBC studios.

—February 20, 1982

AMM: Rowe, Prévost, Tilbury

Laminal, Disc Two: The Great Hall, Goldsmith's College, London
Matchless (MRCD31), 3xCD, 1996

—May 16, 1982

(Various, including AMM)

Cornelius Cardew Memorial Concert
    Impetus Records (IMP 28204), 2xLP, 1985

—December 11 & 12, 1982

AMM: Rowe, Prévost, Tilbury

Generative Themes
    Matchless (MR 06), LP, 1983
    Matchless (MRCD06), CD, 1994

—May 24, 1984

AMM: Rowe, Prévost, Tilbury

Combine + Laminates (+ Treatise '84)
    Pogus Productions (P201-4), LP, 1990
    Matchless (MRCD26), CD, 1995 (includes "Treatise" '84)

—September 3, 1984

Supersession: Rowe, Prévost, Parker, Guy

Supersession
    Matchless (MR 17), CD, 1988, 2015

—January 10, 1987

AMM: Rowe, Prévost, Tilbury, Rohan de Saram

The Inexhaustible Document
    Matchless (MR 13), LP, 1987
    Matchless (MRCD13), CD, 1994

—March 1, 1987 Unreleased session

AMM: Rowe, Prévost, Tilbury, de Saram

Recorded in London

—January, 1988 Unreleased session

AMM: Rowe, Prévost, Tilbury, de Saram

Recorded in London, BBC Maida Vale studio

—May 20, 1988

Tom Phillips (with Ian Mitchell, clarinet; Lol Coxhill, soprano saxophone, voice; Phillips, voice; Birte Pederson, voice; Elise Lorraine, voice; Phil Minton, voice; Rowe, guitar, radio, tapes, cello; Prévost, percussion; Tilbury, piano, radio)

Irma
        Matchless (MR 16), CD, 1988

—July 5, 1989

Keith Rowe

A Dimension of Perfectly Ordinary Reality
        Matchless (MR 19), CD, 1990

—March 31, 1990 Unreleased concert recording

AMM: Rowe, Prévost, Tilbury, Gare

Recorded at the Taktlos Festival, Zurich, Switzerland

—April, 1990

AMM: Rowe, Prévost, Tilbury, Gare

The Nameless Uncarved Block
        Matchless (MR 20), CD, 1991

—October 13, 1991

Chris Burn Ensemble (Chris Burn, piano, toy piano, percussion; Jim Denley, bass flute, piccolo flute; John Butcher, soprano and tenor saxophones; Phil Durrant, violin; Stevie Wishart, violin, hurdy-gurdy; Marcio Mattos, cello; John Russell, guitar; Matt Hutchinson, synthesizer, electronics)

The Place 1991
        Emanem (4056), CD, 2001

        Note: Composition by Rowe, "Pollock #82," performed by Chris Burn Ensemble (Rowe does not perform).

—November, 1991 Unreleased recording

Keith Rowe

Audio Letter to Gino Robair (Frogs)

—July 2, 1992

AMM: Rowe, Prévost, Tilbury

Newfoundland
        Matchless (MRCD23), CD, 1993

—1992

Keith Rowe

(Y)earbook Volume 2
        Rastascan Records (BRD009), 1992

        Note: Compilation contains one track by Rowe, "Untitled"

—August–September, 1993 (& April, 1992)

Keith Rowe

City Music for Electric Guitar (by Frank Abbinanti)
  Table of the Elements (B 5), Vinyl 7," 1993

—1993 Unreleased session

AMM: Rowe, Prévost, Tilbury, de Saram

  BBC broadcast

—April 24, 1994

AMM: Rowe, Prévost, Tilbury

Live in Allentown USA
  Matchless (MRCD30), CD, 1996

—May 3, 1994

AMM: Rowe, Prévost, Tilbury

Laminal, Disc Three: Contextual, Context Studios, New York
  Matchless (MRCD31) 3xCD, 1996

—May 16, 1994 Unreleased concert recording

AMM: Rowe, Prévost, Tilbury, de Saram

  Recorded at Ravensberger Spinnerei, Bielefeld, Germany

—1994

AMM: Rowe, Prévost, Tilbury

Ambient 4: Isolationism
> Virgin (AMBT 4, 7243 8 39810 2 1, 8 39810 2) 2xCD,
> 1994

> Note: Compilation contains one track by AMM,
> "Vandoeuvre," 7:28.

—October 12, 1995

AMM: Rowe, Prévost, Tilbury

From a Strange Place
> P.S.F. (PSFD-80), CD, 1996

—October 13, 1995 Unreleased concert recording

AMM: Rowe, Prévost, Tilbury

> Recorded at the Nagoya City Art Museum, Nagoya, Japan

—1995

Keith Rowe

In God We Trust
> Table of the Elements (Ni 28), Vinyl 7" single-side, 1995

> Note: Compilation includes one track by Rowe, "Untitled"

—April 19, 1996

AMM: Rowe, Prévost, Tilbury

Before driving to the chapel we took coffee with Rick and Jennifer
Reed
> Matchless (MRCD35), CD, 1997

—April 25, 1996 Unreleased concert recording

AMM: Rowe, Prévost, Tilbury

> Recorded in Seattle, Washington.

—June 20, 1996 Unreleased concert recording

AMM: Rowe, Prévost, Tilbury

> Recorded at the Jazzgalerie, Nickelsdorf, Austria

—June 28, 1997 Unreleased concert recording

AMM: Rowe, Prévost, Tilbury

> Recorded in Glasgow, Scotland

—July 21, 1997

Keith Rowe

210797
> *Avant* magazine Sampler

> Note: Compilation includes one track by Rowe

—July–December, 1997

MIMEO (Rowe; Peter Rehberg, computer; Richard Barrett, computer; Jérôme Noetinger, electronics; Gert-Jan Prins, electronics, radio; Cor Fuhler, piano, electronics; Christian Fennesz, sampler; Justin Bennett, synthesizer; Thomas Lehn, analog synthesizer, mastering; Phil Durrant, violin, electronics; Yannis Kyriakides, violin, electronics; Marcus Schmickler, mastering)

Queue

GROB (GROB 005), CD-R, 1998

Music In Movement Electronic Orchestra
    Perdition Plastics (PER 009), CD, 1999

—October 14, 1997

Keith Rowe, Jeffrey Morgan (alto saxophone)

Dial: Log-Rhythm
    Matchless (MRCD36), CD, 1999

—1997

Keith Rowe, Alain De Filipps (tape)

The ReR Quarterly Volume 4 Number 2
    ReR Megacorp (ReR 0402)

    Note: Compilation includes one track by Rowe and De
    Filipps, "Feu Brilliant"

—March 4, 1998 Unreleased concert recording

AMM: Rowe, Prévost, Tilbury

    Recorded in Padova, Italy

—December 15, 1998

MIMEO (Rowe; Christian Fennesz, computer; Peter Rehberg,
computer; Kaffe Matthews, violin, computer; Jérôme Noetinger,
electronics; Gert-Jan Prins, electronics, radio, percussion; Rafael
Toral, guitar, electronics; Cor Fuhler, piano, electronics, organ;
Markus Wettstein, amplified metal garbage; Thomas Lehn, analog
synthesizer; Phil Durrant, violin, electronics)

Electric Chair + Table
GROB (GROB.206/7) 2xCD, 1999

—January, 1999

Zeitkratzer (Ulrich Krieger, saxophones; Axel Dörner, trumpet; Melvyn Poore, tuba; Luca Venitucci, accordion; Burkhard Schlothauer, violin; Michael Moser, cello; Alexander Fragenheim, double bass; Reinhold Friedl, piano; Raymond Kaczynski, percussion)

SonX
Zeitkratzer Records (zkr 99Z2), CD, 2000

Note: Composition by Rowe, "Traces 51 Pollack," played by Zeitkratzer. Rowe does not perform.

—October 14, 1999

Keith Rowe, Günter Müller (electronics, drums), Taku Sugimoto (guitar)

The World Turned Upside Down
Erstwhile (005), CD, 2000

—November 30, 1999

Keith Rowe

harsh,
GROB (GROB 209), CD, 2000

—December 31, 1999–January 1, 2000

Keith Rowe, Evan Parker (tenor saxophone)

Dark Rags
Potlatch (P200), CD, 2000

—1999

AMM: Rowe, Prévost, Tilbury

For Ute/Tower of Ghost
    FatCat Records (12FAT030), LP, 1999

    Note: Split LP with Merzbow, AMM on Side One.

—May 4, 2000

AMM: Rowe, Prévost, Tilbury

Tunes Without Measure or End
    Matchless (MRCD44), CD, 2001

—May 20, 2000

[N:Q] (Rowe, Julien Ottavi, electronics, percussion, voice; Jean Chevalier, electronic, bass clarinet; Christophe Havard, saxophone)

[N:Q]
    Fibrr (fibrr 001), CD, 2000

—June & November, 2000

Keith Rowe, Burkhard Beins (percussion)

Grain
    Zarek (ZAREK 06), CD, 2001

—August 2, 2000

Keith Rowe, Oren Ambarchi (guitar), Christian Fennesz (computer), Paul Gough [as Pimmon] (computer), Peter Rehberg (computer)

Afternoon Tea
     Ritornell (RIT 14), CD, 2000
     Black Truffle (BT03), CD, 2009
     Weird Forest (WEIRD-55), 2xLP, 2010

—October 14, 2000

AMM: Rowe, Prévost, Tilbury

     Video: Audio recording of full performance at ICA, Boston
     - https://www.youtube.com/watch?v=TC19JMog-WQ

—November 5, 2000 Unreleased concert recording

AMM (Rowe, Prévost, Tilbury) with The Stadler Quartett (Frank
Stadler, violin; Izso Bajusz, violin; Predrag Katanic, viola; Peter
Sigl, cello)

—December 5, 2000 Unreleased concert recording

AMM: Rowe, Prévost, Tilbury with the Abstract Monarchy Trio
(Franz Hautzinger, quartertone trumpet; Zsolt Kovács, guitar,
percussion, electronics; Zsolt Sörés, viola, percussion, electronics), Voice Crack (Norbert Möslang, electronics; Andy Guhl, elec-
troncis), and Günter Müller (electronics, percussion)

     Recorded in Budapest, Hungary

—2000

Keith Rowe, Kim Cascone (electronics)

with hidden noise
     Anechoic (a002), square mini-disc, 2000

—February 6, 2001 & May 7, 2002

Keith Rowe, Michel Doneda (soprano saxophone), Urs Leimgruber (soprano and tenor saxophones)

The Difference Between a Fish
        Potlatch (P302), CD, 2002

—April 15, 2001 Unreleased concert recording

AMM: Rowe, Prévost, Tilbury

        Recorded at the International House, Chicago, Illinois

—April 28, 2001

AMM: Rowe, Prévost, Tilbury

        Recorded at the Knitting Factory, NYC

        First Set:
        https://www.youtube.com/watch?v=bSipn0dG-iU

        Second Set:
        https://www.youtube.com/watch?v=NSKe0U-dlYc

—May 20, 2001

MIMEO (Rowe; Kaffe Matthews, computer; Peter Rehberg, computer; Jérôme Noetinger, electronics; Gert-Jan Prins, electronics, radio; Rafael Toral, guitar; Kevin Drumm, guitar, synthesizer; Marcus Schmickler, synthesizer, mastering; Cor Fuhler, inside piano; Phil Durrant, sampler; Markus Wettstein, amplified metal garbage; Thomas Lehn, analog synthesizer), Tilbury

The Hands of Caravaggio
        Erstwhile (021), CD, 2002

—May 24, 2001

AMM: Rowe, Prévost, Tilbury
Fine
      Matchless (MRCD46), CD, 2001

—May 26, 2001

Keith Rowe, Oren Ambarchi (guitar, electronics), Robbie Avenaim (percussion, electronics)

Honey Pie
      GROB (GROB 648), CD, 2002

—May 29, 2001

Keith Rowe, Oren Ambarchi (guitar, electronics), Sachiko M (empty sampler), Otomo Yoshihide (turntables, electronics, guitar), Robbie Avenaim (percussion, electronics)

Thumb
      GROB (GROB 432), CD, 2002

—June 11, 2001

Keith Rowe, Toshimaru Nakamura (no-input mixing board)

Weather Sky
      Erstwhile (018), CD, 2001

—October 29, 2001

Keith Rowe

29 October 2001
      Sound 323 (323-2), CD mini, 2003

Note: This is a portion (21:04) of the entire set, which is unreleased

Note: Videos of two segments of perhaps the same set are available on You Tube (https://www.youtube.com/watch?v=Eb-GPdnfbyI) and Vimeo (http://vimeo.com/27117055), 3:56 and 2:11, respectively.

—December 15, 2001 Unreleased concert recording

AMM: Rowe, Prévost, Tilbury

Recorded at Fonotech, Portugal (no city indicated)

—2001

Keith Rowe, Otomo Yoshihide (guitar), Taku Sugimoto (guitar)

Ajar
Alcohol (ALORS1CD), CD, 2002

—2001

Keith Rowe, Oren Ambarchi (guitar, electronics)

Flypaper
Staubgold (staubgold 32), CD, 2002

—2001 Unreleased concert recording

Keith Rowe

A Response to Treatise

—March 2, 2002

Keith Rowe, Oren Ambarchi (guitar)

Squire
        For4Ears (CD 1762), CD, 2006

—May 10, 2002

Keith Rowe, Christian Fennesz (computer)

Live at the LU
        Erstwhile (043), CD, 2004

—June, 2002

AMM: Rowe, Prévost, Tilbury; Formanex (Julien Ottavi, electron-ics; Anthony Taillard, electronics; Christophe Havard, electronics; Emmanuel Leduc, electronics; Laurent Dailleau, theremin; John White, electric keyboard)

AMM – Formanex
        Fibrr (fibrr 006), CD, 2003

—June 19 & 20, 2002

Keith Rowe, Thomas (analog synthesizer), Marcus Schmickler (synthesizer, computer)

Rabbit Run
        Erstwhile (027), 2003

—July 11–14, 2002 Unreleased concert recording

AMM: Rowe, Prévost, Tilbury

        Recorded at Festival Jazz, Luz, France

—Summer, 2002 Unreleased concert recording

AMM: Rowe, Prévost, Tilbury

Recorded at the CoMA Summer School, Yorkshire, England

—October 18, 2002

Keith Rowe, Thomas (analog synthesizer), Marcus Schmickler (synthesizer, computer)

AMPLIFY 2002 | Balance
　　　Erstwhile (033-040), 7xCD, 2003

—October 19, 2002

Keith Rowe, Toshimaru Nakamura (no-input mixing board)

AMPLIFY 2002 | Balance
　　　Erstwhile (033-040), 7xCD, 2003

—October 20, 2002

Keith Rowe, Tetuzi Akiyama (guitar), Oren Ambarchi (guitar), Toshimaru Nakamura (guitar), Otomo Yoshihide (guitar), Burkhard Stangl (guitar), Taku Sugimoto (guitar)

Compositions for Guitars
　　　À Bruit Secret (ABS103)

> Note: Rowe plays on one track, "Hum," composed by Taku Sugimoto

—October 21, 2002

Keith Rowe, Tetuzi Akiyama (guitar), Oren Ambarchi (guitar), Toshimaru Nakamura (guitar), Otomo Yoshihide (guitar), Burkhard Stangl (guitar), Taku Sugimoto (guitar)

AMPLIFY 2002 | Balance
　　　Erstwhile (033-040), 7xCD, 2003

—November, 2002

Keith Rowe, Seymour Wright (alto saxophone)

3D
> W.M.O./r (w.m.o./r33), 3xCD-R, 2008

> Note: Each disc is a recording of the same event, from three different audience angles.

—2002

Pluramon (Marcus Schmickler, electronics; Julee Cruise, voice)

Dreams Top Rock
> Karaoke Kalk (Karaoke Kalk 32)

> Note: Rowe plays on one track, "Time (Catharsia Mix)"

—2002

Keith Rowe, Phil Mouldycliff (electronics), Colin Potter (electronics)

Circle Line
> ICR Studios, 2016 (?)

—2002

Keith Rowe

45'18"
> Korm Plastics (KP 3005)

> Note: Rowe contributes one track, "Nature." Compilation is a homage to Cage's 4'33"

—January 31, 2003

Keith Rowe, John Tilbury

Duos for Doris
        Erstwhile (030-2), 2xCD, 2003

—February 2, 2003

Keith Rowe, Toshimaru Nakamura (no-input mixing board)

        Video – excerpt (4:30) of live performance, St. Louis, Missouri - http://vimeo.com/8822156

—May 4, 2003;

London Improvisers Orchestra (Rowe, Caroline Kraabel, alto saxophone; Harrison Smith, bass clarinet; Jacques Foschia, bass clarinet; Marcio Mattos, cello; John Rangecroft, clarinet; David Leahy, double bass; John Edwards, double bass; Simon H. Fell, double bass; Louis Moholo-Moholo, drums; Mark Sanders, drums; Dave Tucker, guitar; Pat Thomas, electronics; Steve Beresford, piano; Veryan Weston, piano; Adrian Northover, soprano saxophone; Lol Coxhill, soprano saxophone; Tom Chant, soprano saxophone; John Butcher, tenor saxophone; Alan Tomlinson, trombone; Robert Jarvis, trombone; Harry Beckett, trumpet; Ian Smith, trumpet; Roland Ramanan, trumpet; Charlotte Hug, tuba; Philipp Wachsmann, violin; Susanna Ferrar, violin; Sylvia Hallett, violin; Jaap Blonk, voice)

Responses, Reproduction & Reality: Freedom of the City 2003-4
        Emanem (4110), 2005

—September 5, 2003

MIMEO (Rowe; Marcus Schmickler, computer; Peter Rehberg, computer; Jérôme Noetinger, electronics; Rafael Toral, electronics; Gert-Jan Prins, electronics, radio; Kaffe Matthews, sampler, theremin; Thomas Lehn, analog synthesizer; Cor Fuhler, piano, synthesizer; Phil Durrant, synthesizer, sampler, violin)

Lifting Concrete Lightly
     Serpentine Gallery (SGCD1), 3xCD, 2004

—**November 23, 2003** Unreleased concert recording

AMM: Rowe, Prévost, Tilbury

     Recorded at Instal 03, Glasgow, Scotland

—**November 29, 2003**

Keith Rowe, Axel Dörner (trumpet), Franz Hautzinger (quarter-tone trumpet)

A View from the Window
     Erstwhile (041), CD, 2004

—**December, 2003**

Keith Rowe, Cor Fuhler (piano)

Rowe Fuhler
     Conundrom (CD 3), 2007

—**2003**

Keith Rowe, Toshimaru Nakamura (no-input mixing board)

     Video—excerpt (9:08) of live performance, Auditorium de La Médiathèque de Mons - https://www.youtube.com/watch?v=LW9Jf7_By5s

—**2003**

Keith Rowe, Toshimaru Nakamura (no-input mixing board)
60 Sound Artists Protest the War

Atak (no catalog #)

>Note: Rowe and Nakamura contribute one track, "1 Min. in Texas")

—March 4, 2004 Unreleased concert recording

Keith Rowe, John Tilbury (organ)

>Recorded in Leeds, England

—April 30, 2004

AMM: Rowe, Prévost, Tilbury; MEV (Alvin Curran, sampler, percussion; Frederic Rzewski, piano, percussion; Richard Teitelbaum, synthesizer)

Apogee
>Matchless (MRCD61), 2xCD, 2005

>Note: Disc One, joint performance.

—May 1, 2004

AMM: Rowe, Prévost, Tilbury

Apogee
>Matchless (MRCD61), 2xCD, 2005

>Note: Disc two contains two performances, one by each ensemble: AMM—39:27, MEV—36:40

—May 8, 2004

Keith Rowe, Toshimaru Nakamura (no-input mixing board), Thomas Lehn (analog synthesizer), Marcus Schmickler (synthesizer, computer)

Untitled
> Erstwhile (ErstLive 002), CD, 2004

—May 13, 2004

Keith Rowe, Burkhard Beins (percussion)

Untitled
> Erstwhile (ErstLive 001), CD, 2004

—May 14, 2004

Keith Rowe, Sachiko M (empty sampler, contact mics), Toshimaru Nakamura (no-input mixing board), Otomo Yoshihide (guitar, turntables)

Untitled
> Erstwhile (ErstLive 005), 3xCD, 2005

—June 4, 2004

4g (Keith Rowe; Toshimaru Nakamura, no-input mixing board; Oren Ambarchi, guitar, electronics; Christian Fennesz, guitar, computer)

cloud
> Erstwhile (046-2), 2xCD, 2005

—June 12, 2004

[N:Q] (Keith Rowe (radio); Julien Ottavi (radio); Will Guthrie (radio); Emmanuel Leduc, radio)

November Quebec
    Esquilo Records (ES005|EsVAR002), CD-R, 2006

—September 11, 2004

Keith Rowe, Perlonex (Ignaz Schick, turntables, objects, electronics; Burkhard Beins, percussion, objects; Jörg Maria Zeger, guitar)

Tensions
    Nexsound (ns54), 2xCD, 2006

    Note: Disc One: Perlonex/Rowe; Disc Two: Perlonex/
    Charlemagne Palestine (piano, keyboards)

—November 7, 2004

Keith Rowe, Günter Müller (electronics), Tomas Korber (guitar, electronics)

fibre
    For4Ears (CD 1657), CD, 2005

—December 6, 2004 unreleased session

Keith Rowe

    Jet FM broadcast

—2004

Keith Rowe

LMC 13th Annual Festival Guitar Soloists
    London Musicians' Collective (LMCGUITAR 02), CD, 2004

Note: one track, "Guitar Solo"

—2004–2007

David Sylvian

Manafon
    Samadhisound (ss016), CD, 2009 (other versions)

    Note: Rowe appears on tracks 3, 6 & 9. His contributions were recorded earlier, then sampled and assembled by Sylvian with those from other improvising musicians.

—2004–2007

David Sylvian

Died in the Wool | Manafon Variations
    Samadhisound (ss 021) 2xCD, 2011)

    Note: Rowe appears on tracks 2, 4, 6, 7 & 11, as above.

—April 30 and July 1 & 2, 2005

Keith Rowe, Toshimaru Nakamura (no-input mixing board)

between
    Erstwhile (050-2), 2xCD, 2006

—2005

Rick Reed

Dark Skies at Noon
    Elevator Bath (eeaoa025)

    Note: Rowe appears on one track, "Ceremony – Parts 1 & 2"

—March, 2006 Unreleased concert recording

Keith Rowe, Sean Meehan (snare drum)

> Note: No further information

—March 31, 2006

Keith Rowe, Mark Wastell (amplified textures)

Untitled/Live At I-and-E
> Confront (cps 02/ccs 12), CD-R, 2006/2010

—April 1, 2006

Keith Rowe, Annette Krebs (guitar, electronics), David Lacey (percussion, electronics), Paul Vogel (computer)

Untitled
> Homefront (homefront-1), CD-R, 2007

—July 28, 2006 Unreleased home recording

Keith Rowe

Location (Day & Night)

—2006

Keith Rowe

Debris Field
> ICR (ICR 53), CD, 2006

> Note: Rowe's installation, "Dog and Radio," appears among other installation recordings of work by Loren Chasse, Phil Mouldycliff, Colin Potter, and others.

—2006

MIMEO (Rowe, Cor Fuhler, Christian Fennesz, Gert-Jan Prins, Jérôme Noetinger, Kaffe Matthews, Marcus Schmickler, Peter Rehberg, Phil Durrant, Rafael Toral, Thomas Lehn) (instrumentation unspecified)

Sight
> Cathnor (Cath004), CD, 2007

—June 1, 2007

Keith Rowe

Concentration of the Stare
> Bottrop-Boy (B-Boy 036), CD, 2011

—2007

Keith Rowe

The Room
> Erstwhile (ErstSolo 001), CD, 2007

—2007

The Voltage Spooks (Rowe; Rick Reed, synthesizer, electronics; Michael Haleta, computer, electronics)

Boston 2007
> Austinnitus, 2x File MP3, 2008

—2007

Keith Rowe, Kjell Bjørgeengen (video)

> Video: Excerpt (4:00) from performance in Porto, Portugal - https://vimeo.com/15422576

Paul Baran

Panoptic
> Fang Bomb (FB013), CD, 2009

> Note: Rowe appears on two tracks: "Jackson and Lee" and "Pomerol"

—September 19, 2008

Keith Rowe, Taku Unami (computer, guitar, mandolin, objects)

Untitled
> Erstwhile (ErstLive 006), CD, 2008

—September 20, 2008

Keith Rowe

Untitled
> Erstwhile (ErstLive 007), CD, 2008

—September 21, 2008

Keith Rowe, Toshimaru Nakamura (no-input mixing board)

Untitled
> Erstwhile (ErstLive 008), CD, 2009

—September 21 & 23, 2008

Keith Rowe, Sachiko M (sine waves, contact mic)

Contact
> Erstwhile (054-2), 2xCD, 2009

—February 8, 2009

Keith Rowe, Oren Ambarchi (guitar)

"Treatise"
> Planam (CCCPLANAM)

>> Note: Four pages are realized: 53, 58, 168 and 169.

—March 28, 2009

Keith Rowe

> Video: excerpt (3:24) from live performance at Festival Expozice nové hudby 2009, Czechia, Brno - https://www.youtube.com/watch?v=H0W3COIl8SA

—March 28, 2009

Keith Rowe, Jon Rose (violin, electronics)

> Video: excerpt (8:10)) from live performance at Festival Expozice nové hudby 2009, Czechia, Brno - https://www.youtube.com/watch?v=aJpqb4qBnLA

—June 12, 2009 Unreleased concert recording

Keith Rowe, Martin Küchen (saxophones), Seymour Wright (saxophones)

> Recorded at Café Oto, London

—June 13, 2009 Unreleased concert recording

Keith Rowe, Martin Küchen (saxophones), Seymour Wright (saxophones)

Recorded in Leeds, England

—June 14, 2009

Keith Rowe, Martin Küchen (alto saxophone), Seymour Wright (alto saxophone)

Küchen_Rowe_Wright
> Another Timbre (at29), 2010

—June 15, 2009 Unreleased session

Keith Rowe, Lee Patterson (electronics)

> Note: No further information

—November 15, 2009

MIMEO (Rowe; Christian Fennesz, computer; Kaffe Matthews, computer; Marcus Schmickler, computer; Peter Rehberg, computer; Gert-Jan Prins, electronics; Rafael Toral, electronics; Cor Fuhler, piano; Phil Durrant, sampler; Thomas Lehn, analog synthesizer)

Wigry
> Bôłt/Monotype (BR LP01/monoLP006), 2xLP, 2011

> Video: excerpt (4:56) of live performance at
> Półwysep Nowej Muzyki, Wigry -
> https://www.youtube.com/watch?v=HRZ6aykj77c

—November, 2009

Keith Rowe, Rick Reed (electronics), Bill Thompson (electronics)

November Music 2009
> November Music (NM 013), CD, 2009

Note: Rowe appears on one track of this compilation, "Shifting Currents."

—February 12, 2010

Keith Rowe, Kjell Bjørgeengen (video)

> Video: Excerpt (5:29) from performance at unspecified location -
> https://www.youtube.com/watch?v=VHmJMLiQMy0

—July 8, 2010

Keith Rowe

> Video: Excerpt (11:26) from performance at the Konigsberg Jazzfestival, Konigsberg, Norway -
> https://www.youtube.com/watch?v=TQ2LRPzKpbY

—September 29, 2010

Keith Rowe

> Video: Excerpt (1:37) from a performance at Guilty Guitars, Festival Centre, unspecified location (Germany?)

—November 8–10, 2010

Keith Rowe, Radu Malfatti (trombone)

Φ
> Erstwhile (060-3), 3xCD, 2011

—November 28, 30 & December 1, 2010

Keith Rowe, Oren Ambarchi (guitar, percussion), Crys Cole (contact mics, objects, effects)

Black Plume
> Bocian Records (bcACR), LP, 2012

> Video: Excerpt (3:38) from November 30 performance at The Music Gallery, Toronto, Canada - https://www.youtube.com/watch?v=0PgwReWfkJ0

> Video: Excerpt (10:57) from December 1 performance at Sala Rossa, Montreal, Canada - http://vimeo.com/17398392

—December 5, 2010 Unreleased performance recording

Keith Rowe, Kjell Bjørgeengen (video)

> Performance at Experimental Intermedia, NYC

> Video: Excerpt (1:37) of performance - https://www.youtube.com/watch?v=-VlGc_GWtRw

—December 13, 2010 Unreleased performance recording

Keith Rowe, Kjell Bjørgeengen (video)

> Performance at Instants Chavirés, Montreuil, France

—December 17, 2010

Keith Rowe, John Tilbury

E.E. Tension and Circumstance
> Potlatch (P311), CD, 2011

—December, 2010

Keith Rowe

The Art of War
    Hermes' Ear (aSB/HE 001), CD Mini, 2014

—December, 2010

Keith Rowe

The $100 Guitar Project
    Bridge Records (9381A/B), CD, 2013

    Note: Rowe contributes one selection along with 62 other
    guitarists in a project organized by Nick Didkovsky.

—2010

Keith Rowe

Atomy
    Onement (#4), LP, 2010

    Note: only one copy pressed. As of 2016, still unsold.

—2010

Keith Rowe, Luke Fowler (film), Peter Todd (film)

The Room

    Video: Excerpt (3:11) from film -
    http://vimeo.com/18622282

    Video: Excerpt (1:48) from film -
    http://vimeo.com/19209261

—March, 2011

Keith Rowe

Christian Wolff – Kompositionen 1950–1972
Edition RZ (RZ 1023-24), 2xCD, 2011

Note: Rowe contributes one piece to this compilation, performing Wolff's 1968 composition, "Edges."

—May 13, 2011

Keith Rowe

Video: Complete solo performance (25:57) at the I-and-E Festival, Dublin, Ireland - http://vimeo.com/32251602

—May 13, 2011

Keith Rowe, Paul Vogel (electronics)

Video: Complete performance (24:25) at the I-and-E Festival, Dublin, Ireland - http://vimeo.com/32012422

—September 4, 2011

Keith Rowe, Christian Wolff (guitar, piano)

Untitled
Erstwhile (ErstLive 010), CD, 2012

—September 11, 2001

Keith Rowe

September
Erstwhile (ErstLive 011), CD, 2012

—November 13, 2001

Keith Rowe, Phil Dadson (bowed objects), Jeff Henderson (objects)

Video: Excerpt (8:17) from performance at
The Classic, Auckland, New Zealand -
https://www.youtube.com/watch?v=AktFrU8v2cA

—2011

Keith Rowe, Gerard Lebik (tenor saxophone), Jakub Suchar (percussion)

Video: Excerpt (6:03) from performance at
Festival Musica Electronic Nowa -
https://www.youtube.com/watch?v=CFIN94yuueA

—2011 (?)

Keith Rowe

Video: Complete solo performance, date and location
unspecified - http://vimeo.com/51944882

—October 13, 2012

Keith Rowe

Video: Performance of Frank Abbinanti's "City Music
for Electric Guitar" at Lampo, Chicago, Illinois -
https://vimeo.com/51944882

Video: Excerpt (2:36) from performance
of Frank Abbinanti's "City Music for Electric Guitar"
at Lampo, Chicago, Illinois -
https://www.youtube.com/watch?v=cZb9A93w0RY

—October 14, 2012

Keith Rowe
    Video: Excerpt (3:53) from performance
    at Studio Z, St. Paul, Minnesota -
    https://www.youtube.com/watch?v=2EyEcLlsDNM

—2012

NG4 (Rowe; Julien Ottavi, guitar; Anthony Taillard, guitar; Emmanuel Leduc, guitar)

    Video: Excerpt (3:25) from performance at
    Plateforme Intermedia, La Fabrique, Nantes, France -
    http://vimeo.com/65997618

—2012

Keith Rowe

Unsettlingly Horizontal
    Another Timbre (AZ#4), MP3, 2012

—January 17 & 18, 2013

Keith Rowe, Graham Lambkin (objects)

Making A
    Erstwhile (067), CD, 2013

—February 24, 2013

Keith Rowe, John Tilbury, Kjell Bjørgeengen (video)

    Video: Excerpt (2:01) from performance at
    Samtidskunst, Oslo, Norway -
    https://www.youtube.com/watch?v=4b3EBpTjfs8

—March 10, 2013

Keith Rowe, John Tilbury, Kjell Bjørgeengen (video)

>Video: Excerpt (6:16) from performance at
>Samtidskunst, Oslo, Norway -
>https://www.youtube.com/watch?v=ion_AyI06ls

—April 26, 2013

Keith Rowe

>Video: Excerpt (6:56) from performance at
>the Teni Zvuka Festival, Moscow, Russia -
>https://www.youtube.com/watch?v=2BoaVqHQrng

—April 27, 2013

Keith Rowe, Ilia Belorukov (alto saxophone, electronics, synthesizer), Kurt Liedwart (computer, electronics, objects)

tri

>Intonema (int011), CD, 2014

>Video: Excerpt (11:43) of performance -
>https://www.youtube.com/watch?v=INBpzaxkqe8

—April 29, 2013

Keith Rowe, Alfredo Costa Monteiro (accordion, objects), Ilia Belorukov (alto saxophone, electronics, objects), Kurt Liedwart (electronics, objects)

Contour

>Mikroton Recordings (cd 32), CD, 2014

—November, 2013

Keith Rowe

Live at Fairchild Chapel
> Idiopathic Records (IR 007), Cassette, 2015

—December 12, 2013

Keith Rowe, Thomas Lehn (analog synthesizer), Marcus Schmickler (computer)

> Video: Excerpt (3:12) from performance at Les Instants Chavirés, Montreuil, France - https://www.youtube.com/watch?v=tdgDN1LQNlc

—December, 2013

NG4 (Rowe; Julien Ottavi, guitar, Anthony Taillard, guitar, Emmanuel Leduc, guitar)

A Quartet for Guitars
> Mikroton Recordings (cd 27), CD, 2014

—2013

Keith Rowe, Andrew Deutsch (electronics), Yuya Ota (piano, electronics)

Kannazuki no Uta
> Institute for Electronic Arts (IEA1301), CD, 2013

—2013

Keith Rowe, Rick Reed (synthesizer), Bill Thompson (electronics)

Shifting Currents

Mikroton Recordings (cd 17 | 18), 2xCD, 2013

—March 23, 2014

Keith Rowe, Pascal Battus (electronics, objects)

> Video: Excerpt (9:23) from performance at
> Le Temp du Corps, Paris, France -
> https://www.youtube.com/watch?v=rpJHODssKu4

—March, 2014 Unreleased session

Keith Rowe, Patrick Farmer (objects), Lee Patterson (electronics)

—July 17 & 18, 2014

Keith Rowe, John Tilbury

enough still not to know
> Sofa (SOFA548), 4xCD, 2015

—November 1, 2014

Keith Rowe, Ben Patterson (objexts)

> Video: Complete performance (19:35) from
> Festival Expozice nové hudby, Brno, Czech Republic -
> https://www.youtube.com/watch?v=_O5e0JtWOnY

—August 20, 2015

Keith Rowe, Gerard Lebik (electronics)

> Video: Excerpt (6:39) from performance of Rowe's
> piece, Dry Mountain, Sokołowska, Poland -
> https://www.youtube.com/watch?v=vJmm5WRyLLU

—October 29, 2015

Keith Rowe, Antony Maubert (electronics)

> Video: Excerpt (5:12) from performance at
> Radical db, Zaragoza, Spain -
> https://www.youtube.com/watch?v=Fh1qJ_YABQ8

—October 30, 2015

Keith Rowe

> Video: Excerpt (27:40) from performance in Sion, France -
> https://vimeo.com/148087713

—2015

Keith Rowe, Martin Küchen (alto and baritone saxophones, electronics)

The Bakery
> Mikroton Recordings (cd 46), CD, 2016

—January, 2016

ONsemble (Rowe, Julian Ottavi and others)

> Nantes, France

> Video excerpt:
> https://www.youtube.com/watch?v=FL0rwYaWC5k

—April 7, 2016

AMM: Rowe, Prévost, Tilbury

Video: Excerpts from performance at
Église Saint Merrie, Paris.

https://www.youtube.com/watch?v=p1eybwdSLD8
(19:45)

https://www.youtube.com/watch?v=u-T8rmnHtbg_
(5:10)

—December 1, 2016

Keith Rowe, David Toop, Rhodri Davies, Rie Nakajima, Phil Durrant

Video: Performance at Symposium:
On the Edge, Oslo, Norway -
https://www.youtube.com/watch?v=z1ivV4qG-yc
(performance of the quintet begins at 01:49:00)

—2013–2016

Keith Rowe

The Room Extended
Erstwhile (ES004-4), 4xCD, 2016

Acknowledgments

The author would like to thank most of all Keith Rowe, for his patience, great insight, and humor, and for his deep and warm friendship.

Great thanks as well to Jon Abbey for initially suggesting the project, as well as for consistent support, criticism, and editorial review over the years.

I'd like to express special thanks to members of AMM, past and present, who have graciously engaged in conversation, endured lengthy phone calls, and provided many a tale and observation: Eddie Prévost, John Tilbury, Lawrence Sheaff, Lou Gare, Christopher Hobbs. Huge thanks and love to Stephanie Evans. Thank you to Victor Schonfield, Mike Westbrook, Kjell Bjørgeengen, Wes Del Val, Lizzi Sandell, Phil Mouldycliff, Krystyna Roberts, Jacques Oger, and all the musicians and other kind folk who responded to requests for interviews and information. Thank you to friends and family, especially to Linda Crisol for putting up with everything all those years.

This book was begun in 2003, when the Internet community interested in this area of music was already in full swing. I've found the ongoing dialogue with this community to be invaluable, constantly causing me to rethink aspects of this story and to open new avenues of investigation. I'll be leaving out some deserving people, I'm sure, but I'd like to offer a special thank you to some of the folk who have made this period of my life so rich and rewarding.

Tim Albro, Bill Ashline, Antoine Beuger, Jason Bivins, Nayland Blake, Olivia Block, Julie Boatley, Rick Brown, Mike Bullock, Cyprien Busolini, Bob Burnett, John Butcher, Lucio Capece, Daniel Carlson, Nathaniel Catchpole, Johnny Chang, Seth Cluett, Chris Cochrane, Rhodri Davies, Bruno Duplant, Lutz Eitel, Barnaby Evans, Clem Evans, Joe Farara, Mark Flaum, Joseph Foster, Jürg Frey, Jesse Goin, Jennie Gottschalk, Stephen Griffith, Anthony Guerra, Will Guthrie, Sarah Hennies, Doug Holbrook, Walter Horn, Maria Iacovou, Julia Jacquette, Alan Jones, David Crawford Jones, Richard Kamerman, Vincent Kargatis, James Keepnews, Nina Katchadourian, Robert Kirkpatrick, Joshua Kosman, Annette Krebs, Jesse Kudler, Eric La Casa, Catherine Lamb, Graham Lambkin, Joslyn Layne, Gerard Lebik, Jason Lescalleet, Herb Levy, Mattin, Joe McPhee, Phil Minton, Toshimaru Nakamura, Daniel Okrent, Julien Ottavi, Joe Panzner, Kevin Parks, Richard Pinnell, Michael Pisaro, Nina Polaschegg, Tom Pratt, Ben Ratliff, Johan Redin, Rick Reed, Tara Bhattacharya Reed, Simon Reynall, George Rosenfeld, Michael Rosenstein, Vanessa Rossetto, Philip Samartzis, Gil Sansón, Lucas Schleicher, Craig Shepard, Gary Sisco, Damon Smith, Steve Smith, Nirav Soni, Greg Stuart, Derek Taylor, David Toop, Birgit Ulher, Dan Warburton, Mark Wastell, Christian Wolff, Yuko Zama, Sergio Zamora

And, of course, Betsy Wallin.

Index

Boni, Raymond, 279, 363

Bosshard, Andres, 291

Bowie, Lester, 371

Boyd, Joe, 143, 144

Boyle, Mark, 100, 175

Brant, Henry, 201n

Braxton, Anthony, 71n, 78, 317

Bream, Julian, 31, 315

Brecht, George, 183

Breuker, Willem, 59

Brötzmann, Peter, 77, 151, 271, 302

Brown, Earle, 62n, 86n, 97, 108, 273

Brus, Gunter, 155

Bryars, Gavin, 184, 286

Buckle, John, 219

Bullock, Charlie, 14

Burn, Chris, 304

Burroughs, William, 163

Bussotti, Sylvano, 98

Cage, John, 71n, 73, 79, 80, 84, 86n, 96, 97, 99, 103-105, 107, 108, 117, 132, 145, 152, 164, 169, 176, 181-183, 191, 200, 213-215, 217, 262, 266, 271, 273, 277, 280n, 281, 283, 286, 302, 304, 306, 315, 324, 328, 349, 351, 352n, 355, 367

Cardew, Cornelius, 74n, 79n, 86n, 95n, 96-110, 112, 114-117, 123, 124, 127-139, 141-143, 145, 146, 149, 152-154, 158-166, 169, 171-179, 182n, 183, 186, 191-193, 195, 196, 198-203, 205-214, 217, 220, 223-229, 231, 232, 252, 253, 257, 260-264, 269, 271, 272, 274, 277, 280n, 288, 290, 294, 295, 304, 329n, 351, 353, 366, 372, 375

Cassavetes, John, 144

Catchpole, Nathaniel, 335n

Chadbourne, Eugene, 295n

Charlton, Hannah, 264, 265

Charters-Rowe, Barry, 13, 26

Charters-Rowe, George, 303

Charters-Rowe, Richard, 10, 13

Chiari, Giuseppe, 99

Christian, Charlie, 31, 130

Christie, Lou, 113, 115

Christmann, Günter, 212n

Clayton, Peter, 188

Cohen, Alan, 61, 96, 100, 101, 139

Coleman, Ornette, 30, 50, 53, 61, 69-72, 76, 86, 92, 112, 140, 151, 253, 301

Collier, Graham, 259n

Coltrane, John, 30, 53, 60, 66, 70, 71, 79, 93, 151, 211n, 271, 314, 351n

Common, Tony, 91

Conrad, Tony, 85, 93, 97, 104, 254

Cooper, Mike, 276

Cora, Tom, 314n

Corigliano, John, 288

Coryell, Larry, 254

Coxhill, Lol, 91, 286

Cunningham, Merce, 213

KEITH ROWE:
THE ROOM EXTENDED

Text © 2018 Brian Olewnick

"Blindfold test with Keith Rowe conducted by Dan Warburton" first published in *The Wire* issue 287 January 2008. Reproduced by permission. thewire.co.uk

Published in the United States by powerHouse Books,

a division of powerHouse Cultural Entertainment, Inc.

32 Adams Street, Brooklyn, NY 11201-1021

e-mail: info@powerHouseBooks.com

website: www.powerHouseBooks.com

First edition, 2018

Library of Congress Control Number: 2018937561

ISBN 978-1-57687-864-4

Printing and binding through Asia Pacific Offset

Book design by Krzysztof Poluchowicz

10 9 8 7 6 5 4 3 2 1

Printed and bound in China